PHILOSOPHY
OF
HAPPINESS

PART ONE
COLLECTING OUR SELF

This book is dedicated

to

those who are left to understand the world

and their place in it

and to

those who do not have that good fortune

PHILOSOPHY
OF
HAPPINESS

**A
THEORETICAL
AND
PRACTICAL
EXAMINATION**

PART ONE
COLLECTING OUR SELF

MARTIN JANELLO

Cover, book design, and artwork by Martin Janello

Published by Palioxis Publishing

Palioxis, Palioxis Publishing,
and the Palioxis Publishing colophon
are trademarks owned by Martin Janello

Publisher website:
www.palioxis.com

Book website:
www.philosophyofhappiness.com

This volume is Part One of a two-volume paperback edition

(Part Two: ISBN 978-0-9910649-9-1)

Parts One and Two are also available
as one combined hardcover book
(ISBN 978-0-9910649-0-8)
one combined PDF e-book
(ISBN 978-0-9910649-1-5)
one combined KINDLE e-book
(ISBN 978-0-9910649-2-2)
and one combined EPUB e-book
(ISBN 978-0-9910649-3-9)

Part One
ISBN 978-0-9910649-8-4
First Edition

PALIOXIS
PUBLISHING

Access an index
discuss the book
read associated articles
contact the author
keep updated
& more
at

www.philosophyofhappiness.com

NOTICE

CONTENTS
PARTS ONE AND TWO

INTRODUCTION   1

PART ONE
COLLECTING OUR SELF

SECTION ONE
ORIGINS

CHAPTER 1   WISHES AND NEEDS   13
CHAPTER 2   EMOTIONAL AND RATIONAL MIND   32
CHAPTER 3   PASSING ON   54
CHAPTER 4   AFTERLIFE   68
CHAPTER 5   PRESENT LIMITATIONS   83

SECTION TWO
EMPIRIC APPROACH

CHAPTER 6   EXPERIENCES AND INFLUENCES   99
CHAPTER 7   TRIALS, CONVENTIONS, AND IDOLS   115
CHAPTER 8   OPPORTUNITIES OF EMPIRIC INSIGHT   134
CHAPTER 9   LIMITATIONS OF EMPIRIC INSIGHT   146
CHAPTER 10   THE SUBJECTIVITY OF HAPPINESS   159

SECTION THREE
IDEALISTIC APPROACH

CHAPTER 11   IDEALISTIC AMBITIONS   171
CHAPTER 12   IDEALISTIC CONVERSION   195
CHAPTER 13   CRITICAL EXAMINATION   224
CHAPTER 14   IDEALISTIC SCIENCE   243
CHAPTER 15   IDEALISTIC DISSATISFACTION   257

SECTION FOUR
EXISTENTIAL APPROACH

CHAPTER 16   SEARCHING FOR A BETTER WAY   269
CHAPTER 17   OUR INNER ESSENCE   290
CHAPTER 18   PERSONALITY FORMATION   313
CHAPTER 19   THE STRUGGLE FOR OBJECTIVITY   335
CHAPTER 20   GATHERING PERSONAL INFORMATION   358

PART TWO
MOVING FORWARD

SECTION FIVE
INDIVIDUAL RECONCILIATION

CHAPTER 21   IDENTIFYING OUR EMOTIONAL TRAITS   381
CHAPTER 22   SELECTING THE BEST APPROACH   398
CHAPTER 23   SETTING OUR PRIORITIES   417
CHAPTER 24   THE DEMANDS OF COMPROMISE   438
CHAPTER 25   ALLOCATING OUR RESOURCES   450

SECTION SIX
COLLECTIVE RECONCILIATION

CHAPTER 26   COMPETITION AND COOPERATION   479
CHAPTER 27   CONTROLLED COMPETITION   513
CHAPTER 28   COMPETITIVE STRATEGIES   531
CHAPTER 29   THE INDISPENSABILITY OF COOPERATION   566
CHAPTER 30   COOPERATIVE PRODUCTION   581
CHAPTER 31   COOPERATIVE TRANSFORMATION   607
CHAPTER 32   REDISTRIBUTION AND CHARITY   625
CHAPTER 33   INTEGRATION AND DISSOCIATION   664
CHAPTER 34   POLITICAL CONVERSION   703
CHAPTER 35   COOPERATIVE GOVERNANCE   736

SECTION SEVEN
GENERAL RECONCILIATION

CHAPTER 36   LOST AND FOUND   759
CHAPTER 37   COINCIDENCE   775
CHAPTER 38   THE INSUFFICIENCY OF CONTROL   799
CHAPTER 39   PURSUIT AND FULFILLMENT   811
CHAPTER 40   CONSTRUCTION AND DESTRUCTION   826
CHAPTER 41   SOLIDARITY AND DISCRIMINATION   861
CHAPTER 42   BASIC GENERAL RECONCILIATION   883
CHAPTER 43   ADVANCED GENERAL RECONCILIATION   910
CHAPTER 44   HUMAN INTEGRATION   921
CHAPTER 45   FREEDOM AND PROGRAM   956

CONCLUSION AND EPILOGUE   971

ACKNOWLEDGMENTS

This book has been facilitated by important factors and persons whom I would like to thank. Although its contents developed over time, they came to me without much prodding. I never wondered what I should write next. In a very real way, the book wrote itself. I felt I was merely serving as a medium in memorializing what was, is, and could be. I am grateful for having been there and having had the capacity and experiences to do this work. It took quite some endurance and calm concentration to collect and ponder all aspects I regarded as relevant, express them in communicable terms, and organize them according to their inherent progression. As the entire measure of this effort materialized and I sacrificed important years in my productive prime to it, I was at times daunted. But I also sensed an increasingly unyielding determination that this work was necessary, that I had to undertake it, dedicate every moment I could to it, and not publish it before I deemed it ready. Even diversionary temptations, disruptions, as well as pursuits that I had to abandon or neglect during my writing focused my mind and made me pursue my purpose with hardened resolve. I thank all of these trials for confirming how much this work matters to me.

Most difficult was the solitude that intense writing and deliberation require. Also, I never told anybody what the book was about until it was completed. I sensed I had to keep my work private to develop my thoughts undisturbedly. I was trying to sort my mind about a great variety of issues that I could often barely describe and not fathom yet. I wanted to do that without being distracted by endeavors of others to influence me. I appreciate that I could mature my thoughts independently. I further wanted to see what I could accomplish, and I am glad to have had the occasion of finding that out. My self-imposed isolation meant that I had to be a critic to my work and had to hold myself accountable where I was not thorough enough, went astray, or could express myself better. I am grateful for this corrective reflection. In addition, I came to appreciate how short and precious time is. It flew while I was immersed in writing and when I looked up at events on the outside, I received an unobstructed impression of life's actual pace.

Some of my acknowledgments might sound as if I were thanking myself. But I did not create any of the conditions responsible for this book. They were given to me by circumstances to which all credit is due. Immeasurable recognition has to go as well to persons close to me for their unconditional trust, love, and support. Accordingly, while I am gratified by the completion of my book and by its substance, I am equally humbled by the favorable circumstances that enabled them.

INTRODUCTION

The most direct introduction for this book is the story of its development. That story does not begin with deeply contemplated structures and with high concepts. When I started seriously thinking and writing about happiness almost seven years ago, I was not certain what would come of it. Nothing dramatic triggered this enterprise. I was not greatly unhappy. A fair number of my endeavors were bringing me satisfaction, and I had no lack of ideas about conditions that I believed would bring me more satisfaction. But it had bothered me for some time that I possessed no coherent notion of happiness. All I had was a scattering of impressions about it contrasted by a conviction that happiness was very important to me. I recognized that this state of affairs made it difficult to reach or hold, let alone increase or even maximize happiness. Thus, I decided to assemble and consider my impressions to find out whether I could derive a more deliberate approach from them.

I soon realized that my understanding of happiness could not advance much without further exploration. I began by asking whether my objectives, their pursuit, and their fulfillment were generating the best possible quality and quantity of happiness. That questioning encompassed not only obvious failures but successful endeavors as well. Events of happiness appeared to be of short duration and little consequence. They did not appear to have a lasting effect on my long-term level of happiness, which did not impress me as greatly different now from most other times in my life. Perhaps that equalization was fortunate because disappointments seemed to follow the same trend. Still, I wondered whether the results of all my exertions were worthwhile. It worried me that the measures of happiness I had already experienced should be all there would be. How I fared appeared to depend in large parts on the environment of my endeavors and how other persons behaved. Then again, I could see that much of it was a function of my attitudes and actions. Could I have prevented missteps and unsuccessful pursuits? Could I have enhanced the experiences and outcomes of my undertakings? Was there any value in the failures or sacrifices that I had incurred? Was it prudent to give up some of my ambitions and to instead concentrate on others? I found myself asking whether I could have done better. I speculated what I could have done differently and what my life would be like had I made different choices. Even more, I kept wondering whether I was missing anything right now. Was there something that I should be doing of which I was not aware? Should I abandon or restrain certain pursuits for the sake of others? Was I living my life to its greatest potential? I had the suspicion that I was not.

This concern did not only focus on the generation of higher intensities and quantities of happiness. I also worried about the stability of happiness. I wished I could better hold on to it when it faded or regain it after it vanished. Both my impressions of deficiencies and, even more, possible cures were unclear. I had a sense that there was room for improvement, but I could not see a clear path to more happiness.

I further queried myself why I should rely on my aspirations so steadfastly. How many of my ideas were thought out? It seemed that most of them originated as cryptic bits that had attained momentum over time. Where had they come from? Were they really mine? Were they not defined by circumstances I experienced, by what I found possible, by what I was told rather than genuinely by me? Even if my ideas were entirely mine, what basis did I have to think that they would conduct me to happiness? Even if I was confident about my objectives, did I possess sufficient information and skill to implement them? Did I know how to make myself happy? How could I be certain about my competence in setting and pursuing objectives? Even as I confronted myself with the simple question what happiness is, I could cite a variety of examples but I could not succinctly characterize its essence. My inability to define happiness sealed my conviction that I did not have the best grasp on it and drove me to action. The question now became how to extricate myself from this dissatisfactory situation. I realized I was not merely looking for some ideas to boost my happiness. I wanted to get to the bottom of the phenomenon and solve its mystery.

In an attempt to recognize aspects of assurance and direction, I reviewed what I had learned about happiness thus far. I thought I had picked up a sizeable collection of appropriate objectives and standards of conduct that bring about happiness. Perhaps refamiliarizing myself with them, deliberating about them more intensely, or following them more intently could help me to transcend my lack of confidence. Such efforts might empower me to recognize certain principles as true and to confirm or adopt them as mine. I reviewed what I had learned from my family, from school, religion, and the social and cultural context in which I had grown up. I also reviewed what I had learned about happiness as an adult from my personal and work relationships and from other experiences. My life started with a few basic rules that were imposed by my caretakers or that I learned impliedly in contact with my environment. Most of these made intuitive or practical sense and have stood the test of time. But as I was growing up, additional settings and purported authorities emerged whose presence and impositions were less commonsensical. Many principles impressed or inflicted on me were abstract generalities that stayed disconnected from my circumstances. Where specific instructions filled general principles, they often referred to factual and emotional situations with which I could not identify. Even where that did not pose a problem, they regularly presented less than credible or otherwise unsatisfactory explanations why they should apply. Authorities habitually demanded adoption of principles without any verification or only with perfunctory proof. Moreover, many instructions or implementations were plagued by incompleteness or inconsistencies. When they appeared to contain valid aspects, these were frequently hard to recognize and to evaluate because they were adulterated by incorrect translations, interpretations, modifications, additions, or omissions. Quite a number of instructions had been imposed on me under the authority of possible, often vague, direct or indirect external repercussions. Others appealed to an internally administered sense of shame or of guilt. Even where such pressures were not obvious, their ubiquitous or prevalent acceptance in my environment had suggested them as viable guidelines. For lack of deeper thought or better alternatives, I had tended to comply with them.

As my experience with this guidance had grown, an increasing share of it had revealed itself as detrimental. I frequently found myself disagreeing with attitudes and resulting conditions. Yet that only provided partial instruction about what should take their place. It taught me what not to think, feel, do, or want but less about constructive objectives. I could not even be certain that the guidelines I deemed plausible could be trusted. They frequently conflicted with one another by direct contradiction or indirect competition. Even systems of purported guidance seemed to be afflicted by internal inconsistencies, incompleteness, or inapplicabilities. Frequently, I found in them principles I supported amalgamated with others that I disapproved. If theories appeared acceptable, their practice tended to betray their promise. This meant that hardly any instructions could be adopted free of doubt. It also meant that I could not identify a comprehensive approach toward happiness. My distrust of instructions had grown further with increasing information about their background. They often appeared to have been established or advanced to benefit their initiators and their promoters rather than the persons to whom they were directed.

Not all was lost. I had been able to nuance and supplement the basic guidelines of my youth. I had learned from the concurrences of my experiences with external instructions. I had applied and had confirmed the authority of a number of principles, and I had been able to customize some of them. In addition, I had developed some guidelines of my own through my experiences. In various respects, I had learned what to do if I would find myself in situations similar to those I had already experienced. Even in regions where I lacked experience, the expanded application of trusted principles could give me some guidance. Still, the frame of reference of the guidelines I had approved kept my concepts largely reactive. It was of little help in determining for what I should be searching, in formulating my objectives past the horizon of what I already knew. I had learned how to get along, how to live with reasonable stability, how to contain problems and resolve them with some success. But I had not necessarily found out how to take charge of my existence. It seemed that my experiences, including my experiences with principles, lacked the capacity to convincingly guide me in achieving more happiness, let alone in maximizing it. Basing my pursuits on an incomplete set of guidelines and trying to expand them by new interesting ideas and their trial did not strike me as the best way of confronting the problem. Even if I could generate some progress in this manner, shaping a happy existence this way seemed uneconomical and ineffective. I thought that, despite unique challenges posed by contemporary life, previous generations must have had many similar experiences. By now, there should be an established, solidly founded, and intelligible guidance structure by which humans should be able to advance their happiness. Only, I had not found such a system.

I was aware that various religious and secular doctrines claimed to have resolved the challenges of happiness. I had examined many of them during my formal studies of law and of philosophy and in later years. Some of their principles rang true to me. Yet I did not discover anything that dramatically reformed my mind. I mostly accumulated deeper insights into what I disapproved. I considered that my failure to be positively impressed by any of the formalized recipes for happiness might be a personal peculiarity. After all, many of these doctrines seemed to have significant influence on many other individuals. Then again, the condition of happiness of their originators, proponents, and followers, let alone the effects their application had on other humans overwhelmingly did not live up to their claims. This was often blamed on interpretive error, abuse, lack of dedication, or the difficulty of circumstances. But I thought that a valid message about how happiness can be accomplished should have broken through such impediments. I found this to be the case for fundamental features stated in a variety of doctrines. However, it seemed to me that anybody sufficiently considerate could readily identify these maxims without much guidance. That philosophies acknowledged these did not redeem their incapacity to go beyond and define a practicable path toward happiness. It had mystified me that, after years of studies, I had not come across a general system for the pursuit of happiness and that it might not exist.

Confronting this issue again brought back a vivid memory of an event during my studies of philosophy at the University of Heidelberg. I had been attending an introductory course with Professor Friedrich Fulda, the dean of the philosophical faculty. One of the statements he made engraved itself into my mind down to its exact setting. I can still see and hear the professor pronounce that studying philosophy is not likely to help individuals who are looking for authoritative answers to their personal problems. Rather, it instills a flexibility of thought and tolerance of different viewpoints and gives us the tools to explore and compare these viewpoints. This declaration had not bothered me immediately because I had not chosen philosophy to find answers to personal problems. I had begun studying it in addition to law because of an interest in the foundations of law. But I had not understood why I had that interest. Looking back, I began to recognize that my interest had been all along in happiness and had only been couched in terms of legal theory. I had hoped that the incongruities between assertions of safe and systematic guidance and the reality I had increasingly encountered could be closed by studying sources. That issue had become acute if I was going to represent such guidance in form of the law. I had expected that the study of philosophy would disclose substantive guidance on how to behave individually, as a society, and as a species. I had thought that, similar to wealth and health, happiness was an objective state and therefore assumed that its constituents and principles could be rationally investigated, understood, detailed, and implemented. I had expected that identifying objective normative principles by which happiness operates and can be systematized was feasible. I had trusted that best practices of acting and interacting with others, best principles of law and morality could be deduced as matters of science. I had believed in their derivability from a substance of happiness and that, by following them upstream, that substance could be revealed.

It had profoundly surprised me that someone like the professor, who had such intense knowledge of so many philosophies, should not have found and would not commit to authoritative answers on how to lead a proper existence. I had no problem acknowledging that certain areas of philosophy should be preoccupied with technique. But I had not been able to accept that the study of philosophies addressing human affairs should be a mere exercise of instilling flexibility, tolerance, and analytical skills, that there was little hope of finding one guiding truth in them. As I remembered my struggling with the implications of this apparent limitation, I realized that I had not found peace with it. If there was no singular truth applicable to human existence, there could be any number of legitimate opinions and approaches. This had

not comported with my ideal of happiness as an objective phenomenon then, and I could not accept it now. It seemed problematic to me
that there should be multiple coexisting claims to the truth. I likened
this setting to different positioning in observation of a physical environment. Although the experiences made in different positions might
vary, they would still pertain to the same objective phenomenon that
could be described as one truth by the same principles. It struck me as
odd that human happiness should deviate from this standard, particularly in view of the claim of scientific derivation and objective certainty by most philosophies addressing matters of happiness. Much of that
claim was already suspect to the extent philosophies contradicted one
another. Yet, if their characteristics merely represented one viewpoint
among others, all of them would have to be mistaken in their claim of
objective truth regarding these characteristics. They could not contain
any valid knowledge of what makes humans happy other than subjective preferences and their elaborations. Some of us might be fortunate
enough to find a philosophy in concordance with our views and obtain
applicable guidance from it. The rest of us would be on our own. Further, the subjectivity of happiness called into question the functionality of many laws, morality, and other principles that might be focused
on improving and optimizing human existence. Even where philosophies superficially appeared to agree, their interpretations frequently
left them with little in common. The widespread absence of objective
truth about happiness in them seemed to make the derivation of generally valid principles for human behavior mostly impossible.

I remembered that the lack of guidance revealed by this conclusion had troubled me. As much as I had tried to escape this result, my
studies in the following years had regularly confirmed it. This had led
me to considerable disillusionment about the function of philosophy
in the betterment of humans and humanity. My disappointment with
substantive philosophies and their reflection on law had prompted me
to concentrate on the technical aspects of law and philosophy. In my
practice as a business attorney, I represented a broad variety of interests. I learned to assess the positions, objectives, and arguments of all
participants to a transaction and to negotiate solutions among them. I
became skilled in the safeguarding and the cooperative optimization
of clients' purposes in a shared environment. Developing and applying
these capacities formed a source of considerable satisfaction. Still, as I
assessed the progression from my university days through my career, I
realized that I had become a representation of Professor Fulda's declaration. I had become proficient in understanding, in respecting, and in
harmonizing different viewpoints to design productive arrangements

for my clients. However, I had not come across a philosophy by which I could comprehensively identify and connect valid objectives and systematically enhance and maximize their pursuit. This did not disturb my functioning. Clients hired me to represent their defined or implied business objectives and not to answer deeper questions of what they really wanted or should want. But I had also relented finding these answers for myself. As this insight emerged, I understood why the professor's statement had stayed with me so persistently. For all this time, I had ignored the reminder of an unfinished task that my memory of his statement had continued to submit. I finally decided to pay attention and ask: If philosophies cannot provide authoritative answers to the question how to be happy, what or who can? The answer was obvious. I needed to find my own way. I began to see why I had avoided this task before. It seemed exceedingly difficult. There did not seem to be much to work with even now that I understood the challenge better. The assortment of principles I had gathered up along my path had served me reasonably well. Yet, if I was to improve on them, I had to take a few steps back and gain a better comprehension of happiness. I had to reflect deeper on what my impressions represented and might have to develop and supplement them. To undertake all that, I had to represent my thoughts and thus began to commit them to writing.

As my considerations progressed, I detected an unexpected development. Not only did I assemble a better picture of what happiness meant to me. I also began to notice the emergence of a general procedural concept about how happiness might be found, maintained, improved, and maximized according to an individual's autonomous insights. The development of this method instigated my writing of this book in addition to the personal records I built for myself. It does not presume to know the particularities of happiness for any of us. Rather, it explores how we can identify what will make us happy. It proposes that we must turn inward to accomplish this identification. We have to comprehensively come to know who we are and what we want. The book offers perspectives on how to achieve that knowledge and shows that autonomous acquisition of knowledge is not only possible but is also necessary. Once we have established a topical comprehension of what makes us happy, we must employ this knowledge in its practical context. We have to identify, examine, and select means and strategies to pursue our objectives. That work exceeds immediate technical concerns. We have to comprehend how to harmonize our pursuits within ourselves and with our human and nonhuman environment to obtain the best possible results. A significant portion of this book is therefore dedicated to the transitioning of our ideas of happiness into reality.

Because these processes focus on exploring and expressing who we are and bringing our self into reality, their results are bound to be as individual as our differences. Nevertheless, when we step back from the particulars of our pursuits and compare them with the pursuits of other individuals, we can perceive a larger picture. We can distinguish common denominators that derive from our nature as humans and universally shared conditions of human existence. These commonalities cause us to recognize foundations of our nature in others. They allow us to draw conclusions about happiness and our pursuit of it beyond individual particularities. They permit us to formulate a general concept of happiness, including its purposes, sources, motivations, requirements, detractions, and implications. As a result, we are able to construct a general substantive theory of happiness. Although its tenets may be modulated by particular internal and external conditions, it prescribes guidelines and parameters for our objectives and pursuits that we cannot transgress if we want to be happy. Understanding the nature of happiness is a condition for more comprehensive access to its potential. To prosecute our happiness effectively and efficiently, we must comprehend the topography and physics of its universe and our position in it. This orientation permits us to improve the selection of objectives and methods and to behave in a more purposeful manner. Further, we gain a better judgment of our ability to control our happiness and about how much happiness we might be able to obtain.

The exposition of both the procedural and substantive aspects of a general theory of happiness obligated me to observe stringent requirements. To preserve the general applicability of the theory, I had to keep its presentation separate from the originally intended writing that focused on my person. Still, neither of these writings would have been possible without the other. Exploring and memorializing ideas for the advancement of my happiness alerted me to the manifestation of generally applicable principles. Moreover, the development of these principles benefited from being tested by personal application. In return, applying emerging principles greatly helped me to develop and understand what I needed to do for my happiness. The mutual illumination between theory and practice helped me to develop and sharpen both of these aspects. My hope is that this book can prompt a similar progress of reciprocal discovery between the principled and practical aspects of happiness for its readers. I set forth best efforts to find, develop, and delineate universal concepts. But proving their universality is not my supreme ambition. A critical examination is necessary if the concepts in this book are to serve their function of enabling readers to identify and advance their happiness through their own insights.

PART ONE
COLLECTING OUR SELF

SECTION ONE
ORIGINS

CHAPTER 1
WISHES AND NEEDS

To find out how we can advance our happiness, we must first identify what it is and how it comes about. We may begin this venture by observing how we experience happiness. When we think about our happiness, we tend to associate immediately its particularizations in our existence. We picture past and present conditions, or we imagine settings that we believe or hope to be capable of bringing us happiness in the future. Our awareness of past and present events and our ideas of future events of happiness correlate with a desire to rekindle that past, to hold on to present situations, or to engender particular conditions. These longings to be situated in past, present, or future circumstances and to experience their beneficial implications for our emotional state constitute our wishes. We wish to re-create, attain, or maintain particular circumstances so we can be happy. Our wishes define our happiness and guide our exploration for it. The fulfillment of a wish conveys happiness onto us. We are happy when we get what we want. Because our understanding of happiness is so intricately intertwined with the substance of our wishes, we have difficulties thinking rationally about it or our wishes. Our wishes appear to be phenomena in our mind that precede our rational thoughts. They appear to be emotional incidents, urges that appear to exist independently of what we think about them. We may apply rational considerations to help in their definition and advancement. But even if we find rational reasons why we should not give in to particular wishes, they still tend to persist. The only way we appear to be able to reformulate our wishes is if we perceive that they or other wishes may suffer from their pursuit and we form new, more advanced wishes. In that formulation, our wishes seem to take rational advice and emotionally reconcile. Yet, even then, the underlying desires may continue to agitate and may be difficult to discourage.

Most of our wishes do not materialize by mere willpower. They pose objectives that have to be carried out. This implementation takes place in movements that we can frequently describe in a sequence of changes, in related steps. Simple wishes may feature only one narrowly defined activity engendering their accomplishment. Wishes that are more complex necessitate multiple steps of activity and accomplishment that sequentially build on other steps to bring about the desired result. Many of our wishes require more than a singular chain of steps. They require the convergence or the interaction of two or more parallel sequences or single steps to produce a combined step. That combined step may serve the fulfillment of a wish alone or together with other steps. All steps involved in building to the fulfillment of a wish are means in its accomplishment. We may describe these constructive means as subordinated steps in a strategy to reach its ulterior objective. Because each such means is a step toward an ulterior objective, the accomplishment of each means also forms an objective. When we consider subordinated steps helpful or necessary to reach a desired result, they become subsidiary objects of our desire. Each means to the ulterior objective of a wish is the subject of a subordinated wish. Our desire attaches to them because they enable the fulfillment of our ulterior wishes. Because subordinated objectives form auxiliary targets of our desire, their attainment instills us with increments of happiness as well. Yet even ulterior wishes tend to attend additional purposes. Consequently, ulterior and subordinated wishes appear to be similar in their functionalities and emotional effects. Our characterization of the subject of a wish as a means or as an objective depends on whether we focus on it as a target or as an instrument for another target.

Observing how wishes are positioned in our life as motivations for means and objectives gives us some information about their workings. But it does not inform us much about their nature, the source of their motivation, or even about the motivation we sense. The immediate, emotional, demanding character of our wishes causes us to focus our inquiries regarding happiness mostly on questions about the objects or events that can make us happy, on technical concerns of their fulfillment. We preoccupy ourselves with concerns of how we or others should behave or what we or they should possess or be able to effect to meet the claims of our wishes. Wishes strike us mostly as topical demands. This prompts us to deal with them in a disjointed manner. Their impulsive quality may instruct us to behave in manners that may not be to our advantage. Our mind is continually flooded by an abundance of wishes that might not be reconciled. Before we can improve our happiness, we must learn how they affect our happiness by themselves and in correlation with one another. To judge our wishes competently, we have to inquire deeper into them and ask where they originate, why we have them, and what they do to us. To find the answers to these questions, we might envisage our existence without the fulfillment of our wishes. Without the fulfillment of wishes, we would be without happiness, we would be unhappy. Because our wishes are instruments for our happiness, the enjoyment of our existence is negatively affected by a failure to fulfill our wishes. More than that, we find that if all our wishes would carry on unfulfilled, we could not exist. Thus, at least some of our wishes have to be of existential importance. But not all our wishes are existential in the manner that our existence depends on each of them. Many subordinated wishes may fail without serious repercussions on our existence. If a wish fails, we may reapply the same strategy in hope for better circumstances. We may also formulate a different strategy that is set to avoid the repetition of a previous failure. We may engage several identical or disparate sequences of subordinated purposes simultaneously or successively to pursue the same objective. As long as some attempt succeeds in timely fulfilling an existential wish, a failure of subordinated wishes would not appear to be existential. The only exception would occur if parallel, repeat, or alternative tries would strain our resources or otherwise damage our future chances of fulfilling the same or other existential wishes.

Existential wishes are not optional or interchangeable with other strategies because their fulfillment is necessary to secure our existence. An instinctive command urges us to pursue and satisfy them as objectives in themselves, as ultimate wishes. The compelling and general nature of these demands gives them the quality of needs. We may call needs that directly concentrate on the physical aspects of survival our survival needs. Some of these needs seem to be limited to our individual survival. Our individual survival is predicated on the suitable supply of oxygen, food, water, exercise, and sleep. We depend on controlled pressure, gravity, and radiation, including visible and invisible light and temperature. More generally, we require corporeal integrity and surroundings that assist and do not interfere with it. Beyond representing an ultimate wish on their own, all these needs seem to constitute or to support a principal need for individual survival for which they form necessary instruments. We may designate these needs and the principal need they attend individual survival needs. We can further differentiate needs that constitute or support a principal need to provide for the survival of our species. Among these are the needs to reproduce, to raise progeny, and to protect and support individuals we view as our kind. We may call these needs and the principal need they constitute our collective survival needs. These needs may appear selfless. Yet, through their pursuit, we are following a genuine individual interest that is founded in the desire to have our essence survive and proliferate. We may define this essence narrowly as our genetic or acquired particularities or more broadly on the basis of commonalities we share with other or even all humans. We traditionally identify the strength of our essence in others by how similar they are to us. Historically, our principal criteria to ascertain similarity have been behavior and appearance. We have been sensitive to distinctions despite prodigious evidence of commonality. We may place emphasis on discrepancies in geography, culture, religion, and group membership, obviously physical traits including skin, hair, and eye color, facial features, build, strength, endurance, symmetry, and health, as well as mental features such as intelligence, personality, social attitude, experiences, or style. Any of these distinctions may make it difficult for us to confer protection and support onto other humans. An exclusion from our care may move in gradations depending on the perceived significance of distinguishing marks. We may discriminate against their carriers to a point where we deny all recognition to them as carriers of our essence. We may not only deny them our assistance. Once we regard them as relatively or absolutely beyond the purview of our need to protect or support them to secure collective survival, we may change our behavior toward them accordingly. We may feel free to actively damage them in the pursuit of our needs, including through their exploitation as resources or their exclusion or even elimination as obstacles or rivals.

Apart from needs that obviously serve survival, we can discern ultimate wishes whose fulfillment might not seem to be indispensable for our survival. Still, we sense an instinctive urge that demands their fulfillment with a vehemence that is similar to our survival needs. We may therefore recognize these wishes as needs yet distinguish them as collateral needs. Among these needs seem to be needs for companionship, social interaction, acceptance, giving and receiving love, and for treating other individuals as we treat us that we may also call our need for empathy. Additionally, they comprise needs for peace, justice, harmony, for the control and reliability of our circumstances, and for optimized comfort. They further incorporate our needs for self-determination, privacy, expression, self-realization, and self-respect. Accurately and succinctly describing these needs, if not even ascertaining their existence, seems to be difficult. It seems to be more complicated than determining the nature and scope of survival needs. Because survival needs focus on obviously physical conditions, fulfilling such needs has a plainly detectable utility in support of our own existence or the existence of others. What we require for survival appears to lend itself to scientific quantification and illumination. While collateral needs may involve overt physical requirements and mechanisms and various corresponding secondary effects, their essential concerns seem to express themselves on a nonphysical, mental level. Their deprivation and fulfillment have primary effects that defy attempts of isolation, qualification, and quantification. This complication may cause them to appear as nonessential for our individual and collective survival. We may acknowledge that their deprivation affects our wellbeing to some extent and that their fulfillment adds satisfaction to our existence. Nevertheless, we may believe that we should be able to survive individually and collectively without fulfilling collateral needs. We may regard them as luxuries or even as nuisances that disturb our peace with overwrought demands. This may lead us to believe that we can do well or even better without satisfying them. We may consider them options that we can curb or reject without serious import. We are particularly prone to develop this attitude regarding collateral needs that we struggle or are unable to fulfill. We may discredit what resists us or what we cannot have. For the short term, our disregard of collateral needs may render our life simpler and seemingly without significant repercussions. Yet a long-term omission to fulfill any of these needs, and sometimes their brief deprivation, may have significant effects on our individual or collective existence. Depending on the duration and severity of the deprivation and our further condition, we may experience negative emotional consequences. These may range from temporary discomfort to a state of intense pain in which our existence has lost its appeal. They may precipitate other mental as well as overtly physiological deteriorations. These conditions may weaken our response to threats and opportunities that are relevant for our individual or collective survival.

The nonpursuit of collateral needs may particularly have negative effects because of their numerous correlations with social interaction. Some of them may be fulfilled unilaterally without the provision of means to others. Others may be fulfilled by the protection and support of others without an expectation of compensation activities. Assisting the needs of others may trigger collateral satisfaction in us. But many collateral needs require constructive contributions from others. More than that, they may require contributions by particular individuals. Our inability to fulfill such collateral needs alone compels us to obtain cooperation to satisfy them. Individuals whose cooperation we desire may decline or condition their participation. This affords them power over our happiness if we are not or less willing or able to satisfy such needs by correlating with other individuals. Our dependence on their cooperation may give rise to conflict if they deny, ration, or condition their contributions. Then again, there is a likelihood that other individuals might cooperate because they require assistance to satisfy their own collateral needs of this sort as well under similar conditions. Unless they are satisfied or committed to reaching satisfaction in a relationship that requires exclusivity, they might be interested in an exchange relationship. The social context of collateral needs is intensified because some derive essential means from the pursuit of collateral or survival needs by others. They require that others pursue needs in a direct exchange, by themselves, or in connection with third parties. These dependences may create close mechanisms of mutuality.

Regardless of how firm the dependence of collateral needs that necessitate cooperation from others is, they are vulnerable to disturbances. But such settings may also often possess some resilience against disfunction. The desire to fulfill collateral needs through the cooperation by others may prompt individuals to make advances even if their intended cooperation partners do not currently reciprocate. Together with the protection or provision of means without an expectation of return, this advance may hold the potential of constraining deficiencies of mutuality and of aiding to repair them. Only, such investments may cease if benefactors comprehend that recipients hinder, damage, or jeopardize the pursuit or fulfillment of benefactors' needs to an extent that renders further investments unattractive. Such a determination may be hastened if benefactors have the opportunity to attain superior satisfaction of their collateral needs through other sources. The threat of benefit withdrawal incentivizes recipients to care for the collateral pursuits of their benefactors. The dependences of many collateral needs and the threats noncooperation produces encourage the establishment of social structures, processes, and conventions that protect the fulfillment of collateral needs through mutuality and the creation of a joint undertaking that covers all collateral needs. A failure to participate in the pursuit of collateral needs in conformance with such arrangements can have extensive adverse consequences for a violator.

The pursuit of collateral needs and the mechanisms of care they promote can provide essential or helpful assistance for individual and collective survival. They can organize and safeguard unilateral protection or provision of obviously physical means, their exchange, as well as multilateral cooperation in obviously physical pursuits as means for achieving collateral objectives. Our desire to secure the fulfillment of survival needs may independently motivate us to engage in such undertakings. The social structures and conventions created for the pursuit of collateral needs therefore regularly overlap with those designed to promote and secure the fulfillment of survival needs. This may lead to the commingling and interaction of pursuits and effects. Additionally, collateral and survival needs seem to be substantively connected in many cases. The failure to socially pursue collateral needs may then have significant repercussions on the capability of individuals to satisfy their survival needs, and the reverse is also true. Collective survival needs appear particularly susceptible to this interdependence because they intrinsically require cooperation or are directed toward cooperation. Their extensive correspondence with collateral needs may cause collective survival needs to be particularly affected by disturbances in the pursuit of collateral needs. Individuals who are frustrated in their pursuit of collateral needs and suppress such pursuits to reduce their unhappiness may abstain from engaging in tasks necessary for collective survival because the manner of pursuit and the motivations of the underlying needs are narrowly intertwined with collateral needs. That might even happen if collateral frustration does not arise from participants in collective survival pursuits or individuals with the potential of pursuing collective survival needs. The resulting denial of cooperation may disrupt social interaction that is necessary to secure our species' survival by a mere failure to engage in such an interaction. But a frustration of collateral needs may also be vented by behavior that actively damages collective survival. This destructive demeanor, by itself or by the conflict it incites, may become so effective and so widespread that it devastates or eliminates parts or all of humanity. Short of that, collective survival mechanisms may become so weakened by nonfeasance or malfeasance that humanity or segments of it may decline or expire without any other causes or might be damaged by or succumb to external causes that otherwise could be repelled or survived.

A failure to satisfy collateral needs seems to have a lesser effect on individual survival needs. Frustrations of our collateral needs may weaken our resolve and our resilience to pursue our individual survival needs similar to how they might affect our collective survival needs. In extreme cases, such frustrations may make us lash out against other individuals or ourselves or to cease our pursuits of individual survival needs. However, those needs appear to be intrinsically much less dependent on cooperation by others. Our collateral needs seem less likely to directly affect our capacity to engage in overt physical pursuits to obtain overt physical means for our individual survival. Similarly, our failure to cater to the collateral needs of others may only insignificantly affect our ability to satisfy our overt physical pursuits. We may find sufficient counterparts in the pursuits of our individual survival needs who are willing to deal with us on a level purely concerned with obviously physical matters. It appears possible to create modes of interaction where disturbances caused by collateral pursuits would have only an attenuated effect on the pursuit of our individual survival needs, if any effect at all. Even where the pursuits of survival needs and of collateral needs overlap, the damage might be limited although we might have to sacrifice the benefits of collateral motivations for cooperative pursuits. It even seems possible to survive without any social interaction once we leave childhood disabilities and dependences behind.

Then again, that separation may be difficult to realize if we live in an interconnected world where we regularly rely on others for the fulfillment of individual survival needs. A large portion of our obviously physical dealings may not be directly subject to collateral aspects. Nevertheless, the frustration of collateral needs might affect the capability or the willingness of individuals on whose contributions we rely to provide necessary or helpful goods and services. It may further motivate individuals to interfere with necessary or helpful resources for the fulfillment of our individual survival needs or our state of fulfillment. Such actions may be taken because individuals may connect in their mind obviously physical and purportedly mental means and pursuits. A disturbance of our obviously physical pursuits may be targeted at us if those whose collateral needs are frustrated consider us responsible. But our obviously physical dependence on others could also expose us to repercussions if the actual or deemed source of collateral frustration is located anywhere in our supply chain or if it is situated beyond. Even slight effects might have substantial consequences in an interconnected system, and they might build on one another either by causing negative obviously physical interactions or other frustrations.

Not all disturbances in our obviously physical concerns are coincidental. Individuals regularly mingle obviously physical and mental means for the pursuit of both collateral and survival needs. A separation may be concentrated in dealings with individuals on whom we do not rely for the supply of collateral means. Still, that appears to be unnatural. It may weaken obviously physical commitments and leave aspects of our collateral needs wanting. It may therefore be helpful and even necessary to generally harmonize obviously physical with mental pursuits. The artificial and unsustainable character of separating these pursuits becomes particularly clear when we consider our inability to separate obviously physical and mental aspects within the same need. Every need seems to have obviously physical aspects, if not in its objective then at least in its means. A minimum of obviously physical activity seems necessary in some respects to shape circumstances for the fulfillment of mental objectives, and supplementary obviously physical provisions and protections may be helpful in ameliorating fulfillment. Similarly, every need seems to have some mental aspect, if not in its means then at least in its objectives. At the end of our efforts in all our needs we expect a mental, emotional reward. Even if we acknowledge that every need possesses obviously physical and mental aspects, survival needs appear as physiologically originated needs. Our senses tell us that they correspond to functions of particular parts of our body in correlation with environmental factors. The origin of most collateral needs seems less clear, although we may feel that certain parts of our body are involved in them. Our difficulty to connect them directly to a substantive cause or the functionality of a body part may tempt us to describe them as nonphysical. Yet closer inspection indicates that they must be physical phenomena as well. Our collateral needs connect to physical sensory impressions of physical objects and events in and beyond us. This connection implies a physical format of subsequent processing. Moreover, the presence or absence of certain facilities or conditions in our body determines whether we exhibit certain collateral needs and how these needs are expressed. We seem to draw a distinction between collateral and remaining needs based on a difference between sensory impressions that we connect with physical objects and events and sensory impressions that we connect to mental phenomena. This distinction seems to originate from our natural incapacity to direct our senses toward the physiological processes in our mind and not from a fundamentally different, nonphysical quality of our mind.

We may therefore remain with the classification of needs based on their relationship to individual or collective survival. Although that distinction seems to have immediate merit in grouping the principal functions of our survival needs, it is ultimately superficial as well. Our ability to pursue collective survival needs is founded on our individual survival, and our individual life would be negatively affected by an absence of collective survival needs, or individuals would not even exist. The distinction provides even less assistance in the area of collateral needs because most of these do not appear to distinguish in this way. Its import is further diminished by a variety of interchanges occurring among all types of needs. Effects of collateral needs on individual survival needs may bear on collective survival needs. Effects of collateral needs on collective survival needs may have an impact on our individual survival needs. Beyond effects by collateral needs on our individual and collective survival needs, we can also detect the reverse. Additional correlations can be found between individual and collective survival needs and between the individual and collective aspects of collateral needs. Finally, our undertakings for needs in each of these categories may have effects on the pursuit of other needs in that same category.

Accordingly, there does not appear to be any limit to the variety and spread of interchanges among all kinds of pursuits. Nevertheless, we may regard the ubiquitous presence of collateral needs combined with the resistance of most of them to immediate categorization and a definition that shows them to be in support of our individual or collective survival as particularly problematic. We may believe that they pose a threat of disturbances for the pursuit of our individual and collective survival needs that exceeds the level of a mere nuisance. Even if we concede that survival needs may as well influence one another in detrimental ways, we may view that to be a necessary tradeoff because

all of these needs are necessary to secure human survival. We may argue that the relationship of survival needs should not present a great
problem because it has been perfected since the beginning of life. We
may view many or all collateral needs as comparatively recent developments that cause particular volatility for the formation, spread, and
expansion of disturbances. They do not appear to be as accessible to
reason or clearly bound to the same purpose as survival needs. Their
complex, surreptitious, and frequently interwoven character raises the
risk that disturbances might arise and circulate without effective containment. Their negative effects may not be easily discerned because
they might accumulate in small and diverse increments, develop over
time, or become revolving and increasing causes for one another. This
may make the arrest or the reversal of negative developments difficult.
We might conclude that their troublesome potential makes them burdens from which we have to liberate ourselves. We may also be of the
opinion that such hindrances are largely or entirely unnecessary. References to life forms that are successful in their individual and collective survival without any or most of our collateral needs or with sim-
plified versions of them appear to support that view. Arguably, all positive motivations to secure human survival that are conferred by collateral needs can arise from survival needs as well. It might therefore
seem that we could improve our happiness if we abolished or simpli-
fied our collateral needs because we would reduce our risk of failure.

Nevertheless, when we inspect our collateral needs, we can discern a constructive function of every need for us individually and as a
species. Unilateral pursuits of collateral needs can protect and support
the fulfillment of survival needs for others. Moreover, the pursuit and
satisfaction of interactive collateral needs can generate incentives, organizational structures, and procedures for unilateral and for mutual
protection and support that can not only fortify but also broaden and
deepen our activities on behalf of our survival needs. The resulting effectiveness, efficiency, and resiliency may assist us to overcome adversities and provide a crucial edge in securing survival. The development
of collateral needs and their relative advantages can be traced in related species of lesser advancement. Although the negative potential of
collateral needs if they are not satisfied and the investments and for-
bearances that they demand compete with the benefits they can confer, they seem to benefit humanity and individual humans more than
they detract. In any event, our collateral needs are ingrained in us as
much as our survival needs. This compels us to manage their positive
and negative potential. It invests us with an obligation to fulfill them
that is paired with a threat if we fail or we go too far in their pursuit.

Their influence on our individual and collective existence prevents us from keeping them in a category of lesser importance. Collateral needs must be categorized as survival needs as well. In acknowledgment of this fact, we may refer to what we previously termed survival needs as basic survival needs. To signify the combined importance of basic survival needs and collateral needs, we refer to them as existential needs.

The pursuit of collateral needs may not only markedly increase our chances of survival in terms of a bare continuation of our existence. They also have the capacity and the tendency to render that existence more secure and less arduous. They assist us in forming a buffer of means and strategies that can improve our management of existential threats and challenges. Yet even our basic needs for individual and collective survival incorporate that aspect. We try to reach a level of existence that avails us and our kind of more than a minimum level of survival. We do not merely want to exist. We want to thrive as well. We want to increase and maximize the fulfillment of our needs. With this additional purpose of our existential needs, they present themselves as needs for individual and collective survival and thriving.

Now that we comprehend the basic classes and underlying purposes and effects of our needs, we can turn our attention to our experience of their function. The irresistible character of our needs coerces us to act upon their command. We pursue their impulses because we feel a longing to make them cease. We experience them as emotional discontent. The unpleasant character of the upheaval they cause motivates us to take action that appeases them by meeting their requirements. We may characterize needs by our refutation of their disturbance. We may describe them in terms of our struggle to escape unsettling, irritating, or more painful conditions. We may also brand them by the relief we sense in their resolution and by our attachment to the related objects and events. Defining our needs in positive and negative terms begins to contour our motivations, our underlying concerns and hopes, the extent of potential we seek to bridge. It becomes clear that we pursue the fulfillment of our needs for two related purposes. We try to avoid or escape from circumstances we perceive as painful and to reach or maintain a state of affairs we regard as pleasant. The relation of these two categories differentiates them as the beginning and end points for our drive to satisfy our needs. Our movement between them can be described as a sequence of steps by which we leave pain behind and approach pleasure. Our struggles for the fulfillment of our needs are marked by our movements in a spectrum from pain toward pleasure. We are happy when we avoid or escape from pain and obtain or maintain pleasure. Pain and pleasure are our basic motivations for seeking happiness. It appears that the absence of pain and presence of pleasure represents our ideal of happiness. Conversely, the presence of pain and absence of pleasure seems to epitomize unhappiness. Thus, happiness can be equated with pleasure, and pain with unhappiness.

The ability to build strategies for the satisfaction of our needs occurs on several levels. In their most rudimentary experience of pain and pleasure, life forms react to the immediate sensory experiences of pain and pleasure without foresight or recollection of the same or the opposing type of sensory condition. The immediacy of pain and pleasure informs us whether we are in a state that damages or benefits us. If we could not foresee or recall pleasurable events in a condition of pain, pain would seem to be the sole motivator to improve our chances of survival and thriving. We could only react by fleeing or dismantling causes of pain. If we find ourselves in circumstances that create pleasure, these motivations cease. Pleasure does not seem to generate a motivation of its own in the immediacy of its sensation. We cannot develop a motivation to sustain conditions of fulfillment if we do not have a memory of pain. Once we are in a state of pleasure, its momentary impression motivates us to cease activities of pursuit until a painful state reemerges. Further, without its memory, pleasure cannot be a motivator in the formulation of our wishes in a state of deficiency. The rudimentary duality of repulsion from a state of pain resulting in activity and of satisfaction and rest in a state of pleasure serves organisms well as a simple guidance scheme. Even inactivity upon pleasure may have its merits because it creates efficiency by conserving energy and because it forestalls organisms from leaving or destroying a conducive situation. Still, an existence where we blindly run into pain and pleasure and react only in the moment does not provide the most effective or efficient direction. As important as information of pain and pleasure might be, it is of incomplete benefit. The efficiency of sensing pain and pleasure becomes vastly enhanced if we can avoid incidents that damage the fulfillment of our needs and if we can seek incidents that have positive effects. These adjuncts to pain and pleasure represent the ability to anticipate pain and pleasure. With respect to pain, we call its anticipation fear. The anticipation of pleasure is desire.

Fear and desire enrich the mechanism of our wishes beyond an immediate reflex to exposure. When we fear, we appear to be repulsed by future circumstances we imagine to cause pain. When we desire, we appear to be attracted to future circumstances we imagine to cause pleasure. We can presently sense a shadow of the pain or pleasure we expect from circumstances we anticipate. We might be under the impression that when we fear or desire we make future pain or pleasure present. Yet, in fact, we are drawing on experiences of pain and pleasure and project them into the future. Together with the transposition of past factual circumstances, we transfer emotional impressions that were connected to the samples from which we draw. Fear and desire appear to require a higher-developed mental capacity because they involve recollection and projection of painful or pleasurable results. But fear and desire do not seem to be limited to individual learning about elements of painful and pleasurable events and the application of that knowledge to subsequent occurrences that bear similarity to elements of these former events. Even relatively basic life forms that cannot individually build anticipations from memories seem to possess modes of fear and desire. They may avoid painful situations before their painful impact comes to pass. They may further be able to seek pleasurable circumstances or to maintain such circumstances. In these life forms, fear or desire seem to be instilled by an automatic emotional response that is based on genetic development. Experiences of pain and pleasure may instigate or influence the formation of genetic material. They may install a genetic memory of past events or patterns of events and a program that executes at the sign of partial congruence of indicators with such genetic memory. Then again, developments that instill fear or desire might not be the result of experiences. Rather, they might be the result of variations whose development is inherently programmed in genetic mechanisms or is formed by environmental influences that are unrelated to causes of pain or pleasure. The motivating experiences of pain or pleasure that were selected by these mutations may make it appear as if the mutations were developed in reaction to painful or pleasurable experiences. Such a semblance may be intensified because coincidental mutations may overlay with experience-based mutations as well as projections arising from experiences during an individual's life. The combination of these factors may cause some individuals and species to react more appropriately to threats or to opportunities than others, favoring the survival of them and their reaction modes.

The developmental history of humans makes them continuing carriers for genetic sources of fear and of desire. These sources may be modulated or supplemented by experiences of individuals during their lifetime. However, the long-standing development of genetic foundations for fear and desire demands a presumption of validity similar to our sense of pain and pleasure. Our species might have survived with some genetically prompted motivations that were always or that have become deleterious to our survival or thriving. Only, considering the momentous challenges humankind has faced in its development, such detractions in large number or intensity should have caused our species' demise. Although we may have wishes that might yet cause such a result, no existential needs seem to be intrinsically useless or detrimental. Rather, detriments induced by genetic motivations seem to be confined to issues that concern the context, direction, or manner of pursuits. As we develop, such motivations may require or benefit from adjustment to reflect varied challenges and opportunities. Experiences of pain and pleasure permit us to reinforce, contradict, or supplement genetic impulses. But experiential debate with genetic forces may only be partly effective because these are engraved in our essence. Our genetic motivations may attempt to condition us in spite of experiences. Particularly where contradicting or adjusting experiences are missing or lack strength, genetic motivations may move us to imagine causes that never applied or no longer apply or reactions that were never or are no longer optimized for individual or collective survival and thriving. They may prompt us to form wishes or may influence our wishes in unproductive or detrimental ways. On the other hand, inappropriate pursuits may also result from erroneous interpretations and reactions to experiences that we apply against better genetic judgment.

In their anticipatory context, fear and desire preserve the functions of immediate pain and pleasure differently. Fear forms an extension of past or present pain as anticipated pain. Although similar, that extension can be very useful for the satisfaction of our needs. It retains the same motivating quality of deterring us from and antagonizing us against situations with the potential of harming the fulfillment of our needs. Only now, we can react to harmful events in their nascent stages or can possibly prevent them. Nevertheless, in avoiding or fighting damaging developments, the character of our responses would generally remain the same. Desire, by contrast, exceeds the previously passive function of pleasure as a signal to cease fulfillment activity. Its anticipation of pleasurable events motivates representatives of life forms to pursue circumstances that may serve the fulfillment of their needs. Arguably, fear already incites activities that serve our needs by motivating us to avoid or curtail potentially painful circumstances. Similarly, pain already incites activities that serve our needs by motivating us to flee from or fight actually painful circumstances. Yet desire imparts an opportunity of qualitative departure from these activities. It instills the concept of wishes with a positive counterpart to pain and fear. The ability to instinctively sense and carry a pleasurable notion and to introduce it as an aim is significant. The resulting focus on the satisfaction of needs allows a more purposeful shaping of events compared to the negation of loathsome circumstances by fear and pain. The positive imagery of desired states provides wishes with positive objectives.

These objectives combine with situations of actual or anticipated deprivation to build a developmental motivation that gives our wishes direction and encourages the construction of a concentrated strategy of pursuit. We may call this structure arching between actual and anticipated pain as its starting position and anticipated and eventually actual pleasure as its completion point the pain-pleasure mechanism.

With the forethought of fear and desire, our position becomes proactive instead of being reactive. We gain the opportunity to seek, select, produce, and shape objects and events we favor and to change, prevent, or evade objects and events we disfavor. This ability to generate or affect our future experiences forms a powerful tool in bridging the distance between deprivation and pleasure. Present and anticipated pain and present and anticipated pleasure all drive us toward the satisfaction of a need. Together with actual pain, anticipated pain repulses us from activities that incur, prolong, or deepen our immersion in circumstances that engender such sensations. The negativity of this experience motivates us to take action and terminate, avoid, or at least reduce exposure to a need. It urges us to fight and overcome or to flee and abstain from damaging circumstances and behavior. The motivations that pain and fear can create are vital for our pursuits because they assist us in rejecting and distancing ourselves from what hurts or threatens us. Yet, beyond these reactions, their motivations may only find an expression in incoherent, misdirected, or destructive behavior. Even an emphasis on obstacles that seem to counteract our departure from deprivation or on progress in the departure may be shortsighted. These concerns may not be sufficient to secure our survival and thriving. To make our departures more effective and efficient, we require a positive motivation that infuses direction and draws us toward the fulfillment of our requirements. Anticipatory pleasure sets a beacon toward which we strive. Even actual pleasure obtains essential functions through the capacity of recollection and anticipation. By rewarding us, it generates positive reinforcement for our anticipation and pursuit of pleasure. Its memory can function as reference point for anticipations, and it can contrast and therewith assist to define actual or anticipated pain. Particularly, a current experience of a pleasurable condition constitutes a necessary element for developing a fear of losing it.

Although notions of pain and pleasure, as well as their anticipatory aspects, stand diametrically opposed to each other, pain and fear push us toward happiness and combine with the pull of pleasure and desire. We regularly sense these opposites contemporaneously in the formulation of our wishes. When we aspire toward the fulfillment of a need, we feel the pain of a present deprivation and the anticipation of pleasure. Our unmet desire intensifies our pain because it emphasizes the discrepancy of our current state. We further fear the experience of additional pain until we meet our desire and the uncertainty of obtaining satisfaction. By anticipating the pleasure of fulfillment, we also sense a positive emotion. We perceive an attraction to the anticipated pleasure to be generated by the fulfillment of a wish and to the anticipated relief of our pain and fear. If we presently enjoy the pleasure of fulfillment, that emotional condition and the desire to sustain its presence are paired with fear that the continuation of pleasure might fail, if we believe that to be possible. We fear that we might be exposed to the pain of deprivation and the pain of struggling to regain fulfillment. That fear enables desire to maintain the present fulfillment of a need, giving rise to a potent amalgamated motivation. In the resulting wish to maintain happiness, we sense the pleasure of fulfillment and anticipation of its persistence, but we also fear the pain of its absence.

We may then conclude that in both the state of deprivation and the state of fulfillment, our awareness encompasses pain and pleasure either as existing or as a potential. We inexorably feel the presence of one state and the anticipation of the other. In either state, we experience the contrast between what is and what is not and our emotional attraction or repulsion regarding these states. Thus, every wish is motivated by our perception of both pain and pleasure. To occur, a wish has to encompass a differential between the current and an imagined state. We are incapable perceiving a state as better unless we conceive of another state as worse. We cannot imagine the relief of fulfillment without the actual or deemed deprivation of a need. Every wish by its nature entails a movement from a position that is closer to pain to a position that is closer to pleasure. Our wishes are created by, exist in, and represent the discrepancy between these two points. The urgency of a wish is defined by the distance between the situations of pain and pleasure represented in a wish. It would appear that we are incessantly subjected to our wishes. At any time, we are in one of the two states that give rise to them. We are either repulsed by our present state and attracted to an anticipated state, or we are attracted to a present state and repulsed from an anticipated state. Our wishes preoccupy us with desired or feared change. This state of mind gives rise to a restless existence that immerses us in a never-ending succession of wishes.

Our wishes regularly occur in multiple contemporaneous pursuits of different and possibly the same needs. Although our principal needs for individual or collective survival and thriving are supported by subordinated existential needs, these principal needs do not necessarily impress us as leading motivators. Needs whose pursuit advances them are incentivized by their own immediate concerns and rewards. The emotional objective of each need is its own satisfaction. For each need, we can distinguish a different kind of pain and pleasure, a specific quality of happiness and unhappiness. These differences describe needs and identify them to us as disparate. They share the same general pain-pleasure mechanism to indicate deprivation and fulfillment. We can therefore employ general concepts of happiness and unhappiness on them. Still, when we refer to our need to be happy, we are implicitly referring to happiness in different regions of our being. These variations are necessary to enable us to react appropriately toward different types of threats or deficiencies to our individual and collective existence. We could not function with a uniform concept of happiness because we would have no guidance which underlying factual necessities for survival and thriving must be addressed to create satisfaction. The differentiation of pain and pleasure for each type of requirement enables us to identify the functionalities that are in need of remediation or upkeep. Our pursuits are guided by their state and by their potential for change represented by circumstances for each need.

Experiences of deprivation and satisfaction happen in a natural cycle for a large part of our needs, while other needs are not cyclical. Although some needs are initially experienced in their state of satisfaction, other needs may be initially experienced without any knowledge of their satisfaction. If they enter our awareness as an incident of pain without our prior experience of their satisfaction, we have at best a genetic urge to guide our actions. Our forays may be directed by automated instructions that point us toward means or strategies of fulfillment. Genetic instincts may be able to motivate our wishes entirely or partly. Although their instructions might be precise with regard to means, their ultimate objectives may remain indefinite in our mind as long as we possess no memory of satisfaction to which our mind could aspire. Before the initial satisfaction of a need, we do not know the ultimate conclusion for our wishes. Even genetic instructions regarding means may be nebulous or may not be triggered until we are exposed to them. We may be conditioned to search for them without much of previous a notion of them. All we might be able to formulate with certainty might be a negative wish to escape the state of pain or fear we experience. That negative wish may have us search for its counterpart of fulfillment and hence reinforce the search incentivized by positive generic imprints. Apart from that, we may learn from examples or instructions by others. We may imagine fulfillment to be similar to incidents we experienced concerning other needs. Notwithstanding, until the differential between pain and pleasure gains definition by experiencing it for a need, its emotional push and pull will not have been appropriately expressed. Even if we have access to technical information, we cannot be sure that sequences we formulate will cause fulfillment.

Correspondingly, if we have never experienced a need in its deprived state, we cannot formulate a fully formed wish of preserving its fulfillment. The continuous fulfillment of a need may prevent us from being aware of such a need's existence, even as a matter of genetic instinct because its actualization remains dormant as long as a need remains fulfilled. The pleasure of fulfillment does not provide an understanding of its absence. We must have a contrasting experience. Short of experiencing actual deprivation, we can draw on our experiences of pain from the deprivation of other needs. Our inquiries into potentials of loss may leave us with an understanding of the circumstances that maintain fulfillment of a need. We could impart fear regarding events that might deprive us of these circumstances by actual or by simulated endangerment. But such a fear would be indefinite and likely miss the motivating vigor of fear that is founded in a prior experience of loss.

The dichotomy between pain and pleasure may grant us an idea of the general mechanism at the foundation of our needs. Still, to understand the phenomenon of our needs fully, we have to give scrutiny to their sources. As we embark on that exploration, we are confronted by the question how we apply the term need. It appears to incorporate several aspects that we appear to combine in common usage. We can describe a need as a deficiency of means that we require to survive or thrive, thus describing the objective causes for a need. In addition, we use the term to describe our awareness of a deficiency. Finally, we use the term to describe our mental response in form of our motivation to neutralize the causes and our awareness of deficiencies. While we can distinguish among these three aspects of cause, awareness, and reaction, our usage of need commonly encompasses all these aspects. That may be so because these three aspects form parts of an automatic process in which they are naturally linked. Circumstances of actual and of potential deprivation involuntarily prompt our awareness of these circumstances, which involuntarily triggers the urge to address them. All our needs impress us as such involuntary phenomena. They appear to us as uncontrollable forces of nature that seem to originate, if not dictate, our demeanor. Our at times limited understanding of them, their causes, and the ways in which they impose on us can make our needs appear like strange and mysterious forces although they define us.

Because we come across our needs as involuntary sensory phenomena that trigger involuntary responses, we are describing them as forces that move us, as emotions. Most physiological mechanisms involved in our needs are concentrated in our brain. It is largely the site that processes sensory information into emotional reactions. It generates pain, fear, pleasure, and desire from sensory impressions. It also correlates, categorizes, stores, and retrieves sensory impressions of objects and events that we consider to be associated with emotions and generates directives in response by its instinctive mechanisms. Even a number of sensory origins for needs, particularly concerning collateral needs, appear to be located there. Still, many origins for our needs are located in, perceived by, conveyed by, and possibly partly processed in other parts of our body. While we may call all these phenomena mental processes, we can distinguish perceptive facilities that detect, convert, and transport sensory signals from emotional facilities that process our awareness of and response to them. The quality of our emotional mind, our emotional intelligence, can be measured by how well it pairs sensory impressions with emotional cognizance and responses in assistance of our needs. In humanity's development, perceptive and emotional facilities initially encompassed the entirety of our mind.

Eventually, they were supplemented by discrete facilities of rational thought that we may call our rational mind. Although it seems to depend on the same perceptive mechanisms as our emotional mind and generates awareness, that awareness is only factual and remains detached from the emotional mechanisms of pain, fear, pleasure, and desire and instinctive reactions. Similar to our emotional mind, it relates, categorizes, stores, and retrieves sensory representations of objects and events, but it does so with a vastly expanded capacity. While emotional facilities are limited to processing the fact that certain objects and events or types of them are linked to emotions, rational facilities discern how they happen. Our rational mind processes sensory information of objects and events in a spatially or sequentially correlated manner, and catalogues them according to recognitions of order. The quality of our rational mind, our rational intelligence, can be calculated in four aspects. The first is how well we remember objects and events or connected rational activity in which we engaged. This is our capacity to recall. Another is how well we derive causality from observations. That is our capacity to understand. A third aspect is how well we keep the correlations of multiple aspects present in our mind, our capacity to associate. Finally, rational intelligence is measured by how well we conceptualize new objects or events as means for pursuits, our capacity to invent. These capacities assist similar, rudimentary capacities of our emotional mind and its aptitude to plan and implement the pursuit of our needs. The next chapter examines rational capacities in more detail and how they interact with our emotional capacities.

CHAPTER 2
EMOTIONAL AND RATIONAL MIND

When we review our rational discovery of objects and events, we often find that they consist of components that in turn can be distinguished into subcomponents. Components may serve as subcomponents, and subcomponents may present components in other conditions. Objects or events may be components or subcomponents in larger conglomerations. Hence, most aspects we explore can be designated as subcomponents, components, or composites depending on our focus. We may use the terms object or event to designate the level of combination we are primarily trying to explore, accomplish, or change. To uncover the reasons for the functioning of objects or events, we may not have to comprehend all or any of their components. The combination of their components may be so stable that the resulting properties can be attributed to the objects or events, allowing us to use them without an investigation of their constituents. Then again, circumstances may require that we take more intimate command of objects and events. We may want to enhance them, build, prevent, or guarantee their stability, secure their occurrence, or control them better in other respects. For these purposes, we may need to know to some extent what components create the functions of the entirety and how they create these functions. To achieve that knowledge, we may have to understand the presence, properties, and interaction of components at several successive constituent levels. But it may often be unnecessary to investigate the deepest possible levels to sufficiently ascertain the nature and the source of behavior we are trying to understand, effect, or affect.

We familiarize ourselves with components so we can assemble them to functioning objects or events or so we can control or alter existing objects or events. We can derive some of this knowledge by isolating components. Isolated components may tell us about aspects of their nature by direct impressions emanating from them on our senses or on measuring devices. We may extract important basic knowledge by studying the behavior of components separately. But we may only understand their functionalities sufficiently to support our purposes if we observe their interaction with other components or combinations of components. That requirement may apply not only when we try to assemble an unprecedented or emulated object or event from components but also when we attempt to understand the workings of an object or event to use or otherwise affect it. We add to our knowledge of components by witnessing their effect on one another as parts of the same object or event, on combined aspects of such an object or event, on the remainder of such an object or event, and on the external context of such an object or event. To be complete and to afford us information about possible challenges and opportunities, we may also venture beyond and research the behavior of components in contexts that are not part of an object or event we are trying to build, use, or otherwise affect. To most comprehensively establish our knowledge and reveal useful means, we may observe the effects among components and combinations at different stages of assembly that are unrelated to an immediate intent. We may thus synthesize substances in a variety of combinations and observe their reaction to understand their utility and to use the product immediately or to possess a future example.

However, synthesis alone might not complete our understanding. We gain additional insight by separating components from combinations. Here again, our wishes and inquiries may not always be focused on constructive purposes for a particular object or event. Most basically, we may attempt to separate components from combinations to use them in another context and may need to understand how that can be accomplished. We may also seek to alter an object or event by breaking or diminishing its functions. This may require that we learn to subtract components. To find relevant components for such an undertaking, we might have to test the separation of various components alone or together from their participation in an object or event. Even if we pursue constructive purposes concerning an object or event, we may have to separate or maintain separation of certain components to enable or enhance its functioning. Further, components that we might require or find useful in building, using, or otherwise affecting objects or events may not occur separately. We may have to subtract components from combinations to identify and understand the existence and properties of such components and to test and observe their correlations. When we separate components, we overwhelmingly have an eye on using the result in a synthesized position. In a constructive setting, our observation of components' behavior during and as a consequence of severing their relationship with other components may illuminate them and such other components. We may use such insights to reconstitute the deconstructed object or event or to construct another similar or different object or event. Even when we attempt to disable functions, we may wish to confirm the effectiveness of deconstruction for immediate purposes, future repetitions, and to preserve their reversibility for present and future purposes by comprehending the essential functions of severed components. Thus, when we isolate components, we often record their synthesized state we are dissolving and the processes involved in and resulting from separation to attain control.

We may then conclude that without undertaking analysis and synthesis it may not be possible to understand or influence functions within an existing object or event or to conceive and create a new object or event. Analysis and synthesis appear to be indispensable, connected processes to comprehend the workings of our domain and to shape it according to our needs. As we separate and associate components, we understand participants and relational causalities that constitute objects and events. This also permits us to distinguish relevant components from others that have no material effect on a result or counteract or inhibit the result. To ascertain the involved participants, their properties, and their interactions that create the existence and functions of an object or event, our inquiries move back and forth between separation and correlation. To gain sufficient understanding of and command over an object or event, we may have to engage in such an interchange between analysis and synthesis at several stages of assembly. What we may commonly call analysis therefore often reveals itself as a process of gaining comprehension that comprises both analysis and synthesis. To prevent misunderstandings, further discussions apply the term analysis in its precise sense of separating components from an entirety and use the terms investigation, examination, or their synonyms to refer to the combined process of analysis and synthesis.

Although the limited application of this investigative technique of analysis and synthesis to individual settings may be instructive, it alone does not seem very efficient. Our understanding of the particular causalities in particular settings we explore enables us to train our behavior should we encounter such a setting again. It may also allow us to re-create such a situation and its effects. However, limiting ourselves to the re-creation and the avoidance of identical settings would not seem to be very helpful. Trying to re-create the exact circumstances that have previously induced pleasure and taking precautions solely when we detect circumstances that are identical with those that have previously led to pain are not the most effective ways to use our experiences. We rarely enjoy the luxury of encountering identical circumstances in our attempts to satisfy our needs. The differences in the settings we encounter are at times extensive. If our mental skills are limited to working with identical circumstances, we might not be able to act effectively or efficiently or might not be able to act at all. Understanding the relational causalities of a particular setting may not help us to predict the outcome of different or changed settings. New components may attend or some components may be missing. There may be variations in the number or quality of familiar components or the components may have different allocations. These factors may change the outcome. Incomplete or unreliable data may require us to speculate on foundations of superficial perceptions and extrapolations. We may venture predictions of outcome according to the congruence of some components with settings we have already experienced. Yet remaining factors may disturb that assessment. The components whose demeanor we observed in a particular setting may perform differently in other settings. Our lack of insight into the causation of a particular new setting may prevent a sufficiently secure forecast of its effects.

We may identify changes in new settings by allowing them to play out and by repeating a procedure of analysis and reassembly with every changed context we meet. We may accumulate experiences and have them correlate and overlay to form a library of causes and effects. Such a library would allow us to narrow the deficiencies in our knowledge. But it still would not resolve our problems of predictability if we continue to encounter substantial variations of circumstances. Beyond that, creating a sufficient number of sample experiences can be cumbersome, dangerous, and costly. Even where deviations in the settings we encounter are limited, the threat or burden that particular settings and their variations present may render it unreasonable to go through their experience to understand them. Hence, the capacity to assess the effects of varied settings without permitting them to come to fruition seems to be of considerable benefit. We wish to predict the result of a change in a setting or an entirely new setting without having to experience it. Making such predictions correctly can be of vital importance for the effective and efficient fulfillment of our needs. Anticipating the behavior of our environment and of our body helps us in our efforts of avoidance, control, and use. To plan and implement the fulfillment of our needs competently, we have to build anticipatory knowledge. We must be able to project whether the effect of a setting falls within the range of our requirements, has no bearing, or is detrimental. We also must be able to forecast quantitative and qualitative specifics.

Achieving such authorities of prediction and related skills of assembly and deconstruction in a world of ever-changing circumstances presents a complex problem. However, we can begin to bring order into our comprehension of our world and rationalize our demeanor in it by focusing on the similarity of its phenomena. We must gain an understanding of attributes and reactions among components and their combinations that make them similar. By revealing similar attributes and reactions, we can build our knowledge of a common causative essence. The derivation of this common essence permits us to search for and to employ this essence in other contexts, to sustain it where it has already been achieved, or to destroy it and keep it from happening in

situations we seek to prevent. We can rationalize our activities by recognizing and exercising common themes, common denominators that
we may be able to use to produce or address settings of a certain type.
Understanding similarity can enormously expand our ability to obtain
pleasure and avoid pain. It permits us to venture past the specific processes of our experiences and to expand our understanding to settings
that, although different, share key similarities. To determine similarity, we have to be able to allow for variation from circumstances we already experienced. We may establish similarity on account of partial
identity, our recognition of some ingredients, features, or occurrences
that are the same. Yet deriving similarity from such a partial recognition still relies on the notion of identity, albeit to a smaller extent.
Even such partial identity may be difficult to find and may restrict the
utility of our inquiries about similarity. Moreover, inferring similarity
from a finding of partly identical circumstances is imprecise because it
ignores factors that are not the same. With this definition of similarity, we have not significantly advanced our capabilities and may have
opened our pursuits to error under a false sense of security. It appears
that we can only fully develop the potential of similarity assessments if
we initially focus our attention on the similarity of effects.

The range of relevant deviations we examine is defined by their
positive and negative effects on the fulfillment of our needs. The fundamental quality of being beneficial or damaging moves us to define
effects as fundamentally similar. We may seek the determination of a
range of effects to determine which allocations are better suited or optimized for the fulfillment of our needs. We may also review a range of
effects because we may only have access to modes of fulfillment that
are less than ideal or only such modes may be prudent at the time. We
include effects as long as they bring about at least minimum requirements for advancement of a need or a step. Our goal for now is to find
means that are sufficient to propel us to other means in a sequence to
satisfy a particular need. In this respect, similarity is described by the
ability of a circumstance to serve the fulfillment of a particular need or
any of its steps. We may further seek to determine a range of effects to
determine which damaging circumstances detract from the fulfillment
of our needs more than others so that we can limit damage as much as
possible. In that context, similarity is defined by the capacity of a circumstance to damage the fulfillment of a particular need or any of its
steps. More particularly, we may define similarity by the capacity of a
circumstance to serve or damage the fulfillment of a particular need or
of particular steps with a distinctive quality or quantity of result. The
shared utility or detriment for a particular need or a step in its pursuit

defines circumstances as similar. Depending on our needs and our circumstances, we may demand exactitude of a very specific quality and quantity or allow for a quantitative or qualitative range in our definitions. Our assessment of an acceptable range of similarity may change as our needs and circumstances change. Our acceptance of a range of effects as similar induces us to accept a range of causes and carriers of these causes that are responsible for these effects as similar as well.

The establishment of a definitional range of similarity is generally supported by our emotional mind through its relation of emotions for each need to our memory of emotionally registered factual experiences. When we recall or anticipate pain or pleasure concerning a particular need, we may recollect and refer to the factual experiences related to these emotions. This establishes involved facts as roughly similar. But this mechanism is too blunt to give us much useful guidance. The capability to recognize the relatedness of sensory experiences according to their type without these experiences being identical is not exclusive to our rational mind. Yet its combination with our rational capacity to recognize the relatedness of factual states enables us to be more focused and discerning in grouping phenomena. In our ability to relate similarities, we may be assisted by our shortcomings as much as by our skills. Such shortcomings may consist of limitations in our sensory capacities to perceive differences. They may also comprise limitations in the ensuing processing of sensory information. Our mind may not transport or translate sensory differentiations. It may process sensory perceptions within a range along the same or similar paths, store them in the same or related locations, or retrieve them as identical or related. It may tag and process our impressions according to one or a few aspects of apparent shared characteristics. Such inaccuracies and the consequential commingling or relating of matters of perception in our mind may produce an initial disability or disinterest to distinguish among components and their combinations in relation to their differences. The procedures by which we perceive, analyze, synthesize, categorize, store, and retrieve information may prompt us to group them together under imprecise criteria. When we process one occasion, we are therefore reminded of other incidents that possess some aspect of similarity. While this interrelation can lead to erroneous reactions, its inaccuracy in processing and marking deviations within a range of experiences as being the same or related can benefit us. It yields a natural basis to be mindful of shared characteristics and explore and define them further. As we examine such items of perception closer, we may become able to distinguish them in their dissimilarities and to quantify and qualify their similarities into a range of related properties.

Assessing the factual circumstances associated with appearances of similarity may permit us to better define ranges of circumstances and sequences we regard as similar and to subcategorize these ranges. Sensory distinctions within or surrounding similarities may lead us to describe more detailed experiential aspects by their singular attributes and by those that evidence themselves in correlations. Our experiences might not deliver sufficient information to define the entirety of an applicable similarity range in conditions or in ultimate effects on our needs because of the possible variation of circumstances and a lack of incidents. Additional investigation may be necessary. Still, our existing experiences can suggest possible areas for exploration. They may assist us in establishing a group of related data points as a basis for such exploration. Once we have defined the range of an effect in which we are interested, we have to look at the array of causes that combine to produce occurrences within such a range. These may consist of relatively simple variations. But we may also discover more deeply dissimilar sequences that may produce results within the same range. This implies the use of some of the same components or that different components or groups of components have the same or similar properties. Investigating the circumstances under which similar or even the same effects are produced may reveal the essence that causes them to concur.

Capturing the essence of similarity may initially appear to be an intimidating undertaking because of the apparently endless differentiation of settings. Nevertheless, as we engage in the procedures of deconstructing and rebuilding objects and events, we become aware that they are composed of a limited, more manageable number of components. By acquainting ourselves with these more fundamental components, we come to comprehend that they perform according to rational principles that also conduct their interaction and result in mechanisms of higher organization. We realize that our world is ordered and that it is functioning by apparently immutable elements of substance and standards specifically attached to these elements or even shared by all of them. We recognize that we can understand the great variety of objects and events as particularized combinations of more general components. In our undertaking to organize our world for purposes of our pursuits, we might forgo inquiries into more basic substances and principles. We might instead cast phenomena that have become eminent at higher levels of correlation into not further differentiated substances and principles to enhance their utility for our management of objects and events. That might provide us with adequate orientation regarding phenomena in which we are immediately interested. However, our lack of depth restricts our understanding of how the world is structured and how these structures behave in relation to our objectives. It limits us to the use of superficial aspects of our world without accessing the authority of manipulating their constituents. To use nature's substances and principles comprehensively, we must systematically undertake observations and categorizations at all its levels of assembly. We might resolve to analyze nature into all its types of components and observe these during and after their separation, in isolation, and in correlation with one another or with other components or combinations. We might synthesize them into combinations and observe the results in isolation or in correlation with other components or combinations. We might replace components that we extract from a combination with other components. Through dissociations and associations of components and combinations of components, we learn about the ranges of relevant causes. We grasp what effects they have alone or in combination with a variety of allocations of the same or of another type of component or combination of components.

This method may originally appear to be indistinguishable from acquiring knowledge of specific settings by letting them play out and studying their particular constituents in their correlations. If anything, the scope of playing out settings would seem to increase by the systematic testing of their potential. But there is an important difference that emerges from our insight that the world is organized by a limited array of substances and principles. Although the work required by our systematic exploration might not be immediately useful, it is bound to eventually save us considerable effort. That the world consists of firmly defined substances and that it functions pursuant to properties that appear to be firmly attached to these substances makes the world predictable once we understand all relevant substances and principles involved in a setting. It permits us to formulate substantive and procedural laws of nature at elemental and higher levels. We must only become mindful of these substances, the basic laws represented by their properties, and the laws resulting from the interrelation of substances and their properties. After that, if we can identify substances and their positioning, we will be able to predict their behavior. Moreover, our knowledge of fundamental substances, their properties, and the consequential laws by which they behave and interact, and the manner in which these components compose objects and events allow us to create means for our pursuits. They empower us to use substances and their functions according to our insights of their typical behavior. We may call this approach that systematically tests the activity and interaction of components and combinations of components to understand the substances and principles of nature the scientific method.

The identification of a limited number of firm substances and principles rationalizes our pursuits. It makes our pursuits accessible to our rational mind in as far as our means and their detractions become rationally intelligible. It makes our command over nature a matter of discovering its substances and grasping and applying its organizational principles. Scientific exploration has then the potential to critically expand the effectiveness and efficiency of our ability to manage us and our environment. The detail and great variety of systematic investigations of correlations among components and their combinations may initially elevate the degree of perceived complexity. But the systematic exploration of interrelations by experiments, the consolidation of insights into principles, and the resulting identification and exploration of remaining areas that have not been scientifically ascertained seems unavoidable if we want to gain maximum control over the fulfillment of our needs. The comprehensive scope of scientific inquiry assists us to explore all accessible threats and means in the pursuit of our needs. Apart from that, systematic exploration seems to only be a temporary imposition until we complete the classification of all causes. We may recognize substances and principles long before we exhaust potential combinations and render additional experimentation superfluous. Research that may have initiated open-ended and may temporarily have led to redundant results therefore may soon be reined in leaving us to the acquisition of substance and its allocation in our pursuits.

Even in the beginning, our research is not likely to be aimless or random. It is likely to be focused on challenges to our pursuits that we would like to mend. To meet such challenges, we might engage in experiments without consideration of what might work to achieve our objective if we have no idea of what might be suitable. However, if we can recognize similarities with other challenges we have learned to resolve, we might be able to narrow the range of possible solutions from the start. Even if we are on a general quest to classify the world's substance and behavior, we are led by the initial similarity of phenomena and seek to expand initial experiences of similarity. Phenomena that already appear to us as similar may provide an easier opportunity to access the commonalities of their constituents. They may facilitate the stripping away of disturbances that cause deviations within a range of similarity and to identify shared substances and laws of nature. Where we cannot find similarity at higher levels of combination, we may still seek to establish sourcing from a limited set of substances and principles by dividing them until we reach levels at which such substances and principles become apparent. Our exploration may lead us to objects and events whose similarity we cannot translate into a common source. We may further find that commonalities at a component level do not result in similar or identical objects and events. Barring known disturbances, we may look for other causes in these settings. We may have to discern that otherwise dissimilar components can carry similar attributes and that similarities do not always warrant the conclusion that components will behave similarly in other respects. Thus, we learn to define the scope and consequences of similarities. Where established substances and laws are not sufficient to provide an explanation of an observation, we may have to modify our impressions of such substances and related principles. Alternatively, we may have to identify additional substances that are responsible for or that contribute to such phenomena. Following such inquiries along criteria of similarity and distinguishing causes may eventually permit us to classify all aspects of our world into their constituent substances and principles.

The substances that scientific research uncovers are defined by their characteristic properties and the interactions of these properties. Both these properties and their interactions can be regarded as laws because they seem to be permanently attached to substances. Our notion of a law of nature arises from the concept of an identical outcome of repeated demonstrations with identical constellations. Its validity is based on the reliability of the cause-effect relationship. That reliability prompts us to pronounce laws of nature that are attached to certain or even all substances. A law of nature is proved by showing that single or multiple causes produce a certain quality or quantity of perception. To acknowledge the validity of a law, we may require unquestionable proof of its existence. If we can demonstrate that certain substances or their combinations by themselves or in relation to one another necessitate an observed effect, we may subsequently dispense with demonstrations of reiterations to acknowledge a law. Such trust is strengthened if it is supported by an insight into how a result is obtained. Although we may base our judgment that a law exists on the notion that a result has remained constant, we cannot predict its unwavering recurrence without knowing what causes that result. Our explanation of why an effect results becomes a guarantor that it reliably results.

The predictable qualities of substances and laws that appear attached to them may render additional practical proof of what they or their correlation will produce largely unnecessary once we have established that they fully explain a phenomenon. Still, a setting of known substances whose allocation or quantitative scaling has not yet been explored may introduce experiences that might not be covered by prior explanations. Our insight into the reasons why an effect results may allow us to securely forecast certain ranges of combinations or scaling.

But the omission of exploration beyond particular ranges leaves room for surprises. Previously unexplored regions may carry effects we were not able to discern at more familiar levels, even if that potential may diminish with advancements of detection. Further, as long as there is a possibility that undetected substances might be present, we cannot foreclose the possibility that settings and the substances and laws we consider establishing them might prove to be different or incomplete. Such undetected substances may consist of additional substances or of subcomponents whose properties and interactions compose what we previously deemed to be substances and their ordered derivatives. Undetected substances may uphold such concepts, or they may pose the actuality or potential of supplements, interferences, or deviations. We may be satisfied if we achieve a scientific explanation of all phenomena we can observe. But we may also want to control these phenomena in excess of what seems possible by the substances and laws we detect. Moreover, there might be phenomena that we cannot currently perceive. Even if we possess no information that unexplained phenomena influence our world, we might be able to make use of such phenomena. Hence, only if we can be certain that we have tested and explained all types of scale and allocation of substances and that we have detected all substances and the principles they bear might scientific exploration end. Arguably, our interest might abate once we have secured all knowledge and capabilities required to satisfy all our needs. However, we might not be able to determine that unless we have ascertained all that might assist us or detract from the fulfillment of our needs.

If the reliability of scientifically predicted events is less than total, we may not be able to designate the explanation of events a law. That may not only be the case if we encounter a failure of predictions. To assert that a law is reliable, even a standard of similarity may not suffice. A distinction of sameness and similarity does not matter much if we permit a range of similar effects as acceptable for the satisfaction of our needs. Yet, with increasing development of our knowledge and capabilities, we appear to tighten our requirements. As we explore nature, we become increasingly encouraged to insist on strict precision in the correlation of causes and effects because we increasingly experience that nature is organized in a precise manner. In addition, strict predictability may become markedly more important as we construct means with increasing complexity and interdependence. The behavior of our constructs may have to be fully predictable because only slight aberrations may cause extensive and potentially catastrophic damage. Even in areas where fluctuations remain acceptable, a decrease of variation will ascertain that effects remain within an acceptable range.

With the burgeoning exploration of the contents of our world and their categorization, it appears only a matter of time until we will be able to understand all of them in general terms. Our concept of similarity should increasingly be replaced by a concept of substances and principles, and our concept of possibility should be replaced by a concept of certainty. We may ultimately succeed in rendering the entirety of the world predictable if we can ascertain the presence and allocation of substances. Our ultimate problem in understanding what is and what will be may be a practical matter of adequate sensory impressions of all substances that are relevant for our pursuits and our coinciding consciousness of them in their dimensional placement and their movement. Nature seems to assist us greatly in solving this problem by presenting us with typical settings or states in which we can exclude or ignore the presence or movement of certain substances or take them for granted. Still, arriving at useful practical results for our pursuits in complex allocation conditions might be difficult. We may face settings that involve large amounts of substance of various types in a wide variety of allocations and directions. Even if we had general scientific knowledge of the nature of all of them, we might not know all relevant aspects in our environment by number, type, distribution, or bearing. It may be impossible or impractical to deconstruct and investigate all parts of a setting before we act in or react to it. We may not have the capability or luxury of exploring a setting to a level where we know all its aspects that are pertinent to our pursuits. Even if we knew or we could know the number, type, distribution, and bearing of substances and what laws apply to them, we might continue to suffer significant problems. The correlation of a multitude of parts and processes by which these parts behave may require computational capabilities that we may not possess. Practical certainty may therefore only be a limited possibility. Even if we could become aware of and understand all interactions, we might not be able to regulate them. Hence, we may be unable to secure results according to our plans. The complexity of circumstances may cause the general scientific method to be of limited use in our practical requirements unless we can devise machines that assist us with sufficient effectiveness and efficiency. In the absence of such assistance, we may have to supplement our tactics.

Our difficulty in comprehending and in addressing the detail of complex conglomerations may prompt us to handle them differently. Rather than trying to understand them through the behavior of their parts, we may endeavor to comprehend them through their combined systemic behavior. We may try to understand them by observing their correlation with their naturally occurring circumstances. Yet this may not give us sufficient information. A multiplicity of possible relation-ships of factors within and beyond the system we are exploring might remain. To obtain improved information about causes and effects per-taining to systems that we cannot trace into their significant compo-nents, we may at least apply some scientific exploration by testing the reaction of systems if we subtract, substitute, or add components. Fur-ther, we may correlate a system with external components or systems. These correlations permit us to test such other components and sys-tems at the same time. But we may obtain a better insight if we test a system in combination with aspects we already know and can control because this allows us to focus on the system and to identify its prop-erties with reduced issues of attribution. The insights we derive from these manipulations may assist us in engineering systems by adding, subtracting, and substituting parts or by combining systems. We may also obtain better notions about the results particular systems yield or types of results that types of systems yield. Particularly if the systems we encounter vary so much that we cannot establish typicality among them, this research of systems may be viewed as an application of the topical mode in which we let single settings play out and observe their mechanisms. Depending on the importance of a system, that may be acceptable. But if we stop short of completely investigating the com-ponents of systems and their contributions, we may not possess ade-quate information to understand such systems entirely. We may iden-tify properties that largely direct a system's demeanor and establish a registry of them. Still, working with systems under a condition of lim-ited knowledge exposes us to a risk that they might contain unknown features that may cause them to act or to react in variation to explored aspects. Our absence of knowledge may translate into lacking control that threatens our use of such systems as well as other pursuits.

Our approach toward systems as entireties with insufficient ex-ploration of their constituents then imparts a risk of unpredictability and is only of limited use. We may cast our notions of them as provi-sional assessments and may remain guarded against nontypical behav-ior from them. The detractions caused by such precautions and the re-sidual threat of damage despite them inexorably depress our ability to pursue our needs. These effects may compound as we interact with an environment that comprises a multitude and a variety of systems with considerable complexity. Our body, external biological resources, and various nonbiological resources that we require for our individual and our species' existence are in the nature of, or the product of, complex systems. Many of these systems are connected. Historically, such sys-tems were presented by nature. Our instinctive interaction with them, limited knowledge about them, and limited ability to affect them provided us comparative stability. However, as we have become more numerous and knowledgeable, we have increasingly become capable of destabilizing preexisting systems. We may become initially rather astute in using systems based on their apparent attributes. But uses with such shallow knowledge may cause us to affect them in ways that we cannot foresee or control. Even a deeper research regarding such systems may concentrate on yielding immediate or easily foreseeable advantages or on averting immediate or easily foreseeable disadvantages while neglecting less direct or less obvious effects. We may make similar mistakes regarding systems we construct. We may create and use complex systems whose functions and effects are not sufficiently understood. Moreover, artificial systems could interact with natural systems in ways we do not anticipate or cannot control. With advancing development, we may become more effective and efficient in manipulating systems while still not understanding their entirety and their effects on circumstances we require for our pursuits. This may intensify the side effects of our endeavors even as our knowledge and aptitude increase. As these side effects become more dangerous to our pursuits, we may take notice of them and begin to address them. At that time, however, we may not be able to reverse these effects or may only succeed undoing them at a great expense. For that reason, it appears prudent to take a comprehensive, detailed scientific approach and to supplement that knowledge with a comprehensive awareness of our system settings if we are to become proficient in our pursuits. Until we understand systems and their interactions, we will have to develop arrangements in ourselves, with other humans, and with our nonhuman environment without the entire benefit of comprehending natural and artificial systems. Yet, because overstepping our boundaries of knowledge and control may cause significant damage, we must limit our interference to inevitable necessities until we possess secure knowledge how to interact with systems we need without unduly harming them.

The utility of a scientific approach and an environmental orientation for the pursuit of our needs and the amelioration of our competence in our endeavors demonstrates the objective value of our rational capabilities. They can contribute momentously to the fulfillment of our needs. This may induce us to develop confidence that our rational functions might suffice to ascertain our survival individually and as a species. Fortified with a more extensive comprehension of our rational capacity and its potential for complete correspondence with the order of the world, we may ask whether our rational mind can or should replace our emotional governance. It might appear conceivable that our rational understanding of the requirements of our individual and collective survival and thriving and how these can be met, together with rational assistance in their fulfillment, could engender states of mind approaching those we gain from our needs. Our rational awareness of deficiency and fulfillment seems to imply a capable parallel to a pain-pleasure mechanism that might induce us to redefine happiness. We might describe it as a state of mind that results from an observation of harmony between the rational concept of our existential requirements and the reality of their fulfillment. Our rational awareness of harmony seems sufficiently contrasted by our rational awareness of disharmony in a condition of deficiency. Accordingly, it might seem possible to replace emotional mechanisms that indicate deprivation and fulfillment of a need with rational mechanisms. Still, we seem to be missing a resounding reason for employing such mechanisms. Neither our rational awareness of a state of functional integrity nor our rational awareness of deficiencies by themselves or in combination appear to be able to give us motivation to be repelled by deficiency and attracted to integrity. While rationality can tell us how things were, are, or will be as a matter of causality, it cannot tell us how they ought to be. We may be able to explain what function a particular need and the collective of our needs serve in the advancement of our individual or our collective survival and wellbeing. But there exists no rational reason that we individually or collectively should continue to exist or thrive or that we should fulfill any requirements to accomplish these purposes. The sole reasons we should be interested in these endeavors are our current or anticipated impressions of pain and pleasure. We are attracted to the emotional reward of securing our and our species' survival and thriving and their subordinated requirements, and we are repulsed by the pain and fear related to deficiencies in that enterprise. The inability of our rational mind to supplant the motivational impulses issued by our emotional mind presents a terminal shortcoming that makes any ambitions to substitute our emotional mind illusory. In spite of any problems in registering and reacting to threats and opportunities appropriately with which our emotional mind might be afflicted, its exclusive capacity to motivate us leaves it matchless for leadership of us.

Because the emotional aspects of our mind govern our pursuits, we are in search of emotional gratification in pursuing them. Our supreme wish implied in all our needs is to experience satisfaction. This supremacy of emotion leads us to the conclusion that our rational and tangible capabilities, while necessary, are subordinated. They seem to be instruments that serve the more exalted objective of happiness. Yet this conclusion of supremacy may be only correct if we examine needs from a subjective viewpoint. Objectively, needs are utensils that motivate us to secure individual and collective survival and thriving. Since survival and thriving are the result of their functions, we may conclude that they serve that mission. In the context of that mission, the emotional heights that we experience with the fulfillment of our needs constitute a lure. The pain-pleasure mechanism can be regarded as a means to steer our behavior. Emotional rewards are the result of a collateral mechanism that serves our, and through us and our assistance our species', survival and thriving. Consequently, our emotional satisfaction is objectively not the supreme purpose of our pursuits. We do not know why we and apparently all other life forms follow the mission of survival and thriving, where this mission came from, where it leads us or life in general, what its purpose is, or even whether there is a purpose to the mission. Although we fail to find answers in reason to which we could emotionally relate, our needs advance it regardless.

Our needs seem to incorporate proficient emotional detection, guidance, and propulsive capabilities for the fulfillment of such a mission. They seem to capably support the mission by differentiated emotional motivations that concentrate on the entire assortment of necessary existential support functions. But our emotional mind appears to engage our rational mind to assist its purposes. This warrants a closer inspection of the cooperation between the emotional and rational divisions of our mind. It might not be easy to discern our rational from our emotional mind because both involve parallel, apparently similar processes of relating, categorizing, storing, and retrieving information. More than that, our impressions of our mind's functions are frequently amalgamated products of the emotional and rational aspects of our mind. Our emotional mind identifies actual and anticipated menaces and opportunities for the fulfillment of our needs by generating from perceptive impressions emotions of pain and fear, and of pleasure and desire, respectively. It also forms reactive motivations for activities to avoid, prevent, or remedy threats and to take advantage of opportunities. The corresponding function of our rational mind is to investigate and correctly reflect anticipated or actual deprivation and fulfillment and their causes and consequences for our emotional mind's consideration. It must further recall, learn, or imagine means and strategies, consider alternatives, and gauge and rate the relative effectiveness and efficiency of different reactions in consideration of our needs. It must devise and supervise the acquisition, creation, and management of resources and assist with the coordination of pursuits with the pursuit of other wishes of the same and other needs. These tasks are not confined to antecedent planning because our circumstances develop. Our plans may change with changes in our needs and their relative satisfaction status. Our abilities may increase or diminish. New opportunities may arise or existing avenues may transform or close. We may not have completely thought our pursuits through. Our approaches may be ineffective or less effective because of our mistakes and limitations. We may encounter independent intervening causes that distort, delay, detour, aggravate, or block our progress. Not all countervailing forces can be forecasted. Even if their potential is foreseeable, modalities of their occurrence may not be predictable. Even if these are known, we may not be able to brace against them sufficiently in advance. Even if we had that aptitude, the expenditure of resources might detract from the protected or other pursuits. Considering such possibilities, we may only be able to optimize our efforts if we maintain awareness, flexibility, skills, and other resources that allow us to react to challenges and opportunities as they arise or as we become aware of them.

Practical responses to impressions of threat or of opportunity could also come to fruition under the sole guidance by our emotional mind. Our instincts might control them through automatic reflexes. Still, without a rational identification of causes, means, and circumstances we want to reach, we would be dependent on whether our instincts recognize these. Our emotional mind may be able to broaden its recognition of threats or opportunities and to fashion a more articulated response in direction and intensity by drawing on samples of emotional experiences and related facts it has gathered. Hence, our emotional mind may already resort to experiential assistance within its own facilities. But the experiential capacity of our emotional mind appears to be confined to a relatively rough detection of similarities to experienced or instinctively stored facts and an emotional reaction according to existing emotional associations. That may result in insufficient or in incorrect information about the relevance of facts or their causative context. We remain reactive according to approximations to instincts and memories. Our emotional mind alone may therefore not be very effective in reacting to environmental circumstances, particularly as they transform. However, it may recognize the similarity of rational processes of relating, categorizing, storing, and retrieving information and decide to incorporate them into its deliberations. That decision may be solidified by its experiences of finding rational characterizations and recommendations emotionally confirmed.

Rational processing of our internal and external circumstances and its devising of paths to fulfillment focuses our emotional mind. It enables our emotional mind to dramatically improve effectiveness and efficiency of pursuits by rendering more and better instruments available for detection, decisional processing, and remediation. It also amplifies the capacity of our emotional mind to track conditions with regard to multiple needs and to put together appropriate emotional and practical responses that include the coordination of responses among needs to devise the most promising combined strategies. To assist our emotional mind in its modifications of instinctive responses for optimized fulfillment, our rational mind must translate the nonemotional quality of its results. It can achieve this by presenting comparisons between its results and factual situations to which our emotional mind can already relate based on its prior experiences or instinctive content. This work requires intimate knowledge of genetically entrenched and acquired emotional memories. Additionally, the derivation of competent results necessitates close awareness of our needs and of their requirements in factual terms, as well as of our environment's workings. The capacity of our rational mind to understand us in correlation with our environment, to increase utility, and to curb damaging effects situates rational discovery in the center of our efforts for advancement.

The apparently superior capacities of our rational facilities may make us wonder how much our needs remain or should remain based on genetic predispositions and on emotional experiences that encircle them. The ubiquitous backing by more insightful and flexible rational functions appears to suggest that they have and should have extensive influence on our conduct. Humanity might be approaching a stage in its development where it can take charge of its affairs by adjusting and possibly substituting the content of emotional instincts with rationally investigated determinations that might be better positioned to secure our needs. The adjustment capabilities of our emotional mind indicate that humanity has already developed past a state where its behavior is exclusively directed by genetic programming. We may not give much credit to the modification of our genetic instincts by emotional experiences. But their influence appears to be central for our success. By itself, our rational mind would only represent a second, unrelated manner of awareness. We can solely relate rational concepts to our emotional mind because it has undergone a transformation that enables it to deviate from genetic instincts and relate and become open to experience-based assistance. Our needs appear to not only permit but demand rational processing of our external and internal world and assistance in addressing threats and opportunities. It is the insight by our needs, not their preemption that enables rational facilities admittance to their processes. Our emotional mind can become aware by its experiences that the rigidity of genetic programming may prompt us to ignore more accurate interpretations of factual circumstances and available, better-suited responses. It can recognize limitations in its capacities to supersede these rigidities and may therefore invite and accommodate rational participation. Then again, experiences may also confirm and thereby strengthen the rigidity of genetic instincts or modify them to a result that can reach similar levels of stringency as our genetic programming. While solely our emotional mind can motivate us, and our rational mind cannot replace that function because of its fundamentally different character, we might wish we could overcome ill-considered impulses that arise from such rigidities. Our rational mind might be able to devise and impart experiences that might modify our emotional mind, or it might devise technologies that permit more direct alterations of our instincts. But such alterations would have to be motivated by our emotional mind. We might suspect that such a motivation could not develop if emotional features have attained a high level of rigidity. However, we would be incorrect to think of our emotional mind as an undifferentiated entity. It is composed by our needs. Emotional experiences are also placed in relation to distinctive needs. Needs therefore experience and possess emotional and correlated factual awareness of other needs and experiences and demands of these needs. Needs that are negatively impressed by other needs may recognize the sources of such disturbances and react to them. They may enlist the assistance of yet other needs that are negatively affected by the same needs, as well as of our rational mind, to stand their ground. If it should be impossible to change the rigidity in the attitudes of adverse needs, they may build an opposition to their demands and insist that we curb or refuse activities pursuant to needs that damage them.

Rivalries among our needs may naturally happen because they each have a different objective. Yet it appears that these would be limited among our genetic instincts based on the fact that they are part of an existential totality in which the pursuit and fulfillment of all other existential needs is necessary. That attitude should be strengthened by experiential awareness of our emotional mind. But experiential influences may also change that considerate attitude and give us reasons to change it. Our emotional mind is being exposed to information and to other, more immediate influences that may not coincide with its genetic programming. Although that seems to be desirable if it broadens the decisional horizon of our instincts, it may engender perversions in our instincts or noninstinctive reactions that are not optimized. Even if our reactions are adjusted to the settings from which they arise, they may form inflexibilities that are not optimized for our overall setting. Such influences may accrue as a result of our engagements or of independent occurrences. While forming impressions may emanate by the actions and reactions of any features in or surrounding our mind, they may also be aimed at us by forces that possess and act upon their own needs. Frequently, influences may not alter our instincts but only generate principled adjuncts to them in various grades of stability. Nonetheless, we diagnose that our needs are being or have been exposed to voluntary and involuntary adjustment. Our rational mind seems to be indispensable to reveal and assist us in addressing these influences.

We may wonder how much maneuvering room our genetic and acquired conditioning permits in connection with these remedial undertakings. That conditioning may not only affect our emotional mind but our perceptive and rational mind as well. Because the information processed by our mind primarily originates in impressions of circumstances external to our mind, our environment may have considerable influence over our mental functions. However, our perceptions, emotional and rational awareness, and motivations to react to stimuli are produced by the reflection of information in mental mechanisms that are at least initially the creation of genetic dispositions. These genetic foundations may only permit the acquisition and processing of information to sharpen or adjust our genetically based processing but not to fundamentally change it. As a conduit, perceptive facilities seem to be least affected by environmental circumstances. Our rational mind appears to be relatively flexible compared to our emotional mind. The malleability of our emotional mind seems to be located between these mental facilities. The programmed character of genetic instincts causes them to persist in trying to impose their notions of reality on us.

The genetic foundations of our mind seem to have an inherent tendency of reinforcing themselves even if environmental factors can influence them. Initially, genetic mental dispositions direct us in the acquisition of experiences through perceptions. Although these might subsequently influence our initiating mental patterns, the contingency of such revisions on a fit with preexisting mental dispositions and the processing they tolerate may also strengthen our dispositions. The result molds our subsequent capacity to change mental patterns. Hence, all our mental facilities may develop in genetically predisposed rigidities. In addition, the correlations between our rational and emotional mind may impose each other's persistence on the other, although an opposite effect is conceivable as well. Even to the extent acquired influences can alter our mind, they may contribute to an entrenchment of emotional and rational patterns that do not allow us to change our mind or only allow changes with a great amount or intensity of diverging experiences. These patterns may affect the collection and further processing of perceptions to a degree that makes the consideration or reflection of contradictory evidence difficult or impossible and has us continue in established modes of thought and emotion. These considerations suggest that our rational and emotional dispositions and environmental influences generate programming that seems to make us entirely products and continuing subjects of genetic and environmental indoctrination. This appears to shape and rule our mind in a way that does not seem to leave us free and in charge of our mind.

This conclusion is being contravened by our direct impressions in which our mind appears overwhelmingly as an independent, self-controlling authority that allows us to consider circumstances freely and to act and react appropriately in both its rational and emotional aspects. We seem to be able to refer to incidents where we successfully fought the formation of or domination by mental patterns or where we adjusted previously approved mental patterns in light of new circumstances. However, when we look closer, we have to admit that in most instances we only reluctantly change our mind. Adjustments are regularly maneuvers to arrange our genetic and acquired emotional or rational dispositions because previous positions that we regarded applicable do not adequately secure the fulfillment of our needs. Before we change our mind, we will try to change the circumstances to which we apply its programming. If that fails, we may initially attempt to restrict our mental adjustments to rational conditions because they are most easily changed. We may seek to increase our experiences or improve our rational processing of them. If we are pressured further, we may be prepared to address the arrangement among our needs. Only if we cannot find adequate fulfillment for our needs this way may we consider adjusting our needs. We reserve that option to the end because we understand that changing a need is difficult and may be impossible. But even if we could change our mind, our actions would be dictated by our emotional and our rational conditions as they present themselves at that point. They would also be conditioned by our surrounding circumstances that dictate the setting in which we must apply our emotional and our rational facilities although these may have stopped forming these facilities. We then appear to merely coordinate among our needs, our rational abilities, and their surrounding circumstances. Still, we may insist that this represents an important measure of sovereignty. We may argue that no matter how much we have been conditioned, pain, fear, and desire motivate us to investigate and possibly alter our impositions and to engage our rational mind for these purposes if such a conditioning does not keep us sufficiently satisfied. Even needs afflicted with a high degree of rigidity might not become comfortable by themselves if their instructions do not satisfy them.

While we may then hope that our emotional mind will defend its integrity, we may also fear that the obstinacy of its patterns might prove to be insurmountable. We may further anticipate that our needs might become corrupted to a point where they deem themselves satisfied even if they fail to benefit our individual or collective survival and thriving, although such a state might require a comprehensive perversion of our needs to remain unopposed. More generally, we may view our emotional mind as an unreliable authority on our welfare. Its susceptibility to error contrasted by the scientific rigor that applies to our rational mind may render it difficult to recognize the supremacy and leadership of our needs. We may instead attempt to derive guidance for our happiness from rational considerations measured by how well they serve our individual and collective survival and thriving. We may think that rational constructs and the physical aspects they reflect can give us independence from emotional dictates against our interests.

Even if we submit to the rule by our emotions, as we ultimately must, rational concerns and the physical aspects that they reflect may appear dominant in our mind. Much of our attention is occupied with producing rational and, through them, physical means for which they stand. This practical preoccupation is supplemented by our growing insight that our world is organized and functions by substances and derivative rational principles. This scientific notion appears to confirm physical concerns and their rational reflections as the only sound features of reality. Emotions are revealed as programming compelling us to act in prescribed ways. Because emotions are constituted and organized by substances and laws of nature, they only seem to superficially present a different challenge and can be resolved into substantive and rational concerns. While we may understand the essential function of emotional constructs in our existence, we may also deem it necessary and possible to optimize them by replacing or at least supplementing natural programming and controlling environmental programming.

Our rising capability to affect us and our surroundings encourages confidence. Although we may acknowledge the possible existence of limitations set by the substances and principles of nature and our dispositions, we may believe that there is much potential left for growing and possibly perfecting the fulfillment of our needs. The only conspicuous exemptions to this optimistic outlook appear to be posed by the inaccessible character of the past and by our mortality. Even if we trust that these problems might be resolved by future generations, our awareness that we are foreclosed from accessing our past and will be eventually barred from admittance to the future can fill us with a deep pain. The next chapter explores these obstacles to our happiness.

CHAPTER 3
PASSING ON

Our experiences are encased in an irretrievable past to which we have
no other access than through our memory. All the happenings we can
recall will not occur again. They are lost forever. We comprehend this
most distinctly when an experience of great pleasure concludes. We
will never be positioned quite like this again. The particular happiness
we experienced is locked and lost in the past. If we try to revisit conditions of the past, these conditions will have changed. Even if we manage to approximate earlier circumstances in an effort to experience the
same occasions of happiness they once caused, we and their effect on
us will be different. Further, our happiness will change if we attempt
to preserve and to continue it after we first experience it. Its inherent
dynamics may cause it to abate. Even if we can renew it, the requirements of its maintenance, intervening conditions in us and our environment, and its mere continued presence while other circumstances
develop will render it different. These changes or their consequences
may range in severity. Yet, throughout, we can only create similarities
to former happiness. Our attempts will be limited by the distinctive-
ness of the constellations we are striving to regenerate. We cannot arrest the development of us or our surroundings. We must leave stages
and segments behind to never truly be able to return to them. The
past may lay the basis for future happiness. Still, that does not change
its passing character. We cannot hold on and we cannot go back. We
helplessly watch our experiences drift away. The past is sealed.

There is a fundamental sadness to this experience of our finality. Oddly, this unhappiness applies regardless of whether an event in
our past was bad or good, happy or unhappy. The passing of a painful
event can make us unhappy as well. Once it has happened, we cannot
alter it. We might only manipulate our memory of it as a dissatisfactory substitute. We cannot turn back the course of events to the setting
from which they arose. We cannot recoup wasted time and effort. The
potential to create a happy occasion at a certain moment has passed.
In addition to haunting our memory, past occurrences may define our
present and our future in disagreeable ways. We keep wishing we or
someone else could or would have acted differently, that circumstances would have been different to spare us these afflictions. We mourn
missed chances and our inability to correct past pain-inducing events.
Thus, regardless of whether we cherish an experience or abhor it, we
probably would go back if we could. We would want to experience the
happiness of pleasurable events again and might try to enhance them.

We would also want to relive occurrences that led to overproportional pain so that we could create better outcomes. Such unrequited wishes place us into a difficult situation. We can neither relive pleasure nor correct the causes for pain. Our incapacity on both counts causes us pain because it leaves us helpless. We may try to counteract that pain by engaging our memory to place us in our mind back into former experiences of pleasure. We may replay unhappy events in our mind as if we could revive them and could change or overcome them. Yet, apart from learning lessons for our future demeanor, these mind travels are necessarily hurting us more than they soothe. The pain of perfection haunts us because there seems to be nothing we can do to counter it.

The only possibility we have to combat our pain over the loss of the past is to connect it with occurrences in our present and future. We may try to continue or reopen past events where we find sufficient circumstances for a revival. Where that is not possible, we might try to produce similar circumstances by reenactments that give us an opportunity to derive similar happiness or to prevent similar unhappiness. Even where we do not go that far, we may try to commemorate joyful and mournful occasions to apply them for present and future support and direction. We may let the past serve as a reminder for present and future behavior. We may regard it as a representation of pleasurable conditions we should strive to emulate, regain, maintain, or on which we should build. Alternatively, we may look upon it as a representation of circumstances we must endeavor to avoid, prevent, or change, or for which we must seek redress. These incentives and activities do not empower us to surmount the absolute impossibility of a foreclosed past. We can only project into the present and the future the accomplishments we would seek if we could access the past. By that transfer, we may hope to keep the past from being perfected. We may attempt to compensate for its impenetrability by readdressing our wishes and actions regarding it toward the present or future. Placing past events into the context of similar present and future occurrences allows us to regard them as episodes in a continuing undertaking. The potential of finding similar fulfillment or avoidance of pain to which we were formerly exposed may assist us in coping with the inaccessibility of past events. The semblance of a continuance or iteration may enable us to ameliorate our pain of perfection. Still, no matter how well we fare in compensating endeavors, the pain induced by the closed character of experiences keeps accumulating throughout our existence. The factual and emotional weight of past events threatens to catch up with our efforts to produce new events of happiness. This makes our memory of times when we had fewer of these burdens precious but also bitter.

Short of traveling back in time and of accessing or even commanding the version of us existing at the time, our efforts will lack satisfaction. But traveling back appears to be prohibited by laws of nature. Alternatively, a reversion of circumstances might be permissible, but involve unmanageable complexities. Further, it may not yield the experience we seek because we would generate another event in time without affecting the previous occurrence. Even time travel would not be able to truly set us back into the time. We would want to preserve our experiences since then to savor the satisfaction of going back or if only to act differently at this time with consideration. If either of these methods were possible, they may not have been invented. Even if they were technically available, they would have to be strictly controlled to not unacceptably modify already evolved circumstances in which others have rightful interests. This would require severe limits on both.

Hence, we are now and might forever remain confined to creating new incidents of happiness in an effort to compensate for our loss of the past. Yet, even the already inadequate consolations these compensations can provide are limited because our ability to pursue them deteriorates with our physical condition as we age and will end when we die, if not before. Usual mechanisms of addressing actual or potential pain do not apply here. We are left with the awareness that happiness will eventually be categorically denied to us and that this denial limits the number of our chances to obtain happiness. We are inexorably running out of time. We are withdrawing our pursuits from a restricted account of chances. Every opportunity we pass, false or inept choice we make, obstruction of our efforts, and experience of pleasure counts against our finite ability to create happiness. The finality of our experiences places an additional pall of irretrievable passing on all our pursuits. Our pain about this may be remote as long as we possess life and vitality and no reason to deem them in proximate peril. As opportunities pass, succeed, or fail to emerge, we presumptively have many chances of happiness left. But our confidence wanes and our fear rises as we physically decline and move closer to our life's natural conclusion or when other causes threaten us with injury or death. The only remedy appears to be to safeguard our constitution and life for as long and against as many causes as we can. That might seem to be a technical problem that should be manageable with proper development.

When we inquire why we want to survive, we invariably name pursuits of other needs as reasons. We might therefore doubt that our need for individual survival exists independently. It may be a composite of our other needs that originates in their concern for their satisfaction that is contingent upon the fulfillment of all other existential needs. This shared, equal, multilateral motivation that all our individually relevant existential needs acquire may give us the impression of an overarching need for individual survival. A similar mechanism may apply among our collectively relevant existential needs. The resulting need for collective survival and thriving may comprise all individually relevant needs. However, although our need for collective survival and thriving may be based on our individual existence, it also incorporates needs that aim at objectives beyond. The fulfillment of these may require or may benefit from the subordination of our individually pertinent needs and our individual survival need. That preference seems to mirror the apparent expendability of individuals as tools in the overarching development and continuance of a species. If we are pressed to choose between our individual survival and the survival of our species, we are disposed to prefer the continuance of our species. Moreover, our individually significant needs seamlessly produce a basis for needs directed at collective survival and thriving without our exposure to dramatic choices. That might be concealed by the at times contingent nature of our needs that directly pertain to the support or protection of our species. There may be periods during an individual lifetime when some of these needs are not developed, continuing, or triggered or do not motivate us in sufficient strength. During times when we are not charged to serve or are not fully dedicated to serving our need for collective survival and thriving, we perceive that this service function is not or not solely the motivation for our individual survival efforts. Still, our underlying disposition is to invest and, if we deem necessary, sacrifice ourselves, including our life, when these needs call on us in a fitting context. Conversely, if our continuing existence and our contribution to collective causes seem to us critical or helpful, we will support and defend our life. But this does not represent the entire reason we want to live. We also perceive an independent, self-serving cause.

We may find this aspect initially difficult to explain. The motivations of individually relevant existential needs to achieve fulfillment should be neutral regarding our individual death. Death does not directly affect these needs in that together with our capacity of fulfilling them our need for their fulfillment ceases as well. Arguably, we only have a fear of our finality because it runs against a distinctive need for personal survival. Without it, there should be nothing for us to fear. We would simply endeavor to fulfill our other needs until we cease to function and could fulfill them no more. This appears to be a mode by which most other life forms exist. Humans dramatically diverge from that approach. The distinguishing factor appears to be their expanded capacity to anticipate their death rationally and emotionally. Without such capacity, an apprehension of death may be limited to an immediate awareness of a threat to physical integrity. Many species possess mechanisms for fear that benefit their self-preservation. They may instinctively react to life-threatening circumstances. They might be able to increase or to shape the applicability of their reactions by learning about their environment. Some higher life forms might have some observational understanding of death as a termination of life functions. They might be able to infer the possibility of their own death. But species that do not reach human capabilities to anticipate might not have mindfulness of the categorical limitation of their existence and might possess no concept of nonexistence. Their fear of death might remain tied to certain types of events that trigger their fear of death. Even if they are under constant fear for their existence, their attitude toward existence and their need to survive may not be defined or influenced by the eventual inescapability of their passing. Nor may they possess a concept of the finality of death and the relative time spans of their life and their nonexistence. They would therefore not share the extent of fear and resulting motivations that inhabit humans. Our awareness of the inevitable approaching of our annihilation and our apprehension of final nonexistence critically expand the scope and intensity of our fear of death. That anticipation particularizes a need for survival that seems to transcend our other needs and to form a separate objective.

Even in consideration of our powers of anticipation, the subjective impression of such a detached need for survival seems hard to justify. Our fear of death should be limited to anticipating physical pain that might accompany dying as well as regret about not having satisfied needs and not having sufficiently compensated for past events of happiness and unhappiness. This may incentivize us to pack our limited time with as much fulfillment as possible. If we succeed in leading an existence of fulfillment, we should be contented. Yet, although we can anticipate that our existence will end, we should be able to resign to that fact because we can also anticipate that our needs will expire. This is where our capacity to anticipate appears to fail. Our awareness and our anticipation of death are flawed because we have never experienced our nonexistence. Even if we witness the endangerment of our existence, we have never experienced not being alive. Accordingly, we have no true concept of that state. This inexperience renders our need for individual survival unique among our needs because we have never experienced the entire span between its deprivation and satisfaction. We have only known its satisfaction and possibly its endangerment. In that fundamental ignorance, we might not differ much from other animals. But our higher mental capacity allows us to imagine that state.

Because we cannot imagine our nonexistence, we cannot help projecting a part of us as surviving into the time after our death. We stretch our imagination to a status of being dead in the literal sense, an existence in death. The outward consequences of death are drastically demonstrated by the evidence we observe when humans die. Because there are no physical signs of survival, we may conclude that we will continue in a more restricted manner. This leads us to a claustrophobic vision of an afterlife. We tend to envisage ourselves as beings without substance, as ghosts and spirits, as shadows of ourselves. The termination of obvious life functions suggests that we would not have needs anymore to fulfill these life functions. Still, we cannot let go of the impression of having needs because our needs and the activities in their pursuit define the essence of our nature, of who we are. We cannot imagine our existence without them. As a result, if we imagine our continued existence after death, we have to also imagine the continuation of our needs rather than acknowledge that they will die together with the organism that engenders them. Since that organism disintegrates, we must imagine another basis for our needs to continue. We may therefore try to imagine nonphysical sources for our needs. This increases our fear because we imagine our awareness of our physical disintegration. We further fear the phase upon disintegration. We anticipate that we will be in a state of pain because we foresee retaining our needs but having lost together with our physical existence the capability to fulfill them. We fear becoming arrested in a helpless state where our options to create happiness will have ended but all or some of our mental processing faculties are remaining intact. We visualize a setting where we are conscious, may even remember who we were and what happened to us, but are unable to do anything except stew in our awareness of decay and deprivation. We sense that we might be incapable of generating happiness without a physical existence. This vision becomes a part of our fear of death. The denial of satisfaction over the entire spectrum of our needs and the confined nature of our imagined existence deprive the prospect of a continued existence after death of its appeal. Instead, we contemplate it in horror. Our fear of death and conversely our need for individual survival then reveal themselves as constructs of our existential needs that anticipate a permanent state of deprivation. Without that anticipation by these needs, we would have no fear of death beyond the fear pertaining to the period until death.

To the extent we cannot succeed in surviving, we will have to find strategies to cope with the crushing weight of our fear. One regular strategy is disregard. There would appear to be justification for this strategy if there is nothing we can do to overcome our death. The re-

lated fear does not appear to have a purpose because it will never be
sublimated in the pleasure of fulfillment. It would seem then that the
best we can do is to mask that fear and to distract ourselves from our
awareness of it. On an individual as well as on a societal level, we may
therefore attempt to eliminate the reality of death from our everyday
consciousness. We may try to preoccupy our mind with particular intensity in the pursuit of other needs and their satisfaction. But we may
also consider such a concentration of efforts to be a display of desperation whose effort to produce contrast reminds us of death even more.
We may prefer to live our life as if it would last forever and as if death
did not exist. In either case, we may avoid contact with death so we
are not reminded of it. We may try to relegate it from a lifelong imposition to a minimum at the end of our life or the lives of others where
we cannot avoid encountering it. Upon witnessing death, we may try
to overcome this break in our awareness as promptly as possible. This
focus on denial does not seem to fit with our predilection for accounts
or simulations of deadly violence, death, and related horrors. But accounts of actual events related to death help us to numb our mind, to
immunize us against our fear at a secure distance. Simulations fulfill a
similar function. They additionally permit us to lull ourselves into the
pretense that death does not exist, that it is a product of imagination.
Its convolution with fantasy helps us to neutralize true reminders of
its reality. Trivializing death helps us to ignore it in plain sight.

These strategies to numb or suppress our awareness of death or
to immunize us against emotional reactions to it may assist us to contain our fear momentarily or even for significant distances of time. Yet
our endeavors are ultimately ineffective and might even heighten our
helpless realization that we will die and our desperation over that fact.
We are bound to be confronted with death as persons with whom we
share or once shared closer genetic or other ties or commonalities die.
Based on the knowledge that we are of their kind or similar to them,
their death makes the inescapability of our death conspicuous. We are
further reminded by references to other individuals who have passed.
Every organism we kill, observe dying or dead, or consume insinuates
death. Life itself in all its facets points us to its antithesis of death. The
passage of time, a change of seasons, and any decline we observe in us
and in our surroundings suspend us in apprehension. Annually recurring events prompt our awareness that our ability to experience them
is finite and inevitably decreasing. We are surrounded by a multitude
of intimations that do not allow us to forget. Our unwillingness or inability to deal with death renders us unprepared for it. As we witness
the death of contemporaries, encounter life-threatening conditions or

situations of increased risk, our denial is becoming brittle. When fear pushes into our awareness, we may try to find a more stable way of handling the reality of our death than by denial and desensitization.

Head-on acknowledgment of our finality does not seem to improve our happiness. The apparent inevitability of death may cause us to resign and to not pursue happiness or pursue it with reduced vigor because we perceive it as ultimately pointless. We may be frustrated that we are continuously being tortured by an awareness of our death without the ability to effectively overcome death. This frustration may combine with frustration regarding our incapacity to access the past. We may already turn against the notion of happiness because it taunts us with memories of pleasure that we cannot recreate, as well as past, present, and future pain that we cannot erase but can only hope to reduce. This frustration rises by our insight that the already dubious effectiveness of compensation efforts and our ability to experience non-compensatory happiness are limited by our dwindling lifespan. These incapacities may give rise to a defeatist approach to life. Our attitude may not be reserved to a lack of incentive to fight causes of death. We may welcome and promote its occurrence to abbreviate our suffering. This might be reflected in a lack of pursuit of existential needs, an absence of defense against external interferences, or actions to end our existence. Although we would deprive ourselves of remaining chances of compensation for the sealed past by this deportment, we may view death as a relief because it would stop memories we cannot mend. But if our fear of death should be warranted, incurring death will cause us the very pain we fear regarding both our memories and the end of our life. Our fear of death should therefore have a life-affirming effect. It should direct us to avoid death and to make the most of our life.

Our zeal not to miss any opportunity might induce us to follow any current pleasure we can attain. This view discourages us from investing time and effort into the building of elaborate means and plans. It considers the rewards of building for future fulfillment insecure and dubious in their relevance. It believes that, even at their best, eventual rewards from preparatory pursuits may not compensate for the time and opportunities to be happy we sacrifice in the meantime. This attitude appears to have its advantages. It seems to liberate us from pains of pursuit and from worrying about consequences of our actions and our future happiness. On the other hand, it may render us defenseless against internal and external interferences and unable to use opportunities. Our lack of attention and inquiry may even leave us unaware of them. Our concentration on present pleasure may make us reluctant to defend against endangerment until it interferes with our pleasure or to locate means before we need them. This lack of effort is bound to affect our ability to reach happiness. It may keep us from accomplishing results that are required for proper and timely fulfillment of needs. Moreover, being driven by coincidences may encourage or even force us to act in negligent, reckless, or willful disregard of our future happiness for the sake of current gratification. We may even fail to maintain or protect, and might actively destroy, the resources on which we rely for the provision of future benefits. Our lack of foresight might motivate us to infringe or rely on the resources or pursuits of others to cover deficiencies. Hence, by making our happiness dependent on our immediate grasp of resources that we did not provide, we may expose us and others to avoidable current and future risks. This strategy then reveals itself more as a desperate attempt at a diversion from our continuing frustrations about our incapacity of accessing the past and securing an unlimited future than a usable strategy to fill our life with happiness. Its incompetence in securing success at high levels may not only punish us with deficient fulfillment and the strain of improvisation at the edge of failure but may even render death more likely.

The disadvantages of concentrating on immediate rewards may prompt us to try to maximize our happiness for the entire span of our existence. We may elect to investigate, embrace, and develop our potential to influence, even direct the generation of our happiness. Our awareness of this opportunity may propel us to seek a plan that allows us to maximize the fulfillment of all our needs and with that our happiness as a systematic undertaking. That may comprise fighting proximate and eventual threats of death and other threats as well as constructive undertakings to use the secured space for maximum effect in the support of our existential needs. While the inclusion of all our affairs and of our entire lifetime in our planning and execution creates complexity, it also maximizes our control regarding the fulfillment of our needs. It allows us to produce mechanisms of fulfillment for long-term and recurring requirements of our needs. It helps us to generate balance and security and infuses an aspect of predictability and calming confidence that we are making the best of our situation. We may continue to be subject to unpredictable circumstances, but we may be able to reduce detrimental occurrences or at least detrimental effects. We would let our awareness of our past and future finality serve as an admonition to organize our capabilities to their best effect.

Notwithstanding these considerations, the imposition of death and the associated pain are likely to continue even if we acknowledge that remaining alive is preferable and if we fight to keep our fear and pain contained by living life to its fullest. Our desperation may only be avoided as long as we experience sufficient events of happiness. With their abatement, we may fall back into less constructive, inert, and ultimately harmful modes in our behavior. The damage of such behavior may not be limited only to us. Our connectedness with other individuals in our pursuits and our mere coexistence with others may expose them to unintended collateral impairment. But we may also resort to damaging behavior targeted at others to cope with our frustrations.

Our frustrations may antagonize us against deemed causes. The general character of these frustrations may take us beyond attitudes of retribution toward specific causes that elevated our systemic pain and fear. We may resent the world that generated us to be mortal and surrounded us with mortal potential. We may despise a reality in which we cannot relive our past. We may loathe that we should have to die while life will go on without us or that we should be encumbered by painful memories or societal stigma for past events we cannot change while others may live free of these burdens. These causes may make us wish for comprehensive destructive events as a purported defense or resolution. We may relish their occurrence, even strive to initiate and conduct them, or to support, widen, and intensify their occurrence or impact. The intent to destroy or allow destruction and the defenses by others who are exposed to the consequences of such intent may create a climate of violence. Even if these attitudes regularly do not find expression and can be kept contained, they may lead to an undercurrent of disdain for our surroundings that may erupt depending on how we fare and may elevate the threat for destructive behavior together with other incentives that by themselves might not possess sufficient gravity. These other incentives may be fundamentally manageable because all other areas of human concern offer devices to overcome obstacles. Even the sealed character of the past seems manageable if we have an unlimited future to compensate for it. But the overwhelming certainty and severity of death appear to surpass all other problems and leave us ultimately destitute of a capable resolution or accommodation.

Nevertheless, our desperation may move us to attempt to manage death as we might try to manage other opponents to our pursuits. Beyond direct endeavors of attacking death by prolonging our life, we may attempt a strategy of alignment. We may try to counter our pain of death with the infliction of such pain in an effort to turn the negation of a negation into a positive. Such an attitude may begin with legitimate defensive efforts. We may try to neutralize sources of death by visiting upon them what they impose or threaten to impose on us. Such a stance may be necessary and effective in certain situations. But we may expand this selective concept to general application. We may

believe that we can protect ourselves against threats of death generally
by assuming and exercising powers of death. We may deem that by
aligning ourselves with the force that in the end appears to win, we
too can win or at least protect ourselves. We may hope that, by joining
what we cannot fight, by assisting and reconciling ourselves with what
is set to kill us, we can render it friendly toward us. We may imagine
that we can use death as an instrument, ally, or principal, that we can
edge out a satisfying existence under its overwhelming power and protection. We may therefore seek positions that imitate the supremacy,
unpredictability, and merciless efficiency in the infliction of damage
and pain we observe in death. Even if we apply the power to threaten
or to impose death sparingly or not at all, we may strive to mimic the
power that the threat of death wields over the behavior of individuals.
We may pursue such positions in various contexts and directions over
other humans or even over our nonhuman living environment.

Destructive or dictatorial approaches toward our surroundings
may cause repercussions directly or in defensive response. Moreover,
if we succeed in suppressing or evading these repercussions, this does
not resolve the causes for our frustrations. These shortcomings might
discourage such approaches. However, if their perpetrators carry a defeatist attitude toward their existence, its endangerment, impairment,
or destruction may not be an effective deterrent against their evil.

While we may deem such attitudes to be extreme and thus unlikely to occur, we all carry them in us as contemporaneous potentials
and possibly even pursuits together with distracting and constructive
reactions. Our proclivities might strengthen or diminish depending on
how we fare. But it appears to be unavoidable that frustrations about
the inaccessibility of our past and our future increase as we go on. The
only force that might help us to escape detrimental reactions appears
to be our need for collective survival and thriving. Because the survival
and thriving of our species are the subject of our highest objective and
are represented by a need that can be fulfilled in spite of our individual frustrations, they appear to offer us a superseding objective that is
free of our limitations. Although fulfilling that objective and its supporting needs generates its own satisfaction that may raise our overall
satisfaction level, it can also decrease the pain and fear over individual
frustrations. We may take solace in the knowledge that all or a part of
our physiological essence is directly and indirectly passed on and continues to survive and thrive through duplicates, descendants, and our
species. Even if our individual genetic essence will be lost, we can take
comfort in the prospect that our generic human essence may survive.
We may be aware of risks that our duplicates, lines of descent, or spe-

cies might die and suffer. But these events are less certain or at least more postponed than our own death. The survival and thriving of our duplicates, descendants, and species are not merely surrogates. They constitute physical survival and thriving of our individual or at least our shared biological essence. This grants supplemental motivation to advancing the survival and thriving of our kind. Our need for individual survival and thriving prompts us in addition to our need for collective survival and thriving to expand the boundaries for our happiness beyond our narrow individual concerns. They both instruct us to meet the needs of other humans, to include their happiness in ours.

Still, as rewarding as securing the survival and thriving of other representatives of our species may be, it cannot fully satisfy our need for individual survival and thriving. That is because securing the survival and thriving of our physiological essence in a part or its entirety does not necessarily secure our awareness of that survival and thriving. It does not carry over our experiences and our consciousness that draws on these experiences. The nongenetic information in and about us may be lost. With that aspect missing, much of our identity would be lost. Some of our nongenetic essence might be remembered by persons who knew us and be held present by a few succeeding generations. To avoid being forgotten, we might attempt to make a record of that information or build other monuments that point to our perceptions, thoughts, and emotions. Yet the mere existence of these representations does not mean that they will be deemed worth preserving or that they will be accessed or identified with us in a meaningful way. To achieve even such a meager semblance of continued existence, the memory of our existence and its details would have to be particularly relevant for the existence of future generations. Only few individuals achieve that importance. Even then, we might be mostly remembered as a coarsely sketched silhouette, as a mere caricature. For most of us, who we were is likely to fade quickly in the awareness of others until little or nothing remains. Even if we should be exceptionally fortunate or astute to keep memory of us alive, we would not be aware of that fact. The death of our consciousness places us into a position of insecurity about whether, how much, and for how long we will be remembered. Moreover, it makes this indirect manner of survival as a representation in the mind of others rather meaningless for our happiness. While being remembered may console our fear of death somewhat, it remains insignificant as a matter of our individual survival.

The inadequacy of attempts to console our need to survive and thrive through representatives or representations stimulates us to extend our individual life with the ultimate objective of eventually eliminating our physical death. We may invest efforts into technologies for the preservation and restoration of health and youth and even reanimation. We may further focus on technologies to transfer experiences and consciousness into biological copies or into nonbiological conveyances. Beyond fighting causes of death we consider as natural, we may try to eliminate the remaining unnatural causes. Although advances in fighting death may necessitate targeted scientific research and application, they may also result or profit from efforts to improve the satisfaction of other existential needs by technological, economic, and social means. But our setting may be flawed. After remedies for blocking natural causes of death have been found, implementing and maintaining these remedies as well as securing our existence and improving its quality in other respects may remain arduous and susceptible to inability, error, or imprudent attitudes. If we should succeed despite such detractions, our happiness may still be negatively affected by structural and procedural alterations that the achievement of these improvements may require or yield. High levels of development may present us with new, enhanced, or formerly hidden types of risk and damage.

The most evident threats appear to emanate from the fact that technological, economic, and social progressions facilitate and necessitate large-scale connectedness and organization of humans and their concerns in systems that may also depend on one another. These systems may benefit us by rendering some types of risks and damage, including some threats to our survival, more remote. Yet the scale of potential negative consequences often has grown to match or exceed the achieved attenuation of risk and damage. Integrated systems may be subjected to efforts to utilize their structures for the advancement of particular parties at the cost of others. Even without such usurpation attempts, these systems may be drawn into internal or external turmoil by their integrated functions. Not all such disturbances originate as systemic phenomena. Many large-scale phenomena may have localized and even individual causes. Interdependent circumstances of sustaining and advancing our existence may allow relatively small causes to grow and threaten us regardless how far we may believe ourselves to be removed from them. Apart from fearing such contagion, we may generally suffer from increased fear because integrated systems curtail our control over the pursuit of our needs. We sense elevated vulnerability to interference from others and the impositions of an interrelated society. The frequently complex and remotely organized character of our life makes it more difficult to act as we wish. Our vulnerability to and dependence on other humans, technology beyond our comprehension and control, and large-scale economic and other societal processes and structures may curb our ability to pursue happiness according to individual terms. These attributes of integrated systems place us in fear that we might not be able to effectively pursue our needs or that their fulfillment might be taken from us. They place us in apprehension that assistance or noninterference might be made contingent on our compliance, that we might be controlled. We may fear that our existence, including our life, might be regarded as a mere accommodation in support of common concerns and subjected to them.

Together, these risks of progress confront us with considerable challenges. They may result in severe, including deadly threats for us, others, and future generations or may imperil the survival of our species. We may then doubt that our technological, economic, and social development will assist us greatly in our fight to conquer death or to ameliorate the period until its occurrence. But even if that pessimism should be misplaced, we may have to settle for incremental advances toward perfection of our individual survival and thriving. Even if we succeed in expanding human lifespans and in increasing the quality of life, the eventual denial of our need for survival is bound to continue until we achieve immortality. Even if humanity succeeds in halting or reversing the rate of physiological deterioration and finds cures for illnesses, we would remain susceptible to accidents, catastrophes, and to negligent, reckless, or willful acts. Even if we could solve these hazards of human activity, we might continue to face nonhuman interferences and general developments that could endanger our existence. We additionally would remain exposed to past and possibly continuing contamination, weakening, and depletion of our resources. Unless we can adjust ourselves to become indestructible or take over comprehensive control of our surroundings, the fundamental menace of death to our existence and happiness promises to continue even as our knowledge and skill advance. As long as we cannot securely eliminate death, our fear of death will continue. Our coping with our mortality through destructive reactions may attenuate once we conquer natural causes of death because that would remove a heavy burden of inevitability. This may move us to concentrate more on the managing of causes that lie within our capacities to prevent. But other causes may remain. As long as our fear of death continues, we will only find partial consolation in minimizing its chances of occurrence, filling our existence with more satisfaction and strategies that have some essence of us survive, or advancing the possibility that our species might find a way to eliminate death someday. Short of its complete elimination, no measures we can take or perceive can extinguish our fear of death. The next chapter explores the consequences of our enduring existential dissatisfaction.

CHAPTER 4
AFTERLIFE

As long as our technological and organizational accomplishments do not carry far enough to guarantee unlimited personal physiological existence, we will experience fear of death and a desire to overcome this burden on our happiness. The ultimate terror of being aware of an absolute deprivation of our needs without any ability to change our pain compels us to find a more suitable alternative. To edge out a bearable existence, we must resolve what seemingly cannot be resolved.

We may try to attack the physical evidence of our death by inverting our impressions of it. We may claim that our current physical existence is an illusion, a dreamlike condition or a fantasy into which we are temporarily immersed and from which we will revert to reality upon our death. Such a concept initially appears to present a promising potential of survival. Yet, upon a closer inspection, we find that we have to address many or all of the same questions because our current existence is the only existence of which we are aware and in which we can function with our mental processing facilities. Our awareness and its subjects seem to be provably physical phenomena. The concept of a simulated physical reality compared to otherworldly forms of elevated reality threatens to deprive our contemporary needs of all meaning of which we are aware or which we might visualize. Further, even if we accept aspects of us and of our surroundings as an illusion, we develop similar questions and fears as we display regarding our physical death. We must ask which part of us is being immersed in a simulation and therefore real. Although we might suspect that we will make a transition from this to another, more real world, and that we should be familiar with that world because we emerge from some type of simulation, we possess no evidence for that proposition. We might die and a character that we hosted or emulated might continue. Nor do we have any idea how the world to which we might revert could be more real than ours and how comparable it might be. Because its conditions are claimed to be different in unspecified ways, we cannot define what of us would survive or what that survival would be like. We would continue to face uncertainties that instill us with similar types of fear. For these reasons, we still have to find a solution to our fear of death.

That solution is offered by the same mechanism that causes our fear of death, by our inability to imagine our death. We consider the absence of definitive information about awareness after death to be an uncertainty. We may view it as an opening to consider and convince ourselves of alternative settings that can help us to overcome our fear.

In imagining more favorable circumstances, we may attach impressions of survival to our physical remains. We may picture that our awareness, personality, or capacities continue to be attached to them. Such a position is not entirely unreasonable. All physical aspects of an individual except those whose absence caused the death appear to be as present immediately following death as they were immediately before death. The only difference seems to be that they are not animated. If we could immediately repair the cause of death, they should be working again. Where that is not currently possible, we might be able to preserve a person's body as it was immediately after death until the lethal damage could be repaired and thus bring such a person back to life later. Yet, short of such measures, we cease to exist as a physical organism and decay into disorganized and further disconnecting arrays of atoms. Even under best efforts, visions that relate our live attributes to the decayed matter of our body are tenuous and not very satisfying. They require the acknowledgment of a radical deconstruction that is not compatible with our compulsion to imagine that all or at least some of our human characteristics will survive. We may therefore abandon theories of survival that include physical aspects.

Instead, we may pursue evidence for the survival of an ethereal essence that leaves our body and continues to exist independently. In our mind, there is reason to believe in such a reduced continuation of our existence. Although our mind comprehends itself to be located in our body and our experiences allow us to point to our head as its main repository, it is immediately unaware of the structures and processes that constitute it. This makes it unsurprising that our mind lives in a resulting awareness that regards itself as separate from our body in its sourcing and its existence and assumes to have a nonphysical quality. Even as our direct impressions are supplemented by science, and science progressively ties our mind to our physiology, we may resist accepting these insights against all evidence because our direct impressions seem to contradict these discoveries. Even if we partly submit to reason, we may maintain that position for any parts of our mind that science has not verified to be physically sourced. We may invoke the concept of a spirit that is distinct from our physical existence. We may acknowledge that there is a bond between our physical and nonphysical properties during our physical existence. However, we may believe that it can be severed because of the separate nature of our ethereal identity. We may believe our mind or parts of it to merely inhabit our body. Under this belief, the essence of our mind is not affected by our physical death beyond losing its physical setting and instrumentation. Once we submit to our intuition, we can rationally maintain hope in the existence and survival of such a nonphysical essence because we are not confronted with positive proof to the contrary. In contrast to the stark evidence of physiological death, there is nothing to evidence the demise of ethereal attributes. If they existed, their nature would make them characteristically impervious to physical proof.

In the absence of a requirement to provide scientific proof, we cross into the domain of belief. The character of our nonphysical essence and the parameters according to which our existence continues are exposed to speculation that carries as far as our imagination. We may envisage that our essence undergoes a metamorphosis. We may posit that it splits into aspects of being or that it combines with other essences. We may imagine it to include or exclude all, part, or none of our current perceptive, rational, and emotional capacities, our experiences and memories, our personality, and a nonphysical copy of our body and its functions. We may imagine that this essence continues in a nonphysical form on earth or somewhere else or that a physical body is constituted for it to inhabit and that this body is a human body or the body of another life form on earth or in another locale. The range of these often incompletely considered conditions of our existence in the afterlife may engender a wide variety of views about our existence after physical death, our environment, and our interaction with that environment. To find satisfaction in imaginary constructs of our afterlife, we must create a vision that affords us with an impression of sufficient continuity to warrant our conclusion that we will survive. This requirement sets functional limits for our fantasies. But we may soon discover that even basic constructs are afflicted by this concern.

The foundation for such a concern is the fact that, regardless of what else we may conceive to be the aftermath of our physical death, we imagine being reduced to our nonphysical aspects when we die. To convince ourselves that we will continue, we must expound how this state and any subsequent state or states we imagine to develop from it preserve our essence. That may seem to be most problematic if we believe that we will remain in a nonphysical state after death. To distinguish such a state from the terrifying vision we fear, we do not want to be haunted by physical needs that we could not pursue and fulfill. To distance ourselves from the vision that generates our fear of death, we may imagine that these needs will terminate. Arguably, the changes of our personality would be natural and not coerced. Once our principal need for individual survival has been fulfilled and no longer depends on the functions of its supporting needs, these needs should naturally disappear. Even our need for collective survival and supporting needs would seem to lose their purpose because our personal survival would secure the survival of our kind. To the extent existential needs previously prosecuted their own purposes, the loss of their physical context might neutralize them as well. Without a physical basis, we might not feel needs related to that basis anymore. We may therefore expect that we will adjust to our new being spontaneously without pain. But such a reduction raises the question what needs or aspects of needs would remain and whether these would allow us the attainment of adequate happiness. To preserve some remaining needs that might continue to bring us happiness, we might attempt to distinguish between needs or aspects of needs that we acknowledge to be physical because they are tangible and other needs and aspects whose physicality we deny due to their relative intangibility. We might ponder that the happiness we are to experience might be sourced in the absence rather than the fulfillment of needs we consider to be physical. We might believe that we will enter a state of clarity, of peace, of rest, of freedom where our essence is released from the vexations of physical pain, fear, and desire, is liberated from the toils and sorrows of our physical existence.

While this may initially appear to result in a desirable state, we may have difficulties picturing how we would then create happiness. We would have to acknowledge that most of our existential needs and most aspects of our principal needs for individual and collective survival and thriving are needs for physical survival. The termination of our tangible needs would cause us to lose the satisfaction of their fulfillment. Even if we would not miss that fulfillment because our related needs would have terminated, our experiences of happiness would be diminished. We may believe that some intangible needs or aspects that we might deem separable from a physical existence might retain a continuing purpose. All of these needs or aspects would be collateral needs and thus, by definition not define existential core concerns but perform assisting functions. Without tangible references, our pursuits of intangible needs or aspects would lose their function as existential needs in the service of our tangible survival. Even if we held that our needs serving survival contain a nonphysical aspect, survival would no longer guide us because there would be no remaining function if we secured our ethereal survival. Without issues of survival, the concept of thriving would be reduced to identity with the remaining needs. To still produce happiness, these needs or aspects of needs would have to form objectives that we regard worthwhile in themselves or in the advancement of other remaining objectives. But the continued existence of purportedly intangible needs or aspects is difficult to imagine because all of them appear to require tangible means and strategies or a tangible setting for their generation or at least their expression.

The concept of a nonphysical situation leaves us without references regarding our intangible needs. It would also deprive us of most, maybe all, reasons that we should care about the preservation of our awareness or our essence. Everything about us would change so dramatically that it is difficult to consider the result a continuance of our identity. Such a state does not appear desirable to us. The reduction it implies does not seem to fulfill our need to survive but to confirm our death. We may try to imagine an existence that allows needs and aspects of needs we deem to be nonphysical to emerge from their current physical context and to be elevated into an ethereal existence. We may envision the further development of these needs and aspects of needs. Yet, even if intangible needs would develop to constitute their own purposes or to take on other purposes in an ethereal context, we may question whether they would possess the capacity to equal or exceed the happiness we could develop under the entire spectrum of our present needs. To match the potential of our earthly needs for happiness, additional, presently unknown unearthly needs and manners of pursuit might have to arise. But we cannot fathom what forms of happiness could replace the happiness we would lose by the elimination of tangible needs. Even if we had a description of our adjusted and our new ethereal needs, we could not emotionally attach to them and the state of being they imply. They would be fundamentally alien to our current form of existence. Apart from a nebulous notion that nontangible needs and aspects survive, we have no perspective about how we might be able to derive happiness in an ethereal state after our death. Even if we could be assured of happiness in such a state, we might not attribute much value to it. Our essence would have to pass through a radical transformation so we can engage in a new existence defined by adjusted and by novel nonphysical needs and manners of pursuit. The alterations to our being that might be required to make happiness in nonphysical form achievable call even more into question how much of our identity, of our personality could remain intact. This renders it difficult to conceive of a nonphysical afterlife as a desirable state.

Even if former needs had lost their purpose and we had novel ways of achieving happiness, our memory of former types of happiness whose achievement would be foreclosed might infuse us with a sense of loss. We might not have specific desires and wishes for the fulfillment of earthly needs anymore. Still, it would seem that, as long as we possess an emotional cognizance of happiness, we would emotionally connect to former experiences of happiness, particularly if they are of a different type. We would perceive pain about the absence of earthly pleasures, circumstances for their pursuit, and our inability to sample them again. In addition, we would have to feel loss about being radically and irreversibly pulled out of all familiarity and emotional connections we had, regardless of whether our needs have changed. These effects might only be averted if our memory of former happiness were extinguished. This prospect that, in excess of our physical identity and most or all current needs, our awareness might be wiped out as well heightens our apprehension further. The likelihood that such a radical break of our consciousness and departure from our nature might be required for a happy afterlife violates the idea of continuity that is implied in our need for individual survival. The existence we might gain threatens to be unrecognizably distant from who we are in this life.

Our anxiety over that possibility combines with our doubts that our afterlife should be happy or even happier than our present existence. The sweeping reduction of our needs and our insecurity about what needs could remain, whether they might increase in impact, and whether needs might be added leave us in great anxiety over whether we will be able to produce any or much happiness. Although such a future state might not translate into pain because related needs would not have survived, we cannot help considering such a state as unhappy. An important reason to regard an afterlife as desirable and potentially superior in supplying us with happiness is that it fulfills our need for survival. If our physical features and related needs do not survive, we might be left to derive a major part of our happiness from the survival of our remaining essence. We may wonder how much happiness we could feel about the survival of a fraction of our essence even if we would not be cognizant of its reduction. Also, building on our survival from a former life as a source of our happiness assumes that we will be aware of having survived our death at least in these aspects. That may not be possible if we are to secure a new existence without mournful memories. However, even if our awareness continued, we have no reason to presume that our survival would result in happiness beyond a period of initial joy. A memory of an existence with risk of death may fill us with appreciation for some time. Yet, after we have achieved a secure state of survival, that memory will fade in importance because it serves no further function in the pursuit of a need. Our guaranteed survival could therefore not be a sustained source of our happiness.

Our reasoned doubts concerning an existence in ethereal form give us little reason to ease our fear over our physical death. Although our mindset induces us to believe in an afterlife, it is difficult for us to assuage ourselves with concepts that are beyond our capacity to comprehend. Visions we develop about how our nonphysical essence may continue to exist may look to us like improvements compared to the frightening fundamental vision that induces us to engage our imagination. But the characteristic limitations and unfamiliarity of a nonphysical state and our limitations in imagining it seem unable to instill sufficient confidence that such a state could persist or that it would make us happy. We might therefore conclude that we are overreaching with our expectations of a continuance. We might suspect that our essence might not be commensurate with our mind. We might deliberate the evidence of the physical nature of mental functions and admit that at least some mental functions even beyond our physical needs and the satisfaction we collect from them might be of a physical character and will be left behind. We may entertain similar considerations regarding more obvious features such as our physical sensory facilities and rational facilities. Yet it is difficult for us to see what might remain of us after we subtract all these aspects. The loss of all that we can perceive our mind to encompass would deliver us back to our existential fear. More than that, we cannot help interpreting the loss of any mental facilities, any curbing of our awareness or capacities to produce awareness as a partial death of our mind. Hence, we cling to concepts of the afterlife that leave our mind intact. Such a result can only be achieved if we assume that all physical aspects of our mind possess a nonphysical equivalent that mirrors their capacities. But we then encounter the problem that, with the cessation of a physical environment, our mental facilities lack sufficient material with which they could engage to produce satisfaction. This would raise again the horrifying specter of full awareness in absolute paralysis. We may imagine this to be mended by being placed into an illusion that mimics our earthly existence and gives us the perception of a physical environment. Only, such an existence might appear to us as a consummate deception. It suggests that our existence would be without substance, without purpose. Even if our existence might already be an illusion, this is not what we perceive it or want it to be. Nor is it what we wish to be our setting after our earthly existence ends regardless of whether our present existence has substance. From our current point of view, a coming state of illusion appears more like a punishment than a reward. We may therefore not embrace the prospect of a nonphysical emulation of a physical existence or the continuance of an illusion if that were our present.

This leaves our reinstallation into a physical body in a physical environment as the only solution that could effectively neutralize our fear of death. Because all the happiness we know is a function of our earthly needs, we cannot picture happiness in the afterlife in any other way than the happiness we experience during our contemporary existence. Any purported new type of happiness is beyond our comprehension because it is outside the horizon of our reality and our imagination that is based on it. Accordingly, we regularly base our concept of an afterlife on the assumption that the conditions and the principles of our happiness will generally remain as they are during our lifetime. The best setting we can envision would be a re-placement into a human body and into a physical environment that closely resembles our earthly realm. We might also picture some enhancements to our body, mind, and environment that would make our afterlife more fulfilling. Yet paradise would be more of the same or higher levels of what we already desire. We might then imagine our existence in the afterlife as an endless lifetime. Unless our current reality is eventually sublimated into the state of the afterlife, the environment for such endless physical existence would have to be a location apart from our contemporary world. As an alternative, we may envisage undergoing repeated, perhaps endless cycles of birth and death in the same or other worlds.

This alternative of cycling through lifetimes confronts us with an immediate notion of limitation. Even if we should be reinserted on earth or elsewhere into a comparable physical existence with an array of familiar needs, amnesia about our former life seems necessary to allow us to lead happy lives. That may already be necessary if we merely change over once into an endless afterlife. But a memory of repeated lifetimes would have us accumulate burdens of not being able to access the past that might depress us to levels we can now only faintly imagine. Although we would possess repeated lifetimes to compensate for past experiences, such compensation would be particularly inadequate if the settings for our lives lacked continuity. We would mourn former lives and attempt to connect to and continue living them. We would attempt to live one integrated life through disjointed episodes. There might be other grounds we would not want to remember past lives or even that we had past lives. If we trusted that we automatically slide into a new existence that is not affected by our previous life, we might use our lives without care. We might even die intentionally so we can advance to a new setting. This might lead us to an existence of neglect, recklessness, or willful disregard for us and others. We would have to cope with the effects of our and other individuals' behavior in our current existence. Even if we believe that we can escape immediate repercussions by moving to a new life, we might hesitate because that escape still would come at the price of losing our identity. Moreover, we might return to a world where we experience the fallout from shortsighted conduct by us and by other individuals. Without our and their care, the conditions of unconditional reincarnation would deteriorate. These realizations might move us to appreciate the opportunity of each of our lives to create and experience happiness and to invest ourselves into creating better circumstances for our future lives. But these aspects of general care might not permit us to overcome frustrations about a continual separation from all personal connections. Regardless of our speculation about the reasons we could not remember the content or factuality of multiple lifetimes, our amnesia would be evidenced by our current inability to recall former lives. Unless we are all new participants in a scheme of successive lifetimes, we should recall our past lives unless such access is blocked. A showing that such memories might reside deeply sequestered in our mind might give us some suggestion of mental continuity. Yet, unless we can access that memory as ours in the presence of our mind and identify it as ours, it might as well be someone else's memory. That is particularly so if successive lives are not connected by genetic particularities and leave only generic human commonalities. Here again, we may ask whether we would lose too much of us to regard this progression as our survival. That question rises in intensity if we consider that we might not only transition among human forms but reemerge in other life forms.

These considerations distill what we really wish. If we must die, we want not only our mind to survive intact. We also want to be reinserted into a genetic copy of our body. Moreover, we would want our inability to access the past addressed. To the extent that is not possible, we hope to be placed into a setting of continuity in which we can reconcile with past happiness and pain. Hence, the solution we might desire most to overcome our fear of death is that, if our life cannot be secured without the experience of death, we will be reconstituted and inserted in an environment in all aspects as if death had not occurred. While we may additionally ask for improved conditions in our self or in our environment to make our afterlife happier, we may wish to retain as many of our circumstances as we consider conducive. The wish list born from our fear of death, frustration over our inability to access the past, and from possible frustrations in achieving the fulfillment of our needs during our lifetime, can then be extraordinarily ambitious.

Regardless of what we imagine or wish our afterlife to be, the complexities of arranging and maintaining it make us wonder how it might be achieved. Even the feared vision of an existence in paralyzed awareness would seem to require a creative act if not maintenance of our facilities and their setting. Our involuntary imagination of such a state does not demand evidence for us to believe in it. But that is not the case regarding states of survival that deviate from this default. We may find evidence for such states partly in the correlation of our inability to imagine being dead with our wonder regarding the existence of the world and our existence. Because our current world by far exceeds anything that we could create, we may surmise that it must have been generated by an intelligent and omnipotent entity. Once we acknowledge the existence of such an entity, we are led to believe that it is also responsible for the world of the afterlife. Our belief in the existence and power of such an entity is particularly strengthened because of our belief in an afterlife. We may deem any continuation after physical death to be supernatural because it occurs contrary to all physical evidence and the rules by which our present world seems to operate. Further embellishment of such an entity is fostered by our desires regarding an afterlife. Fulfilling these desires would require inordinate skills as well as intense consideration, planning, and execution.

Yet, beyond finding comfort regarding the issue of capacity of a supernatural power, we must answer the question why such an entity should dissever our life into different existences and why it should accommodate our desires. The involved complexities suggest that there must be a reason. We may speculate how the entity that created this scheme might profit from it. In narrowing our speculation, we might query why results could not be accomplished in our continued earthly existence, through our expansion into additional habitats, by creating more worlds, by having us perish without an afterlife, or by disclosure and even direct intervention. Such speculation takes us so much outside our experiences, including our motivations, that we have difficulties finding plausible answers. We might therefore resign not to fully understand the motivations of a creative entity. But we might still impute meaning to the separation and the transition we purport to observe from our position. We might picture that the creative entity has prearranged our transition into the afterlife as an automatic, unconditional event. It might encompass a development through multiple existences. We might imagine a metamorphosis at the end of that process or immediately after our current life ends as a natural progression whereby our essence, after having seasoned in our body, leaves it behind and assumes its adult form. Then again, the traumatic separation of these worlds by our physical death suggests an interruption rather than an organic progression and that our welfare on the other side requires a saving act. That in turn implies that the selection of possibilities for an afterlife might depend on our worthiness. We might imagine that upon our natural death judgment is passed what our experience will be. We might contemplate that our worthiness will be determined according to our preceding behavior. Our qualifications might be virtues displayed, lessons learned, or the pursuit or achievement of other acts. We might believe that a preset, automatic decision mechanism or a regulated bureaucracy causes our actions during our lifetime to have certain consequences. We might speculate that we decide our own fate based on insights we attain in the afterlife. Alternatively, we might believe that the quality of our afterlife depends on the discretion of the originating power or an agency. We might ascribe human characteristics to such a decision maker and deem the process to be influenced by such characteristics. Based on our experience with humans, we may deem submission, service, faith, respect, and flattery to be effective means to earn a favorable decision, particularly during our lifetime when the existence or powers of such a decision maker may seem uncertain or remote. Even if we should fail to securely qualify by our actions, we might hope that contrition, a commitment to future compensation for failings, or appeals for mercy might still qualify us.

We might deliberate whether the reward for qualification may be entry into the afterlife, while the punishment may be our exclusion from it. However, since our incapacity to comprehend death compels us to presume our continuing existence in the afterlife, we could not fathom being entirely eliminated. Our compulsion to fear death forces us to conclude that the decision at the end of our natural life will not be a resolution of whether or not we enter the afterlife but what the conditions of our afterlife will be. The envisioned conditions might include a range of gradations. They might comprise conditions in which some or all needs, the satisfaction of some or all needs, or some degrees of satisfaction are foreclosed. But we may wonder how happy we could be in an afterlife even if we were not subjected to any restraints. In contrast with the ultimate form of punishment, we might imagine our ultimate reward as the fulfillment of all our needs. Although this may initially appear like an obvious choice of the best situation we can imagine, we may develop misgivings whether the fulfillment of all our needs would equal ultimate happiness when we contemplate the consequences. To experience happiness in an existence after death, it appears necessary that we tolerate its counterpart, unhappiness, to some extent. The rooting of our idea of happiness in a pain-pleasure mechanism renders it impossible for us to segregate pleasure from pain in terms of its definition and as a required experiential counterpart. Experiencing pain without being able to do anything about it would subject us to a state that we seek to prevent. However, the unconditional fulfillment of all that we need might impose a painful paralysis as well on the other end of the spectrum that we visualize. To escape this paralysis, it appears necessary that we should be exposed to the potential if not the reality of deprivation and that our acts and omissions would have to be responsible for the enhancement of fulfillment conditions.

Hence, we can only imagine experiencing happiness in the afterlife if its mechanisms for the creation of happiness would be similar to how we accrue happiness in our earthly existence. We might raise our happiness by an improved quality or quantity of means made available to us and improve our choices based on insights we could gather during our life, during transition, or in our new setting. Yet these advantages would have to stop short of making our pursuits superfluous.

Such conditions even seem to be necessary for our need to survive in the afterlife. Without the continuing threat of death, we may not perceive a need for survival anymore. Although our fear of death would subside if survival upon physical death were guaranteed, our pleasure about our survival would fade as well. Without the function of supporting and protecting our survival, our existential needs would also lose their ultimate purpose. That might prompt us or give us latitude to engage in behavior that might cause us pain regarding existential needs. Even if that pain would motivate us to fulfill them, we may give preference to the pursuit of other impulses if we deem such preferences to be protected by the impunity of our survival, therewith creating an imbalance. To continue our happiness about being alive and avoid damage in the pursuit of existential needs, our existence upon our death may have to be threatened by further possibilities of death. That would not seem to be a problem in a scheme of multiple cycles of life in which we would be kept unaware of our previous existence and confronted with frightening visions similar to our existing experience. But in a scheme that involves knowledge of successive lifetimes or a permanent afterlife where individuals could witness reconstitution after dying, the threat may have to involve more severe and perhaps final consequences to maintain an appropriate apprehension of death.

These are issues about which we might not worry at this point. For now, we have to consider what we can do to ensure that we obtain an adequate standing upon our transition through death. We do not know whether any of our notions about the hereafter or conditions of entry are correct. However, the stakes of our survival are so high that they may prompt us to attempt to improve our fate in case it exists and a qualification process applies. We may try to forecast the effect of our comportment and to determine what we can do to advance our chances of a happy afterlife. We may try to understand what a judging entity or mechanism might deem important in a decision. We may try to deduct such principles from the imagined nature of the afterworld and its organizing principles. Still, our ignorance and insecurity about the modalities and transitory processes of an afterlife make such planning difficult. We may be longing for leadership that can save us from falling into any of the negative states we can imagine and place us on a course for a state that is advantageous to our happiness. This yearning may motivate us to give power to individuals and groups who suppose or pretend to possess answers to our questions regarding our afterlife. The function of such purported authorities may range from an advisory capacity to strict governance of our conduct. Their common denominator is that they declare to have knowledge required for guiding us in matters of existence after death. Mostly, they assert that we have a conditional opportunity to escape the pain of disadvantageous states. The opportunity is usually stated to be conditional because it is claimed to depend on our thinking, feeling, and behaving in ways that are prescribed by authorities. Our acknowledgment of such authorities may have us follow their commandments in any aspects of our existence they wish to govern, thus allowing them to take advantage of us. Even if we do not submit to a particular authority, we may be careful about the possible consequences of our thoughts, emotions, and actions. If we believe in an afterlife or at least consider it a possibility, we will want to avoid circumstances that make our transition to it less secure or our standing in it less desirable. We may let the potential consequences motivate us to build and maintain our own guidelines.

Ideas and guidelines about how to optimize our existence in the afterlife with actions in our present existence may be beneficial for the amelioration of present happiness. They may support the instructions we already obtain from the composite of our needs. However, there is a considerable risk that the principles of behavior we consider necessary to secure a happy afterlife might conflict with the instructions for a happy lifetime. The prospects of punishment or reward may loom so prominently in our mind that they may devalue the significance of our current pleasure and our current existence. If we regard qualifying for the afterlife as the function of our lifetime, we will not place as much importance on the optimization of our current existence. Rather, we are likely to view it as proving ground for our worthiness. We may imagine or be promised compensation in the hereafter for not acting up in favor of rewards in this existence and for obeying adverse instructions that we or purported representatives attribute to the determining entity. This attitude may amalgamate with an interpretation of our pain-pleasure mechanism whereby our pleasure will increase the more we endure pain. A belief that our rewards and their certainty will intensify with suffering disposes us not only to endure pain but to affirm and pursue it instead of pleasure in perversion of our needs. It further may render us agreeable and even zealous victims of exploitation, preclusion, and other injury in social or surrounding circumstances.

A focus on the afterlife by which our current existence is viewed as a mere conveyance may also not bode well for the happiness of others. The actions we take against our own happiness may weaken our advancement of our needs for collective survival and thriving. In addition, a utilitarian vision of our present existence carries a tendency of devaluing current happiness in our treatment of other humans as well. Depending on what we deem the requirements of qualification for an afterlife to be, we may pursue our salvation not only at our cost but also to the detriment of others. With the overwhelming significance of otherworldly happiness at stake, we may fight anybody we perceive to not serve or to impede our salvation. Our intolerance will grow if we perceive that judging authorities support such behavior. It will further grow if we are told or suppose that the conversion of others to our beliefs and behavior constitutes a benefit or a requisite for our salvation. Such a mission may compel us to extend to others the burdens and resulting painful experiences that we regard to be qualification requirements or positive contributions toward a happy afterlife. We may then easily move from a defensive stance to an offensive interference in the pursuits of others. We may consider individuals or groups that do not comport with our zeal as agents of evil who would preclude us, themselves, or others from obtaining ultimate happiness. We may have few scruples to counter such apparent destructive forces with purportedly defensive destructive force of our own. We may declare that, because individuals who do not comply with our impositions will be excluded from a successful afterlife, their relegation to suffering is certain. We may therefore believe that we function as instruments of supernatural intent if we punish them. The devaluation of happiness in our earthly existence and the pain we cause by the application of our convictions may create a high level of unhappiness that increases our yearning for the afterlife. Our desolation may condition us to seek or at least to not avoid death for us or others. As a result, we may produce the opposite of the happiness for which we yearn. We may create hell on earth.

The belief that we must suffer in our earthly existence to gain happiness in the afterlife requires inconsistencies in several aspects. A creative entity would prosecute contradictory objectives with the creation of life before and after death. It would engage in the creation and advancement of life and reward us for acting contrary to that manifest intent. It would intensely motivate us to pursue individual and collective survival and thriving only to punish us if we follow that motivation. Moreover, if we believe in or suspect the existence of an afterlife and that we might gain happiness in it with our behavior in this life, it is reasonable to assume that our efforts to produce happiness in our lifetime determine whether we enter the afterlife or how we fare in it. Such a behavior would be consistent with our behavior in the afterlife and prepare us best for the behavior expected from us in such an afterlife regardless of whether our needs then were similar. The division into a present dedicated to the pursuit, enduring, and infliction of suffering and an afterlife of happiness arises from our assumption that a decisional authority is afflicted with the worst human depravities and weaknesses. Such an assumption may be inevitable if we imagine an all-powerful creative entity that infuses us with irresistible needs for survival and thriving, exposes us to the absolute denial of these needs in death, and skewers us in lifelong agony of its expectation and the insecurity about an afterlife and its conditions. This realization may cause us to revise our views about that entity and whether we expect our afterlife to be happy. Beyond these concerns, we also must be concerned with the substance of our loss. Without the pursuit of happiness in our present realm, we would miss a unique and precious experience of pleasure. That would particularly apply if a focus on happiness should be missing from the afterlife or there should be no afterlife. But even if there is an afterlife and happiness in it is possible, this outlook retains validity. If our emotional awareness should continue, our regret of missing happiness during our life would remain as a pain of loss regardless of the happiness we experience in the afterlife. Even if we would lose our emotional awareness of our current existence in a permanent transition or when we enter successive lifetimes, this could not change that we would have irretrievably squandered experiences of happiness. Whatever we imagine the potential of an afterlife to be and regardless of whether there is an afterlife, there is no good reason not to value, not to maximize our happiness during our lifetime. The pursuit of happiness during this lifetime can only benefit us. It cannot possibly harm us now or in the eventuality of an afterlife. If there is no afterlife or if it is not organized by happiness, we gain by maximizing happiness for our lifetime. If we possess an afterlife and it is organized around happiness, we win on both accounts. There is no downside to our pursuit and maximization of happiness. We will experience disadvantages if we disengage from them. We may therefore decide to cherish this life's opportunities and maximize happiness in this lifetime.

Yet, even if we entirely focus on generating happiness with our best efforts, we frequently fail or fall short in achieving the happiness we imagine. The causes may not always be clear. Our chances of wisely investing our efforts may benefit from identifying the types of limitations that we can encounter and the general characteristics of their intransigence. The next chapter focuses on laying that groundwork.

CHAPTER 5
PRESENT LIMITATIONS

Our experience tells us that the best manner to get what we want is to influence our surroundings by our actions. Some of our objectives may come about independently without our involvement or may be offered to us to be used. But most of our needs, most of our wishes do not fulfill themselves. We must make them happen. We have to edge out our happiness from neutral circumstances and against various adversities, using tools that support our objectives. Maximizing our happiness requires work. Whether we obtain what we want can depend on a multitude of factors. These may include individual intelligence, knowledge, skill, vision, logical scheduling and implementation, preparation, flexibility, commitment, and physical strength. They further comprise environmental factors such as the state of technological, economic, and social development and our access to its results and resources for our purposes. They also consist of the more correlative factors of our connections and bonds, social status, attractiveness, and abilities to influence. They finally contain dispositions of other humans, their cooperation, resistance, interference, or competition regarding our pursuits.

Some of these factors may not be accessible to our control, or at least not to the degree we need them to be to make our wishes come true. Still, quite a number of them seem to be in our hands or can at least be swayed or acquired. This partial malleability empowers us. It means that we can improve the effectiveness and efficiency of our efforts by improving the effectiveness and efficiency of these factors. To accomplish this, we have to consider the requirements of our needs, the approaches for their fulfillment, and the consequences of our actions. If we implement our insights with circumspection, we should be able to increase the success of our pursuits. Improving happiness may then appear largely as a matter of acquiring knowledge and its careful application to the other resources we have available. This conclusion seems obvious. We spend a considerable number of years in upbringing, education, and training to develop instruments and strategies for the pursuit of our happiness. With sufficient dedication and preparation, we should go far. Yet we might wonder how far these attributes can take us. What should be our expectation? We might be subjected to powerful encouragements assuring us that we can control our fortune. Apply yourself to your ambitions and you will succeed. Where there is a will there is a way. You can do anything if you put your mind to it. This is what we are told. If this is posited as the promise of our existence, it forms the standard by which we measure our success.

For most of us, the practical application of this principle is not working to our full satisfaction. Eventually, we find the promise broken that we can get whatever we want if we give it enough effort. We may find ourselves at a distance from our ideal of happiness. We may be satisfied with one or another aspect of our existence. Nonetheless, a discrepancy between our state of affairs and having all of our wishes become reality may remain. Regardless of how circumspect and dedicated we may be, some and often considerable room continues to separate our situation and what we consider to be ideal happiness. There are always aspects of our existence that leave something to be desired. We cannot always get what we want, no matter how much we might try. Sometimes, it even appears that the harder we push, the more we insist, the less we obtain what we want. We run into resistance, experience limitations, fall behind, and we fail. These deficiencies keep us occupied asking ourselves why they occur. We may consider the possibility and admit that the encouragements for perfection we received were exaggerations. But we may still desire to identify why we did not succeed. We may investigate our failures or inabilities and try to find the causes that slow us down, block our rise, or make us slip up.

In that investigation, we tend to divide the possible causes into those that lie with us and those that are attributable to external factors. We seek fault either in us or in our surroundings. If we find fault in us, we may take responsibility. We may admit our error, inadequacy, or failure to rise to the challenge. We may concede that we could not formerly and perhaps cannot now deal with certain circumstances. We may commit to change our ways to avoid the same or a similar failure from recurring in the future, or we may resign to our inability. Then again, even if we find fault in us, we tend to express it in correlation with external circumstances, in terms of our interaction with our environment. This expression is facilitated by the prevalent lack of a clear distinction between internal and external causes. Our inabilities and failures usually accrue as a result of our relation with the outside world, as do our successes. We and the outside world seem to be prerequisite components for the pursuit and creation of most of our happiness. This relation to outside factors may cause us to shift attention from us to external causes. To the extent we perceive a cause of a failure or inability to be found in external conditions, we may look at our problem as existing external to us in its entirety. We may let the great number of external causes and influences on us lead us to the conclusion that our entire existence is the product of outside forces. It might seem that our creation as the result of our environment and its effect on us delineate all we are and the entirety of our demeanor. In completion of this reasoning, all our failures and inabilities would be the product of external forces as well. We may sense that such a sweeping conclusion may not be correct. We experience that we can use or influence outside forces and their effect on us, that they can be blocked, attenuated, overcome, or turned in our favor. We also experience that where that is not possible, it may be possible to modify our position in relation to such unchangeable outside forces. If we want to make our mark, if we want to achieve our objectives, we will have to work with outside forces. If we cannot use them as they are or if they interfere in our pursuits, we will have to change, obstruct, or destroy them or arrange ourselves relative to them. Our demeanor toward outside forces greatly determines our happiness. Although we appear to be largely a product of external factors, we might often be able to shape or select their influences and thus take at least partial charge of our fate.

Nevertheless, we may continue to ascribe great power to external forces that interact with us. Even if we perceive that we can influence our environment, we may continue to perceive us and our actions to be influenced if not controlled by external forces. In spite of our best efforts, we remain broadly exposed and subjected to the nature and behavior of outside forces. Even if we apply everything in our power to control them or to position ourselves in reference to them, we might not succeed in dominating or evading them. External forces continue to have great influence over our happiness that is independent of our endeavors. We may therefore contend that they are in great part responsible for our fate. Following such thoughts may lead us to become hostile against our environment or to reject responsibility and resign our fate. We may accept less than ideal conditions, accommodate pain, and not pursue our happiness to its greatest possible extent. However, acknowledging the unalterable presence, effect, and causality of external powers does not warrant that we attribute responsibility for our happiness or unhappiness to them. External powers may have no or only conditional interest in our happiness. Even if they take an interest in us, attributing responsibility for our happiness or unhappiness to them fails to acknowledge that they follow their own agenda. Their interference, neutrality, or assistance is a function of their trajectory, their objectives. We as individuals are the sole force unconditionally committed to the fulfillment of our wishes. Because only we have an uncompromised and immediate interest in our happiness, our happiness and unhappiness are wholly our responsibility. Once we acknowledge this, we can approach the context in which our happiness occurs as a directional relationship between us and everything else in which we must extract what we need from our circumstances.

It would seem that to increase our happiness, we have to limit the influence of external aspects over us and gain control over them and use them as means to fulfill our wishes. But our attempts of fulfilling our wishes are imperfect because we have limited power. Moreover, our efforts are embedded in an environment that is also populated and controlled by independent circumstances and powers that might not yield. This leaves us with limited opportunities to achieve our wishes, a limited ability to be happy. The limits of our ability to transform our wishes into reality can be divided into two main categories: general and individual impossibility. General impossibility means that what we wish for is currently impossible for any human or combination of humans to accomplish. The category of individual impossibility includes all results that are generally attainable but cannot be presently reached by a particular individual or groups of individuals.

The area of general impossibility includes areas of science and technology humans have not discovered as well as all claims that violate the substances and laws of nature that have been found to exist from observations of nature. From these observations, one can derive a set of seemingly universal abstractions, a code by which they can be expressed. Although these abstractions are derived from specific observations of our world, our observations of some facts and principles seem to be unopposed wherever we look. This universal confirmation may inspire confidence in us that such facts and principles contain independent, immutable, universal truth by which every substance must abide. These general abstractions are regularly called mathematics or logic. To differentiate them from attributes that are limited to certain substances and their behavior, we may refer to logic and mathematics as universal laws of nature. We may refer to the principles that seem to be attached to particular substances as specific laws of nature. We may designate the efforts to derive universal and specific laws as science. We may further call the efforts to employ these insights on substances for the production of means technology. As we explore and lay open the structures and processes of nature, we gain knowledge of the substances and laws by which it is organized. These insights may increase our selections to shape us and our natural environment and to make us and it compliant with our wishes. They raise our knowledge of what is possible and shift our impressions regarding the boundaries of general impossibility forward. But our developing understanding also apprises us of boundaries in substances and their principles of organization. The ordered character of the world we discover constrains us to proceed within and by its rules. The absolute nature of such limitations warrants calling them boundaries of absolute impossibility.

Boundaries of absolute impossibility may describe limits of specific laws and intrinsic logic that cannot be surmounted regardless of our efforts. But judgments about absolute impossibility are frequently unreliable. Like all other impressions of impossibility, they may refer to a current objective or subjective inability to accomplish a task that might be resolved by sequences building toward that task. There may be unexplored potentials that we might be able to uncover as our understanding develops, thus allowing us to dissolve concepts of impossibility. Our impressions of impossibility may derive from instinctive dispositions but primarily arise from our experiences. Scientific methods seek to exclude error from the conclusions we draw. To that aim, we seek to establish laws from our observations that seek to cover the entire extent of a phenomenon and grant us comprehensive guidance. After we gain a partial footing in observations, we venture theoretical forecasts about the entire spectrum of a phenomenon that we perceive or imagine. While we render assumptions about the scope of applicability of laws, scientific insights stretch only as far as our practical experiences will support them. As long as we have not covered the totality of our predictions with confirming experiences, we might find contradictory circumstances. We therefore cannot be definite whether a result contradicting a law we posited is absolutely impossible. Similar reservations have to be allowed regarding the depth of a phenomenon. As we understand more about components and about possibly successive component levels, an impression of absolute impossibility might dissolve into manageable constituents. Hence, we cannot exclude that our concepts of absolute impossibility will change as our practical capabilities reveal more of the workings of nature. What we call absolute impossibility may not only represent a matter of missing breadth and depth of inquiry. Humans may also lack the capacity to detect some of the circumstances of nature or to comprehend the substances or principles they imply or even their unordered nature. We may face a general impossibility that is based on human limitations in the processing of information rather than absolute impossibility. We may refer to this as our general conceptual impossibility. It may be permanent, or temporary if it arises from remediable deficiencies in the development of the human mind or of assisting facilities to which it can connect.

Even if we develop an accurate idea of what exists and is permissible or mandatory under the laws of nature, we may lack the ability to implement the resulting potential on the scale or in the context we desire. We thus meet the barrier of general practical impossibility. It pertains to technology that is deemed possible under the substances and laws of nature we have derived but is beyond anybody's capability to create at the time. General practical impossibility appears to have two causes: a lack of knowledge or a lack of other resources. Humanity may lack the requisite knowledge to make objects and events work according to what should be possible under the provisions of nature. We may be at a stage of collective development at which no individual or group can currently devise a workable strategy to create a certain result although we cannot find it barred by laws of nature or can establish with certainty or with encouraging probability that it is permissible. Further, even if humanity may know how a certain result can be obtained in practical terms, it may still not have the necessary practical means to fulfill a wish. It may lack access to the resources it would take to accomplish the objective. When we consider these two aspects of general practical impossibility, we discover that the issues of knowledge and of resources are often related. There may be a wealth of resources available, but we may lack the knowledge to locate, access, extract, develop, shape, or employ them. Knowledge may then be merely one among a number of other resources. Some practical barriers may remain insurmountable. Yet the marshaling of resources may eventually be possible if the substances and laws of nature allow it and if sufficient amounts of the pertinent substances exist and can be reached as a result of technological development. Humanity might have or develop the mental capacity and be able to set forth the necessary efforts to attain the required knowledge and technology to allocate such substances. Under these conditions, general practical impossibility would be temporary. Barring general conceptual impossibility, it would only last until observations and trials have uncovered scientific insight and our practical capabilities have caught up with that insight.

Our ability to explore and understand nature allows us to formulate practical objectives based on what we have found possible toward which we can orient our implementation efforts. As possibilities appear and are found to be worthwhile, humanity engages individual and cooperative efforts to mend its practical deficiencies through the development of technology. Our recognition that the deriving of substances and laws of nature and the synthesizing of objects and events from them elevate our practical capabilities spurs us on to expand our exploration of nature and to reduce our conceptual and practical impossibilities. Consequently, humans customarily desire scientific and technological development to expand their practical capabilities past their current state and to come into the possession of means that they believe to be necessary or helpful for the advancement of their happiness. That desire may be broadly shared. Nevertheless, most individuals do not personally push the boundaries of scientific knowledge and the resulting state of human practical capabilities forward. The complexities of science and technology at the forefront of exploration may reserve the advancement of these to a comparatively small number of experts. Behind such experts, there may be other individuals or groups with the necessary resources and with their own motivations to establish and maintain certain developments. Unless we participate in such circles, we may not be aware of the efforts that have been and are being undertaken to push the theoretical and practical boundaries of development. If we are sidelined from undertaking or sponsoring scientific and technological development, we remain relegated to using scientific knowledge and existing technology to which we are permitted or can independently gain access. In this area, we contend with individual conceptual and practical impossibility. The conceptual or technological capability we seek might exist, but we may not have intellectual or practical access to that capability. We as individuals or a group may lack resources that others possess. Particularly if we are aware of our shortcomings to realized potential, we might try to improve our capabilities to match or to exceed the conceptual or practical state of others. We can undertake to close the differential autonomously or by obtaining resources from or in combination with other individuals or groups, including those who already possess desired results.

If we cannot implement a wish in spite of our best efforts at the time, we may deem its fulfillment impossible regardless of the reason. We may not distinguish individual and general or other aspects of impossibility. This lack of distinction may have a negative effect on our motivation to keep pursuing an objective and our success from such a pursuit. Understanding the distinctions of apparent impossibility may be determinative of our chances to overcome our current impossibility and the strategy we might pursue. If we recognize that a deficiency of means is attributable to individual impossibility, reaching such means moves within a more likely field of possibilities because it excludes absolute impossibility. Further, if the result we desire has already been accomplished by others, it becomes more likely that we might develop such a result or acquire it. Although our chances might be remote, the achievement by others of what we hope to accomplish indicates that we might succeed as well. To estimate our chances of success, we may explore by comparison whether our obstacles are of a practical nature or arise from a lack of our autonomous or assisted capacity to process information. We can then concentrate on compensating our deficiencies. If a result should be generally unavailable, an alternate approach may be needed. The nonexistence of what we seek may give us pause. It may mean that nobody has tried what we endeavor to achieve, that all others failed, or that they found the result to be unattractive. Examining their thoughts and efforts might be instructive. Beyond that, risks, costs, and benefits are usually less calculable in undertakings to overcome general impossibility. To obtain a maximum of information about these aspects, it might be helpful to understand whether we are confronted with a matter of general practical, conceptual, or perceived absolute impossibility. Overcoming a perceived absolute impossibility appears to carry the highest risk of failure and may involve the greatest effort because it controverts our collective experience. Surmounting general conceptual impossibility might challenge us similarly. Forays to overcome absolute and general conceptual impossibility might present problems whose solution attempts exceed what one or a few more individuals can or are prepared to bear. In addressing a general exploratory or implementation problem, the adversities may be more definable. Yet even solving such a problem may involve risks and investments of resources we might not be willing or able to carry alone. Arguably, the fact that nobody has succeeded in overcoming obstacles of general impossibility does not necessarily mean that they could not be overcome other than by a collective effort. Still, even if individuals advance to obliterate general impossibilities, they may have to rely on cooperatively obtained means or find such reliance helpful. Moreover, it seems likely that efforts to overcome individual impossibility could benefit from cooperation by others who wish to overcome their individual impossibilities as well or from assistance by individuals who already have accomplished the goals to which others aspire. Accordingly, cooperation seems to offer itself as a possible universal facilitator.

Not all individual impossibilities that we encounter are so fungible that they permit fulfillment by acquiring processing or practical capabilities from other sources. There seem to be individual impossibilities that we ourselves must defeat to obtain fulfillment. Even if the objectives of needs can be fulfilled entirely by exterior sources or by us with their help, our happiness might be disturbed because we did not provide that fulfillment ourselves. In these cases, not only the results particular attributes enable us to achieve are important for our happiness. We additionally value our possession of the enabling attributes, the capacities they convey to us, and enjoy the exercise of these capacities. This nonfungibility burdens our pursuits because the attainment of attributes we seek may be relatively difficult for us and at times impossible. The impossibility to be satisfied unless we generate means is different from the other types of impossibility that are concerned with practicalities. We may call it personal impossibility. It can cause grave consequences because much of the satisfaction we gain from the fulfillment of our wishes is produced by achieving objectives through our personal attributes. A lack of certain personal attributes may not curb our wishes to possess them. It may strengthen our desire. If we cannot close the discrepancy between these wishes and our reality, we may have no other choice than to obtain assistance to prevent larger losses. But the nontransferable character of personal attributes and their application may prevent us from finding adequate satisfaction of an array of needs ranging from needs that pertain to social correlations to needs for self-determination, privacy, expression, self-realization, and self-respect. These wide-ranging deficiencies threaten to fill our existence with mounting frustration of these needs and resulting pain.

Possibly, technology could create or help us create certain personal attributes. This might involve nonbiological as well as biological conditioning or supplementation of our mind and tangible aspects of our body. Such artifices might not satisfy us because they may remain foreign even if we personally create them. We would always know that such attributes are not genuinely ours but that they were added to us. We may not be able to accept them as our own. Yet, even if changes or supplements to dispositions of which individuals are already mindful should not be accepted, their infusion from the beginning of individuals' awareness would likely prevent their rejection as foreign. Even if individuals were aware of their conditioning, they might not be burdened by results of external assistance because they would know engineered characteristics only as attributes that have always been with them. They might be missing additional attributes whose introduction might burden them with suffering similar tribulations regarding their authenticity as previous generations that were confronted with novel attributes. However, with their already existing acceptance of technological alterations to furnish attributes that can enhance their potential for the pursuit of needs, issues of personal impossibility might be greatly diminished or entirely fade away. Humans may grow to incorporate technology into their concept of self. In time, technological attributes might become indistinguishable to their carriers from natural attributes and their development. That would seem particularly likely if they could be seamlessly incorporated into direct impressions of an individual's self. Beyond such developments, they might also become accepted because individuals might not want to be left behind in the development that added features empower. Enhancements regarding common needs may encourage them to condone them in idiosyncratic areas as well. With the development of enhancing technologies, issues of personal impossibility might be disappearing to where humans may overcome all personal impossibilities at least relative to one another.

To the extent we cannot or we cannot satisfactorily address deficiencies in our attributes with technology, we might be able to compensate for them by our diligence. In many cases of missing or insufficient personal attributes, we can take steps that advance our position. We may improve our mental and tangible abilities by studying, practicing, or changing our approach. We may unlock and maximize our potential through instruction and training. While we may compensate somewhat for lacking original disposition with dedication and strenuous work, such exertions meet boundaries. They may improve underdeveloped attributes but may not be able to replace missing attributes. We may still fall short of overcoming personal impossibilities according to standards we set. As unrealistic as it might seem that we should possess certain qualities, we might continue to agonize over their absence. Depending on our wishes and the gravity of our shortcomings, personal impossibilities may continue to pose considerable problems for our happiness. Barring a fundamental change of our mental or our tangible capabilities, this problem may seem impossible to resolve.

But cooperation might provide an avenue to resolve or at least relieve concerns about personal impossibilities. Many of our needs inherently necessitate cooperation from others to provide unique means that we cannot generate. To bring about such a cooperation, we may have to engage our personal attributes in return. As long as we possess valuable attributes that we can offer, we may naturally accept the reciprocal application of other individuals' attributes. This may become progressively familiar for us as our cooperation expands to needs that we could pursue and satisfy ourselves. We may adopt a general mode in which we maximize the effectiveness and efficiency of our pursuits by exchanging efforts or their products or contributing them to shared results. This may permit us to more comprehensively use our personal attributes as indirect means toward our objectives because they serve the purposes of others. This use of personal assets may satisfy us sufficiently to accept assistance in areas in which we lack personal assets. Cooperating with others may let us leverage our strengths to compensate for our weaknesses. The valuation of our attributes in exchanges or joint efforts may help us to not only decrease conceptual and practical individual impossibilities but also personal impossibilities. It permits us to reduce our reservations toward accessing external attributes we wish we had because we earn desired means by application of our personal capacity. The mutuality of assistance counters the pain over our personal deficiencies with the pleasure over the benefits our personal assets provide. This may permit us to be content with the result as the best attainable solution. Rather than engaging in futile efforts or wasting resources on approximating attributes that only come to us at undue expense, we might maximize the overall effectiveness and efficiency of our pursuits by focusing on improving and using attributes we already possess. We may further diminish our pain over personal impossibilities by helping others develop talents and capabilities that we lack. Through our assistance, we become partly responsible for and can savor their success even if the attributes we advance are not our own. Our need to support the survival and thriving of other humans offers the foundation for obtaining such vicarious fulfillment.

Technological, economic, and social advancement and cooperation present impressive instruments for pushing back many barriers of individual and general impossibility. Still, we and others might be left quite a distance from experiencing reliable satisfaction of all basic survival needs, let alone all of our existential needs. The progress of technology renders general material deficiencies a diminishing part of our problems. When we search for examples of detrimental circumstances in our existence, we recognize that, apart from accessing the past and overcoming death, most of our relevant wishes should not be affected by general impossibility. Nor does there seem to be a good reason why individuals should suffer great pain over boundaries of individual impossibility. There appear to be enough resources as well as conceptual and practical capacities to accommodate the existential concerns of all humans with the noted exceptions. Even the ability to conquer death with technological and social developments seems to be within reach. But a dearth of mental clarity encumbers humanity in realizing its developmental potential. Many individuals seem to have trouble understanding how to employ their conceptual or practical capacities or following that understanding. They may not have well-rounded, mature concepts of objectives they should pursue or the manners of pursuing them. Even if they possess sufficiently developed technological skills, they may therefore procrastinate or pursue erroneous or less than optimal strategies. They may select the wrong type, strength, timing, sequence, or combination of means. They may not use their resources in the most effective ways. They may lack motivation to address matters that lie within their capabilities because of unwarranted fear or disregard. They may interact with others in ways that do not optimize their interests. They may be disinclined to cooperate, have incompatible requirements, or be unaware of the advantages of cooperation or how to organize it. Deficiencies may also result from a preclusion of access to resources and from exploitation that deprives humans of the fruits of their labor or of other possessions. Perpetrators and victims may both suffer from the struggle engendered by this abuse. Problems may further arise from the abuse of natural resources that may negatively affect individuals who did not participate or benefit as well as offenders. Such abuses may be caused or tolerated by ignorance or errors regarding one's own and other parties' needs and rights. But we also often find willful ignorance or disregard for the sake of gratifying dominant needs. We can further detect destructive acts that do not seem to follow such motivations and appear to be without purpose. Responses to actual or deemed violations of needs and rights, and replies to those, extensively add to deprivations. These factors of human irresponsibility are material causes for individual and general impossibility. Even if we should fare relatively well in such a setting, its strife and damage necessarily leave the level of our satisfaction short of its potential. Our needs seem to call upon us to solve our self-imposed limitations.

Beyond these limitations, other boundaries are and become visible whose dissolution may be helpful or necessary to increase the fulfillment of our needs. In many aspects of our individual and collective potential, we may be only at the beginning of what we can discover or achieve. The individual and collective determination and tenacity to fight limitations of our pursuits appear to be deeply embedded characteristics of humanity. Overcoming limitations is our individual and collective preoccupation, perhaps even our obsession. We incessantly determine and implement strategies to ameliorate our happiness. We dedicate our existence to the realization of our wishes, to the pursuit of our happiness. Nevertheless, our efforts might not yield the happiness we expect from such a towering investment. Although we might achieve moments and periods of happiness, some and perhaps many of our pursuits do not appear to produce the satisfaction we had expected. There may be simple explanations for such a shortfall. Besides our own errors and carelessness, we may be subject to obvious interferences and limitations that do not allow us intact pursuits or to savor such pursuits and their results. It is much more confounding when we encounter a failure of happiness where we seem to act responsibly toward us and others and suffer no recognizable encroachments. We may make adequate progress and achieve what we had set out to do. We may be reaching the objectives we thought would place us into a state of happiness. Yet these accomplishments may not translate into the satisfaction we had imagined. The objective validity and success of some pursuits may not be matched by our subjective impression. The reasons for such a shortfall are enigmatic because everything seems to be arranged according to our needs and proceeding as planned. Our dissatisfaction may prompt us to inquire whether we are truly pursuing our needs and how much happiness we can rightfully expect.

Tragically, we might never or only rarely and fleetingly be confronted by occasions that make us pursue such inquiries with the necessary profundity or extent. There might always exist some detraction from happiness that we might blame for our not being as happy as we imagine we could be if everything went our way. The imperfections of our pursuits render it difficult for us to distinguish causes for our unhappiness that are generated by nonintrinsic inadequacies from those that lie in the nature of happiness or our failure of identifying and following what will make us happy. Our lack of distinction may cause us to concentrate on addressing technical optimizations of our pursuits. However, before we can enhance our happiness through technical optimization, we must ascertain that the underlying objectives can convey the satisfaction we seek. We must first find out what we want and do not want, as well as what the necessary implications are. Our preoccupation with forestalling and solving technical disturbances might alone not permit us to gain adequate clarity about such issues.

We may negate such a lack of clarity and refer to motivational foundations that we consider to be securely competent. We may have favorite pursuits that we know are bringing us happiness. We may be certain about the needs these pursuits fulfill. We may reject the possibility that we might derive more happiness from these types of pursuit. But we may also identify pursuits that we regard with more ambivalence. If we inquire why we engage in such pursuits, we may find a somewhat undefined urge that is only described in general terms. We may respond with a declaration of values and principles that are important to us. It is often hard to trace how these became settled in our mind or how we know that they should guide us. We may not or not consistently live by these maxims that we apparently hold in some esteem. We may not have given them much thought or our considerations may have been largely abstract without much particularization. We may practice them merely in a perfunctory manner. There may be exceptions to this vagueness. We may know more regarding the background and meaning of some of our convictions than others. We may fully embrace some of them and try to live according to them. We may approve of some of them on account of their practical instruction, rationale, or an emotional bond. We may believe that some of them and perhaps all of them, contain important and useful insights about how we should live. Nevertheless, a few general statements like these cannot possibly constitute sufficient guidance to create, increase, maximize, and sustain our happiness. They cannot replace a clear definition of our needs. Beyond that, their capability as practical guidelines may be questionable. They are often too general or too specific to grant us sufficient knowledge for resolving varying convolutions among needs and the situations in which we find ourselves. Many of our principles may then turn out to be thin layers of commonplaces. We may coddle ourselves in their purported security and resign to a life of mediocrity and partial frustration in which we battle problems whose resolution only vaguely represents our desires. To the extent we decide that our familiar values and principles are insufficient and that we want more, we struggle because we do not possess a well-developed idea of the internal and external circumstances and mechanisms that make us happy or unhappy. In such areas that lie beyond the refuge of guidelines we deem sufficient, we are bound to address issues of our happiness in ways that expose us to risks of damage. We are forced to consider and define our happiness in an erratic and fragmented manner. We may detect causes of happiness and unhappiness and address them as they arise and claim relevance. If we attempt to plan for our objectives and their fulfillment and engage in longer-term strategies, we run the risk of pouring substantial efforts into sequences that prove to be inapposite. Either way, we would not be in command of our affairs.

We experience that this is not a proper mode to maintain, let alone to improve or maximize our happiness. We would be more efficient and effective in our happiness if we could lead our life in a more confident fashion. Thus, we look for a strategy that places us in front of, in charge of events before they occur, a strategy that gives us control over our existence to the extent persistent impossibilities and uncontrollable interferences allow. Finding such a strategy does not appear unmanageable. We are not the first to seek happiness. Every human who ever lived has been confronted by the same fundamental difficulties of achieving happiness. Even if personalities, circumstances, and means differ and humanity has undergone development, principal needs and principal choices pursuant to them have remained similar. There must be models from which we can learn. Likely, we have been exposed to constructs that claim such an authority and we may have adopted some or all of their teachings. But the fact that we are not as happy as we wish to be places them in question. Although their proponents and we might blame us and other causes for shortcomings, technical optimization only becomes an issue to the extent we can be certain that our model guides us competently and that there is no alternative that can offer better guidance. If we are to gain control over our happiness, we must be able to make that determination. A similar determination is necessary if we are not predisposed by any model. In either event, we must become able to judge whether and how models match our needs. The next section begins to explore that endeavor.

SECTION TWO
EMPIRIC APPROACH

CHAPTER 6
EXPERIENCES AND INFLUENCES

If we knew nothing about what makes us happy, we could still call on basic facilities to help us in determining a fundamental concept of our happiness. The most direct facilities would be our senses and their immediate emotional effects. They would assist us in establishing a basic framework of our happiness by indicating what feels painful and what feels pleasurable. Our facilities are further amplified by our capacities to analyze, synthesize, memorize, project, and compare facts we connect with these emotional events. We can apply these mental facilities to formulate not solely our immediate responses to pain and pleasure. We can also use them to influence our future, to evade or prevent pain and to obtain pleasure. When we involve these forward-looking abilities, we determine the happiness or unhappiness of circumstances at a distance instead of relying on our impressions at the time of their occurrence. The detection of whether a prospective cause serves or hinders a need does not arise through our senses at the time. It is a result of our mental processing of past sensory information, of experiences.

When we introduce our experiences into determining whether a prospective course of action will cause pain or pleasure, the relationship between cause and effect in a predicted occurrence is a construct of our imagination. We will not know whether our predictions of pain or pleasure and our reactions are correct until and unless the anticipated result occurs, fails, or at least begins to occur or fail. We may be able to predict a result with reasonable certainty a few steps before we stand to incur pain or pleasure if we possess a sufficient understanding of the factual setting and involved causalities. Yet, if we lack guiding experiences, face new ingredients or constellations, or are subjected to interference by other powers and actors, we may not be able to determine future causalities with adequate reliability. Known and unknown, foreseeable and unforeseeable causalities may overlap and intersect. We may not know of actual or potential events or may not sufficiently understand them. We may not possess enough experience to predict particular outcomes reliably or even with a reasonable margin of error. The correlations may be so complex or foreign that we cannot forecast them or even decipher them after they occur. We may have to close such deficiencies by making assumptions, drawing parallels, relying on conjecture, and allowing for possibilities. This invites the risk of misinterpretation, omission, error, and ensuing detriment or failure into our pursuits. These threats likely prompt us to widen our experiential horizon so we become better equipped in our forecasts.

We may attempt to accomplish this widening by obtaining information about the external sensory impressions of other individuals or of machines with sensory capabilities. In addition to including such information from sources beyond our own, we may incorporate the rational and emotional processing of this information by such sources, including internal sensory phenomena, into our mental processes. As we combine these sources with our facilities of judging what makes us happy, we move away from the direct proof of our senses and our processing of their signals. We progressively rely on the experiences and judgments of other sources for a determination of what does and does not benefit our happiness. This reliance is problematic even if it only pertains to communications of external sensory impressions. Our removal from the immediacy of these impressions exposes us to an elevated risk of misconceptions. The external sensory information we obtain from other sources may have been captured, contained, translated, reproduced, transmitted, or received in ways that do not allow us full access to the entirety of relevant information that could have been observed. Its collection may have taken place at locations, at times, or under circumstances that do not permit a complete account of what happened. Beyond that, the information we receive may not be a true reiteration of the original external sensory impression. The medium or technique of recordation, storage, or relay of such information may filter, modify, exclude, or enhance aspects of available information. Such alterations may be unavoidable in consequence of the technical limitations of a medium or the ways by which information is located, captured, translated, contained, reproduced, transmitted, or received.

Such inadequacies of external sensory information related from other sources may afflict humans and machines. However, human involvement provides an additional factor of unreliability and intentional or unintentional manipulation. The information would inescapably be processed not only by the sensory but also by the rational and emotional apparatus of the perceiving and relaying individuals. Although a certain treatment would happen as well in the acquisition and subsequent processing of information by machines, their construction may exclude or limit rational and emotional processing. Further, individual variations in human perception and in other mental processing appear more difficult to reveal and assess. We may encounter not only diversity in the ability but also in the willingness to register or to relay sensory information. The acquisition, storage, and communication of external sensory information may be influenced by the interpretation of its context. That interpretation may be subject to previous experiences, the mental attributes, and the current attitude of the observer. The influence of such processing may be difficult or impossible to contain. The person obtaining a sensory impression may try to extract rational and emotional responses before passing on sensory information. Then again, such a person may give in to or embrace rational and emotional treatment and may try to influence others to whom external sensory information is passed. There may be an agenda to manipulate others under the use of selected or skewed external sensory information. Information may even be produced for purposes of communication and for the manipulatory effect it may have. Such tendencies may be concealed by the use of information gathering and communication technologies, methods, personnel, or institutions that purportedly provide assurances of authenticity but are in fact used for ulterior purposes.

The perils of intentional and unintentional falsification by humans and by limitations of communication technology are often multiplied as we become more removed from witnessing objects or events. We may rely on sources that in turn receive their sensory information from other sources. Each station through which information passes on its way to us may be subject to the same or to other shortcomings that may compound until the information reaches us. If we wanted to prevent these contaminations, we would have to investigate and confirm all external sensory information on which we rely. This proving process would ideally require that we observe the original circumstances. We might also be satisfied with duplicating events or gaining access to recordings that contain the relevant content in which we are interested in relative fidelity. Yet such access is often not possible or only possible in part. Beyond that, even if all information were directly available to us, we may not possess the individual capacity or inclination to address all of it. Undertaking the necessary inquiries to prove the accuracy of sensory information may require skills and resources that we are not able or willing to invest. Further, we may not be able or willing to shoulder additional inquiries regarding occurrences whose impression might be necessary to provide a complete picture of a phenomenon. To overcome these impediments, we may look for assistance. We might defer to sources that can find, collect, ensure the completeness, reduce the complexity, derive, and summarize information. We might also look for agents that can explain the significance of external sensory information on our behalf. The risks involved in the conveyance of external sensory information become compounded if we additionally place reliance in processing of external sensory information by other sources that exceeds conveyance. Any such processing may exacerbate the problems already involved in its conveyance. It removes us from source materials even more. We now allow other persons or machines

to evaluate facts they observed or relay and to present us with conclusions with regard to their meaning. Sources that engage in such a processing may not fully reveal their sensory basis or the processing from
which they derive presented results. Interpretive processing may depend on the interaction of a wide variety of preexisting and accompanying factors. Because we now rely on an interpreter's judgment, we
become exposed to all factors that facilitate and influence such judgment or its pretense. This expansion infuses an additional dimension
of subjectivity into a process in which we invest hopes of objectivity.

If we lack the means or the willingness to verify informational
sourcing and processing, we incur a risk that we may not have accurate and complete information. This risk poses a principal issue for the
planning and implementing of our pursuits. We may try to avoid it by
operating only on the basis of our direct sourcing of information and
our mental processing. But our needs and our existence in a connected environment may not make such behavior a viable choice. Moreover, the problem by far exceeds immediate issues of information processing. Our presence and pursuits in an interdependent setting necessarily expose us to the conduct of others as receptors and providers
of information and to resulting circumstances. It is often not feasible
that we verify information and how it is used in areas that affect us.
Our shared environment and our interactive pursuits frequently make
it necessary that we subject ourselves to or that we engage in activities
with unverified sources, if not directly then indirectly in terms of the
circumstances they produce. The ways in which we acquire or are subjected to information and to its results join with the conditions under
which we acquire resources or are subjected to circumstances that are
not of an informational quality. But many of these are likely to be affected by information. We will want to know information about them
and their sourcing that we deem relevant to our dealings with them.

Within the parameters of human interaction, we have to decide
whether we need to, want to, or can afford to resort to our own faculties, assistance from others, impositions on others, and how we might
react to similar considerations and activities by others. Both our withdrawal from interaction and our engagement carry potential risks and
limitations. Our refusal to incorporate informational or any other assistance leaves us with consideration that is constricted to our perceptions, our knowledge, our imagination, and our capabilities. We may
have reason to resort to such practices. We may in particular look for
a removal from adverse encounters with others. But our restriction to
self-sufficiency may hinder or prevent successful or at least optimized
pursuits. More than that, it may expose us to conflict with others and

to losing such conflicts based on lacking socialization. Relying on ourselves may then be impossible, too cumbersome, or too risky or costly. On the other hand, reliance on information and other assistance from other sources or on their noninterference exposes us to their incompetence, negligence, and willful misconduct. Apart from becoming subject to the qualifications and the circumstances of others, participants in interactions with us engage in these with motivations of their own pursuit of happiness. We cannot trust that they have our interests in mind, much less that they solely have these in mind. All activities by other individuals, including all their communications and all purported undertakings on our behalf or with regard to us, are performed in the pursuit of their happiness. The attitude of others toward our objectives depends on whether and how much fulfillment of our needs is necessary, neutral, or adverse to their interests. The promotion of our happiness is coincidental to its consideration as a potential means in serving their benefit. This may make it hard to obtain or to be certain that we obtain information or other deportment from other individuals that benefits us or is even capable of improving or maximizing our happiness. Together with the potential that others might not be capable of generating results we require or might be otherwise precluded from producing them, our uncertainty about the motivations of others places an extensive burden on us. We must assess the extent to which a course suggested or taken by others is useful, neutral, or harmful to the fulfillment of our needs. We cannot unconditionally trust others.

Arguably, we suffer comparatively few problems confirming the adequacy of goods and services we acquire if they are standardized or regularly offered by particular purveyors. We can contract for a particular quality and quantity of a product or these might be imposed by law and even supervision. We and legal authorities might possess legal or legally authorized recourse if the product does not meet the applicable legal standards. Moreover, purveyors of products may guarantee the attributes of products they offer for fear of losing customers. This may give us reason to presume that products relevant for our pursuits comply to certain standards. Similar conditions may prevail regarding effects of circumstances that reside within the responsibility of others for other reasons. We may have the right to insist that these circumstances do not affect us or do affect us in certain ways and may have legal or legally authorized recourse if that does not occur. The accuracy and completeness of information might be established by these or similar criteria as well. These assurances gain importance the less we are able or willing to undertake external sensory or interpretive activities and instead rely on the capacity and motivation of others.

However, many concerns of our life are not organized according to rules of legal responsibility or guaranties. There may be more informal ethical tenets under which individuals are held or hold themselves to criteria of conduct. These may be partly effective to warrant an expectation regarding their compliance with certain standards. But such rules may contain substantial latitude and uncertainty and may weaken in spite of rising contact and interdependence because of the great scope and variety of interaction. Information flows appear to be particularly affected by a lack of reliability. As information we receive grows in variety, scope, and complexity and is easily generated, modified, and proliferated by an increasing number of sources, and because it is often provided without any assurances of reliability, we may have difficulties or may fail to establish its credibility. We may be subjected to a torrent of information in which external sensory information and interpretations by multiple and concealed sources and intermediaries may be amalgamated. This leaves us increasingly at a loss in confirming compliance with standards of truthfulness. Our inability may have us resign because we may not see how we can resolve it. Even where a resolution seems possible, we may deem ourselves unable or unwilling to invest the resources that are necessary to detect informational deficits and to cure them. This may keep us from producing an informed judgment regarding our pursuits. Besides specific clarity, we may lack more general insight about the opportunities and risks our surroundings contain. We may have an incomplete and incorrect understanding of reality. Even if we undertake a serious effort to verify facts, we may not make large gains against the mass of unverified information. To still meet, improve, and maximize the fulfillment of our needs, we may have to incur some risk that the information or demeanor we incorporate into our pursuits might turn out to be different. Not relying on any information and underlying circumstances may expose us to unwarranted anxiety and indecision. Chances to use opportunities or address threats may pass us by if we wait for verification of all relevant facts. We must rely on information about the behavior of others and the effects of their deportment in many respects with limited or no recourse if we want to maintain, develop, or maximize our happiness.

Notwithstanding, in view of the risks of relying on informational and other conduct, we may attempt to ascertain the trustworthiness of our circumstances. We may try to keep some level of rational control before and while we rely in our undertakings on positive, neutral, or negative circumstances. We may try to use our autonomous senses and considerations and a maximum of otherwise available information to determine the merit of information and our expectations regarding other conduct. In areas where we must rely on the assistance or non-interference by others or might derive a benefit from such reliance, we may require proof of competence and intent. We may require operational assurances that the acquisition and the processing of the information we seek meet certain standards and that our own impressions are accurate. We may want to possess unmitigated access to the activities and considerations of involved parties. We may require that they lay their sources open and give us the ability to trace them and the process in which the resulting information is formed. We may want to know at what junctures and how external sensory information was obtained and processed or interpreted. We may require that our sources declare the deficiencies or limitations of their activities or results. To assure the full use of their capacities in the gathering and consideration of information, we may demand that sources must be motivated to serve us or that their motivations are sufficiently analogous. Where this is not the case, our verification procedures might have to be more stringent. We might resort to continual testing or other information collection to justify our continued reliance. But this collateral information forms an additional layer of information. Because performance verification may exceed our capabilities or inclinations, we may rely on others to perform such functions. That reliance regarding external sensory and interpretive information remains subject to similar potential problems and control requirements as the informational aspects it is to verify. We may have to engage agents to monitor other levels of agents. Similar structures may be required to obtain other assistance or to react to adverse circumstances. Where possible, we may strive to keep direct control over sources of information and other assistance. Only, the burdens of establishing their compliance with our standards may be so involved that they may interfere with our pursuits.

Such complications are a large reason we rely on legal or ethical enforcement options in many relationships that are of sufficient importance for us to establish and maintain high degrees of assurance. But there may be a number of valid reasons why we may not rest upon such assurances and seek verification. Much damaging behavior may not be covered by legal or ethical commandments, or these might not be accepted. If there are applicable legal restrictions, we might have to confirm that the party on which we legally rely is capable of carrying the burdens of noncompliance. That in itself may be a reason to undertake reliability investigations. Further, there may be settings where legally bound parties cannot be sufficiently relied upon or compelled to abstain from violations of their obligations or to answer and compensate for breaches of their obligations. Even if we could receive adequate compensation in an event of breach, we may wish to avoid the burdens of legal enforcement proceedings. Similar and possibly even more compelling considerations may be appropriate for enforcement proceedings under ethical rules. Moreover, we may seek relationships that exceed what can be compelled under legal or ethical impositions. We may strive for a quality and quantity of resources, the stability and duration of their provision, or the development of a relationship that can only grow from high levels of dedication. While much of this dedication may depend on how we conduct ourselves, we may also look for signs that our investment into such a relationship is warranted.

The inquisitiveness of parties may be limited if they do not consider the expected benefits or the potential risk or damage from a relationship to be worth inquiry efforts beyond a certain level. But there may be many circumstances where the curiosity of parties is limited by other parties' resistance to verification. Such attitudes may be particularly widespread in collateral, coincidental, or casual interactions. Deeper inquiries or demands for information are likely to be more tolerated in relationships where one or both sides have substantial exposure to harm. Yet, even under such conditions, there may be limits to the accommodation of curiosity. Parties subjected to an inquiry may resent intrusions into what they regard to be their affairs, particularly if inquiries occur before a relationship is entered. They may interpret certain levels of inquiries as unwarranted imputations of wrongdoing or at least undeserved demonstrations of distrust. The levels at which offense is taken may vary broadly depending on the form and the substance of inquiry, the subject matter of the parties' relationship, their individual history and preceding relationship, their relative standing, and the general attitude of parties toward themselves and their environment. Further, parties subject to inquiries may determine that the potential benefit from a relationship does not warrant the disclosure or intrusion. They may wish to protect sources or trade secrets or limit disruption. They may be concerned about unfavorable revelations pertinent to the interests of an investigating party that may dissuade that party from acting in their interest. They may try to avoid possible efforts they might otherwise have to undertake to obtain approbation or to accommodate demands for remediation. They may fear the disclosure of unfavorable information that does not pertain to the rightful concerns of a requesting party or might also pertain to the concerns of other parties and whose dissemination might expose them to damage. They might not have an interest to dissipate concerns of the inquiring party because such concerns might benefit them. The extensive range of possible justified or unjustified reasons for disclosing or withholding information may render arriving at satisfying arrangements difficult. Unwarranted demands as well as unwarranted defensiveness may stand in the way of harmony. In most circumstances of human interaction, conventions have grown and may develop that define generally accepted levels and methods of verification. But tension may prevail in remaining deviations from common settings or in situations where no general or more particularized usages have been established.

The necessity for verification efforts may diminish over time as the relationship among parties is carried on in a satisfactory manner. Even if we initially employ stringent inquiries whether our sources are reliable, a record of consistent performance may build rational trust. Such a record may prompt us to eventually dispense with most or all requirements of rational verification. Still, it may often not be possible or desirable to build long-term relationships that allow us to reduce or relinquish verification. The parties may not wish to be involved in potential adversities arising from verification. Inquiring parties may not want to become exposed to disappointment or employ protracted verification campaigns before they can trust another party. Nor may their counterparts tolerate to be placed on probation for all this time. Additionally, the increasing ability or need to select interactions in a broad variety of matters with a broad variety of parties may cause us to demand more readily available indications that other parties or that circumstances connected to them perform to our requirements. We may refer to auxiliary indications in supplementation of legal security and guaranties. We may require professional qualifications, peer approval, and a record of activities and accomplishments in other relationships. We may refer to social standing, reputation, and other positions of accountability. We may require examinations, certifications, a lack of a negative record, positive references, or other convincing evidence that others depend in their pursuits on satisfying us. Alone or in combination, such indications may give us sufficient reasons to extend trust.

We might combine these and other rational criteria to establish or reinforce our assessment of trustworthiness. Yet rational considerations of trust or proof often might not be able to confer sufficient indications of reliability. We may have to decide based on incomplete or unclear rational indications. We may also look for levels or categories of means or for manners of provision that exceed rational considerations and invoke emotional aspects. To assist us in such situations, we may supplement or replace rational criteria with emotional criteria of assessing trustworthiness. Even if rational factors re available to us in sufficient scope and clarity, we may be disposed to add emotional considerations. Emotional criteria can wield momentous influence in our decisions to trust others or their products. They may be so strong in some contexts that they override rational considerations. Frequently, we are predisposed or conditioned to trust or distrust particular influences based on nonrational criteria. Depending on the relative weight of these influences among one another and in relation to rational considerations, we may ascribe varying degrees of trustworthiness to different sources. The most fundamental source for the establishment of emotional trust appears to lie in the relationship with individuals who care for us during our upbringing. At a young age, we depend on their love, support, protection, direction, teaching, and approval. We have an instinctive existential emotional bond with them. We begin our relationship with these individuals without skepticism and reserve. We presume that they are knowledgeable and proficient, will promote and protect us, and have our best interests in mind. To some degree, we extend this emotional confidence to other family members. Our tribal instinct and the particular empathy for members of our family and our need to secure the survival and wellbeing of our kind through them cause us to believe in reciprocity. We presume special, mutual bonds among individuals we regard as family that induce them and us to act in the interest of one another. If this presumption of trusting and being trusted is disappointed, we are incredulous and suffer deep-seated emotional pain. A relationship of trust with our family appears to constitute a basic wish whose satisfaction or dissatisfaction lingers to bear heavily on our happiness. We continue to carry an emotionally motivated focus with us of what the relationship with members of our family was, is, could have been, should be or should have been, or what it should or could be in the future. The strength and persistence of our desire of trust among family members may lead us to suspect that it has a genetic basis over which we have no or only limited control. This conclusion is supported by observations of similar practices of giving and seeking protection and support among related individuals in other species that are mainly or solely guided by genetic programming.

We may expand the scope of emotional relationships of trust in the context of love relationships, friendships, relations with mentors, teachers, or idols. Beyond that, we may invest emotional trust into relationships with other individuals whom we recognize to be similar to us, individuals who share objectives, experiences, attributes, or certain aspects of their environment with us. We may project part of us onto them and conclude that their partial congruence should give rise to at least some of the confidence we customarily reserve for ourselves. Our identification with such persons leads us to assume that they act with similar motivations and performance standards and that they act in our interest because we assume that they identify with us as well. We may have even higher expectations regarding persons who appear to have achieved a position to which we aspire. We may infer additional emotional bonds with such persons because of their purported leadership. Similarities may then cause us to transfer the devotion we originally reserve for our family. We may further invest trust in individuals who share characteristics with other individuals we trust. Finally, we may instinctively invest trust into a variety of social, economic, religious, political, and military associations that remind us of a family.

Frequently, the emotional quality of a relationship of trust may be fused with a rational basis into a hybrid. The advance of emotional trust may be affirmed by rational circumstances. Conversely, relationships that are at first rationally based may convert into a state where trust becomes in parts or entirely emotionally motivated. We may interpret the rational basis for trust and the actual or potential benefit it confers onto us as an invitation by our benefactor to engage in emotional mutuality. We may infer that motivations by other individuals to assist in the satisfaction of our needs are attributable to their need to protect and support us. Accordingly, we may read motivations into the participation by others in rational transactions that appear to warrant a response of emotional trust on our part. Such inferences may be in error. Yet the apparent instinct in humans to grant and seek protection and support among one another favors the development of emotional motivations from rational relations of reciprocity. These motivations come naturally to us and seem to be unavoidable because they precede rational causes for cooperation. An emotional motivation may still be instrumental to initiate or to strengthen a cooperative relationship that is founded on rational criteria. A climate of emotional trust may be helpful or even required to uphold or develop such a relationship to full fruition. We may therefore unintentionally or intentionally signal our willingness to extend emotional bonds to parties who are or might be cooperating with us in a rational context. Even if we do not actively encourage emotional reciprocity, we may not foreclose it. Because rational foundations for trust are often not absolutely secure or able to guarantee performance, emotional trust can present a welcome binding agent. Not extending or responding to emotional trust might signal possible estrangement and disloyalty, especially if other participants indicate that they wish to engage in a relationship of emotional trust. It may cast doubt on the effectiveness and reliability of a rational cooperative commitment. It may give rise to suspicion that rational assumptions in favor of extending trust may not be warranted. The inconsistency implies a cause for the limitation or cessation of trust.

The development of emotional trust can also produce negative consequences. Once we develop emotional trust, our emotional bonds may become so entrenched in our mind that we may have trouble relating rational proof of untrustworthiness and experiences of unhappiness to unjustified emotional trust as their cause. Past, present, or expected satisfaction may motivate us to follow the influence of persons and groups we trust without any or with reduced indications of trustworthiness or in spite of positive indications that counterparties are incompetent or do not have our interests in mind. We may only react to the betrayal of our trust if rational indications of untrustworthiness translate into emotional responses in us that are so severe that they fundamentally weaken or break our emotional attachment.

Because emotional trust carries a sizeable risk of blindsiding us, founding our determination of what will make us happy on emotional trust may not be the best strategy. Yet large portions of our concept of happiness may be influenced by relationships of emotional trust. That influence is usually most invasive during our childhood. We build our autonomous capabilities generally by learning from sources we trust. During this process, we brace our dearth of experience and decisional aptitude by relying on sources of emotional trust. Ideally, their influence should in time empower us to discover our needs and define our wishes, to generate and strengthen mechanisms of rational trust, and to render competent independent decisions about our happiness. At the end of our development, we should be self-governing. Still, chances are that, when our childhood ends, many of us have not learned the skills to competently investigate our needs and how to pursue them best. Few of our early influences may teach us to be independent decision makers. While some may seek to condition us to assure our happiness, others might have more sinister objectives. Either way, many appear to be set on utilizing our unconditional trust to bias us toward adopting certain patterns of thought, emotion, and deportment. Such conditioning may disable us or leave us unprepared at the end of our upbringing to render our own deliberate choices regarding our happiness. But our needs and the wishes they ignite may not conform to the patterns of pursuit we have been taught. Thus, we may enter a period of rebellion toward the end of our childhood. We may try to find independence from taking someone else's word or command. We may test and endeavor to overcome unwarranted trust and to become self-initiated and self-considered. We may have tried to assert our self before. However, our impending adulthood is a time when this becomes critical because we have developed sufficiently in many respects to exercise autonomy and soon might be left to fend for ourselves. We are crossing a threshold where we can chart the course for fundamental aspects of our existence for the first time. We expect and often are expected to take responsibility for ourselves. We may want to or have to determine how to support ourselves, how to behave, how and where to live, whom to love, whether to enter into commitments, and how to address such commitments. Previously, these decisions were made or prescribed by others or were not relevant. Now, suddenly, we are or desire to be in charge. We work on issues and make choices we have never faced before that may carry implications for large areas and long stretches of our existence. In exercising or struggling to establish our freedom, we might not know what to keep and what to discard.

Coming of age poses a complex problem for us to which neither continuing prior patterns nor totally breaking with them may be an adequate answer. The problem and its solution may be more complex. Our determination to reject prior influences may be so strong that we select opposites. These may not be in our interest. Automatic opposition to former guidance does not show independence. It demonstrates continued direction even in its reversal. Further, by rejecting prior influences, we may open ourselves to new influences, merely replacing one external authority with the domination by another. We might also reject both old and new influences in an effort to develop or defend our autonomy. In an attempt to gain distance from influences and develop our own person, we may discard beneficial together with detrimental aspects. We may not be able yet to fill that void. Venturing out in rejection of all influences is near impossible because we would have to generate all principles that guide our actions. For many of us, undertakings to break free from influences are therefore ineffective and short-lived. Our lacking experience, resources, deliberation, and planning renders it often problematic to gain and maintain independence. Our mind contrasts this state with the relative safety of a familiar environment of dependence. Even if we dislike such an environment because it forecloses the potential that independence appears to hold, its comparative security may stay appealing. Societal pressures may place the powerful lure of relatively safe satisfaction of needs upon compliance and the threat of a more difficult existence upon noncompliance before us. If we have not been provided with enough encouragement, respect, and freedom to become a self-considered person and to value our independence over comforts, our adherence or return to conformance is probable. We would have problems overcoming the inhibitions and influences of our ingrained dependences and to suddenly be self-actuated and emancipated upon coming of age. Once we are retained in dependences and settle in, we are unlikely to overcome them later.

Even with the best education and attempts to facilitate our development into self-considered persons, there is a novelty to our independence. It still gives rise to a foray into the unknown. With luck, the foresight of our environment and care on our part, we may ease into new functions and succeed keeping painful learning experiences to a minimum. However, in many situations, we will be ill prepared and be prevented from taking on our new position of independence with certainty. Committing and learning from mistakes may be an unavoidable process at that stage. That we might not be ready to generate fully reflected autonomous decisions does not acquit us. Eventually, we will have to make up our mind. Not having a plan, not selecting a career, not picking a partner, not choosing a purposeful existence, not knowing what we want may be regarded as a defect by us and by our social surroundings. We perceive pressure to do something or run the risk of being excluded, marginalized, or dominated. We also understand that, if we fail to make decisions and act upon them, our situation may advance to where our selections may become progressively more limited or may run out. We loathe the thought that we might remain or again become dependent or that we might lose our freedom to control or at least impact our happiness. These prospects prompt us to decide and follow our decisions at the risk of being wrong rather than remaining uncommitted. When we inquire into the underlying reasons, we may not find much depth of guiding contemplation. Some determinations may be superficial and may seem to be the product of coincidence and whim. We may revoke them swiftly if they do not succeed. But some decisions appear to have deeper motivations. They elicit strong, continuing hopes and convictions. If we cannot trace these focal points to a self-considered process, they can only result from our innate genetic mental dispositions or influences exerted by external sources.

When we try to trace our decisions to their motivations, we often encounter unconsidered impulses that have enigmatic origins. We appear to be particularly susceptible to such impulses with regard to life-altering and existential topics. The smaller an issue is, the more the solution seems to lend itself to logic and consideration of the facts. When we ponder larger, more complex issues regarding our existence, our ability to exercise rational judgment appears to weaken. Yet, upon closer review, this occurrence does not seem to depend on the size of a challenge alone. Even large technical challenges may not derail our rational decision-making and proceeding. Rather, the problem seems to be connected to the circumstance that we make fundamental decisions with regard to our needs, our happiness. Here, related impulses tend to circumvent our rational facilities, critical thinking, and emotional reservations. This positions us at partial odds with our impulses. We are not in charge of them. Instead, they seem to control us. We may deem that being at their mercy may not be in our interest. We may reason that being thoughtful and deliberate, placing our rational mind in control may prevent us from following damaging impulses. In an attempt to gain control of our impulses, we make an effort to learn, we try to better our odds at making decisions that are suitable for us.

Unsure of ourselves, we may seek the advice of others. Some of those sources may be the same as in our childhood, some may be new. Some advice may be instructive. Other individuals may possess sufficient distance to see circumstances more clearly that our proximity to ourselves prevents us from distinguishing. They may help us by investigating for us or with us. They may provide us with the tools to examine ourselves, including our needs and potential courses of action related to these. On the other hand, following answers offered by others puts us at risk of making choices that reflect their ideas of happiness, not our own. No matter how much another person may try to identify with us and to comprehend us, that identification and understanding has to remain limited. The person providing advice remains separate. This separateness is the source of potential bias. It poses a viewpoint that is not ours. We receive suggestions of what to do if we were more like the advising person, if that person were more like us, or a combination of both. Even at its best, external guidance involves an at least partial superimposition among individuals and therefore has to result in at least partial inaccuracy. But opening ourselves to external guidance also exposes us to more insidious risks. It gives others the opportunity to use us for their purposes. This influence may evolve beyond a state of mind where we follow the advice of others. It may reach a level where we allow someone to govern our personality at least in parts. With such control, it may take little effort to make premises, thought processes, and actions seem legitimate that we otherwise would reject. Worse yet, once a manipulation takes hold, the subjected person becomes a superficially autonomous participant in pursuing the installed objectives. Such a person becomes a seemingly self-directed tool that in fact stands in the service of foreign needs, wishes, and pursuits.

One might assume that this type of brainwashing is reserved to unique constellations in which individuals whose mental immune system has been severely weakened are victimized. However, many of us are dangerously disposed to having our personality deeply affected by outside influences. We tend to follow certain individuals and groups we trust rather uncritically with answers to fundamental questions of our existence. We habitually trust assertions and explanations by presumed experts and authorities to tell us where we come from, why we are here, what we should be doing, and where we should be going. We accept their guidance on various levels of abstraction from the general parameters of our existence and our environment, over specifics of our life, down to our thoughts and emotions. We allow them to direct our ethics and our behavior, the formulation of our objectives and means. Once we acknowledge their authority, we rarely ask for proof or explanations before we go along and execute their instructions. We tend to trust their opinion and to not reserve judgment in matters that we concede to be under their authority even if they directly concern our happiness. If this trust in authority is misplaced, unfortunate and tragic consequences may occur. Our uncritical acceptance may induce us to overlook indications of incompetence, inapplicability, error, obfuscation, deception, and abuse. We may unwittingly follow foreign purposes that are not in our interest or at least not in our best interest.

To ascertain whether a particular piece of guidance is suitable for us, we would have to understand its effects on our needs. External guidance is only secure if we have the capacity of subjecting it to our critical assessment. Without such capacity, the risk is high that we will be influenced by guidance that does not match our requirements. We may use guidance to assist us in the process of exploring and identifying the objectives, means, and strategies that make us happy, happier, or happiest. Still, the risk of intentional and unintentional undue influence by these sources may render their application even for exploratory purposes misleading and possibly dangerous. Following external suggestions to direct our endeavors might embroil us in so many misdirected trials to ascertain worthwhile pursuits that the fulfillment of our needs may severely suffer. Further, we may be led into directions or required to make investments from which we cannot or can solely retreat under significant cost. This places us into a difficult situation. We have to find a way for validating the applicability of external guidance before exposing ourselves to it. If we cannot trust external direction to establish our needs and wishes, we may try to take a more direct, empiric approach that cannot be falsified. We may try to witness the application of external guidance to other individuals who are sufficiently similar to us to warrant a presumption of transferability. Better yet, rather than listening to what persons say and have others do, better than having us and others become test subjects for their ideas, we may try to find proof that their ideas are applicable from what they do to find happiness. We may be willing to adopt such ideas if there is sufficient similarity between us and them. The next chapter addresses whether such practical examples can provide competent guidance.

CHAPTER 7
TRIALS, CONVENTIONS, AND IDOLS

When we look for principles of happiness, it might appear reasonable that we should consider principles that sizable numbers of individuals hold dear and exercise in their own matters to satisfy their existential needs. Turning to such established systems of seeking happiness provides us the relative security that others have already considered and judged certain behavior and circumstances to be satisfactory responses to needs we all share. That a large number of individuals can agree on what renders them happy might signify that they are on to a valid principle of happiness. We might extract common denominators from observations of what makes many or the most persons happy. A practical example would become increasingly convincing as more persons subscribe to it. To find guidance, we would then mostly look at larger groups of similar or identical conduct and try to identify the concurrence of motivations that direct such conduct. We may trust that valid views are expressed in prevailing moral, religious, and legal principles, in written and in unwritten social conventions. We may presume that such principles are applied because they result in happiness. Yet their existence does not necessarily tell us how effective they are in creating happiness for individuals to whom they are applied. Nor does it reveal whether there are other principles that might be more useful.

The reasons individuals apply established standards may not reflect their foremost ideas of happiness. These principles may not have been fashioned to make individuals who are subjected to them happy. Nor may such individuals have selected or acceded to them. Principles may have been imposed by an authority or may have grown as a matter of tradition. They may represent inapplicable, ineffective, or outdated models that individuals are forced to accept if they wish to exist in a particular environment or even if they wish to leave such an environment. Even the apparently free sharing and application of conventions do not prove that these constitute principles of happiness. The underlying grounds not only for consent with preexisting conventions but also for the active shaping of conventions can be resentment, fear, error, insecurity, and any other causes that create or promote unhappiness. Compliance with existing principles or their selection may reflect compromise, containment, adjustment, defeat, or resignation. Individuals living by these principles may conform to them because they regard compliance with them as the best way under the given circumstances to fulfill their needs. Then again, these conventions may only allow modest achievements. They may not reflect what complying or shaping individuals would do if they could freely imagine and select their path to happiness. Even if individuals should not consider themselves constrained by principles and should regard them as the best solutions they can conceive, the existence of such an accord does not automatically give credence to the agreed conventions as meaningful principles of happiness. Agreement regarding a common denominator of happiness does not mean that the endorsed behavior is effective or efficient. Individuals may abide by paradigms because of their lack of capacity, knowledge, imagination, or effort, or because they have been misguided by others or by themselves. That others share an erroneous outlook does not make it correct. Even if the shared behavior represents a common denominator by which happiness can be produced, it may not constitute a particularly high-yielding denominator. A larger acceptance then does not prove that the shared principles constitute a better or the best possible idea for building, increasing, or maximizing happiness. It seems that there is no great assurance in numbers.

Nevertheless, the common foundation of existential needs that is shared by all humans, their common needs, should render us hopeful that we can find principles that guide us to fulfill a particular type of need better or best. If we wanted to assemble valid principles, we would therefore still look for behavior patterns by which individuals achieve what they consider to be supreme satisfaction or approximations of that state. It seems relatively easy to distinguish certain core behavior patterns that are better suited than others or best suited to fulfill a need if such a need pertains directly to fundamental survival functions. Although some variations may exist, these closely relate to principal shared fulfillment functions. With regard to collateral needs, however, we may find it harder to identify behavior patterns that are universally recognized as superior or ideal. The reasons for such increased variation are not immediately obvious. They may relate to the plasticity of mental structures and processes that form the prevalent setting for collateral needs. With regard to all existential needs, differences in preferences may be due to individual conditions that are not shared. These may be of a permanent or of a temporary nature. Not all individuals share the same intensity potential in their needs, the same individual faculties, the same environment, the same past and current position in an environment, or the same fulfillment state. Even if they share identical needs in principle, the variety of possible combinations of needs depending on individuals' disposition and situation and their setting can lead to different strategies. These differences result in a variety of approaches that yield a variety of objective success and a variety of subjective satisfaction. Even if a large majority should claim that a behavior conveys superior or ideal happiness, it may not be able to claim universal application. It might be limited to claiming that a path certain individuals have chosen is superior or ideal for them. The failure of some individuals to adopt these preferences demonstrates that even a broadly shared path constitutes only one approach toward fulfillment among others. The existence of possible alternatives poses a problem for us if we try to obtain guidance from the behavior of others to determine which path will provide happiness for us. The consequences of an erroneous adoption may be more than negligible gradations of happiness. What may be entirely helpful for some may be unsupportive, dramatically less helpful, or counterproductive for others. Our differences may appear to define us as much as our commonalities. Hence, our trust that principles of behavior shared by a multitude of persons can show us the way to happiness might be misplaced.

Notwithstanding such reservations, we may consider behavioral patterns at least as possibilities whose broader following makes them worthwhile to explore. The question becomes then how to select from different pathways to happiness that we notice being pursued by other individuals. If an item of common accord strikes us as a principle we possibly may want to guide us in our search for happiness, we may try it. If the application of such a principle in fact brings us happiness, we might be inclined to adopt such principle. We may decide to continue to identify such principles by observations and by imitating trials until we assemble a collection of principles that can guide us in all respects. However, even if we derive a measure of happiness from an approach we emulate, there is no guaranty that it constitutes the best way for us to find happiness. Even if we explore several possibilities, we could only claim that we have found the best way among those that someone else has already established and of which we have become aware. As long as we follow someone else, we do not know whether there might be a personally unknown, existing manner of behavior or a new, generally unexplored manner that better suits our needs. In solely trying and adopting approaches already applied by others in their pursuits of happiness, we may hold ourselves back from finding the best possible way for us. To open ourselves to finding the best possible happiness, we would have to transcend the approaches offered by convention and consider all approaches that could possibly serve our happiness. New strategies that are not reflected in the examples offered by other humans may make us happy, happier, or happiest. We would have to test all of these possible alternatives to find out whether they can improve our happiness. To cover all these possibilities and make our selection, it would seem necessary to engage in a systematic, scientific process.

Using a detailed scientific method, we can establish firm principles for the behavior of an array of occurrences. Once we have formulated such principles and confirmed their application, we can use them as reliable tools for our pursuits. We can plan and implement our pursuits according to their descriptions of cause and effect. Yet, in our reality, our use of such scientific principles is limited. That may be due to the fact that we have not understood all applicable principles. But the problem is often not so much unfamiliarity with the involved science. Rather, it may be that we face an overwhelming multitude of parts and processes whose presence or interaction we cannot ascertain. We may therefore be limited to exploring such settings at a system level that includes parts or all of them. Even if comprehensive detailed exploration is possible, that undertaking threatens to make us lose sight of higher levels of phenomena about which we can find valuable information by exploring them as systems, possibly through interaction with other systems. The interdependent complexities represented by our environment, our body, and their relationship warrant approaching these phenomena as systems. Subdivisions of these systems seem to be necessary or helpful for better study. Regarding humans, our mind and particularly our emotional mind warrant such an attitude at least initially for all reasons that suggest system orientation in scientific research. Human emotions resist their scientific classification. While the rest of our mind can be more readily understood in its reflective and its logical functions, our emotional mind appears to be moved by more enigmatic forces. Additionally, the interdependence of its processes makes it an integrated body part whose interaction with the other parts of our body and our environment we must understand.

If we know little about the inner workings of a system, we can find out about it by testing how it reacts to different conditions. Once we have found a particular reaction, we may test how this reaction behaves when we change circumstances. Because we may not know what causes the system to react in the manner we observe, we cannot safely predict how it might react to different associations. We would have to put speculations to the test. We might build some understanding of involved causes by accumulating knowledge about ranges of behavior and aspects that break acceptable ranges of similarity. In that respect, our exploration of systems is not different from fundamental scientific research. Yet it may lack the certainty of a detailed scientific process that arises from establishing cause and effect and derived principles. System-oriented research may therefore consist of a collection of methodical observations that resembles prescientific methods and may only partly advance to scientific standards of deeper understanding.

The ways we collect experiences about our emotional mind and its correlations with our environment are usually not methodical. We develop such experiences as we are confronted with our needs and try to fulfill them as much as we can. Because of this preoccupation alone, the reality in which we must pursue our needs often allows us neither exhaustive detailed nor system-related research regarding our needs. We may not be able to establish the presence, effects, or interactions of factors within their system, in other systems, or beyond these that might have relevance for the welfare of our emotional mind. Nor may we be able to experience sufficient activity by or interaction within or between such systems or between systems and nonsystemic factors to ascertain reliable knowledge. The completeness and certainty of our experiences may vary widely. Even if we collect a sufficient amount of experiences in a particular setting, an investigation may lose relevance once the external setting in which we pursue our happiness changes or if our internal disposition changes. Because of our lack of knowledge, we must often pursue our happiness based on vague notions and generalizations about us and our environment. We may have to determine our course founded on what we consider possible or, if more information is available, based on probability assessments. We may have to act on the basis of the incomplete knowledge we have derived, or we may defer a decision in favor of finding out more so we can render a better-founded decision later. Depending on our assessment of risk and potential damage, we may plan safety margins into our pursuits.

In many respects, we can only cope with the complexity and variety of our emotional mind and our environment by treating them as phenomena about which we have less than complete knowledge. This appears to lower our chances of finding exact ways of improving and maximizing our happiness. We may substantially ameliorate our pursuits if we can procure scientifically verifiable information from other sources. Beyond that, others may impart nonscientific information to us. We must treat this information with reservation because it might be imparted in the interest of other parties. Nevertheless, if we proceed with caution and insist on sufficient signs of reliability, including such information into our considerations may be helpful. We may find not only technical assistance arising from the experiences of others instructive, but also their experiences regarding the satisfaction of their needs. Here again, we will have to be wary of attempts to influence us according to the interest of others. But we may learn from such experiences. As individuals continue through life, they accumulate an increasing fund of experiences by their pursuits or by being subjected to environmental events. These may give them an improved understanding of their emotional mind in relation to the rest of their body as well as to environmental systems and factors. Less experienced individuals might benefit from such wisdom. It might help them to avoid the pain of hard lessons and increase their opportunities for happiness. While some aspects others learn about happiness might be generally transferable, the utility of numerous insights may depend on a congruence of needs and circumstances that may frequently be missing. Moreover, identifying relevant internal and external commonalities may be difficult if we have not had occasion to find sufficient clarity about our needs and applicable methods and lack experiences we could compare or foresee. Further, there might be differences in personality and circumstances with other individuals of which we may not be aware.

To the extent we cannot recognize guidance in the experiences of others, we are left with our own impressions of what might bring us pain or pleasure. Unless we have accumulated appropriate experiences in relevant aspects, we may have to engage in trials to gain control of our happiness. Yet, when we formulate a wish, our ignorance of how it can be brought about is usually not total. If we have experienced the deprivation and the satisfaction of the related need, we can usually determine two points to which we can connect our comprehension and related circumstances. Even if we have not experienced the full range of pain and pleasure regarding a need, we can produce some construct of experience and imagination. This narrows the focus of our efforts to closing the practical difference between two states of affairs. We may build up from the starting circumstances of deficiencies that we can explore in relative detail to circumstances we have experienced or imagine to constitute the conclusion of a need. We may analyze that end state into components and steps that we already know or imagine to be necessary or useful for its occurrence. Even if we do not have direct knowledge of components that might be involved, we may be able to take reference to similar phenomena of progression and to their components. We might adjust them to the task challenging us. If we possess or can develop knowledge in this manner, we may be able to produce some idea of how a desired result might be brought about. Based on a combination of knowledge and speculation, we can usually think of some framework, reference, or construct, however rudimentary, incomplete, implausible, impossible, or inapplicable it might seem that might apply. It would appear to be exceptional that we could not produce some theory, some vision of what it may take to obtain a wish or to fulfill a need. Even incomplete or inapplicable states of knowledge enable us to improve our position because they reveal circumstances from which we may be able to learn and potentials that we can test.

As we prepare for the construction of a path from the beginning to the conclusion of a need, we divide the process into a sequence of parallel or successive steps or components. In defining these steps, we may be able to call on resources that are already sufficiently defined into means. Where resources are not yet defined accordingly, we put the same method we applied to our larger vision to work to determine what might produce the means that we picture. As an outline of a sequence or a combination of sequences emerges, we can identify tasks that are familiar and appear possible and others that are unfamiliar or unknown to us. Once we have contracted the context of our exploration by isolating the possible uncharted increments, we have to find a way to close these deficiencies. If our own experience fails, we may obtain the necessary knowledge by transfer from others. If that strategy fails as well, we must acquire that knowledge in different ways. Scientific extrapolation might assist us. But the reliability of this method is limited to known ingredients and processes, principles, combinations of components, and systems. Once we introduce unknown aspects into our theoretical development, our anticipatory capacities deteriorate. We may not be able to predict the effect of these new aspects securely even if we identify them. Similarity of aspects may provide us with some reasons to assume similar results. Then again, there may be areas where parallels may mislead us. To understand and reliably cure the deficiencies in our capacity of pursuit, we may have to build new knowledge and skills. Analyzing and synthesizing desired objects and events in our mind and arranging our knowledge of components to build them may assist us to advance our knowledge and practical capability in this area. However, ultimately, we must acquire knowledge through practical observations and testing. Thus, our trials in search for what makes us happy may also have to involve technical trials.

These technical undertakings are limited. Because our trials regarding happiness are described by our experienced starting positions and imagined end positions, the selection of components for technical trials is defined to some extent by the space between these positions. We can further build on our existing knowledge of connecting intermediary steps. As we manage to define the shortfall in our knowledge more narrowly, the type and number of possibilities to cure that deficit through trials become more concrete. There is only a limited array of potential means that can connect to the beginning or end points or intermediary components we have already identified. An even smaller group of these implements has the possibility of bridging them. Moreover, we may only have restricted access to resources. With an accordingly sharpened focus, we may find it feasible to test different means from the field of possible candidates to cure remaining deficiencies in our knowledge. That we can set up experiments from familiar factors demonstrates that we are not entirely powerless regarding most problems we encounter and that we possess some potential to succeed.

Although trials offer a useful and ultimately the only way to expand our knowledge, they are not without disadvantages. Our objective in undertaking them is to expand our management power, to understand and control additional aspects of our world. Yet, to gain that understanding and control, we have to create settings and undertake acts that are beyond our understanding and control. Our control over the events we set in motion in experiments is by definition imperfect. We experiment because we do not have a firm grasp on what we are about to test. We lack full knowledge and lack the capacities resulting from such a knowledge. Experiments could result in material setbacks and inflict lasting damage on our efforts to fulfill our needs. In our attempts to achieve understanding and control, we may set incalculable and uncontrollable reactions free. Some settings may allow us to contain such hazards effectively because we can forecast the demeanor of at least some components based on an established range of observations that encompasses similar conditions. However, if we test ingredients or settings with reduced or no prior experience, we may be unable to contain these risks effectively. We may encounter such situations particularly in systemic settings with unknown components. Because we may not be able to emulate such systems on a smaller scale, we may be unable to reduce the risk by scaling down the experimental setting. In addition, the variability of systems due to unknown factors may make it difficult to find a useful understanding that can be translated into control. Even if we can control a system, the control of variations may demand continual testing. Further, the requirement to try varied constellations to gain understanding and control may create or invite the very repercussions that we seek to avoid by trials. Avoiding risks of negative consequences might be difficult because finding adequate results might be elusive. We may not know whether or to what extent we will find what we are looking for before we embark on a trial and confirm that what we find performs effectively or efficiently for our purposes. We may have to test a range of constituents and of constellations to determine what will or will not work and which positive results will improve or optimize our pursuits. If dangerous combinations exist in the field of our inquiry, we will come upon them in the course of comprehensive testing. Trials then present an inherent risk that we might lose control in attempts to expand control. Deleterious consequences may outstrip the potential benefits of better control.

These threats may prevent us from engaging in trials and may thus induce us to forgo an expansion of our capacities. More reasonably, they may move us to set conditions that take the potential of detriment and failure into account when we engage in experimentation. Before we employ trial methods in a situation beyond our control, we must explore closely the type and magnitude of uncontrolled factors and our ability to narrow them. To prevent failures from derailing us, we may want to engage in methods that are reversible or at least terminable and permit us to recover from involved losses. As long as we plan our activities so we can extract ourselves from them without too much damage, we may allow trials to exceed our control. Our general focus would be to give up only as much control as we need to advance our search without materially jeopardizing the achievements we have already reached or hope to reach. Where we might exceed that principle, we must decide whether the risks we incur are in reasonable correlation with the result we seek and its likelihood. Our considerations must exceed the narrow confines of the experimental setting at hand. They have to take account of potential effects of trials on our extended environment and the possible repercussions we may suffer as a result. Repercussions may occur because our actions may directly or indirectly impair or destroy means or sources of means that we require for the pursuit of our needs. They may also consist of defensive measures that resist our infringements or respond to the infliction of damage.

Unless we carefully manage risk, experimentation may not be a very promising method to achieve happiness. Still, all our care cannot eradicate the fact that we cannot entirely know the results of our trials before we engage in them. Although we may be able to apply foresight and precautions based on experiences and deductive insights, we may not have sufficient knowledge and control to avert all negative consequences. Some, and at times significant, risk may remain. We cannot wholly avoid incurring that risk. Experimentation may at times be the only way to advance an objective. Advancing it may not be optional. It may be existentially required. Even where such stakes are not indicated, we may have little choice but to sustain risk if we want to develop our capabilities and to improve or maximize our happiness. That drive appears to be so strong that we individually and collectively are committed to experimentation and inclined to incur inevitable risks.

In addition to incalculable damage we might incur from uncontrolled experimental reactions, trials may impose significant losses on us because we may invest resources in their pursuit that are not compensated by their outcome. Trials may be completed without reaching a satisfactory result, yield only partial success, or call for the expenditure of disproportional resources to accomplish success. They can be involved, lengthy, and potentially costly proceedings with indeterminate outcomes. We may succeed in limiting our cost exposure if we already have some knowledge of the trial subject and trial environment. Yet the remaining undetermined nature of our undertaking may still engender significant resource requirements that might not or not adequately be rewarded. Experimentation in regions that are not already sufficiently definite in their possibilities can strain our resources because of its lack of predictability. Particularly if trials require the pursuit of multiple variants, a sizeable segment of our investments might flow into strategies that will not advance a cause. Even a small number of variables may confront us with extensive trial requirements. These negative factors are increased if we are not merely searching for minimum adequacy but for an improved or maximized result. In that case, we would not stop once we have found a workable solution. We would continue to experiment until we can establish a result commensurate with an exalted standard or the best possible solution. Depending on the number of possible alternatives, trials may therefore present a potential that we may lose our way and our resources in trying strategies that do not work or that are not optimized to fulfill our needs.

Direct costs and collateral damage may then involve us in trials that threaten to cause more damage than benefit. Often, determining the risk of loss or its possible magnitude is difficult before we engage in trials. It may be unproblematic to discern and dismiss trials that are clearly ineffective or damaging. We may be able to render such judgments based on our experiences, the experiences of others, or after a partial pursuit. Notwithstanding, as long as a manner of pursuit might serve the fulfillment of a need, we may not be able to exclude it as inapplicable or inferior before its conclusion. We may only know upon completion of its suggested path how objectively successful it can be and how happy its manner of fulfillment can make us. We cannot ease our burden by categorically excluding paths that include disturbances and pain. They may be worth pursuing because their yield may be superior. The proper measure of whether our investment is worthwhile may only become visible when a wish is finally being fulfilled and the net gain of pleasure is tallied. Further, we may only know upon completion of all other paths with a reasonable potential how each pursuit compares. Our experiences during the implementation of an approach may not provide clear indications of the ultimate success or happiness to be achieved. Distinguishing effective objectives and strategies from less effective, ineffective, or damaging objectives and strategies might be difficult before they reach completion because their yield is by definition incomplete. Even if we pass judgment only at the end of a pursuit, we cannot be assured of our assessment. A path may display disturbances and pain during its implementation that are not systemic to the pursuit. Rather, they may be caused by coincidence through intervening circumstances that happen to intersect with our path or avoidable omissions, detractions, or other errors. In other pursuits, certain disorders and pain may be systemic. Our negative experiences in either type of pursuit may make it difficult to judge the relative or absolute capacity of a pursuit to convey satisfaction to us. Pursuits with coincidental deficiencies may become proficient if we can limit or avoid these deficiencies. Pursuits with systemic problems may be modifiable to where these problems are diminished or eliminated. Even in the absence of such issues, we would have to evaluate whether and by how much our strategies could be improved. To explore and judge the potential of alternatives, we may have to try them, learn from them, and adjust them to our preferences and situation. In the advancement of our happiness, such a comprehensive approach seems unavoidable.

Experimentation and suffering its potential fallout may then be an arduous and at times painful manner of acquiring knowledge and skills and reaching our objectives. It would appear to be an inefficient tool to identify principles of happiness. The vagaries of trials require us to invest much of our time, effort, and other resources. Even if we cautiously monitor results, they may require us to commit many mistakes and to suffer extensive frustration and unhappiness on the way to finding what will make us happy, happier, or happiest. We have to be prepared to live our existence in an experimental state of pain until we have found what we are looking for. Trials may carry an important and indispensable function in vital circumstances where we have little other indication of what will work. But they do not seem to represent a promising regular technique to determine what we want and how to reach what we want. The demands and consequences of embarking on alternatives that do not serve our happiness as well, do not serve it at all, or even damage it threaten to overwhelm us. Even if we succeed in securing some measures of success, we may become bogged down in futile pursuits. We may run out of energy, time, financial or other resources, out of opportunities, out of life if we follow this method. We may recognize the importance of experimentation in exploring subject matters that are more definitely accessible to scientific methods. Only, explorations of happiness often involve issues of such complexity and variability that trials may not lead us easily to success. For these reasons, we may decide that we must look for less exasperating means of insight in our attempts to ascertain what will make us happy.

In the apparent absence of other available methods, many of us prefer therefore to take guidance from conventions we observe in our environment. Although these may not guarantee happiness and may not maximize it, we may believe that established patterns of behavior hold a better promise of deriving principles of happiness than following our imagination and playing through all possibilities with potential. If happiness follows at least in part principles that are transferable among humans, it would make sense to explore avenues already traveled. Other individuals may already have gone through similar trials in their search for happiness. They may have extracted valid principles of happiness over time. We may concede that looking for solutions in the largest common denominators might not necessarily work for us. Still, we may maintain the hope that we might be able to discern patterns that apply to us. We should be able to find helpful constituents for the fulfillment of each existential need that we can adjust to reflect our goals. Taking account of established patterns by which other individuals pursue their happiness may at least narrow the field of alternatives and help us to render our experimentation more manageable.

Our trials are further confined because the principal choices for experimentation may not be as extensive as they seem in theory. Even if we might be able to overcome some limitations, our resources may be limited by our capacity and by the environment in which we pursue them. To succeed with the pursuit of our needs, we have to adopt pursuits that can prompt conducive responses from that environment. We have to adjust our experiments and pursuits according to what we can undertake. Aside from matters of absolute impossibility, our individual capacity and our environmental capacitations are mutually influencing each other or they have that potential. This phenomenon is not limited to us individually but also applies to groups of individuals and to humanity as an entirety. In its development, humanity increasingly shapes its surroundings by individual pursuits. The commonality of existential needs and conventions that reflect them should have increasingly cast our existential setting into conformance with common needs. Since the same fundamental needs motivate us, there may only be incremental differences between the results of our pursuits and already existing conventions and conditions. Diverse individual expressions of common needs may have found reflection in such a system as well because differences have existed all along and demanded consideration. They may have affected standards of how to find fulfillment of common needs by giving rise to a range of strategies that accommodate individual particularities. We may attempt to build our happiness based on such a traditional groundwork of convention and reality.

The evolvement of a system through generations in which conventions and our environment have melded into each other to create one contiguous environmental setting may make it appear reasonable for us to respect and to adopt the provisions of such a system for the pursuit of our happiness. We seem justified to grant it a presumption of correctness and wisdom that might surpass what we can derive, at least with regard to the pursuit of common existential needs and the range of individual pursuits it accommodates. Yet, in embracing such a strategy, we might overestimate the common sourcing of prevailing practices and their openness to the accommodation of idiosyncrasies. Although we may be able to discern a general development in that direction, we may also be compelled to point to pervasive conditions of pain engendered by error and intolerance that have permeated human evolution. This means that we cannot trust tradition and have to view it with progressing reservation the longer it reaches back into human development, at least until we reach genetically optimized instinctive levels. We may overrate our ability to distance ourselves from prevailing practices to the extent they do not cover the requirements of our needs. That may be because we may overestimate our proclivity to establish critical distance, to test alternatives, and to implement changes that reflect our resulting insights. We may even be convinced that our setting fulfills all our needs and that we do not possess differentiating desires. Our approval of conventions may not be deliberate. Our entrenched existence in an environment and familiar ways to cope in it and our relative unfamiliarity with alternatives may preclude us from realizing how uncritical we are in our acceptance of our surroundings and their ways. We may be so thoroughly influenced by the physical, cultural, economic, religious, ethical, legal, and political standards of our environment that we adopt them as ours without awareness.

Even if we preserve idiosyncrasies in our needs, we may consider that we benefit in some ways if we behave in conformance with given standards. We may conform for fear of repercussions. We may fear embarrassment, economic and social difficulties, marginalization, exclusion, violence, loss of freedom, dislocation, or diminishing chances in an afterlife. But the pressures of agreeing with conventional objectives and manners of pursuit may also be subtler. It may seem possible that we could pursue different paths from those most traveled in a society. There may appear to be sufficient freedom within the parameters of permissibility set in a society. There may be some tolerance toward others who do not pursue their happiness in conformance with conventional pathways. Still, within these confines of what is permissible or accepted, there are usually narrower parameters of customary,

entrenched, generally approved ways. Established structures and processes, as well as the failure of these and of individuals conforming to
them to advance deviating practices and individuals may encourage
conformance. They may make it more difficult to pursue or maintain
idiosyncratic behavior or to find sufficient happiness with it. By placing ourselves outside the regular pathways of a system, we may have
to relinquish the assistance and tools that may exist for more regular
manners of pursuit. We may struggle more to advance our happiness
independently than as a participant in conforming activities. We may
have to maneuver separately or carve out exceptions from established
methods. This decision may place a heavy burden on our ability to advance our interests even if these do not clash with ordinary pursuits. It
may require increased investment of resources and produce increased
risk of damage for which the benefits of alternative paths do not adequately compensate. Thus, even if such paths are available, the selection of adequate alternatives may be small or nonexistent. This realization may make us conform because working within governing conventions diminishes our exposure to insecurity and other detriments.
Although we would sustain adjustments to pursuits, the convenience
and security of conventional paths and structures may confer higher
degrees of happiness than we could hope to gain from deviating practices. We may therefore give up pursuing idiosyncrasies to the extent
they interfere with the benefits of a conventional existence.

Arguably, this is not the only consequence we may deliberate. If
conventions and the related environment do not reflect our needs, we
might consider changing them. However, implementing such change
may be problematic because we have to persuade affected individuals
that they would fare better under our proposed modification. Interests
that would be detrimentally impacted would have to be compensated,
which would reduce or might extinguish the utility of change. Further
complications arise from the correlation between conventions and environmental expressions they have produced, as well as by impositions
of independent conditions that might have partaken in forming both.
Resulting ingrained factualities may call for substantial resources and
determination to surmount difficulties in implementing a change. We
may not succeed in changing minds unless we can give a credible perspective that our plans can succeed. Because change may involve a period of upheaval and uncertainty, we must at least warrant its reliable
management. Beneficiaries may have to tolerate a temporary decline
of benefits. Progress may be marked by inherent problems, extraneous
interferences, and residual resistance. The interruptions and volatility
involved in change may amplify the reservations of many individuals.

Before we might convince others, we have to first convince ourselves. Even if adjustments of conventions and environmental aspects might appear desirable, we may not be able or willing to pursue them. We may fear that the results are too uncertain or that changes cause unintentional consequences. We may further believe that the potential result does not stand in reasonable proportion to the required effort. Changes may demand resources that we alone or in conjunction with others may not possess or have an ability to develop. We may not be willing to risk our resources, wellbeing, or existence in an attempt to alter a system that might oppose such change. To pursue our own path despite such obstacles, we might remove ourselves from an unsatisfactory environment and generate or insert ourselves into another that may be more conducive to our requirements. In, or as a result of, a change of venue, we may have to give up benefits and face a potentially wide range of adaptation pressures. This may prompt us to question whether we can fare better in such an alternative environment.

As long as we can reach a bearable level of satisfaction for our needs in our current system, we may therefore relent. We may decide that we are better off conforming to what is commonplace and what is possible and permissible. Compared to the benefits of compliance and detriments of noncompliance, aspects where our happiness deviates may appear insignificant to us. We may consider certain external and self-generated restrictions on exploring and on acting upon our differences with established conditions as a fair trade. We may engage in or allow the contortion or suppression of at least some of our wishes that we know or suspect to be capable of ameliorating our happiness so we can fit in and fare as well as possible under the reigning circumstances. We may even avoid exploring our idiosyncrasies for fear that our full awareness of them might cause us problems. But we may also be cognizant of our environment's shortcomings in relation to our wishes and still carry on in its preservation through collaboration. The system may keep us at bay by offering sufficient rewards for compliance and discouragements regarding noncompliance, change, or secession. Our willingness to accede to an existence in such a system may grow with increasing benefits accruing from remaining in it. Such benefits alone may discourage us from prosecuting alternatives. A thinner margin of benefits may raise the risk of systemic upheaval. But even a thin margin of benefit or a detriment from compliance may not deter us from compliance. Even if a system leaves us free from exterior limitations to build a more satisfying existence within that system, to change, or to leave the system, these possibilities may remain theoretical for us. A system may be so inculcated into us and we may be so dependent on it that we may not be able to conceive alternatives. Allegiance to the system may have been absorbed from or imparted into us by parents, peers, communities, religious, governmental, and educational institutions, as well as general economic, cultural, social, and security conditions. Even if we know that it weighs on our happiness and can conceive of alternatives and understand how to implement them, we may lack conviction that these would fulfill our needs better. We might resent and fear the as of yet unexperienced quality of an alternative even if we could gauge the risks and costs in obtaining it. We may therefore align ourselves with a system even at a considerable harm to our happiness. Often, though, we are not aware of the mechanisms that exert this cost and prevent us from deviating because we are conditioned to perceive them as normal circumstances or causes of our happiness.

Hence, even if the established parameters of our system are not favorable, we may not seriously question them and only find fault with some aspects of their implementation by us or others. To optimize our happiness within the strictures of a system, we may attempt to adjust ourselves not merely to its requirements but to its ideals. For guidance concerning these ideals, we may look to individuals who have found a successful existence in the system. We may try to find someone with whom we can identify who already seems to live in a way in which we imagine we could become happy. We may try to emulate individuals whose life we deem to be happy and most appealing to us. We may be attracted to persons who appear to possess what we regard as indicators of happiness. We may consider individuals to be successful if they have earned material wealth, if they command respect and acclaim, if they are smart, skilled, and self-assured, if they have a thriving family, if they attract friends and love. Our observation of these and other attributes of successful individuals makes us want to model ourselves after them. They become our idols. We may attempt to copy the mechanisms, the pursuits by which we presume our idols to have achieved success. Yet rarely do we know whether our idols are happy and how much the perceived manifestations or causes of their happiness effect the satisfaction of their needs. Nor do we know whether we would be happy in their position and how much the perceived manifestations or causes for their happiness would reflect on our happiness. If we were able to fully or at least essentially copy the personal and environmental attributes, developments, and achievements of our idols, we might find out whether their way of life can make us happy. Only, in many cases, we are unable or unwilling to follow the path that led to the accomplishments we venerate. Rather, we may grasp at superficial, outward causes or manifestations of their status and strive to copy these.

Even if we do not have a personal idol, we can fall into a similar thinking by idolizing a lifestyle we observe. By finding or creating circumstances similar to those we perceive to work in the production of happiness for others, we may focus on attaining appearances of successful pursuits instead of these pursuits themselves. By pursuing implements that signify accomplishment or the capacity of fulfillment, we hope to fulfill our needs. Because frequently outward appearances of successful pursuits are all we can detect, we may place ourselves under the illusion that these contain a key to happiness. We may assume or hope that a shortcut to them will infuse us with the happiness we impute. We may have difficulties understanding that this may be an illusion, that outward signs of happiness may be byproducts or consequences rather than grounds for happiness. We may fail to see that, even if the examples we pursue can be causes for happiness, they may only carry that function once other, more important needs are already being fulfilled. The circumstances we cherish may represent a state where individuals whose needs seem to be securely met engage in frivolous, luxurious pursuits. We may also discount the possibility that they might engage in them as detractions because they cannot fulfill other, more important needs. By emulating characteristics of such a stage, we are signaling to us and others a status of fulfillment that we in reality may not possess. Understanding that status symbols are illusions may not come easily because we can often point to needs they fulfill. We must recognize that their pursuit may keep us from pursuing more important needs and from more meaningful and necessary means to fulfill our needs. The longing and false sense of achievement they convey to us may prevent us from trying to understand our true requirements.

That we would deem it necessary to seek and emulate idols or status symbols, that we desire to be somebody else, demonstrates how much our ability to understand and fulfill our needs is lacking. We focus on creating the stage sets and characters in and through which we hope we can play out our ambitions. Yet, when we arrive at the stage and try to assume the role we had dreamed would change our life, we may be disappointed. We may realize that we were so busy building outward appearances and mannerisms that we forgot to think of the play we wish to enact. We may have failed to develop the underlying plot that brings the sets, the characters, us to life. Even if we succeed putting on a play, we may realize that this is an existence of pretense. We may recognize the error of our assumption that the environment with which we surround ourselves and taking on a character in it will engender a change in us or for us that can make us happy. Nevertheless, we and other actors in our environment may encourage us to live our existence as a pretense. The system in which we live may use our tendency of self-delusion to create compliance. It may encourage us to seek idols and status symbols that bind us into its mechanisms. In addition, more particular forces that populate or govern the system may use and manipulate these tendencies in us for their pursuits.

Our intrinsic weakness to be misled by superficialities is being used and manipulated by advertising. If advertising informs us of the function of objects or events as means for our needs, it can be useful. It can afford us necessary or helpful information that allows us to determine whether and how they can be used in the implementation of our wishes. However, advertising is disposed to intentionally or unintentionally exceed this function. It may not or not exclusively assist us with information for building realistic plans in which the advertised object or event can take a useful place. Rather, it may encourage us to discount, if only for the moment of purchase, the entire sequence of steps necessary for attaining an objective and the function of the advertised item in such a sequence. It may persuade us to identify an advertised object or event with the result of satisfaction for a need even though such a relationship is attenuated, conditional, or nonexistent. Advertising has made an art and a science of that short-circuiting, of not selling us goods or services so much as a dream of a happier existence. By characterizing products as capable implements to partake in the lifestyle of our idols or in more general ideal circumstances, it uses our desires. It may also use our fears of losing or not attaining the fulfillment of our needs. By reinforcing, guiding, and defining these desires and fears toward a particular product, advertising undertakes to foreclose and to supersede our rational judgment regarding the functionality and value of an advertised product for us. It tries to motivate us to acquire means or engage in strategies that are not properly adjusted or optimized to our needs or our circumstances or that do not offer us adequate return value. It may take advantage of our confusion about our needs and manners of fulfilling them. Advertising can only influence us because we do not possess a clear concept of our objectives or how we wish to satisfy them. It uses that weakness to have us advance the purposes of someone else. In that abuse, advertising may not differ from other sources that try to utilize us. But its marketing of goods and services to us can be particularly successful because it can build on our naturally occurring illusion that we can create fulfillment and avert unhappiness by obtaining symbols of fulfillment. The tactics of advertising may not be limited to the marketing of goods and services in a commercial setting. They may extend to any kind of social context in which individuals or groups attempt to influence others to accept their suggestions. Accepting a suggestion requires those receiving it to recognize its implementation as a means in their pursuits, as a reflection of their needs and wishes. Ideally, they would fully consider the causes, requirements, and implications of a suggestion. However, such a thorough contemplation might apprise them that a suggestion lacks in its basis, does not benefit them or at least not to the suggested extent, and that its primary objective is to serve others. In such circumstances, parties that are interested in having their suggestions accepted might divert our attention from closer examination and implant a pretense of achievement by tactics similar to advertising.

The question then becomes how we can avoid falling victim in our search for what will make us happy to external as well as our own deception. We may abstain from unverified claims and ideas. We may search for more comprehensive personal and situational matches with others, and we may emulate their activities more substantively. In this manner, we might be able to find some helpful guidance. Still, courses of action others have taken could only provide secure guidance if such persons shared all applicable external and internal circumstances with us. We may have difficulties ascertaining what these features are and whether they are shared. In the absence of that knowledge, we might focus on identifying individuals with as many similarities to us as possible. But we may struggle to find persons with sufficient likeness. The number of possible pertinent variables among individuals may render an identification with others illusory. Even if matching persons existed, it is improbable that we would be able to determine that they exist, except possibly as a matter of coincidence. Evaluating whether we match other persons might require a detail of intrusion into our and their private aspects that few might tolerate. Even if we found similar individuals, they might not have much suitable guidance to offer because their experiences are fused to their circumstances over time and to their previous choices. Moreover, we would have to find individuals with matching personalities and experiences who have selected one of each of the possible choices at a point very similar to what we are facing. This impossible sampling requirement appears necessary to gain a complete understanding of the potential consequences of our choices. Yet, even if we could find such examples, it is unlikely that we could build a workable concept of our happiness from them. We would have resigned to topical imitation instead of developing a concept of what can make us happy. Therefore, following others is not a reliable mode for pursuing, improving, or maximizing our happiness. This threatens to leave us without effective and efficient guidance. The next chapter addresses how we might begin to recover from this discouragement.

CHAPTER 8
OPPORTUNITIES OF EMPIRIC INSIGHT

To achieve reliable insight into what will render us happy, we can neither follow the suggestions nor the example of others. This inability to
garner decisive guidance on what will make us happy from the behavior of other humans may be difficult to condone. After all, we possess
a common set of existential needs and of basic environmental settings
that are necessary to fulfill these needs. Even if we have to cut through
individual differentiations, we should be able to develop general principles of happiness from concentrating on our commonalities. If such
general substantive principles of happiness exist, they have to apply to
every human. While that does not mean that such principles would
presently be recognized or exercised by all humans, all humans should
be able to confirm them. It would further seem reasonable to assume
that at least some humans would have experienced behavior and practices from which such principles might be derived. To locate and identify generally applicable principles, it seems necessary that we employ
a more comprehensive method than a topical search for advantageous
guidelines or examples, or our orientation according to what someone
appears to have successfully implemented. Nevertheless, our observations are indispensable beginning points to determine the existence of
such principles. We may be able to apprehend a more general essence
of happiness and its workings if we comprehensively collect and compare particular incidents where happiness has been created. If we can
detect similarities in patterns of behavior that result in happiness, we
might be able to strip our collection of particularities and extract evidence for common strategies that can lead to happiness. We may be
able to formulate general principles by which certain common factors,
types, or groups of factors must correlate to produce happiness.

The question becomes then how we can derive such factors and
rules. In spite of common fundamental principles by which happiness
occurs concerning our existential needs, individuals and their circumstances seem to differ in many respects. Arguably, common strategies
of happiness should be discernible in spite of any particularities of circumstances because all humans possess the same underlying existential requirements. Particularities might have enough influence to distort and suppress the pursuit of common needs and prevent the detection of principles applying to pure common needs. Still, we might be
able to detect core commonalities beneath a layer of peculiarities. Our
detection of common features and the derivation of common principles would be based on our observation of naturally occurring pursuits

or experimental pursuits. A broad empiric basis is essential for the establishment of general principles by which happiness can be obtained. But examining a representative group of individuals may be adequate. A general principle may be destroyed by even one inconsistent occurrence that cannot be explained as a result of genetic or external pathological influences. However, unless we venture across genuine alternatives to what appear to be shared human needs, we may presume that all humans can fulfill their common needs pursuant to the same principles unless they suffer pathological conditions. Although particularities might add to or detract from the effect of common laws of happiness, they should not be able to abrogate them. We may therefore find principles of happiness akin to laws of nature as a matter of science.

The proposition that we should be able to apply scientific principles to concerns of human happiness and formulate substances and laws of happiness might appear novel. We are accustomed to engaging in empiric exploration of our experiences to reveal natural laws in the physical world. It is accessible to our rational mind, and it can be increasingly explained in rational terms. As we explore the more physical aspects of our world, we become familiar with apparently unalterable truths about it. We recognize substances and properties of these substances, and we develop additional laws by which our world works through the interactions of substances defined by their properties. We discover that our world is ordered. In consequence of our comprehension of substances through their properties and interactive laws they engender, we can organize the more obviously physical features of us and our environment. Our insight that our world is organized by substances that act and react consistent with principles affords us massive utility. It relieves us from having to experience, learn, and react to every object or event we encounter on its own separate terms. Substances and laws of nature and our understanding of them are the keys for our ability to function intelligently in our world in two ways. They permit us to react appropriately to challenges and opportunities posed by our physical presence and environment, and they allow us to shape us and our environment proactively. Our increasing awareness of substances and laws of nature and our use of them make us confident that we can employ them to generate and preserve fulfillment. We must only learn to arrange substances to activate, modulate, or preclude their natural tendencies or arrange ourselves with regard to these tendencies.

We may doubt that the same approach can be successfully applied to the apparently nonphysical, emotionally laden problem of our happiness. The enigmatic, conclusive immediacy by which we become apprised of our mental functions induces us to consider them, particularly emotional functions, to be separate from the physical world. We may deem ourselves to be spiritual entities that, because of their separate nature, can move beyond compulsions of natural laws. That freedom together with the apparently commanding position of our mind may imply to us that our mind is superior to the physical world. In an attempt to build support for the notion that our mind or parts of it are detached and superior, proponents may declare categorically that the spiritual world consists of its own spiritual substances, properties, and interactive laws and that our mind or at least its essence only answers to them. They may further assert that the spiritual world abides by its own separate logic. These constructs liberate claims about purportedly spiritual matters from having to contend with proof propositions or logical demands of the physical world. But they do not absolve proponents of such ideas from clarifying the substances, properties, and logic of the spiritual world and explaining its functions. Moreover, if the spiritual world were simply another area of physics, albeit possibly alternative physics, it should also be accessible to science. If our mind is part of this world, it should be open to our scientific exploration. Proponents of a spiritual world would also have to establish how claimed spiritual substances and principles interface with those of the physical world. They owe such an explanation because our mind is the essential instrument by which we perceive the physical world, reflect its attributes, and form concepts and incentives of interacting with it. They would have to explain how an organ that is preoccupied with physical functions and is progressively verified to consist of physical functions could leave room or be connected to a nonphysical governing essence. Resolving all these issues is of essential importance for our happiness and our advancement of it. The inability of spiritual claims to convincingly address these issues demonstrates their fundamental fallacy.

Claiming separateness and superiority of our spirit might have extensive detrimental consequences for our attitude toward the natural world, our own perceived natural aspects, and our happiness. Distinctions and attributions of different importance and value between the natural world and a perceived higher world might encourage us to ignore, depreciate, or mishandle the natural world and, because of our connectedness with and dependence on it, ourselves. This neglect may threaten to dispossess us of the basis for our continued individual and collective existence and thriving. Beyond that, such attitudes may prevent us from obtaining the necessary insight and motivation to change our fate. We may surmise that because our essence can exist and continue to exist separately, our physical existence is expendable. In addition, the presumed supernatural character of our mind may foreclose attempts to engage in its scientific investigation and comprehension. This may foreclose or diminish attempts to systematically explore and address our needs as existential phenomena and to improve our existence in the physical world. The supposition that humans are in parts exempt from the dictate of natural laws causes problems in explaining the emotional aspects of our existential needs. This is most noticeable regarding our demonstratively physical basic survival needs. Their requirements and our sensory detection and other processing of these needs seem to be explicable by natural laws. This may move points of view that attribute a supernatural quality to our mind to exempt such obvious physiological functions as base, animal functions that do not involve the spirit. However, emotions that have no obvious physiological functions can be shown to have physiological sources as well. If we apply scientific methods of exploration, we can observe physiological causes for all our emotions. As we proceed with our exploration of the human mind, we detect without exception natural substances and principles at work. We are hence bound to conclude that we are their product. This implies that all problems of human existence, including emotional concerns, should be solvable by the exploration and application of physical substances and laws. Emotions and with them happiness should be subject to empiric exploration of physical phenomena. We might think differently if we have not understood the natural aspects that are at work in this area and are unable to trace the complex, concealed functions of our emotional mind. Yet, even if we could trace the physical mechanisms of our emotions, their demands would remain in control of our existence. Further, their intuitive immediacy compared to the detail and dispersion of facts to the contrary would continue to make them appear at least partly separate and superior.

To a lesser extent, our disbelief also plagues us in our impressions of our rational mind. We may proclaim our apparent freedom of choice as evidence for the proposition that our rational mind is different, separate, and superior to the laws of nature. We appear to possess freedom to position substances or us with regard to them and to thus activate and deactivate their characteristics for our purposes. Through this power, we control to some extent whether a particular substance or law comes to bear although we cannot change the substance or law itself. In this indirect manner, we can avoid, prevent, select, congregate, set in motion, accelerate, delay, or stop the application of certain substances and laws of nature to us and our surroundings. We can use that capability to shape us, our world, and our position in it. What we perceive as freedom to decide is in part a reflection of our mind's investigation, consideration, and judgment of different approaches. But we must work with the prearranged substances and laws of nature. Our choices are mere selections that bring out certain constellations, qualities, or quantities that are based on the substances and laws we find. Our ability to select does not contradict the applicability of natural substances and laws to our selection mechanism. Rather, there is indication that our rational mind is controlled by natural substances and laws because its functions are a reflection of them. The derivative of logic is used and proved valid by solving physical problems. Moreover, whether we apply logic or not can be shown to be a function of the physical facilities in our mind. Faced with such evidence, we may be willing to concede that our rational mind follows representations of substances and laws in its ability to reflect, understand, and allocate the natural world and its capacity to monitor and emulate some of its functions through technology. We may even concede, where we cannot deny the evidence, that our rational mind does not only reflect but also is a product of the natural world. Still, we may reserve the qualification that the capabilities of our rational mind demonstrate aspects that cannot be explained by the interaction of natural substances and laws. Our scientific and technological competence seems to present us with capacities that appear to exceed anything nature can attain without our assistance. We may let our apparently unique capacity of understanding and applying nature's substances and laws instigate us to presume our superiority and authority over nature. This presumption derives from a disproportion between our scientific and technological development and an underdeveloped understanding of ourselves as a product of nature. It might not even be corrected if we could accomplish a full scientific understanding of our mind. Our immediate sense of our self may keep stubbornly insisting against our better knowledge that our rational mind is a force that is to an extent free of direction by natural substances and laws and can assume control of nature.

Our illusions of our independence and superiority are strengthened by our apparent ability to conceive principles about how humans should behave toward one another and our nonhuman environment. We create our own laws to alleviate the burden of having to undertake a full consideration of circumstances with every step we take and with every obstacle we encounter in our pursuits, and to make our world more predictable and conducive to our pursuits. These laws may govern our behavior, the behavior of others, and the use, protection, and support of our nonhuman environment. They seem to be different and in addition to the laws of nature. Even if we acknowledge that we are a product of the substances and laws of nature and function by them, we perceive that not all of them automatically work in our favor. Some of them may be categorically neutral or unfavorable to the satisfaction of our needs. Some may become favorable, neutral, or adverse to our interests in variance with the circumstances. More generally, we may perceive the interaction of objects and events in nature to be too unpredictable and coincidental without our ordering influence. We want to be in a position to make the results of natural conditions and processes come about, to prevent them, and to control them in their rate or their amplitude of occurrence. We perceive that we have to shape circumstances or to regulate human positioning and interaction with regard to them and one another to achieve and maintain satisfaction of our needs. We deem that we have to place ourselves, others, and objects and events into situations where certain substances and laws of nature must, can, or cannot apply categorically, under certain conditions, or to a certain extent. Human laws form positive and negative operating instructions that constrict what is possible according to the substances and laws of nature to what those who conceive these laws regard as good or bad for the fulfillment of their needs. These powers may suggest that we are superior to nature because we seem to be able to change its preset arrangements and to create a higher organization that approaches the reiterative qualities of a law. It might seem mistaken to compare any of these forms of organization to laws of nature because they do not apply without imposition and enforcement. They appear to lack the intrinsic compulsion of natural laws. Still, the fact that these laws are a human creation and that they depend on our enforcement seems to imply an independent quality of our behavior that does not seem to be an extension of natural substances and laws.

This impression prevails even though it can be shown that human laws have to result from and reflect natural substances and principles. By producing us, our needs, and our capacities for conceptualization and execution, natural substances and laws are the causes and are in control of our higher levels of organization. Arguably, our unawareness of their functions increases the automatic character of their applicability. That we can condition ourselves, one another, as well as our more extended environment does not abrogate our natural sourcing. It only shows that humans may have graduated to a development level of nature that allows the superimposition of higher levels of organization on natural substances and laws. These higher levels of organization do not modify and are conditioned upon the presence and functions of substances and laws of nature. The principles we produce share the characteristic that they signify mere allocation rules of substances and processes of nature and the objects, events, and persons that these form and permit to be formed. All principles of human behavior, regardless of whether they are genetically imparted, whether they are conditioned by experiences, or whether we can create, adjust, or eliminate them fit this category. We may distinguish these allocation rules as human laws. Although we give them the designation of separate laws, they are derivatives of natural laws and are not matters of our independent invention. They only constitute and express natural laws at higher levels of combination. That should make it possible to understand them by reference to their natural law constituents.

Our objective with all rules we devise or follow is to secure the fulfillment of our needs. This viewpoint is bound to color our opinion regarding the rules by which we deem we and other humans should abide or how the world should be ordered. We may discover that others naturally share our ambitions. This may lead to a voluntary common acceptance of principles by all individuals that are subjected to a law. However, laws may also promote the interests of some humans over others. If individuals can and wish to impose their will on others, the interests of others may not find equal consideration. The law of the stronger becomes the law by which others behave. That may be so regardless of whether the needs of others are the same or different because the focus would be on safeguarding the needs of those imposing their requirements. The ability of others to satisfy their requirements may be negatively impacted from the preference or reservation of fulfillment to those imposing the rules. Even if laws are not produced to secure the satisfaction of needs for some at the cost of others, it might be difficult to reflect the interests of all subjected to a law because of their differences in internal and external dispositions and positioning. Opinions among individuals regarding their interests often differ considerably. The content of laws humans produce therefore depends in significant part on who participates in their creation. This may cause problematic results if a law is established by less than all individuals subjected to a law even if it is produced with the intent to provide extended or universal benefit. The ideas of the forming individuals may not be reflective of other opinions. An increasing involvement of those who would be subjected to a law in its creation renders it likely that its principles will reflect a larger accord of what is commonly regarded to be in the advancement of happiness. It intensifies the prospect that it will benefit the fulfillment of needs for more individuals. Such involvement would appear to be unavoidable once subjects understand their needs and the pursuits that will serve their satisfaction best. Because we have an interest in enabling and safeguarding the pursuit of our needs, we are likely to state a claim regarding rules that affect that pursuit and ultimately our happiness unless we are being prevented.

In addition to the overpowering of others in the assertion of the same claims, the imposition of variations in what individuals regard to be in their interest prevents the creation of generally applicable laws. Both may turn laws into instruments of suppression of some individuals' pursuits for the benefit of others. Such laws reflect unequal power structures and a willingness to pursue one's needs to the detriment of others rather than universal principles of happiness. Only if a claimed human law finds reflection in the views of humans regardless of their position may we conclude that such a law represents a common principle for the pursuit of happiness. To make the establishment of such laws possible, individuals have to refer to objectives and pursuits that lie at the core of their common existential needs beyond their idiosyncrasies. Because we share our requirements for the satisfaction of our existential needs with all other humans, we are inclined to regard the pursuit and the satisfaction of those needs as fundamental rights that equally apply to all humans and that are to be protected and supported by fundamental law. Initially, we might not possess the insight to acknowledge the preservation of other individuals' fundamental rights as part of our needs. Nevertheless, we might be willing or forced to extend our protection and support to the existential interests of others to prevent their interference with our fundamental rights. If individuals subjected to fundamental laws establish them by a comprehensive discourse and collection of concerns, all existential needs should find consideration because participants similarly depend on them.

Still, individuals may diverge in how they define these common needs because of idiosyncratic viewpoints that skew their concept of these needs. Moreover, the development of fundamental laws is often not characterized by the congregation of equals for mutual protection. The recognition of fundamental rights may be a contentious struggle because interests that profit from inequality may seek to define or apply fundamental laws in disparate ways. They may deny to others the support and protection of which they already benefit or that they seek for themselves at the cost or the exclusion of others. Further, interests that already enjoy protection and support or seek it may be indifferent to the equality of others even if their privilege is not conditioned upon the suffering of others. Consequently, fundamental rights are often asserted and placed into law under the pressure or by the victory of individuals and groups whose fundamental rights have been violated. Such efforts most immediately crystallize around basic survival needs. There may be accessions to this center until the pursuit of most or all existential needs is protected. The enabling of fundamental rights, at least in its initial phase, may be defensive in the form of rules of noninterference. As the acknowledgment of fundamental rights advances, the recognized scope of their application may expand to include a mutual right to protection against third party interference. The last increment in the claim and recognition of fundamental rights seems to be the right of active support in the constructive pursuit of existential needs. However, once parties recognize a mutual right to a protecting assistance, the transition between these concepts is fluid because the protection of others from third party interference involves active assistance as well. Regarding both the right of protecting assistance and the right to constructive support, efforts for recognition and their acknowledgment may again initially focus on basic survival needs. The existence and the extent of active obligations may be more in contention than noninterference because they necessitate an investment and possibly sacrifice of resources on behalf of others without a guaranty of compensation. The concept of assisting others may imply one-sided circumstances in which means are drained from some individuals to satisfy the needs of others. A right to active support may be particularly controversial because it may invite abuse. To prevent the exploitation of assistance by those who undeservedly claim it, the imposition of qualification criteria may be necessary. Yet, even if concerns of abuse can be put to rest, a motivation to actively assist in the fulfillment of other individuals' needs may not come easily. Our need for collective survival and thriving alone may not suffice to have us broadly assist other members of a society. But practical considerations of mutuality may bring such as well as narrower, even idiosyncratic interests under active mutual support and protection. Every member is likely to find it necessary or helpful at times to rely not only on the absence of direct interference but as well on the protection of liberty and on the support of constructive pursuits. Even if that should not be the case, the knowledge that such an assistance is available if needed can allay many existential fears and substantially improve our happiness.

Besides fundamental laws, we can frequently identify a class of laws that constitute executory tools. By permission, prohibition, and command, these laws set practical standards for the pursuit of common needs. We may call these laws derivative laws because they derive their mission from fundamental laws. Derivative laws may undertake their task in several correlated ways. They may define and declare the protection and support of pursuits or of spheres within which we are free to pursue needs. In that, they acknowledge and delineate the scope of our fundamental rights. Further, derivative laws may contain technical provisions for building and maintaining structures and processes that create, apply, and enforce substantive regulations. Because derivative laws are focused on the practical implementation of fundamental rights, both of these types of derivative laws have to be open to developing views on fundamental rights. Moreover, as circumstances of pursuit and as practical capabilities improve or decline, a society is challenged to match these changes with a collective understanding of their effects on protected and supported needs and with corresponding regulation and implementation to safeguard fundamental rights.

Derivative laws are often contested by efforts to adjust them to settings and fundamental views. But they may also be challenged because their regulation and enforcement interfere with the pursuits of individuals subjected to them. Their function of supporting and protecting the fulfillment of fundamental rights makes them focus on areas where pursuits interfere with other pursuits or where the refusal of protection or support may leave individuals deprived. This places derivative laws into the position of arbitrating the relative merits of pursuits. Some activities may be directly addressed by fundamental laws without a necessity or possibility of interpretation. In addition, much derivative regulation may be largely unopposed because it pertains to core concerns that are generally recognized. However, the coverage or treatment of other concerns might be sufficiently unclear or unsettled to require interpretation. In particular, there might be disagreements whether claims represent common or idiosyncratic aspects or whether or to what extent such aspects should be subject to protection or support. Even if individuals recognize a right to noninterference, protection, and support regarding existential needs, they may have reservations regarding the expansion of such rights to idiosyncratic features. All individuals may strive to preserve idiosyncratic practices as a fundamental right because they all have idiosyncratic needs. Yet their familiarity with their own idiosyncrasies and estrangement from the diverging idiosyncrasies of others, as well as dissimilarities in the consequences of idiosyncrasies, may dispose individuals to discriminate regarding the acceptability of idiosyncrasies. Contending views may further derive from opportunistic considerations. Even if individuals are generally committed to improving the happiness of others as a part of their own endeavors and accept associated rights and obligations, they may prefer their immediate concerns when these are challenged.

The variety of interests that derive from particular internal and external dispositions and situations of individuals may render it difficult to obtain a broad accord in the area of derivative laws. Ideally, derivative laws should translate the generality and abstraction of fundamental laws into the preservation and support of fundamental rights. But if different views of how the fulfillment of needs should be protected or advanced compete in a legislative, judicial, or enforcement process, the winning opinions may not offer solutions that protect and support the fundamental needs of all individuals they regulate equally. Because derivative laws define the practical parameters and functionalities of fundamental laws, they give life to fundamental laws or may result in their denial or curtailment. The practical import of derivative laws threatens to reverse the sequence of derivation. Because derivative laws define and implement fundamental rights, the damage to the ability of losers in the struggle for governmental power to fulfill their fundamental rights may be significant. In addition to applying general inequality, winners may protect and support their idiosyncrasies and impair the idiosyncratic pursuits of others beyond a level permitted by fundamental laws. This threat is likely to intensify the competition for the power to generate, apply, and enforce derivative laws. The unhappiness of losers in the struggle and their mistreatment by the winners may motivate protective, retributory, or corrective strategies.

The division and struggle for power of different viewpoints may substantially damage a society and its members. It appears that a society can only approximate its constructive, cooperative potential if derivative laws are held to requirements that prohibit the infringement of fundamental rights. Only, fundamental laws may be so general that they may not by themselves grant sufficient guidance on the scope of their requirements. They may have to rely on derivative laws to define and implement their content. If these derivative laws are subjects of contest, fundamental laws they are to flesh out may be weakened or skewed. To safeguard fundamental laws and their practical concerns, it may be imperative to build a mantle of interpretive derivative laws around them and to give these heightened protection. To defend these laws and their underlying fundamental laws, supporting interests may agree on noticeable and onerous requirements for changing them. The procedural laws that state and safeguard the implementation of such requirements may themselves be accorded a heightened status of protection. Together with the fundamental laws they protect, we may call these substantive and procedural provisions whose function is to protect central aspects of fundamental rights constitutional law. We may then claim that securing the fulfillment of needs in a societal context requires a constitutional framework. Still, constitutional law cannot categorically prevent infringements. The ability of a society to maximize its members' opportunities to fulfill their needs seems to require a commitment by its members to hold each other and their government accountable and to protect and to support one another's pursuits and fulfillment according to a comprehensive level of consideration.

An important principle of satisfying individual needs in a society appears to be to preserve the character of individual pursuits as an innate right that can only be curtailed if pursuits infringe on protected rights of others. To the extent there is no illegitimate infringement, we maintain the right to prosecute common and idiosyncratic needs. The guaranty of this freedom by a fundamental law should garner broad-based support because of the shared interests in that freedom. Where fundamentally protected pursuits conflict, derivative conventions can set preferences. However, apart from emergencies that require us to concentrate our efforts, derivative laws must protect and support the meaningful pursuit of all fundamental rights for all participants since they all have an identical right to have their fundamental rights safeguarded. Since this identity mandates equality, it entails that interferences by legitimate rights with one another have to be reconciled by a compromise that affords equally meaningful fulfillment even to different needs. The compromising of pursuits may not seem ideal. Nevertheless, it may decrease interference from others, avoid repercussions from interfering with their pursuits, and prevent the harmful effects of strife. It may reduce the suffering of deprivation. It may therefore pose the best practicable and most stable solution to promote happiness in a society. Achieving reconciliation among individual positions promises to be an involved process. It requires negotiations and voluntary curtailment by a multitude of participants in a multitude of contexts and blends of needs that may exceed the formality and the capacity of laws. Still, it appears possible that with appropriate effort and respect for equal fundamental rights, compromised conventions and solutions can be found that maximize the overall happiness of each participant. Accordingly, we may add compromise as a fundamental law by which happiness in a society can be maximized. Compromise also appears to be a necessary principle by which we achieve the maximization of our benefit on an individual level. Our understanding of common and idiosyncratic needs provides a necessary basis for such arrangements.

Because we can define fundamental rights and devise individual and social structures and processes that optimize their establishment and preservation, one might argue that these principles form parts of a substantive science of happiness that applies to all humans. It seems that such a framework promotes happiness in all humans and that its absence universally detracts from human happiness. But the direction that it and its constituents afford us in arranging our pursuits cannot give us guidance on what will make us happy beyond a certain level of commonality. The next chapter explores whether we can obtain additional universal principles of happiness through empiric insight.

CHAPTER 9
LIMITATIONS OF EMPIRIC INSIGHT

Common existential needs, their apparent purpose, the requirements of mutuality, and fundamental rights impose basic general parameters and rules for the pursuit of happiness. These are joined and greatly influenced by the requirements posed by other common conditions for the pursuit and maintenance of fulfillment of our needs. These common principles by which all humans are bound in the creation of happiness should be detectable in pursuits that produce happiness even if they are modulated by idiosyncrasies. It appears possible to observe, describe, collect, and correlate occurrences of happiness and to derive a catalog of practical guidelines, of wishes and strategies that describe how to best satisfy existential needs and how to keep them satisfied. We might even derive some general guidance regarding the pursuit of idiosyncratic desires. The detection of commonalities that apply without any contradiction to a representative sampling group would indicate the existence of general principles for the pursuit of happiness.

To undertake such a substantiation, we would have to engage in sizeable empiric studies. The subjects of our inquiry may not have already come upon and employed the strategies that we are looking to identify. We might have to engage subjects in experimentation. Such mass studies multiply the practical problems that threaten individual trials. To assess relative happiness for different grounds would require us to observe and to record the effects of all alternative pursuits that hold potential on a broad variety of individuals. To the extent happiness can or must be generated by cooperative pursuits and such ventures are not spontaneously occurring, the experimental comportment of subjects would have to be coordinated. Although a comprehensive trial approach might be the most direct manner of gaining broad empiric knowledge, it can also be risk-laden, cumbersome, and costly. It may congest and scatter the pursuits of subjects and thereby frustrate the efficiency, effectiveness, and purpose of experimentation. We may hope that disruptions arising from experimentation might only last for a unique phase until scientific results are derived. We might make experimentation more bearable by distributing trials over several representative groups or generations. Alternatively, we might minimize intrusion by sampling nonexperimental settings. But such less systematic coverage may delay conclusions until we find sufficient information. Further, it may result in a less comprehensive data assemblage. Some manners of pursuit with potential might never be tried, causing us to draw conclusions without a sufficient basis and exposing us to error.

In our experiments and field observations, we would search for causes that make subjects similarly happy, happier, or happiest. Such commonalities might be of great importance and their existence must be explored. However, empiric research into the phenomenon of happiness may be severely hampered regardless of whether we choose observation of events that occur independently of us or experimentation. The recording and evaluation of the resulting information are exposed to error if we cannot measure happiness in numerical quantifications. The behavior of individuals gives only vague indications about their state of happiness. Reading expressions is further complicated because the type and amplitude of behavioral expression seem to vary considerably among individuals. We may therefore perceive that we can obtain more detailed and correct information about causes and effects of happiness if we ask individuals to describe their emotional state in relation to certain objects and events. Yet, when we try to measure happiness as a function of verbal expression, we quickly recognize that we encounter problems similar to those with behavioral expressions. We possess no reliable manner to conceptualize and express exact or near exact measures of happiness. We have merely crude absolute quantifications at our disposal. We can describe humans, including ourselves, only in terms of feeling unhappy, fairly unhappy, somewhat unhappy, not happy or unhappy, somewhat happy, fairly happy, and very happy, or some combinations thereof. But not much more nuance can be expressed about an individual's happiness in absolute terms. In spite of word choices and details, descriptions are bound to remain so general that they can give rise to different interpretations. The understanding of these terms is subject to interpretation according to an individual's emotional capacity, experiences, imagination, and expectations.

Our inability to articulate our happiness in scalable, numerical terms carries through into a united account of our happiness and unhappiness. The rudimentary quantifiers we can muster for every incident make it difficult to gauge how they relate to one another and our overall happiness. But there appear to be further difficulties. We may consider gains in happiness positive deposits in an account. Conversely, disappointments about failing to achieve happiness and the loss of happiness might seem to be withdrawals from this account. However, the concept of an account may not be a suitable parallel. The status of happiness and unhappiness does not seem to move simply by addition and subtraction. We do not know by what formula or method experiences of happiness or unhappiness accumulate or whether they accumulate at all in constructing our happiness or unhappiness. Our experiences tell us that happiness and unhappiness are largely ephemeral.

Their initial intensity soon dissipates. We cannot keep account of how events of happiness or unhappiness figure into our overall emotional state. That problem is exacerbated by our inability to quantify happiness. When we are prompted to describe our combined state of happiness, we do not appear to have more exactitude at our disposal than in quantifying particular incidents. We can express somewhat higher complexity when we compare incidents of happiness. We can express that one cause makes us happier than another. We can determine this by considering which we would rather give up if we had to choose between them. Because we cannot undertake detailed quantifications of our happiness, we may use this method of relative valuation to create a hierarchy among our sensations of happiness for each need. We may assign a ranking to causes depending on whether they make us comparatively happier, as happy, or less happy. We might preselect candidates for such general comparative determinations by filtering out and dismissing less likely grounds by rudimentary noncomparative judgment. We might extend a listing of our preferences into the region of unhappy events if we were to research how to prevent or contain pain in application of common principles. We could have other individuals apply the same method to the same causes and derive a general impression of how causes fare in generating happiness or unhappiness.

These methods only permit us to provide rough descriptions of absolute and relative effectiveness of causes, but they do not help us much to understand the mechanisms of happiness. That lack of understanding may not only be attributable to technical shortcomings. It may also be caused by our disability to define the emotional quality of happiness or of unhappiness in rational terms. It appears that our rational mind and our emotions do not speak a common language. More than that, they do not appear to relate to the same subject matters. In applying scientific treatment to emotions, we are trying to describe in rational, substantive terms a phenomenon that we perceive to happen beyond these parameters. The seemingly nonsubstantive character of emotions renders them inaccessible to our rational concepts. It omits them from our vocabulary that appears to describe obviously physical objects and events and their rational abstractions. Because needs and wishes can often be described in terms of their obviously physical and rational objectives, pursuits, and results, our inability to describe their emotional dimension may be overlooked. We can describe the span of unhappiness and happiness in rational or obviously physical terms by recounting the circumstances of deprivation, what we wanted, how we went about attaining it, and to what extent we succeeded. Still, these observations cannot describe the emotions we experienced. A description of the emotional substance of happiness and unhappiness proves strangely elusive. We may describe happiness as pleasure, elation, joy, delight, pride of accomplishment, and unhappiness as sadness, sorrow, depression, or melancholy. But such descriptions are mere synonyms or antonyms and do not describe the essence of happiness and unhappiness. We may try to describe how we feel by focusing more on the consequences of that feeling. We may try to describe how happiness renders us optimistic, self-confident, forward-looking, and hopeful, how it energizes us and motivates us to work on the fulfillment of other wishes. We may express how it motivates and helps us to transcend melancholy, open up to the world, become lighthearted, friendly, and contented. We may ascribe opposing conditions to unhappiness. Only, such references refer again to feelings whose content is not directly represented or to occasions that follow from but do not embody happiness or unhappiness. We encounter these problems as well when we try to describe unhappiness. This inability of words to carry emotional content makes communication of emotional concepts very difficult if not impossible. Whichever way we attempt to explain the feeling of happiness or unhappiness, we lack the ability to concisely express emotional content in words. Our emotions leave us speechless.

Such a claim may appear counterintuitive because we can refer to experiences where emotional concepts were successfully communicated to us or by us. Yet our inability to communicate emotional concepts through words becomes self-evident if we envisage employing language to represent an emotion to a person who has not sensed that emotion before. It seems impossible to describe happiness or unhappiness regarding a need to someone who has not already sensed these emotions. This might not be a problem for us because we regularly use preexisting knowledge in other individuals to bridge our incapacity regarding a direct conveyance of emotional content. We relate emotional information to other individuals by having them refer to their own experiences. We attempt to trigger their emotional references by factual representations and count on emotional reactions to these causes in recipients to prompt the desired emotional effect. Factual representations may consist of words and other symbols or descriptions, direct perceptive impressions of circumstances, or behavioral indications of emotion. These ways of communicating emotional concepts might not seem to differ from a communication of representational factual concepts. Unless we desire to communicate a perceptive phenomenon itself, we rely in factual communications that recipients correlate communications to a preexisting understanding as well. Such communications are often the foundations for emotional communication. What is different when emotions are communicated is that emotions are of a character that does not allow us to easily access their constituents and to compare and calibrate individual understanding. Because emotions are internal states or processes, there are regularly no external criteria that readily show their existence, properties, or amplitude. They cannot be reconciled by referring to a materialization or rationalization of concepts, and there is no standard by which emotions relate to a factual setting. This makes it difficult for the person communicating and the recipient to determine whether elicited and communicated emotions match. Emotional communication is therefore less interchangeable than representational factual or perceptive communication.

Using rational representations or direct sensory impressions to evoke emotions can be an effective tool. We may use such techniques to convey experienced emotions to other persons. They may also be used to elicit emotions in others that we do not share. The creation of an emotional impression by making the recipient generate the emotional content may be an efficient way to communicate emotions or to manipulate others emotionally because it may prevent having to place them into actual experiences that lead to such emotions. While emotional communication may be inadvertent, the requirements to create particular emotions are demanding. To prompt a precise response, it may be necessary to customize a communication to the particularities of the recipient's profile. The sender has to determine the information that induces an intended reaction in a particular recipient and has to create or find and communicate such triggering information. The efforts and complications of open or clandestine observation and experimentation, the characteristic difficulties in recognizing emotions, and the construction of information to correspond to research results can render accurate communication of existing emotional states and emotional manipulation complicated undertakings. In time, we might be able to gauge reactions of certain individuals to allow such customization by employing our knowledge of recipients' emotional triggers and mechanisms in reaction to other occurrences. But the requirement for customization encumbers the scope of emotional communications. It may only allow us to elicit a certain emotion in persons with the same information if they have the same emotional response profile. A wider distribution of an emotion would necessitate multiple, separately customized communications. Short of that, we are relegated to provoking general types of emotional responses that are common to an extended spectrum of individuals or to eliciting a variety of emotional responses. This might be sufficient or even desirable for some purposes. Yet it is inadequate if we seek to effect accurate emotions and responses.

The desired emotional effect of communications may in certain incidents be realized through a conveyance of factual impressions that remain truthful or by the generation of facts that can be truthfully reported. However, eliciting particular emotions can be problematic because obtaining the intended emotional response may require misrepresentations of fact. Such misrepresentations may be difficult to maintain and may destroy the intended effect once they are revealed. The manipulation of emotions through the manipulation of facts or of impressions can only succeed if the emotional effects remain sufficiently strong upon the recipients' discovery of manipulation or if it remains hidden. Manipulation might be acceptable if the learning of emotional lessons is beneficial for recipients in their considered judgment. However, unless they know of a simulation for purposes they approve, they might object to factual manipulation even if it is intended to truthfully communicate an original emotion because it would misdirect their rational mind. Separate messages might appear to be required to convey rational and emotional content. Then again, such a partition appears impossible because it relies on inconsistent communications that a recipient would scrutinize both under rational as well as emotional criteria, thus causing irreconcilable interference between messages. The complications in communicating emotional concepts through factual communication therefore frequently seem insurmountable.

Apart from abuses for emotional manipulation, emotional communication may only succeed if the relevant emotional conditions of the sender and the recipient are sufficiently similar. Individual differences may cause interference and may wholly prevent such communication. The rarity of sufficient correspondence may severely limit our choices for maintaining relationships that include complex emotional communication. It may dramatically encumber our capacity to satisfy needs that rely on the existence and functioning of close emotional relationships. To find fulfillment for these needs, we may be relegated to pursuing them in less particularized, less profound, and consequently less satisfying emotional relationships that can be built on the basis of more common parallels in emotional processing. In addition, the difficulties in the communication of emotional concepts hinder the comprehension and scientific categorization of emotional phenomena and thus the discovery of how we can produce happiness. Even if emotions could be reliably shared by certain persons, not much would be gained because emotional impressions would be limited to them. A compatible recipient could describe emotions in the same inexact terms as the individual who originally sensed the communicated emotion. But this does not render that emotion more accessible to scientific insight.

We may then determine that the communication of emotional concepts does not lend itself much to the scientific assemblage of information about the happiness or unhappiness that circumstances inflict on individuals. We may attempt to overcome these difficulties of articulating emotional concepts by describing and measuring them as physiological phenomena. We may grow capabilities to measure physiological changes that occur with happiness and unhappiness, and we may increasingly succeed in tracing their physiological causes and effects. However, before we can assuredly attribute physiological measurements to happiness and unhappiness, we must consider that physiological occurrences may be mistaken for indicators unless they can be shown to be direct causes for triggering these emotions. If the type and intensity of happiness or unhappiness can be shown to be related to the type and quantity of a particular substance or substances or the type and quantity of physiological events, we may imply a causal relationship. But such correlations may be indicators of precursors, tools, parallel, collateral, or consequential phenomena that are not qualitative or quantitative representations of happiness or unhappiness. If we can identify physiological causes for happiness, we will likely become capable of sensing differences that define discrete needs either in substance or location. Yet, even with such knowledge, we might have difficulties relating physical measurements to a precise emotional effect. We might not be able to determine reliably whether the quantity of a physiological indicator translates into a corresponding intensity of an emotion in a linear or other function. We might be unable to map a functional relationship with adequate precision unless we can measure an emotional experience separately from the factors that cause it. A lack of experiential measurement may have us look for possibly less precise and hence possibly misleading physiological aspects.

If we can overcome these potential complications, a physiological understanding of happiness might give us the ability to better express absolute and relative happiness that alternative strategies might produce than the unrefined measures and comparisons we can verbally express. The detection of the physiological foundations for our experiences of happiness may encourage the concept that these foundations can afford us with generally applicable guidance regarding causes of happiness. The attendance of physiological indicators of happiness and physiological causes may enable us to prove that the fundamental physiological structures and processes pertaining to happiness are the same for every human. The possibility of a revelation of physiological commonalities that might instill us with generally applicable guidance on finding happiness cannot be excluded and might be significant. It would not be proper to prejudge the results of research into the physiology of happiness and their utility. Yet the existence of an objective method for measuring happiness and a common physiology of how happiness is generated does not imply that all causes for happiness would have to be universally shared the same way. There might be physiological variances among individuals that cause them to react differently to external and internal stimulants. While we may be able to discern general substances and rules of happiness, these general aspects may not suffice to competently guide our understanding regarding the requirements of individual happiness. Common physiological substances and laws by which happiness is created may be applicable. Still, the mechanisms that perceive and process causes and generate the substances of happiness may be differently developed and articulated in individuals because of genetic and environmental differences. Overt physical attributes of our body might participate in the fabrication of happiness and of unhappiness as well. But the susceptibility of our mind to variation by genetic, sensory, or more obviously physical influences and their processing may lead to a greater individual differentiation. The resulting physiological dispositions of our mind dispose our perception and subsequent processing of information. These dispositions for the processing of impressions and the formulation of our motivations appear to be complex constructs that can carry a great variety of differentiations. They may direct sensory phenomena into different avenues of mental processing. They may give rise to different thoughts, emotions, and activities. They may cause individuals to have distinctive views, fears, and ideals and to select a variety of objectives and pursuits with more particularized preferences than the underlying existential needs might suggest. They might even exceed the range of what would seem conducive under existential criteria. The diversity of individual processing structures renders it improbable that one could empirically determine common principles of happiness in addition to general fundamentals. The variety of individual differences may cause large aspects of our happiness to remain unexplored. It may also make general principles of happiness appear distant and impractical.

It therefore seems to be necessary that we move beyond establishing general principles of happiness and engage in the scientific exploration of individualities. The considerable durability of idiosyncratic features of happiness offers us a stable target for research. But that durability also makes it difficult to put derived knowledge to decisive use. Some dispositions of our mind may be more permanent than others. Genetic conditions and their consequences may be impossible or comparatively difficult to transform. Other direct physiological influences and their consequences may be more accessible to change. Even if our mind suffers from physiological burdens or injuries, it may overcome these under its own power or recuperate after these are removed with external assistance. Experiential influences seem to be most flexible. The forming influence of experiences may be counteracted or reversed by new experiences. Nevertheless, the sum and interrelation of genetic, other direct physiological, and experiential influences seem to generate a relatively stable mental physiology. Its ingrained structures and processes are likely to lead to a lasting rational impression of our world and its aspects as well as of our existence in this setting. Our physiology further tends to yield a related emotional disposition that acts and reacts in characteristic ways. Our rational and emotional dispositions form baselines from which we begin our thoughts and emotions, with which we are likely to keep, and that we are likely to confirm. Because of such rational and emotional dispositions, some individuals may exhibit a more optimistic or pessimistic, a happier or unhappier outlook than others generally or in particular areas. They may not only shape expectations of happiness but lead us in creating or at least contributing to our happiness or unhappiness with our attitudes because they may have us seek impressions and interpret impressions in conformance with their baseline. They constitute self-reinforcing or at least gravitational mechanisms that regulate our understanding of, our emotional approach toward, and our interaction with the world. With direct or experiential nonconforming events of or related to deprivation and fulfillment, we may display temporary departures from our rational and emotional baselines. However, these events may have only momentary or no power to overcome the weight of our accumulated mental dispositions. Single occurrences generally do not leave deep and lasting effects on our rational outlook or emotional setting. Such an impact is reserved for events that radically transform us, our environment, our placement in it, or our perceptions of such circumstances. Less dramatic occurrences consolidate with preexisting dispositions to form a pooled result. The product is often close to the previous state because of the great weight of prior experiences and the entrenchment and impermeability of nonexperiential dispositions.

Besides absorption into the background of previous causes, our awareness of events and their effects is subject to sublimation and supersession by coexisting, new, or revived causes. As other events and their effects arise, continue to occur, or are recalled, the resulting coexistence and interaction may affect our ability to keep causes and effects for each incident distinct in our mind. While our mind seems to be relatively astute in recording and keeping rational events separate, our emotional experiences appear to have a higher tendency to merge with other emotional impressions. That propensity may be irresistible unless we bind emotional experiences to the distinct rational episodes that are responsible for them. In blending together, our experiences of happiness and unhappiness appear to compensate each other to some extent even if they originated in different needs. In addition, emotional experiences seem to lose their emotional intensity on their own. We might thus only be able to trace emotions as short-term phenomena, restraining us to short glimpses of their causality. With increasing distance from a cause, emotions tend to wither away and become drawn into an undercurrent of preexisting, concurrent, and subsequent emotions. The passing nature of our emotions may tempt us to conclude that the relevance of single events might not warrant our inquiry and measurement. Potential confusion about the causes of emotions may further dissuade us. Yet the largely momentary and fleeting nature of our emotional impressions does not make them less important. They pertain to the present in which all our registrations of happiness and unhappiness occur. Moreover, the melding of momentary impressions into the background of prior impressions might, through its confirming or modifying influence, affect our long-term state of happiness by itself or in convergence with other experiences. For these reasons, the ephemeral character of emotional impressions and difficulties in tracing their causes do not relieve us from trying to understand them.

Our mental dispositions and the overwhelming profusion in the nature and assortment of their contributing factors and of coinciding and overtaking factors threaten to frustrate our derivation of scientific insight into general and individual causes of happiness. The problems in isolating causal relations do not vary greatly when we make use of experimentation. Arguably, it should be easier to detect principles of happiness when we can create controlled circumstances. Some of that control appears achievable by inoculating participants with the same potentially happiness-inducing or happiness-reducing cause. We may also be able to isolate subjects sufficiently to suppress external interference. Still, even if we were to assume control of all environmental settings, subjects would carry their acquired and genetic dispositions with them. Relative to the gravity of preexisting variances, controlled settings might be abridged in their equalizing significance. Unless we equalize preexisting dispositions, we may not succeed in creating sufficiently level conditions to isolate a common causal link. Further, unless we equalize circumstances other than those responsible for an idiosyncrasy, we may not be able to prove an individual causal link. This leaves our research for general and individual happiness challenged.

We may therefore question how useful empiric efforts can be to ascertain principles of happiness. Not all our empiric research may be fruitless. We may apply empiric research to gain insights into the particular causal correlations that stimulate individuals to select one path over another. Comparing particularities among individuals may offer a foundation from which we can explore these mechanisms. Physiological readings of events of happiness and unhappiness that stop short of complete explanations may afford us indications of processing differences among individuals. We may locate factors that generate certain types of individualizations, whose presence or absence produces, contributes to, or detracts from individual happiness or unhappiness. An inquiry into how individuals find satisfaction may also help us to derive or more comprehensively define general common denominators. It may assist us in defining parameters we must observe to satisfy existential needs. It may further help us to designate the scope of protected activities under fundamental laws in a social context and to build competent derivative laws. However, such empiric research might only point to requirements that are already sufficiently known or knowable by considerations of obvious common requirements and their social implications. They might already be implied in the designations of our existential needs and pronounced in the instinctive demands they pose. It is in the nature of our needs to provide us with emergent concepts of what will satisfy them. Where our awareness of our instincts is blocked or suppressed, insight into the nature of such needs in others may assist us to find access to them. A comparison may illuminate our difficulties in granting some of our needs articulation. It may also indicate that some of our needs are overassertive or distorted and may impair other pursuits. A collection of what others uniformly or mostly determine to be inadequate to fulfill a common need may afford us a foundation for dismissing pursuits as incapable or unlikely to fulfill a common need. In addition, assembling the pursuits they all or some of them consider to be acceptable may show us a spectrum of strategies that might fulfill our needs if we were to resort to them. It may give us choices whose consideration may facilitate finding our preferences. It may serve the function of listing potentially viable alternatives that we might consider and try and from which we might garner pursuits that are more technically conducive or more satisfying than others.

As useful as such research might be as an orientation tool, it is limited to pointing out possibilities. It cannot advise us on what matters we should pursue if we have a choice. The potential differences of dispositions and in circumstances that other persons carry prevent us from assuming any of their choices as ours without our corroboration by consideration or possibly by trial. In determining which manners of pursuit we should adopt, the group of generally capable means may be narrowed by a subjective filter of individual preferences and aversions. We might derive less or more satisfaction from one selection than another. Picking random means and strategies from the spectrum of apparently functional means may therefore not be sufficient to maintain, let alone improve or maximize an individual's happiness. Humans often require conditions that cater to their individual wishes in excess of generic functionality and fulfillment capacity. A functional fulfillment may only convey a minimum of happiness. We all yearn for better and ideal satisfaction. Yet permanent and temporary dissimilarities in individuals' conditions may lead them to rate the capacity of a cause to convey happiness differently. The same cause or category of cause can have markedly diverse effects on different individuals and on the same individual in different circumstances. The reason may be a mere matter of varying and at times opposing functionality aspects of an object or event. That specific functionality depends on the manner in which it is used and the context of established, coexisting, and overriding internal and external circumstances into which it is inserted. Moreover, the amalgamation of our genetic mental dispositions, direct environmental conditioning, and our experiential rational and emotional conditioning may react differently than the dispositions of other individuals with a particular object or event. This may generate practical and emotional variances of effects over the entire spectrum of possibilities. These settings do not only affect the parameters of whether happiness or unhappiness is produced but also how much happiness is produced and how long it will endure. Hence, common principles of happiness appear to frequently be obscured, modified, or specified by a seemingly impenetrable clutter of individualization. What will or will not satisfy the needs of a person and what will satisfy them better or best are then matters that cannot be well determined by a survey of the preferences of other persons or a more scientific research into them. To discard inapplicable pursuits and identify the ranking of satisfying wishes for an individual, we must investigate that individual specifically.

The individualization of happiness might be too diffuse to allow the general standardization of happiness-inducing strategies beyond a rudimentary level of universal commonality. Although we can identify certain principles of happiness with regard to common needs, such insights are likely to be of reduced practical relevance because of the individualization of needs. Nevertheless, we may be able to bring scientific explanation and simplification to what we observe in individuals. We may be able to identify patterns of conducive pursuits by categorizing individuals according to type based on their similarities and by confirming certain correlations of causes and effects for such types of persons. We could describe these patterns by applying statistical assessments to display approximate causal relationships between certain factors. Modeling of this type may give us increased probabilities concerning the grounds and effects of happiness for certain types of individuals. We may become adept in predicting how certain types of persons might feel, what they might think, how they might regularly behave in relation to their dispositions or when they are exposed to certain circumstances. This information might be useful in matters that focus on larger societal circumstances, on a tendential or quantitative compliance by a multitude of individuals with a model. However, the results can only be of limited individual guidance because they would be subject to the same individuality and variability problems that have plagued our investigation all along. Even within a typical group, individual variations may frustrate the creation of happiness profiles with any certainty of accuracy. Although we might be able to calculate the chances of compliance, we cannot assure that members of a group will react predictably to the introduction of a considered cause. Remaining individual discrepancies might limit us to only derive probability patterns for some personality features and environmental circumstances with at times sizeable margins for error. It is doubtful that we could determine models of what makes individuals happy in excess of typological generalities. The best we can hope to derive from statistical assessments is a strategy for our consideration aggregated according to likelihood. We might abbreviate our deliberations and trials by focusing them on possibilities that are statistically more likely for us. Yet, if statistically recommended choices do not deliver us the happiness we forecast, we have to continue our search. The categorization of statistical information then appears to fall short significantly. It cannot deliver generally applicable principles of happiness as a matter of empiric science by which we can competently fulfill our needs nor provide us adequate specificity to securely guide our individualized search.

These considerations lead us to conclude that empiric studies of how other humans pursue and meet the fulfillment of their needs are limited in helping us find happiness. Because important aspects of our happiness are founded on individual particularities, we are limited in drawing on similarities with other humans. This may be a distressing insight because we deem ourselves left alone to find large expanses of our happiness. Our insistence on having things our way places a responsibility on us to know what we want. The following chapter explores this condition, its reasons, and its consequences in more detail.

CHAPTER 10
THE SUBJECTIVITY OF HAPPINESS

The application of scientific research to happiness as a common phenomenon leads us only to incomplete success. The observation, experimentation, collection, description, comparison, and categorization of occurrences of happiness in others have only limited use in guiding us to the realization of our happiness. Besides differences in available resources and in external restrictions and opportunities, personal differences do not seem to permit us to identify a coherent, full set of principles by which we can produce happiness. These differences frustrate our ambition to find an objective, scientific way to achieve happiness. The utility of scientific exploration of happiness is based on the notion that we, our environment, and our correlations are comprised by certain substances and follow certain laws. We might have hoped to use such predictability to construct higher, human laws of recommended behavior. Such laws appear to prevail at the general level of existential needs and general requirements to fulfill them that can be reflected in fundamental human laws. However, fundamental laws only inform us of some general requirements and parameters regarding our pursuits. Such laws seem to be rather helpful in guiding us to improved and optimized interaction with other humans. They also can assist us to understand our existential needs better. But they do not help us to order our pursuits within the parameters they provide where we are free of external fundamental impositions to organize our pursuits. The ascertainment of generally applicable laws appears incomplete in directing us toward happiness because it leaves our idiosyncrasies unexplored.

Before we become overly upset about this lack of guidance, we might want to consider what such a guidance would entail. If our individual pursuit of happiness were directed by general laws, we would be locked into following them. They would curtail our movement and force certain activities on us. Such a prescribed path does not appear to be in the interest of our happiness. We could only do as we are told or sustain the punishment of unhappiness. We appear to be happier if our pursuits are not imposed, if we have options, if we can shape our happiness according to our individual judgment. We may ask why we feel this way. If the fulfillment of our existential needs is our ultimate emotional objective, we should be glad about a manual that prescribes how to achieve it. Still, we have a need to determine and to follow our own path. If fundamental and other general laws were sufficient to direct us to the best possible position of fulfillment success, our need for self-determination would be a developmental error. It would counsel us to move away from practices that maximize our chances of individual and collective survival. The existence of this need proposes that it may be essential or at least helpful in securing our survival. It suggests that an individualized approach toward the fulfillment of needs might be more successful than a generic approach. Enabled by the flexibility and progressive features of our mind, this need for self-determination contains an opportunity to react to particular conditions. Its variability permits humans to occupy specialized positions and functions that can improve individual and collective survival and thriving.

Then again, the existence of a need for self-determination also seems to indicate that we are on our own regarding the fulfillment of our needs beyond the instructions provided by fundamental laws and their derivatives. This conclusion is tempered by our realization that we can refer to empiric knowledge and the substances and laws of nature for technical support. They establish our practical parameters and equip us with tools and substances for our pursuits once we set objectives. But they do not tell us which objects and events we should seek, create, use, or avoid except for instrumental, factual insights of effectiveness and efficiency. They do not give us an answer to our question what will make us happy. Some guidance to answer this question can be provided by our common needs in correlation with the application of natural substances and laws. Typically, there are multiple technical ways to fulfill an underlying existential need or to fulfill a combination of them. The different levels of satisfaction these strategies attain for our needs inform us which of them will make us happier or happiest. What we regard as freedom would be our ability to choose among the group of endeavors that qualify for satisfying our underlying needs according to our individual preferences. To find out what suits us best, we would still have to try the available alternatives. However, research by trial to maximize the fulfillment of our needs can be inefficient and ineffective and might endanger our principal needs. This appears to be the reason the development of humanity has favored the individualization of needs through a combination of genetics and acquired dispositions. It seems to be an attempt by nature to help us adjust to environmental particularities. That attempt may date back to periods before we were able to summon higher rational capacities that engender choice. The programming of specialized instinctive features automates activities and responses and relieves us from or reduces requirements of autonomous, specified assessments as well as the risks and costs of trials. The generation of these individualized mechanisms has allowed humanity to adjust to its circumstances and streamline the pursuit of common needs into approaches with a greater chance of fulfillment.

To understand whether and how idiosyncrasies can fulfill that promise, we have to examine them in some more detail. Each pursuit of a common need seems to be subject to several factors of individualization. It is influenced by our particular environmental circumstances and our ability to operate in correlation with that environment. Many of these particularities may be momentary, remediable, or superficial. Environmental settings may be changeable, and individuals might improve their comprehension of their needs or the means and strategies that might satisfy them. However, they might also abstain from or fail in such developments or they might encounter limits that they cannot transcend. Additionally, the particularities of our pursuits depend on our fulfillment status. Our motivations may change with changing absolute and relative satisfaction levels for each of our needs. Further, needs may undergo fundamental changes during our life that modify our attitudes toward their deprivation and fulfillment and our pursuit of them. All these factors may combine to result in a unique positioning for individuals with regard to their needs and the means by which they pursue satisfaction. Differences in our pursuits might then be at least partly explained by differences in our historical and current positioning regarding our environment and the phasing of our needs.

If these were the only factors contributing to the individuality of our needs, they might be relatively easily avoided in relevant parts. If we experienced needs with the same intensity, faced the same environmental circumstances, and possessed the same resources as others, we might engage in similar pursuits. Yet we observe that not all individuals approach their endeavors in an identical manner even if these factors are similar. While there is considerable overlap in how similarly situated individuals perceive, think, feel, and behave, we can detect extensive remaining idiosyncrasies. This segment of idiosyncrasies appears to have been with us since we can remember or for a long time. They may stem from particular genetic conditions and the physiology these are encoded to create. They may also originate in environmental factors, which encompass all other factors beyond our original genetic constitution. Such factors may interact with the development, composition, or integrity of our body in addition to or in deviation from our genetic blueprint. They include physical, chemical, or biological forces that might generate obvious changes in our body as well as influences acquired through our senses that might be harder to trace. These sensory influences constitute and trigger less palpable physiological reactions in our body and particularly our mind. Because these effects are less accessible to a scientific exploration, we may discount their presence. We may only recognize formative influences that are caused by momentous events. Nevertheless, we seem to be susceptible to subtle influences as well. Our upbringing, education, and social environment mostly form or affect our thoughts, emotions, and behavior gradually with an apparent concentration in our earliest years. Environmental factors then wield important influences on the formation of our idiosyncrasies. Although the development of idiosyncrasies beyond the effects of direct physiological interference is initially conditioned upon genetically shaped mental structures and processes, there seems to be extensive room for experiential individualization of our mind. We may in significant part become who we are through these experiences.

Genetic rational dispositions may already diverge substantially among individuals to delineate our rational capacity and to direct our thoughts. Even if they do not implant us with substantive impressions, they may determine particularities in the processing of information. Environmental influences may further variegate rational aptitudes and thought processes within genetically set limits. Beyond that, variations in genetic and environmental sources seem to particularize our needs. They also may vary the facilities with which we receive, translate, and transport information for processing by our rational and emotional facilities. As gatekeepers, our perceptive facilities possess important influence over the formation and operation of rational functions and the emotional registration and response mechanisms that constitute our needs. Conversely, rational functions and needs may affect the perception and transport of information or at least their receipt of it. Additionally, the joint focus by rational attributes and needs on our pursuits generates a developmental and a functional correlation between them. The interaction among our perceptive, emotional, and rational mind is conducted by general subdivisions and idiosyncratic particularizations of traits that may span across these partitions. We may refer to general subdivisions as common perceptive, rational, and emotional traits and to their particularizations as idiosyncratic, particularized, or specific traits. Perceptive traits comprise features that receive and deliver raw information. Rational traits are involved in the abstraction of knowledge about the workings of the world from that information. Emotional traits use raw and processed information to register pain, pleasure, and their anticipations and produce motivations that we detect as needs and wishes. These mechanisms form our mental traits that we may abbreviatedly call traits. Since their interaction creates our personality, we may also call them personality traits. Dispositions defined by more obviously physical properties may affect our mind as well. But they stay distinguishable because they do not manage sensory signals, formulate rational reflections, or issue emotions.

The lasting effects of mental traits may cause individuals to differ fundamentally in their needs and how they regard these best pursued. Motivations, processes, and extensive parts of our results may be fundamentally shared. Still, the fulfillment of our common needs that are amended by specific emotional traits may appear incomplete, deficient, or even miscarried unless this fulfillment abides by the demands of these specific traits. If we attempt to cut through the particularities of individual happiness to common needs, we can bring a sense of objectivity to the inquiry. Yet we deprive the subject matter of much of the articulation that gives it relevance in our pursuits. The importance of particularized aspects of emotional traits for our happiness often rivals the insistence of existential needs. The intensity of their demands makes clear that the satisfaction of the compound needs they constitute with underlying existential needs is not a generic process aiming at a generic result. These ingrained idiosyncrasies in combination with perceptive, rational, and situational idiosyncrasies may force the pursuit of significant segments of human needs to become individual undertakings. In spite of the solidness of their underlying foundations in shared attributes, they may not allow us to establish a comprehensive general model of happiness in terms of objectives or strategies.

The problem with establishing a substantive general model of happiness appears to be that it has to either ignore or reject and overcome personality differences. The governance of mental traits by personal variances despite fundamental commonalities may cause confusion. To the extent our perceptions, thoughts, and needs are overlaid by idiosyncrasies, we might be incapable of relating to other individuals although the commonality of underlying traits suggests this should be possible. We might presume that, as members of the same species, others perceive, think, feel, and act as we do. If others are restrained within particularized reference points of their mind, and even more if we are caught in dissimilar reference points of our own, we might not be able to understand their perceptions, thoughts, needs, or behavior. We may presume without question that our ways of perception, thinking, and feeling epitomize the common standards for human mental traits. We may be tempted to judge the mental processes and behavior of others as erroneous or ineffective. We may posit that they would be better off if they followed our perceptions, rational approaches, emotions, and behavior. Failing to discriminate differences or discounting their importance may also lead us to err in assuming that we can uncritically adopt other individuals' approaches to satisfy our needs. We can only avoid falling prey to these conclusions if we understand the discrepancies between our and other individuals' mental dispositions.

We may question where our idiosyncratic traits leave us in our struggle to improve our happiness. Particularized needs may not suffice to securely guide us toward happiness. To illustrate this issue, we may use the analogy with a game setting. The technical structures and procedures ordained by substances and laws of nature, our existential requirements, and the fundamental rules resulting from them govern. They set the playing field, general objectives, limitations, and ground rules and provide the resources and some of the implements by which we can operate. However, they leave it to us to meet game objectives by using our individual capabilities and preferred strategies within the sanctioned maneuvering space and means. Our options or choices of strategies might not work to our satisfaction. We might have to develop strategies that better interrelate our capacities with these settings. Further, our strategies might have to be flexible. We might encounter aligned, competing, or opposing players whose involvement, capacity, or strategy might change. The playing field and conditions as well as our conditioning and attitudes might change. This requires us to work with a number of variables. Some of them might be unpredictable. We might not fully understand them even after we encounter them. Upon such a background, we target fulfilling our objectives and we tune our strategies as game constellations present themselves and progress.

The pursuits of our needs are additionally complicated because we have separate objectives for each need and multiple playing fields that may be connected in some aspects. More important, our idiosyncrasies appear to pose irresistible internal requirements with which we must comply while we have to also abide by the rules in a game. Their sourcing and rigidity may make adjustments to the opportunities and the requirements of our setting difficult and maybe impossible. Still, it may be difficult to convince us that we should abandon or modify our mental idiosyncrasies, even if we could identify them. To us, following our mental traits is not merely a strategy. They represent objectives in themselves without which reaching the main objectives is diminished or meaningless. They represent requirements that we have to obey regardless of whether we recognize that they cause us pain. This applies more obviously to our emotional traits. Yet even our rational and perceptive idiosyncrasies appear to insist that we maintain them. Beyond the mere impositions of their own factuality, emotional traits may actively perpetuate perceptive and rational idiosyncrasies because these often participate in the formation or maintenance of emotional idiosyncrasies. The immediate motivational leadership of emotional traits may cause our mental traits to appear entirely under the leadership of our emotional traits even though that may only be partly warranted.

Arguably, much of the trend to emotional idiosyncrasies is the result of successful economic activity, social arrangements, and technology. These factors are regularly intertwined in their development. They have given us better command to change our circumstances and implement our needs with an increased quality and quantity of means. We have eminently increased the effectiveness, efficiency, and availability of means for satisfying common needs. It might therefore appear that our focus on economic activity, social arrangements, and technology has been fueled by common needs and by technical proficiency in their service alone. It might seem that idiosyncrasies have merely proliferated as a byproduct of the resulting increased offerings of means, that our pursuits have dispersed opportunistically within the range of possibilities as these became unlocked by economic activity, social arrangements, and technology. Then again, if quantitative and qualitative augmentation of means to satisfy common needs were the exclusive incentive for idiosyncrasies, they would have little variety. Efforts to meet challenges would yield provisional variety until means proved their superiority and varying conditions were brought up to standard. Variety would only be a function of different tasks, different situational challenges, or a lack of knowledge or development. There appear to be independent origins for a diversification of idiosyncrasies that predate economic activity, social arrangements, and technology although they may interact with them. This interaction may have had and still have a mutual effect on the development of both. The intensity of this interaction may make it hard to separate the two types of sources.

Considering the intensity and variety of idiosyncratic pursuits, idiosyncrasies may seem to extensively contribute to human development. But even if we recognize that emotional idiosyncrasies are more than side effects of existential development, we may doubt that their development carries a significant, let alone an indispensable function. We may still view them as deviations that mostly detract from existential pursuits and only collaterally lead to some progress. They seem to lack ulterior purpose and appear to become their own purpose. Even if they stimulate human development, they also occupy a large, possibly overproportional share of results. That domination seems to be growing. The increasing availability of differentiated means appears to exert formative effects on us that motivate us to set ourselves apart even more. There does not seem to be a limit for individual differentiation. This threatens to lead humanity into an existence of superficial eccentricities. But humans may develop existentially advantageous differentiations as well that might become prevalent generally or in particular settings to which individuals become adapted. Idiosyncrasies seem to constitute reactive or proactive trials by which our species develops and fills its potential for survival and thriving. Considering this assistance, misguided differentiations may seem like a necessary expense.

We may also approve differentiations with regard to our needs for individual survival and thriving. The variety of ways in which humans define and pursue existential needs might suggest to us that we can review the range of that variety and have the liberty to select from it. We seemingly advance in our powers of self-determination to shape a satisfying course that is closely customized to our desires. Yet such an optimism may be short-lived if we consider that our idiosyncrasies, including our idiosyncratic desires, might represent inadequate trials to cope with our environment. Genetic variations or traits imposed on us by our environment might increase our dissatisfaction because they may negatively impact the satisfaction of other needs or we might not succeed satisfying them. Our pursuits of and attributions of resources to particularities may cause deficiencies in existential pursuits, even in the existential pursuits to which they are attached, as well as in other idiosyncratic pursuits. External circumstances or the superseding urgency of existential needs may not permit us to make the choices idiosyncratic needs demand. Either way, the disharmony among our traits may result in lifelong suffering and may affect our chances of individual survival. Beyond that, our impressions of self-determination and of freedom to select from a wide variety of means turn out to be an illusion. Our idiosyncrasies do not appear to be a product of our free determination and do not seem to be amenable to adjustment. Further, the accumulation of restrictions they impose reduces the area of strategies we find useful. Our freedom of choice appears to be additionally constricted because our particularized needs motivate us to ascertain the best solution for their requirements. Finally, idiosyncratic pursuits may lock us into factual settings and narrow our selections that we are positioned to actualize subsequently. For these reasons, idiosyncratic emotional traits do not represent freedom. Arguably, we are subject to similar curtailments by the demands of our common needs. But our fund of possible pathways to achieve fulfillment is less restricted. This enhances our opportunities to meet underlying existential needs with the greatest effect. Additionally, the developmental history of existential needs and their common purpose appear to have shaped them to allow us the pursuit of all of them in mutually beneficial harmony.

Our potential for pain from the frustration of idiosyncratic pursuits intensifies in a social context because our idiosyncrasies may interfere with or may be affected by pursuits of other individuals. That potential may already be high in connection with existential pursuits by multiple individuals. But the fact that these individuals have their own idiosyncrasies provides additional incendiary potential and unpredictability. Idiosyncratic pursuits carry a high risk of incompatibility among individuals because they may not partake in conventional structures and processes of mutuality but may pose obstacles to them. Moreover, the restricted or missing sharing of idiosyncratic emotional traits among individuals detracts from their social legitimacy, particularly if they encroach on recognized pursuits. The resulting social conformance pressure encroaches on the apparent individual importance and the immovability of idiosyncratic emotional traits. It threatens to engender a continuing struggle among individuals and between individuals and the systems of interaction and governance they establish. The unconventional diversity of idiosyncratic needs and their disturbance potential appear to render it necessary to regulate their practice with particular care. If idiosyncratic pursuits cause interference with the common needs of other individuals, their supplemental character suggests that they must yield unless they can be shown to have superior existential importance. However, the collective and general individual importance of idiosyncratic pursuits also suggests that they be given some space. This might mean that existential rights might have to suffer some curtailment in matters that are considered nonessential for their pursuit or maintenance. The balancing between interests this may necessitate may be difficult, but it may be accomplished in a general fashion. A determination may be significantly more problematic where individuals contend with one another concerning their idiosyncratic needs. The variety, subjective complexity, and lack of broad acknowledgment of many idiosyncrasies may prompt a legal order to refrain from regulating particular interferences. It may instead confine itself on the protection of fundamental rights, including the right to practice idiosyncrasies within limited, equal zones of liberty.

If societal pressures demand an excessive sacrifice of pursuits, it becomes less advantageous for individuals to partake in a society. Excessive sacrifice may be spring from the uneven recognition of existential rights or the imposition of idiosyncratic opinions over individuals who do not share them. But even if societal arrangements can be instituted to resolve such conflicts and they endeavor to optimize societal interaction on the basis of equality for all, they may exact detractions from ideals that individuals may deem too costly. Societal cooperation or coordination may prove to be a problem if our objectives and paths of pursuit have drifted too far apart. Cooperation may become illusory where we do not share the desirability of what could be accomplished by cooperation or if we and other individuals do not provide sufficient means that would be useful for one another. As internal and external differences in how we pursue happiness increase, we may be unable or less able to provide or acquire coordinated behavior. These correlative limitations may combine with the autonomous limitations that our idiosyncratic mental traits leverage on our pursuits to create or exacerbate difficulties in meeting our common needs. Our insistence on particular manners of pursuit and our exclusion of other capable strategies that do not comport with our personality may then have significant consequences. They may create circumstances that threaten our individual and collective survival and thriving or at least reduce fulfillment by narrowing our selections. If sufficiently pressured, we may cope by resigning to fundamental objectives and pursuits. However, even if this saves or benefits our existence, the curtailment of idiosyncratic emotional traits is bound to negatively affect our happiness.

Behind a pretense of freedom of choice, idiosyncratic emotional traits appear to impose unnecessary complications in meeting our existential needs. They raise our potential for incurring pain if we do not possess the luxury of satisfying our existential needs in our preferred way. The subjective character of our happiness and of its requirements seems to make it more difficult to obtain and maintain happiness. Diversified traits may have some benefits because they can provide and fill opportunities or requirements for diversification. But their inflexible cogency may be more a hindrance than an asset for the fulfillment of our needs. As much as we may be accustomed to and value our personality, we may also feel the pain it causes us. Other individuals may be happy with particulars that are easier to achieve and still be able to meet their existential needs. We may realize that, because our happiness is staked to particular conditions that are harder to achieve, we may be less probable to achieve a level of happiness others may enjoy. The larger the spread in the ensuing capacity to produce happiness is, the more we may consider our more demanding particularities or our inability to fulfill them as a curse. We may be discontented with who we are. We may wish we could modify our idiosyncrasies to a format that would be more successful in drawing happiness from our circumstances. In addition, we may be discontented with the knowledge, the skills, or the physical means we can generate or locate for the satisfaction of our needs. This discontent may motivate us to look beyond the limits we find in us or in our environment and possible incremental improvements. Our empiric inquiries may appear to give dissatisfactory answers to our question what will make us happy and how we can reach it. We may try to avoid these problems by construing ideal conditions for happiness. The following section examines that approach.

SECTION THREE
IDEALISTIC APPROACH

CHAPTER 11
IDEALISTIC AMBITIONS

We cannot appear to derive satisfactory empiric guidance from others on what will make us happy. Studying the behavior or advice of other humans does not provide reliable guidance because they are likely to possess different concepts of happiness. The apparent anarchy of pursuits and the dearth of efficient guidance from empiric explorations in the presence of an overwhelming multitude of circumstances leave us wanting for clarity and reliable assistance. The complexity we face in our struggle for happiness makes us wish for a mechanism that would reduce this complexity. We would like to anticipate, plan, and control our path as much as possible so we can extend the enjoyment of our existence to its maximum. We wish we could find a manageable set of instructions that could bring order into the seemingly confused state of our search for happiness. This motivation was already the source of our empiric investigations. However, their failure to satisfy our desire for guidance incentivizes us to search for an alternative approach. This alternative approach is suggested to us by the insight that empiric explorations largely fail us. This insight may provoke a radical departure in our method. Rather than searching for what will make us happy in the circumstances we find, we may undertake to create circumstances pursuant to our wishes. Instead of letting our strategies be defined by what is, we may define them according to what we desire our circumstances to be. This might appear like a circular approach. If we are not familiar with our needs and the circumstances for their fulfillment, we do not know too well what we want. We can only react to topical urges presented by our needs and the means given and constrictions imposed by our situation. Thus, we may inquire for a method to identify our needs free from the constraints of pursuit. We may believe that we can short-circuit the discovery process and begin it with concentrating on its end points of pleasure. We may perceive that we can form a reality according to what we consider as best, our inventions, our ideas. We may contemplate that we can escape empiric ties and achieve pure knowledge of what happiness means for us through our imagination.

In this undertaking, we attempt to imagine an ideal state where our needs are being fulfilled. We try to build methods that can achieve this ideal without at least initially referencing our present state. Based on the ideal conditions of fulfillment, we ask what has to occur to obtain these conditions. To determine the necessary means for our transition from dissatisfaction to satisfaction, we step downward from the most proximate requirement for fulfillment to the next proximate requirement and so on. We may proceed in this way until we arrive at a condition that we can create as a proximate step up from the basis of where we are. Once we have established such a sequence of steps, we can define our subordinated wishes as constituted by these steps. We then trace the sequence of deducted steps back in implementing these steps and their corresponding wishes in the reverse order of their deduction. We build the circumstances we imagined to be capable of fulfilling each need. Hence, our needs form the starting points as well as the end points of our pursuits. It seems that, in this reflective movement, our needs define their factual necessities, the premises for their fulfillment. Our needs become ultimate premises. They become facts in relation to which we seek all other facts. To the extent these other facts cannot be readily obtained, we search for them and we endeavor to shape our environment to fit the purpose of fulfilling our needs.

Beginning our investigation from the ideal of our needs appears to be the reasonable answer to our empiric struggles. These struggles seem to have attacked the problem from the wrong side. They seem to have focused too much on circumstances as they are and on distancing ourselves from the deprivation of these circumstances. By trying to reject and distance ourselves from circumstances as they are, we do not appear to obtain sufficient guidance to steer us toward the fulfillment of our needs. Such negative guidance might give us part of our motivation to transform our circumstances. However, the negation of what we find and attempts to extricate ourselves from certain circumstances or to ameliorate them stop short of adequately defining what makes us happy. They leave us aimless because our vision remains focused on deprivation instead of being set on a state of fulfillment. If we are to maximize happiness, the positive guidance by our desire of fulfillment seems required. Being guided by our ideals of fulfillment appears to enable us to transcend the limitations of our experiences.

Ideal happiness does not strike us as a function of the world as it is or as we have experienced it. As a state of fulfillment, its distinction seems to be largely its differentiation from our reality. It seems to be the very nature of a wish that it designates a state of affairs that is not, at least not yet. In this quality, it appears to have the capability to surpass empiric status. We may wish for something that is absolutely impossible or something we cannot manage to arrange. If existing circumstances do not provide the answer to our wishes, we are willing to consider processes that go beyond circumstances we have already experienced. When we form a wish in excess of customary constellations and functions, the method we employ does not appear to be an empiric deduction, let alone a scientifically founded process of building up from underlying circumstances and their organizing principles. Ideal wishes often do not represent current or past conditions. Rather, they may appear as leaps that are founded on our conjecture of what might bring us satisfaction. Notwithstanding, when we examine our wishes, we appear incapable of inventing circumstances that are independent of anything we have experienced. Even if we do not follow substances and laws of nature in a scientific or technologically possible sense, we arrange elements of our experiences to form our fantasies. The premises of our needs are empiric as well. We become aware of those needs through direct sensory impressions, emotional reactions, and physiological states that are prompted by deprivation and fulfillment. These impressions are authentic empiric phenomena. Arguably, their unreflected immediacy renders them the most empiric of our experiences. Their characterizations of pain and pleasure provide us with the most important sensory impressions in our pursuit of happiness. All aspects of our pain-pleasure mechanism that stimulate us can be categorized as empiric events. The distinguishing quality of empiric and idealistic aspects of our mind is not that one is more based on experiences than the other. We experience phenomena of our mind, including its motivations, as much as any other aspect of nature. Rather, the distinction lies in the character of one as a rationally ascertainable experience and the other as an emotional experience. It might thus be more precise to distinguish rational empiric and emotional empiric phenomena.

The use of the word ideal with regard to our concepts of happiness cannot be justified as signifying a phenomenon that is separate from our experiences. But our needs comprise an element that is ideal in terms of the meaning of the word that designates perfection. That ideal is the concept of ideal happiness as the complete absence of pain and the complete presence of pleasure. We possess this ideal, even if we have never experienced such condition, simply as an extrapolation from the direction implied in our pain-pleasure mechanism. That ideal is based on experiences as well because we merely purify and continue the movement between dissatisfaction and satisfaction to its ultimate conclusion. Even if we only harbor a vague notion of relief and bliss, its anticipation is a result of empiric impressions. There can be no ideal separate from empiric constituents. As all mental occurrences, all ideal concepts are in their essence empiric. However, this does not keep us from forming ideals of our ultimate destination of perfection. Our experiences suggest to us that the complete absence of pain and complete presence of happiness represent our consummate ideal. They would indicate that all our needs are fulfilled and that we would not have to fear any circumstances that might change that fulfillment.

As we turn to potential means for fulfilling our needs, the basis of our experiences remains indispensable. The demands of each need are articulated by references not only to what we presently sense but also to our preceding impressions of its deprivation and fulfillment. We cannot help being influenced by these experiences as samples in ascertaining our objectives and pursuits. If we can distinguish objects or events that bear similarity with sampled objects or events that provided adequate satisfaction before, we may apply the most promising of them and improve them if that is possible. We may have to use our imagination of potential components to build planned pursuits based on our experiences. We may replace, add, or subtract components in naturally occurring objects or events. But it may not be sufficient to deconstruct and reconstruct objects or events we find preexisting and to engage in their variation, even if it is a significantly improved variation. To accomplish means beyond these, we may have to disassemble objects and events and to scrutinize the possibilities their components hold to interrelate in unprecedented objects and events. That we possess such creative capacity seems to be evidenced by human technology as well as feats of social and economic organization. Its results often appear to reflect a departure from nature. Historically, the fulfillment functions of our needs were met by naturally occurring objects and events. Objects and events we invent to fulfill these functions in a more developed state may seem dissimilar from anything nature provides. Yet, in spite of that appearance, we take all our cues of what is possible from nature. Even means and functions that we newly develop or revolutionize for the pursuit of our needs often appear to be inspired by objects and events we observe in nature. Although we might not work with traditional objects and events anymore, we frequently emulate their functions. Our search and coordination of subordinated functions derive from this principal orientation. This is not surprising because the ultimate resulting functionality of products must often be identical or similar to natural products if they replace these products to be useful for the contentment of our needs. A similarity in resulting functionality implies a requirement for similar components.

While our development is hence substantially characterized by copying nature, we appear to be able to discern allocations of components to which we can more fittingly attach the label of human invention. By drawing analyzed components and characteristics of components from separate objects and events together to synthesize new objects and events, we may not only build functionalities that are identical or similar to existing objects and events. We may combine components in unprecedented ways with unprecedented results. We can undertake this expansion of our knowledge and technical ability without an intent of emulation. Instead, we would systematically examine the combination of nature's components, try to find out how they react, and see whether we might be able to use the result. This implies that we play through possible combinations of given or extracted components. We can also try to abbreviate the process by taking reference to experiences to determine what combinations have not been explored so far. Further, we can arrange experiments under the use of settings we have already experienced. However, by these methods, we merely discover what is already there, what nature already provides. Our scientific research is destined to bring such preexisting factualities to our attention. The attribute of invention is even less deserved where we stumble upon knowledge that is new to us in a coincidence. We may then restrict invention to situations where we search for and find solutions for particular problems. Yet even here we are bound to the empiric acquisition of knowledge and the advantage of using prior empiric knowledge to concentrate our inquiries. Finding solutions with such undertakings is not fundamentally dissimilar from broader systematic endeavors to amplify our knowledge and capabilities. Nor is it fundamentally different from gaining insight as a byproduct of accidents or attempts to meet needs, or from observations of occurrences in which we are not or not intensely involved. While such techniques may pose differing requirements regarding our talents, knowledge, or efforts, we can only discover what nature holds in store for us. The belief that we can invent anything is born from a lack of comprehension.

Although our mind may have experiences within itself that are not the result of external factors, these cannot be called a product of our independent creation. Our knowledge or speculation about what we might find and the dedication and sophistication of our search or confirmation efforts do not change the derivative character of our activities. Our sole contribution appears to be an intentional or an accidental arrangement of factors that bestows on us particular experiences from a larger fund of possibilities. But the motivations of our needs that guide us in these undertakings and our other faculties are products of nature as well, and we experience all of them involuntarily. We do not create. We merely realize potentials within us and in our environment that are already granted and whose development through us seems to be imposed by our dispositions and dispositions in our surroundings. We may be able to imagine and implement circumstances in variation, rearrangement, qualitative enhancement, or quantitative augmentation of what we have experienced. Nevertheless, the concept for such activities originates in and is defined by sources beyond our control within us and our surroundings. When we deconstruct experiences into their components and apply them individually or allocate them into the same, similar, or new correlations, we react to and use what is presented. New correlations are mere extensions of what already exists and the realization of its preexisting potential. Allocating what exists from the basis of our knowledge of substances and principles or chance may be unprecedented and complex. But neither our ideals nor the means for their fulfillment are independently ours. The capacities and determinations of our mind seem inexorably rooted in what is and what we are by the grace of nature. Our insights and activities merely catch up with the potential of us and of our environment. Our potential or the potential of nature may or may not be competent to meet our ideals. Still, through our practical pursuit of our ideals, we are reconciling empiric reality with empiric potential to some extent.

Insights regarding the empiric nature of our needs may be disappointing at first. But they give us renewed hope that we might derive happiness as a scientific result. We might succeed if we approach our research from the viewpoint of ideal satisfaction, by posting it as a hypothesis from which we derive and toward which we develop a systematic science of happiness. Such an idealistic position and method seem to come naturally to us. Our needs represent the ideals to which we aspire. They confront us with the idea of their satisfaction as our objectives from which all our organizational efforts and activities flow. The empiric aspects of what is or may be possible and how it may be possible provide tools that the idealistic aspect attempts to use. They also place practical limitations that the idealistic aspect might attempt to obliterate or at least expand. Yet the undefined experience that we are not satisfied, that we can anticipate more pleasure when we detect the presence of pain, creates an idealistic edge on which our development essentially depends. This idealistic edge drives us to develop our empiric knowledge to where our capabilities and their application will match our aspirations. It is the vanguard of our knowledge and practical abilities. At the outer edge of our skills, we may know what we are looking for only by sensing a discrepancy in our pain-pleasure mechanism for a need. Our perceptive, rational, and practical efforts are set in motion by that emotional discrepancy. Our mind connects empiric impressions of an emotional void with its memory of similar impressions and corresponding remediation efforts. Our needs incentivize us to meet their requirements as well as possible. Where empiric circumstances that cause ideal satisfaction are missing, they encourage us to develop these. We may then search for such circumstances under the leadership of our needs until we become able to meet our ideals.

Our ideals focus us on experienced or imagined circumstances of pleasurable events. The at times speculative nature of our happiness or of imagined opportunities for its advancement exposes us to considerable risk. The emotional character of our ideals may have our rational mind guessing. Because they might exceed our practical experiences, we might not be able to call upon sufficient knowledge or other resources to generate the necessary conditions. Even if circumstances can be imagined and produced, they may fail our emotional expectations. Our emotional ideals set our development objectives in a sometimes indefinite manner. They compel us to engage in pursuits even if we cannot be certain of their aptitude or success. Their impulses and means at which they make us grasp may at times be reckless and misleading. Nevertheless, the achievement of improved levels of satisfaction and aptitude in its service appears to depend significantly on letting the impulses of our needs motivate us. The idealistic aspect of our mind encourages us to develop knowledge and other resources to fulfill our needs better. This makes an idealistic approach essential for advancing our individual and collective survival and thriving beyond the levels that are secured by automatic instructions of our instincts. Without the leadership of our emotionally inspired ideals, our means may not develop past the levels we have already reached. Their uncertainty of fulfillment seems to be a price we must pay in exchange.

Unless we have experienced ideal fulfillment before, we cannot securely anticipate its circumstances. We will only know whether our ideal has been reached when our pain of deprivation regarding a particular need subsides. Besides projections we may venture based on observations, our only ability to better define our needs and what will satisfy them is to explore more of us and our reality and make it part of our experiences. To understand what our needs are and to arrive at ideals of their fulfillment, we have to refer to and build on experiences with them. Apart from instinctive instructions, our needs only give us guidance with respect to whether approaches fulfill them and whether some experiences fulfill them more or less than others. They appear to be incapable to tell us what will satisfy them beyond such experiences. To the extent we do not have instinctive knowledge or experience regarding what means fulfill them better or best, we have to rely on empiric observation or experimentation. We may have to engage in trials and revise our approaches depending on their results. Finding the best solutions may require experiments in addition to those undertaken to locate better solutions. Depending on resulting advancements and approximations toward an ideal state, we might modify our concepts of ideal applied circumstances that will or might live up to our emotional ideals. In spite of all its shortcomings, this empiric method appears to be the only feasible process we can devise to obtain better knowledge about our needs and their fulfillment. Our trials must be largely individualized because our needs are modulated by our particularities. To obtain guidance on what will make us happy, we must try all reasonable possibilities. But we may identify areas of worthwhile experimentation by referencing previous experiences of happiness and unhappiness that might indicate directions for improving our happiness.

To construct ideal concepts and ideal circumstances according to them, we have to seek a concept that reconciles experiences regarding singular needs and their correlation. As we accumulate experiences through natural pursuits and intentional experiments, we develop a roster of incidents that we can translate into a guidance scheme. The basis of this scheme is the combination of incidents of satisfaction and pain with factual circumstances. On some occasions, we might be able to assess and record circumstances regarding single needs. But mostly, our experiences in the pursuit of needs will intersect and overlay, generating a netting of happy and unhappy correlations among our needs and of linked factual conditions. The association of happiness and unhappiness in a variety of types and intensities with certain categories of occurrences may allow us to develop some principles. Hence, it may in part reflect scientific abstraction. More immediately, it may provide us with a topographical map of what can cause us pain or pleasure and to what extent. We may refer to this composite as our existential philosophy because it gives us orientation regarding what we deem to secure and advance our existence. The formulation of an existential philosophy seems to be a natural process in all of us as our experiences grow. The context of these experiences may enable us to ascertain regions in which we are missing sufficient guidance, and we may decide to gain more experience in these areas to build a more comprehensive philosophy for our existence. We may deliberate how we should react if we were confronted with alternative settings and what alternatives would be conducive to what degree for the contentment of our needs. Even so, such a philosophy must remain deficient if its entries are insufficiently integrated into a comprehensive, reflected scheme. Without such a system, we may not have the necessary oversight and criteria to rightly assess, correlate, or supplement our experiences. Our experiences may have been affected by factors that cloud our judgment. Our philosophy may further suffer from a limited scope of our experiences. We may only achieve approximations of happiness, or not even that. Our existence proves that we have succeeded in satisfying basic survival needs up to this point. But some of our collateral needs may stay unfulfilled, and collateral and basic survival needs may be under-fulfilled. That might also be applicable to idiosyncratic features of our needs. Needs may compete and damage other needs and lack reconcil-iation. Even if we can experience happiness at one moment, future or continued fulfillment may be endangered. As long as we sense pain or fear and we yearn for more satisfaction, we have not experienced ideal happiness if we deem it to consist of pure fulfillment. Because our phi-losophy might not be able to attend to these issues effectively, it may fall short in helping us to dependably define our ideals. To elevate our happiness, it appears necessary that we transcend the limitations of a scientific approach to our means and apply it to our objectives.

How we can undertake that may not be immediately accessible for us. To expand our reach, we may extrapolate from what we know and may picture ideal conditions that can be assembled from compo-nents in our mental repertoire. We may attempt to integrate the con-cepts we have collected and derived into a comprehensive system that gives our experiences overarching sense. We may use such a system to supplement areas in which we have insufficient experience or to shape areas in which we have no experience. We may build a philosophy as a speculative, ideal construct. However, if we want to ascertain that our constructs afford us applicable guidance, we must engage in corrobo-ration. We will have to generate a reality in which the practice of our imagined ideal pursuits becomes feasible. Often, the building of such a reality may surpass our personal capabilities. That insufficiency may not only be due to a lack of personal or nonhuman resources for mo-mentous rearrangements of our nonhuman environment. It is also at-tributable to the fact that a number of our philosophical ideals require or benefit from cooperation with other humans, by exchanges or com-mon ventures or by the mere survival and thriving of our species. We all wish we could shape the world to cater to our needs. But achieving our ideals may require extensive and at times massive undertakings.

Our desire to adjust the world to our liking and the potentially vast changes we imagine stand in stark contrast to our particularities and their possible insignificance for large-scale developments of hu-manity. Considering the context of our pursuits and our interest in the survival and thriving of our species, our desire to have our idiosyncra-sies accommodated must appear frivolous to us upon deeper contem-plation. The shape of our existential philosophy and the success of its implementation are in large parts determined by our particular inter-nal and external circumstances. It is therefore likely that this philoso-phy will solely pertain to us. We may reserve the right to shape imme-diate circumstances to satisfy our particularized requirements. But we

may acknowledge that such pursuits must not interfere with our ultimate objective to support and protect the survival and thriving of our
species. Even if we have not graduated to these insights, the fact that
our idiosyncratic ambitions to arrange our surroundings are not likely
to be shared in much of their detail by other individuals and that such
individuals are likely to have their own diverging ambitions must impress us as an overwhelming presentation of obstacles to our ideals.

Differing wishes among individuals that result from their particularized needs and circumstances make it unlikely that a homogeneous system of pursuits under one philosophy could be created and
maintained by them. We may therefore question to what extent harmonious coexistence and collaboration is possible in the face of idiosyncrasies. They seem to require limited unity to support and protect
underlying common interests but also the preservation of large areas
of autonomy. We may further query how we should arrive at comprehensive guidance for matters of our happiness if we each have to develop and implement our unique existential philosophy. It seems that
our attempts to form ideals do not help us much to overcome our dependence on trials and exposure to their detriments. To obtain competent guidance for our happiness, we have to largely sustain our own
experiences from which we might then construct such a guidance. But
this threatens to defeat the purpose our seeking guidance. We want to
avoid having to suffer through experiences of failure, frustration, and
pain. We do not want to waste time, efforts, and other resources on
endeavors that might not fulfill our needs. We may fail in our experiments because of personal and environmental adversities. We might
remain ensnared in a variety of continuing trials without significantly
improving our happiness. Even if our trials eventually succeed and we
become better able to understand our happiness, we might have wasted much of our existence in arriving at appropriate insights. We might
have expended large amounts of our resources on misadventures that
could have been better spent in the production of happiness. We may
view the loss of most resources with mitigated regret because we can
regenerate most of them. Yet we may regard time and the particular
constellations of circumstances in our life to be different. We stand to
spend much of our existence trying to comprehend ourselves and our
relations with our environment. By the time we obtain sufficient wisdom so we could benefit from our exploratory hardships, many occasions in which we could have applied that wisdom may have irretrievably passed. We may be robbed of the products of our educational investments by becoming debilitated by physical decay and annihilated
by death. We may also lament that, as our insights mature and might

lead to a happier life, we may be deprived of choices by the surroundings we built. We may seek to reduce our frustration over these facts
by trying to view our insights that result from our struggles as accomplishments in themselves. We may attempt to make sense of our tribulations as an apprenticeship that prepares us for higher destinations
in a life following death. But these appeasements cannot change that
we might not advance much in our comprehension of happiness and
that we might not have much occasion to apply our knowledge. These
difficulties might be compounded by technical problems of finding or
producing conditions that correspond to our requirements because of
internal and external deficiencies and obstacles. We might also mourn
that the lessons we draw from experiences should be of little relevance
for other humans. We might regret that they should have to contend
with their own particular internal and external circumstances without
being able to build upon our insights. We may therefore conclude that
gaining knowledge of happiness by exploration is an inefficient, ineffective undertaking even if it is guided by our ideals. Further, the idealistic method we tried to devise seems to add little. We have been following the exhortations and reactions of our needs for improvement
all along. Even if identifying and striving toward ideals gives us ultimate direction, the reality of how we must earn more detailed knowledge seems to be unchanged. We still follow our hunches and react to
results, albeit in a more systematic fashion and with greater expectations. The painful development of perfection through trials may make
us suspect that we cannot reach it without additional guidance.

We should be confident that at least some guidance can emerge
because not all our efforts are defined by our particularities. We might
succeed in learning from, constructing together with, and passing on
to others existential principles that focus on common needs and the
individually and collectively ideal pursuit of such needs. Such general
existential philosophies should generate essential contributions to the
happiness of individuals and humanity. Much could be accomplished
if humans could be motivated to acknowledge their existential needs,
their apparent purpose, and their requirements, including the protection and support of one another's fundamental rights and the practice
of mutuality. This might naturally incentivize them to pursue an existential ideal. Such insights would situate idiosyncrasies into a guiding
context on the basis of which they might be explored, evaluated, and
possibly adjusted. In looking for comprehensive guidance on a general
theory of happiness, we might take notice of partial insights other individuals have gained in these matters. But we might hope that a professional philosophy would have established a general framework.

Upon forming this hope, we may immediately question whether professional philosophy can assist. For many of us, philosophy may appear to be a lifeless or at least an irrelevant science. There does not seem to be much of a demand for philosophical services. References to philosophers may summon images of unworldly university professors, marble busts, or rows of dusty books. We may think of it as an association of scholars that predominantly focuses on its history and continuance, that endlessly discusses problems but never arrives at broadly recommended solutions. To many, philosophy signifies the abstract treatment of arcane subjects that are only of academic importance to a few experts and whose content is inaccessible to noninitiates because it is phrased in incomprehensible jargon. Philosophy is widely regarded as a science without much practical applicability, as erudition for its own sake. But we may also carry a suspicion or even the conviction that this lack of relevance is as unnecessary as it is undesirable. We understand some of the power of philosophy because we are aware of the search for and applicability of some of its principles within ourselves and the reliance of social organization on philosophical principles. Still, for most of us, philosophical propositions remain unknown, distant, or disconnected. We may want to know whether someone has developed a comprehensive concept that can make our life better.

What we are looking for may hide beyond questions of means. We may want to know how we can find more satisfaction with them. There is good reason to believe that philosophy should give us at least some of the guidance we seek. Its Greek name that translates as love of knowledge implies an inquisitive mind that tries to understand its surroundings and itself. The implication is that once we know about phenomena and how they work, we can put these insights to use. We may say that philosophy is in part an abstract science because it tries to derive mental representations of objects and events and attempts to describe and categorize them and their relationships. But we can also claim this abstraction as a necessary precursor for our ability to competently influence our environment. When we look at how philosophy developed, we can detect such a practical effect if not intent of philosophy. Originally, philosophy covered all ranges of science. The relative lack of knowledge of humanity prompted philosophy to inquire into all directions where knowledge could be located. As knowledge grew, the amount and complexity of knowledge and its practice in particular areas as well as the requirements for further exploration in these areas led to the specialization of knowledge into segments. Thus, the original pursuit of acquiring knowledge separated into sciences that were largely autonomous in their subsequent inquiries and resulting knowledge. They were only bound together by their shared boundaries and a common basic method. As areas of exact science were carved out of the body of philosophy, it increasingly resembled an emptying husk, whose developments of knowledge have fruited and fallen out, germinated, and begun growing on their own. Even the foundations of science became self-contained. Philosophy became increasingly restricted as a backward-oriented science that reviews, compares, and classifies its own development. However, it has preserved authority in trying to explain the shrinking array of matters that have not yet become accessible to proof. In that area, it retains the nature of an exploratory science according to procedures that take account of proven facts, disclose unproven assumptions, and develop conclusions in their interrelation according to accepted standards of argument. Only, the subject matters it is left to address frequently exhibit such an undefined complexity in their elements and correlations that speculation may build upon speculation. The resulting theoretical proof might require practical application to confirm the correctness of its speculative conclusions. Philosophy has then retained some practical scientific aspects.

That remaining function to discover subjects for practical confirmation through speculation seems to be curtailed in areas that adjoin practical sciences because these may undertake their own speculations. Although these dispersed speculations may consist of smaller steps, have a smaller scope, and insist on more immediate proof, their development may catch up with philosophical constructs. Where that is not the case, philosophical research appears to contribute to its replacement by exact sciences by pioneering and confirming through its conceptual results worthwhile directions for more practical investigations. As speculative concepts that still remain contained in philosophy become accessible to proof, they either form their own sciences or become integrated into an existing exact science. With the progress of practical sciences and speculative philosophy, speculative philosophy is relegated to ever smaller areas that eventually will completely give way to exact knowledge. Hence, the mission of philosophy to find out what there is to know seems to be programmed to expire as a result of its success. As the mother of all sciences, it is set to retire and live in its memories of its productive years. Until that time, speculative philosophy may help to define areas that remain to be explored and provide an initial framework of possible explanations that motivate more exacting research. It can serve as a temporary advisor that preliminarily explores uncharted areas and attempts to give us orientation. While philosophy might remain instrumental to practical sciences and ultimately to human pursuits, its functions seem to be remote at best.

However, this contemplation of philosophy is evidently incomplete. It never was only preoccupied with what is but also with what should be. It has never limited itself to explaining the workings of the world and assessing how and with what results they might be applied, only to leave determinations regarding the application of knowledge to us. It has always concerned itself with what we should do with our knowledge once we have developed it. As we acquire knowledge and through knowledge achieve command of other resources, we are confronted with choices that exceed and distance themselves from the automatic instructions of our instincts. Our rising powers make our wisdom in using them increasingly important. Philosophy can help us in that determination. It may keep an overview over all specialized sciences and incorporate their insights into a comprehensive system that avails us of the ability to apply them for optimal benefit. That service is needed because the specialized sciences and their coordination can only assist us to find out how something functions and how to achieve something. They can describe to us the consequences of acts or omissions. But they cannot instruct us why we should or should not apply what they make possible beyond considerations of technical effectiveness or efficiency within their subject. Questions about purpose and instructions that flow from its designation form a second, higher level of our love of knowledge. It is the task of philosophy in its existential concerns to answer these questions and to prepare those instructions or at least to bestow the development of our own competent conclusions. As the originating point from which humanity ventured out to discover its surroundings and itself, philosophy still presents the focal point of human concern. All our technical knowledge and our capacity converge on it to determine what we should undertake with them and ourselves. The only adjustment in a continuation of this function will be that the speculative nature of its considerations will be progressively substituted by scientific optimization. That result develops from the practical confirmation of its speculative premises and deductions. This time, however, the comprehensive ambition of the philosophical foray suggests that philosophy is to maintain the administration of the subject matter even after its speculative explanation has been confirmed. That is because the comprehensive scope of its purview fundamentally differs from the specificity of the sciences that previously departed.

Our acceptance of a philosophical leadership in existential concerns is ultimately determined by our identification of what we want in a philosophy. To be legitimate to us, an existential philosophy, even after its speculation is factualized, would have to reliably designate or assist us in designating what we want. Our mind judges all knowledge it acquires and applies all science under the criterion of whether they assist our wishes and, if it is wise, the entirety of our needs. Existential philosophy may help us to recognize our needs and understand how they can correlate for an overall maximized level of fulfillment. Existential philosophy then seems to be a science to find out what pleases us and how to maximize our pleasure. The inquiry by philosophy into the nature of our world and the particularized sciences that developed from that inquiry seem to constitute subordinated efforts to obtain instruments for achieving this ultimate objective of happiness.

Considering the apparent significance of existential philosophy, it is difficult to explain why we do not avail ourselves more of its suggestions. One reason seems to be that there are many existential philosophies that remain unreconciled with one another. Another reason might be that existential philosophies resort to speculative constructs to fill gaps in matters of knowledge until these aspects have developed into a science that can successfully comply with demands for practical proof. The presence of speculative concepts creates a dangerous opening for risk and damage in our optimization efforts. That is particularly so if speculation leaves scientific methods behind and takes flights of imagination with diminished care in defining premises or disclosing its speculative character and methods of developing conclusions. The conclusory nature of a nonscientific speculative philosophy decreases our opportunities to evaluate its presentations and may cause us to rely on superficial concordances in its premises, arguments, and conclusions with what we suppose or want to be true and want to attain. The paucity of its scientific clarity may combine with our lack of ability to investigate its claims. But we may also condition ourselves to avert our mind from what we could find and understand. We may want to believe that speculative concepts are correct. This may have us rely even more on superficial concordances. They might even be embedded to sway us in favor of a philosophy that we might otherwise not adopt.

Mistakes in nonscientific speculative philosophies should reveal themselves during and after their implementation. Only, this type of proof can subject us to great risks of damage. Even after we incur such damage, the factually untethered nature of a nonscientific speculative philosophy may forestall us from determining the true causes for our failure. To avoid such consequences, an existential philosophy has to adhere to a scientific method of speculation that reveals its premises, allows us to follow their application, and limits its claims to what the argument allows it to conclude. But we may not take it upon us to review and to differentiate accordingly and may mistrust all speculative philosophies, particularly after being apprised of warning examples.

Perhaps most of all, we may resist considering speculative philosophies because we have already been taken in by a speculative philosophy that precludes us from considering other speculative philosophies even if they are scientifically legitimate. Notwithstanding, unless
we are completely satisfied with the guidance such a philosophy gives
us, it appears useful to review legitimate alternatives. Our considerations might be rewarded by establishing a better approach toward the
pursuit of some or all our needs, if it is only by helping us define our
own premises and philosophy in differentiation from what we review.
To facilitate such considerations, scientific philosophies have to make
themselves available. This requires that they avail individuals of technical access to them. Only, that may not suffice because many philosophies are restrictive in the substantive access they permit. For one,
they are often difficult to understand. That may have various reasons.
Some of them were recorded or have reached us only in fragments. Issues of language, style, and organization might pose a problem. Translations may be imprecise. Archaic terminology may make writings difficult to understand. Authors may have had problems in clearly expressing themselves. They may not have been aware or may not have
cared that they left important presumptions and parts of their arguments unexpressed or poorly described. Writings might build on their
authors' interpretations of other philosophies that are not explained in
sufficient detail. They might use arcane language that their authors or
other philosophers coined. They may give new specialized meaning to
commonly used words. These problems make it frequently difficult if
not impossible to find clear meaning in the statements of a philosophy
or to compare or correlate the substances of philosophies. They often
prevent or limit direct access by those who could benefit from it.

These problems require that persons with studied knowledge of
these philosophies become intermediaries. The at times considerable
communicative shortcomings of philosophies may also pose a significant burden on the resources of academic philosophers who might try
to become such intermediaries. Many of their activities may be preoccupied with deciphering, translating, explaining, and speculating what
original philosophers have expressed and in the discussion of their insights with other researchers of these philosophies. It might appear to
be a relatively minor stride to make that work accessible to a broader
audience. Yet, often, researchers become so enveloped in the universe
of a philosophy they are reviewing that they succumb to many of the
original or grown communicative shortcomings of that philosophy. In
an effort to obtain intimate understanding of an original philosopher's
mindset, they may assume that philosopher's terminology to elucidate

that mindset. For this reason, it may be difficult among specialists in different philosophies to truly understand one another. That may not only be so because each philosophy might use unfamiliar terminology but also because each philosophy may attribute partly different meaning to common language. While experts may enable competent comparisons by gaining proficiency in multiple philosophies, that does not significantly assist the dissemination of a philosophy if their explanations continue within the particularities of one philosophy. This does not change much if they create translation mechanisms between philosophies. To make veiled philosophies more accessible, they will have to be translated into commonly understandable terminology.

The absorption and maintenance of the original code of philosophies may be an understandable and partly necessary requirement to become familiar with and understand works that are often extremely challenging and to succeed in not falsifying their meaning. Translating a philosophy carries a high risk of misinterpretation. However, experts who comprehend its meaning should be able to express it in commonly understandable terminology. Such a popularized expression should also be in the interest of such experts because remaining within expert jargon may prevent a philosophy from making its case and conferring the benefits it promises. It sentences an existential philosophy and its endorsers to a speculative state and its potential beneficiaries to a relatively unhappy existence. Having dedicated their life's work to an existential philosophy, specialists in it should believe that it has much to give and they should be uniquely motivated to popularize its content. That an existential philosophy has not been popularized may indicate that its experts may not have an interest to disseminate its message.

One reason popularization is not undertaken might be that experts wish to reserve the philosophy with which they are occupied to elites and desire to forestall broader access. They might form part of a power structure that attempts to subject other parts of a society to the rule of the initiated. Another reason experts might not desire to popularize a philosophy might be that it represents an agenda that might not be accepted if it is fully revealed. The resulting veiled indoctrination may be broadly employed or focus on subjects who go on to positions in which it can operate in favor of objectives that originators and expert promulgators want to have promoted and prevail. Even if they are not aware of bias in their positions and regard them as scientifically justifiable and able to withstand critical scrutiny, they may fear additional adversity. They may be concerned that representatives of other philosophies or attitudes they deem erroneous might attack them, their philosophy, and its followers if the philosophy gains attention.

Another motive for not popularizing an existential philosophy might be that experts are prohibited from doing so. However, their reluctance appears to continue in societies that do not encumber their freedom. In such settings, experts might occupy themselves with such philosophies for reasons other than their confidence that these could benefit humanity or even a segment of humanity. They may keep existential philosophies alive in their minds because of considerations related to the teaching of philosophy and its institutions. Academic institutions may be charged or permitted to keep an extensive scope of speculative philosophies alive. Their commissioned inclusiveness may be sourced in the ignorance of sponsors regarding the merit of philosophies or the reluctance of these to become involved in deciding such matters. Nor may those administrating philosophical schools want to interdict the teaching of any accredited philosophy. A selective curriculum may be viewed as an affront to freedom. It may be regarded as an overt act to suppress an undesirable philosophy or as an opening to future unwarranted discrimination. New philosophies are more likely to be excluded. Academic institutions may require that they establish themselves in certain ways before they are given a place in an institution's curriculum. Yet, once philosophies are academically established, they may be very difficult to remove. They may assume an encapsulated status that may neither pursue nor tolerate their improvement. Academic treatments may focus on interpretations of the original works.

There may be valid reasons to maintain a broad offering of existential philosophies in their original substance. One may be the establishment of foundations on which later philosophies build without repeating these. Another may be that philosophies define themselves by differentiations from other philosophies and can be better perceived if these are understood. A further reason would be lacking development or verification of their substance. Beyond this, there may be interest in establishing and keeping a historical record of how existential philosophy has developed. Keeping a wide range of speculative philosophies present may further be a matter of academic stature and tradition.

Experts may also be interested in a broad, stable curriculum for reasons of their employment. Since teaching institutions are the sole employers for professional philosophers, it is in their interest to maximize the positions that can be justified in such institutions. That justification is easiest if a broad range of speculative philosophies can be maintained and if their speculative nature is not resolved. Expertise in any acknowledged philosophy might secure a desirable academic position regardless of such a philosophy's relevance. Once their position is dependent on the philosophy they teach, they might be disinclined to

concede its irrelevance or failings. Nor might they be disposed to facilitate ready access to the philosophies they oversee for concern that an
understanding of them by others might invite assertions of irrelevance
or failings. But even if reasons to make such assertions are known, col-
leagues might be reluctant to attack the relevance of philosophies col-
leagues administrate. They might have concerns about becoming subjects of such attacks as well or exciting a greater discussion about the
funding or justifiability of philosophical institutions or their positions,
compensation, and other benefits. Philosophical experts may then habitually skirt issues of practical relevance for economic reasons.

However, if existential philosophies are to have any purpose in
accordance with their claim of existential importance, their mere academic preservation is insufficient. Any philosophy that purports to offer guidance in existential matters must present itself in ways that allow such guidance to be understood, considered, accepted, practiced,
dismissed, or improved by intended beneficiaries. Hence, experts that
take the philosophy they represent seriously must render that philosophy accessible. There might be obstacles that an offering cannot control. Individuals might be biased by philosophies already residing in or
influencing their mind against considering other existential philosophies. But even if this makes it harder to gain consideration, this must
not keep an existential philosophy from making its teachings available
if it is to possess any chance of realization. Yet there may be another,
more justified and resolvable issue that might foreclose consideration
by designated beneficiaries. They may be unwilling to entrust their life
to a philosophy that represents one viewpoint among others that are
presented by competing philosophies. Even if specialists could render
their philosophies generally comprehensible, nonexperts might not be
able or prepared to commit the time and effort to immerse themselves
in a diversity of speculative philosophies. They might demand that experts examine one another's philosophies, discuss their validities and
shortcomings, and present their findings in ways that comply with the
same communicative standards as their initial presentations. That appears to be an appropriate demand because professional philosophers
are trained to review and critique the logical structure and substance
of arguments and can consecrate more time to such efforts. Their assessment of one another's philosophies may add a clarifying pointed-
ness to such an undertaking. Nonexperts may further demand that experts in these philosophies undertake reconciliation work before they
submit them for practical implementation. That seems to be a legitimate requirement because the reconciliation of philosophies promises
to be difficult and time-consuming even if these were to be translated

into the same terminology and comparative opinions were presented. Reconciliation may necessitate a partial or total abandonment or adjustment of philosophies. In addition, the involved considerations may give rise to important new developments. Experts appear to be in the best position to render such decisions and their determinations could be presumed to be reliable because their consent after initially divergent positions is likely to reflect a fully considered change. If speculative aspects of existential philosophies do not allow present clarification into one construct, experts would be uniquely qualified to lay out the alternatives of scientifically legitimate speculation and to describe the scope and consequences of this multiplicity of models. They might also give advice on how speculative concepts might be practically confirmed and thus advance existential philosophy. They would be duty-bound to attend the development of existential philosophy until one comprehensive solution to common and general matters of our needs is derived. The application of scientific principles to interchangeable human characteristics has the logical result that proof will successively and ultimately entirely reduce our search to one result. It generally portends that the speculative aspects of existential philosophy will ultimately transform into an exact science of human happiness. Experts in existential philosophies may hence provide a critically useful service to humanity. Their assumption of responsibility may even be essential for individual and collective survival. Our development and ascent in power may not leave us much room for experiments and injudicious choices in addressing existential problems. Even if philosophical guidance should not be a matter of life or death, any lack of guidance may unnecessarily cause large numbers of humans to be afflicted with pain and restrict their thriving. Unless philosophers admit that their work is pointless, they must claim that they may be in possession of at least a partial recipe for an antidote to human distress. Their failure to perfect it and make it available may strike us as cruel and irresponsible.

Experts in existential philosophies may not be comfortable with their responsibility. Fulfilling their vanguard function may demand a drastic change in their outlook and practice. They must overcome the divisions of their particular orientations. They may have to supersede reverence for particular philosophers or their philosophies with a general commitment to existential philosophy. They have to emerge from academic seclusion and place their activities in the center of public interest. Moreover, the exercise of their responsibility may be burdened with danger and personal sacrifice because the assumption by philosophy of its rightful leadership in human development may meet with resistance. Such a resistance may be caused by fear of transformation even if current circumstances leave room for improvement. It may also be attributable to interests that benefit from an antecedent state of confusion or the relative order they manage to maintain. Both the fear of losing ground and the fear of losing overproportional benefits may motivate countermeasures against active scientific philosophical practice, its originators, and its promoters. These measures may entail the necessity to respond defensively. Additionally, nonscientific philosophies may pose independent threats of irretrievable damage that may suggest defensive measures against them. Philosophers may thus become involved as leaders in human affairs. Although scientific existential philosophies have already participated and made progress in shaping human pursuits, they have often suffered perversion and suppression at the hands of unscientific philosophies or due to the pressures of attacking and defending against them. Where scientific philosophies were successful in motivating individuals to shape their life according to them, their inherent errors or lack of development as well as incomplete or erroneous acceptance or implementation may have added obstacles. These problems frequently left them discredited and their supporters desolate. Many humans have therefore come to distrust schemes purportedly aimed at improving their happiness.

There may then be daunting problems that philosophy has to overcome if it is to fulfill its mission. But who else could competently undertake this mission? History instructs us that a void of competent philosophical leadership will be rapidly occupied by nonscientific impostors to whom humanity will look for guidance in its confusion and pain. Regardless of whether their guidance is well-meant or offered for nefarious purposes, following them may cause avoidable detrimental consequences. Although scientifically based philosophical movements may derail and falter from their own deficiencies, there does not seem to be any alternative to scientific progression. The development of a unified scientific existential philosophy requires that professional philosophers establish it and see it through to a stable existence. Without their initiative, hope wanes that humanity can advance and realize its potential. The preservation of philosophies by academic institutions reveals itself as an invaluable foundation for this reorientation. They have been able to enshrine sources of enlightenment similar to some monasteries, schools, and libraries that were their keepers before, despite a world governed by unprincipled behavior, nonscientific, superstitious philosophies, or misguided scientific philosophies. Most technical aspects of philosophy have succeeded in freeing themselves from the paralyzing grip of nonscientific powers. These powers have largely receded and transformed to exclude technical sciences. Yet, in many respects, they have continued their domination over the application of technical sciences and human life beyond them. To complete its mission of illuminating the world, philosophy must complement the establishment of a first level of scientific technical knowledge with the institution of a second scientific level of knowledge about purpose.

However, the generality of this philosophical positioning would disregard the particularizations of needs that weigh so heavily on our happiness and thus would be only of limited utility. Existential philosophies that venture beyond commonalities into individual particularities can only hope to account entirely for the principles that apply to the happiness of one person. Comprehensive guidance would have to accommodate a large number of variants to establish optimized happiness for individuals. This might entail the fragmentation of the philosophy every time personalities could differ. It would splinter an existential philosophy into unmanageable multitudes of philosophies. Idiosyncratic differences necessarily render a comprehensive substantive philosophy with universal pertinence impossible. We may attain some success in drawing on particularized existential philosophies that apply to us and others if we share sufficient particularities with them. An existential philosophy that embraces idiosyncrasies should be able to increase the depth of its applicability as it narrows its scope to certain shared types of particularities. Such a specialization might empower a philosophy to provide capable assistance to some groups of individuals in some areas. Yet, to the extent interests it addresses do not exist alone, the differences in the remaining context of individuals' pursuits may still burden such specialized philosophies with problems of subjective divergence. To avoid being embroiled in such intractable problems, specialized philosophies may exclude coverage of such aspects. But that may dispossess such philosophies of much of their utility because they would leave us to manage the dissonance of particularities in us and in our relationships with other individuals on our own.

The failure of the idea of a comprehensive substantive existential philosophy that can securely guide us in all our affairs might be a disappointing result that we are not willing to suffer. We may not be willing to let the potential of essential commonalities among humans be overruled by separating idiosyncrasies. We may claim that idiosyncrasies keep us from acting in our true interest and denounce them for causing irritation and insecurity within ourselves and with one another. We may see in them the cause for unnecessary complexity in our search for happiness and our inability to find happiness. We may view individualized aspects of happiness as a result of errors, inadequacies, and deformations. We may therefore believe that we must transcend and extinguish these idiosyncrasies and generate an existence that is based on commonality if we want to achieve a maximum of happiness. For such a system to take hold, we may not deem it sufficient to only suppress idiosyncrasies because they persist as inherently virulent and because their dissatisfaction still leaves us unhappy. We may consider it necessary to remove idiosyncrasies with their root by removing their causes. We may think that it should be possible to shape an ideal society of humans with superior capabilities of creating and maintaining happiness. This may necessitate that individuals comply with a genetic standard. To form sufficient similarity, individual genetic substance might have to be unified to where individuals are mere copies of one another. In addition, such individuals would have to be exposed to the same or at least similar circumstances, experiences, information, and education and would have to live and pursue activities without significant differences. To achieve this, needs for self-realization, expression, and self-determination would have to be neutralized. An effort to improve happiness thus may produce a temptation to streamline us, others, and other conditions so the pursuit of happiness becomes scientifically traceable, predictable, and manageable. Such a rationalization of our production of happiness might appear as a reasonable response to the problems that individual differences cause. These make it difficult to administrate the pursuit of happiness in a society. They can lead to interference, estrangement, and friction. The interaction of distinctive pursuits increases problems in the establishment of an environment in which participants can find fulfillment. It further renders coordinated behavior for the achievement of coexistential objectives more difficult to arrange. The management of idiosyncratic pursuits necessitates far more extensive protective regulation, enforcement, judgment, negotiation, self-restraint, and vigilance compared to common pursuits.

Only, an equalization of personalities and of environmental circumstances would not necessarily solve the problems of interference, estrangement, and friction among individuals. If we were all the same and engaged in the same activities to satisfy the same needs, we would require and might compete for the same means. Arguably, these problems might be solved by an undifferentiated philosophy. But it is hard to see how differentiated means we require for high levels of pursuits could be created if all humans had the same abilities and had to apply them without specialization. We would each have to be able to create or find all the resources we need autonomously or by bundling parallel individual efforts. Unless we are highly advanced on an individual level to secure means for ourselves, or a society has evolved to where independent structures and processes provide our means, our ability to satisfy our needs would be severely limited. It is also challenging to conceive how we could progress to an advanced state of development under such strident conditions of equalization. More than that, all developments would have to come about exactly in the same manner for each individual to maintain equal conditions. This may cause unmanageable logistical problems. Trials would impart the additional burden of being universally undertaken. Failures and mistakes could therefore cause more severe consequences. Even if we should manage to initially create a functional society of identical personalities and pursuits in an identical environment, it is difficult to envision how such a world could be maintained. All activities and circumstances would have to be controlled in ways that would prevent material deviations. Even if intentional eccentricities could be foiled, such a system would have to control the potential that individuals might meet with different occurrences that might give rise to unintentional differences. We could not empower selected humans to manage such a system because this differentiation would destroy the uniformity of all participants and could easily lead to our disadvantagement by ruling individuals or classes.

To avoid such a result, we might hand over control to an independent nonhuman entity. Then again, subjecting ourselves in such a comprehensive manner to a mechanism of human fabrication entails similar dangers of abuse. This transfer of control may also breed dangers of malfunction that might cause us to recoil. Our subjection to an external authority exposes us to unacceptable risk. As a better alternative, we might attribute control functions to each individual to be exercised in an identical and integrated manner by all. But our imagination may not be able to grasp a setting where we are all the same and live under the same circumstances. The prospects of the requirements to construct and keep such a system stable, of what might go wrong, and what the effects of such a system might be on our happiness and our survival and thriving may cause concern and apprehension. Even if adjustments should succeed, homogeneity and the requirements for its maintenance may require or threaten unacceptable repercussions. Notwithstanding, the questionable feasibility and benefits of a radically equalized society have not kept humans from rejecting individuality and setting forth and endeavoring to implement substantive equalization. Such efforts, even if they are only incremental and stop short of being comprehensive, may engender many of the same problems that full-fledged equalization efforts might entail. But individual superimpositions on general aspects may pose an even more insidious threat in the purported formation of general existential philosophies and in equalization efforts. The next chapter examines these threats.

CHAPTER 12
IDEALISTIC CONVERSION

The subjective beginning of existential philosophies is reflected in the beginnings of many such philosophies. They often originate in or are ascribed to the views of a single founding individual or a group of only few. Existential philosophies rarely represent an amalgamation or collection of the viewpoints of many in their inception. In consequence of this genesis, existential philosophies tend to be heavily influenced by the individual experiences and the personalities of their founders. Their bias about the nature of happiness and about its workings is often quite obvious. Such philosophies regularly focus on certain experiences of pleasure, desire, pain, or fear over others. They also claim certain forms of pain or fear as more abominable than others and certain forms of pleasure or desire as more exalted, important, or rewarding than others. Their bias toward particular ways of happiness is usually accompanied by a bias against other forms or manners of pursuit.

The subjective origins of existential philosophies are bound to create results with limited or no shared applicability. The effectiveness of such a philosophy for any aspect of our happiness is questionable. The details of our personality and our circumstances may, despite all similarity, differ from those of the originators of such philosophies in significant ways. An existential philosophy might only contain a recipe on how happiness can be achieved for those individuals who share its premises on a particular topic or a range of topics. This might permit originators to establish a group of followers, an interest group, whose members share opinions and emotional attitudes about certain causes of happiness. Some of these causes may be important or even critical. Still, the remaining diversity of positions will likely cause persons who share one or more interests to disagree on multiple others. Individual differences may further result in disagreements regarding the intensity and modalities of pursuit for shared interests. This restricts the possible coherence among individuals even if they share certain interests. Thus, even under most favorable conditions, the systems established by idiosyncratic existential philosophies would have to leave supporters free to pursue their divergent interests independently or in other associations. To maximize happiness, we would have to be able to opt partly into or out of an existential philosophy depending on its correspondence with our individual situation. Such practice would create a system of modules, of topical philosophies that we might join to promote a particular item of pursuit and leave if they do not sufficiently promote our happiness or their purpose is fulfilled. A philosophy that has our interests in mind or respects these interests will admit its limitations. It will concede us the freedom to contemplate and debate its principles so we can decide whether and to what extent they benefit our pursuits. Although it may publicize its knowledge, it would leave it to us whether and to what extent we follow its teachings. It would grant individuals the privilege to join and depart without compulsion.

That idiosyncratic existential philosophies may not take such a liberal position demonstrates that their promoters desire to take advantage of others by having them subscribe to their philosophy. Such an attitude may develop from a variety of positions. As promoters of a philosophy, we may be interested in assisting other individuals. Their survival and thriving may satisfy or help to satisfy some of our needs. We may desire that individuals for whom we care adopt philosophies that we have learned to acknowledge as helpful or necessary to maintain, increase, or maximize our happiness or that we deem to be beneficial for these individuals. This may motivate us to overcome their resistance to the acceptance of such philosophies. However, because the happiness of such individuals is our objective, we may be sensitive to the question whether and to what extent the imposition of a philosophy on them promotes that happiness. We may ask whether assisting others to develop their own philosophy based on their particular conditions might yield better results. But we may reserve our interest in the happiness of others and related scruples toward the imposition of a philosophy to a relatively small number of individuals. Our desire to impose a philosophy on others may also spring from the fact that our pursuit of happiness intersects in further contexts with the pursuits by other individuals. We may determine that we need the cooperation of others for the fulfillment of our needs or that we suffer from their interference with our pursuits. That other individuals pursue happiness and that we need to deal with their pursuits while pursuing ours complicates our planning considerably. We have to consider and include into our plans that other individuals possess diverging ideas regarding their happiness and that their schemes may detract from our pursuits. The benefits we desire may be conditioned upon the subscription of a sufficient number of other individuals to a compliant philosophy.

Our philosophy may find sufficient assistance from individuals whose interests are aligned with our interests. If a philosophy is formulated to benefit a particular group of beneficiaries, their assistance may be expected. Yet the number of individuals whose compliance or noninterference would be necessary or useful often exceeds the number of individuals to whom that philosophy applies. We can try to address the potential interference and lack of protection and support by other individuals through the threat or exercising of adverse activities. Still, in an interactive system, other participants may try to compel us to curb our interests and to promote their interests as well. Even if they do not take an aggressive stance, they may try to defend their interests and independence, recoup their losses, or obtain retribution. This places us at risk of confrontation and not being able to maximize our happiness because of strife or the pall of its continuing potential. We may therefore determine that we can better advance our needs if we avoid the application or threat of adversarial activities concerning others. To make a philosophy function without compulsion, we might resort to manipulation. We may deceive others about our intent to use them so we can extract means for our pursuit of our happiness from or through them. We may conceal or misrepresent our activities against their interests to avoid their defenses and to obtain and secure means from them or otherwise at their cost. Conversely, we may be subjected to attempts by others to manipulate us for their benefit. The discovery of manipulations creates a high risk of repercussions because victims and those in solidarity with them may take protective, retributory, or corrective action. That action may take similar forms as a reaction to coercion. The ensuing risk of conflict makes the pursuit of happiness through manipulation seem antithetical to our goal of improving our happiness. In consideration of the risks of coercion and manipulation, we might not be certain that we can gain and maintain our advantage in such competition. We might doubt whether we can prevent significant repercussions from defensive reactions to our impositions or our endeavors in defending ourselves. Alone the preparatory and preventive preoccupations and barriers we and others maintain may severely restrict our potential. We may realize that coercion and manipulation are not the most effective or efficient manners to advance our happiness. To maximize our happiness, it seems necessary that we arrive at a better arrangement with others that renders their behavior compliant with our wishes. Such an arrangement appears possible if we could convince others to act voluntarily in ways that advance our interests. We may convince others to serve the interests of our happiness in a more secure manner if we can convince them that doing so will serve their happiness as well and if such a conviction is based in fact.

To that end, we will have to devise a philosophy for those individuals whose compliance with our requirements we desire and convince them that this philosophy applies to them. We may have a philosophy that cannot permit others to pursue happiness in the same way or must reserve certain portions of activity if we are to succeed in our objectives. To motivate others to protect and support such a system of our philosophy and keep them from interfering would require that others follow a compliant but different philosophy. Such a mode of coexistence would confront us with considerable complexity. We would have to build and maintain a philosophy for ourselves and at least one other philosophy, or a more restricted philosophy, for those whose submission we require. It seems unlikely that such a dual system of beneficiary and subservient philosophies could remain stable, particularly if it is openly employed. It still would take advantage of the pursuits of certain individuals to facilitate the pursuit of happiness by the beneficiaries of the system. A dual system may allow for some fulfillment to those who cater to the privileged group's fulfillment of needs. But it is instituted with the primary objective of securing the integrity of privileged pursuits. This inequity threatens to expose an auxiliary existential philosophy devised for such purpose as a sham.

If the ability of subservient individuals to produce happiness for themselves under that auxiliary philosophy is significantly lower and such individuals become aware of that fact and the difference in philosophies, they might question their philosophy. They might ask why there should be separate philosophies. This would lead to the question whether the philosophy devised for the subservient class by the privileged reflects the best manner of pursuing the happiness for subservient individuals. They might deem themselves better served by adopting the philosophy of the privileged class or a third philosophy. These considerations may arise even if a dual system seems to provide sufficient means to members of the subservient class. The philosophy that benefits overproportionally from the protection, support, and noninterference by the subservient class might still appear to be preferable, inducing subservient individuals to adopt that philosophy. However, because the privileged philosophy relies on generating compliance by others according to a different set of rules, the accession of others to the same philosophy would render them competitors for privilege. Beyond that, such accession threatens to leave an insufficient quantity of individuals in the service class to adequately cater to the needs of the privileged. Accessions into the privileged class would create the interferences and the failure of protection and support that the system was built to avoid. They would threaten to make the continuing existence of the privileged class impossible. When the inherent instability of a dual system comes to bear, the privileged class of such a system might harden its interior boundaries by coercion or manipulation. If such attempts are unsuccessful, a dual system may give way to the pursuit of independent philosophies. Such a mode of relating to others may succeed in the form of a cooperative or independent coexistence. It may also deteriorate into a competitive struggle of philosophies or unprincipled, topical pursuits. Privileged individuals in a dual system may try to foreclose the destabilization of their system by concealing its dual nature as much as possible. They may attempt to hide their subscription to a different or a supplemented philosophy compared to the philosophy they employ in motivating others to cater to them. Yet maintaining this illusion may require restraining contortions by the privileged and a considerable investment of resources into control measures. Moreover, such a system would still carry the hazard of exposure and severe harm to the privileged upon the discovery of their fraud.

If we wanted to avoid the considerable complexities, fragilities, and risks of a dual system entirely, we might fashion one philosophy that is geared to apply to the entire system. The organization of a system according to one philosophy does not necessarily mean that such a system must be peaceful. Even if all members of a society shared the same philosophy, that philosophy might permit or encourage them to prey upon or to otherwise abuse one another. The philosophy might approve total freedom in that undertaking, or it might subject behavior to certain rules. It might sponsor the same right of all members to pursue their needs even if that pursuit damages others. Some individuals might secure desired advantages by leveraging relative strengths. However, the threat of conflict and deprivation may cause even them to lose confidence that they could maximize their concerns in such a system. To pacify such a system, it must be effective for the advancement of all its members. This requires that we reconcile the behavior of individuals. Motivating others to abstain from interfering with our pursuits and to instead assist in our pursuits entails that we relinquish attempts to obtain overproportional benefits and that we practice mutuality. As we expect others to protect and support our pursuits and to abstain from interfering with our happiness, we have to do the same in return. Such a single philosophical system of mutuality appears to carry a potential of providing some benefits to us. But it also appears to require us to give up the exclusive pursuit of our interests to the extent they would unduly infringe on other individuals' legitimate pursuits. Commitment to the mutuality of protection, support, and noninterference involves the principle of equality in what individuals can demand from one another because they can only call for what they are willing to give. Such a system may require that members compromise what would make them happiest for the sake of securing a stable level of happiness below the perceived maximum potential. This poses the question whether the sacrifices required in a compromise of an individual existential philosophy to include others are worth the benefits.

This question may be difficult to answer for us even if a system of mutuality works flawlessly. The difficulty may be attributable to our inability or unwillingness to test alternative systems or to develop our own philosophy. As a consequence, we might lack the competence to tell whether we would fare better in a mutual system, a system of duality, or in another system. Depending on our personality and circumstances, we may estimate the success of our participation in a system posited by an existential philosophy differently. If we believe that we are vulnerable, we may deem our chances improved if we are part of a unified system based on mutuality or another form that provides protective and supportive structures and processes. If we consider ourselves cunning and influential enough, we may think that we can fare better in a dual or in an unregulated single system. To bring about the same effect without the formal institution of a dual or a liberal single system, we may modify our participation in a mutual system. We may try to achieve the benefits of the system without honoring our obligations to the system. We may only pretend to be constructive participants and manipulate the system so we draw more benefits than others. Such deviations, if they are sufficiently pervasive or severe, may translate a mutual system into a dual system that institutionalizes an imbalance surreptitiously. Beyond that, we may perceive ourselves to be so powerful that we would have a better chance of obtaining happiness without being tied to any system, rules, or parameters. We may therefore promote the absolute freedom of individuals to pursue happiness according to their own philosophy or without a philosophy.

Individuals may form and change features of their personal philosophies as the fulfillment level for their needs fluctuates and as they deem themselves more or less capable to compete successfully and secure advantages over others. These and other assessments may be only partly based on examinations of facts and their logical development. They may also be founded on emotional factors. In addition, individual philosophies may contain a strong aspect of speculation about past, present, and future circumstances. That speculation may hinge on incomplete indicators or indications may be ignored, insufficiently understood, or misinterpreted. These aspects may condition individuals to create inapplicable philosophies of their own or to deem inapplicable external philosophies appropriate for them. A lack of applicability should naturally limit the maintenance and spread of an idiosyncratic philosophy. To the extent individuals have built their own philosophy, they might adjust it relatively easily to their deviating experiences. Adjustments may be more challenging if we are caught in a philosophical system. As reality catches up with and disproves mistaken approaches, discredited philosophies should cease to attract individuals. This outcome would seem to be unavoidable even if proponents apply deceptions to mask the subjectivity of their views. Existential philosophies that involve others are destined to reveal their feasibility through the compatibility of developments. Only, despite that inevitable clarification, the complexity and scale of activities that are claimed to result in happiness may delay the emergence of convincingly positive or negative effects and may thus intensify their possible detriment. Inapplicable existential philosophies may also be hard to shed if their principles have permeated our environment. The harm they may cause until and after disillusionment sets in may therefore be devastating.

The threat external existential philosophies pose for our happiness should render us suspicious and disinclined to adopt them. However, such considerations may not overcome our inclination to trust external philosophies. That inclination may be founded on instinctive mechanisms by which we adopt philosophies from our caretakers. We may be genetically or environmentally programmed to imitate and assume their behavior and underlying mental processes. We may also be programmed to fit ourselves into the social order of our environment as well as the actualities of our environment generally. These acquired manners of pursuit merge with our genetic programming that already instructs us how to behave as a matter of instinct. Hence, the idea that we develop an initial existential philosophy of our own as a matter of our consideration appears to be a fiction. We are or become generally conditioned to pursue our needs in a set way and to regard these pursuits as attending our happiness. Our genetic and acquired instinctive mechanisms condition us to evaluate these matters according to their signals of pain and pleasure. It is only within these presets and their mandates and restrictions that we begin to develop our own considerations about happiness. Our philosophy may not be adequately developed because of our unreflecting familiarity with our genetic and acquired instincts. We may not reflect much on our needs or instinctive formulas for pursuit and whether they are in our interest. Our lack of reflection may cause us to seek solutions in technical inquiries to improve our happiness. Because our needs seem to have already decided what will make us happy, it appears legitimate that we concentrate on the creation of means and develop and harness technology in an effort of fulfilling our needs more effectively and efficiently. Such advancements cannot give us purpose. It cannot uncover for us what we want, what would satisfy us and make us happy. All technical issues we pursue are subordinated to answering his question. Nevertheless, a technical stage may be vital in advancing our cognizance of our needs. As we become more astute in pursuing and fulfilling needs, that capacity and its application contrast our relative lack of knowledge what those needs are, how they interrelate, and that their automatic guidance of our behavior might not optimize our happiness. That realization may motivate us to fill our void in knowing what will make us happy. We may attempt to develop guidance on our own by referring to our experiences and explorations. We may also look to external sources or allow them to inform us at their initiative. While we may derive some guidance from such personal and external references, they may omit or misaddress important features of our desires. As long as we can arrange a tolerable way of living, we may console ourselves. We may not believe that a more useful philosophy might exist or that it would warrant the additional efforts that might be necessary to bring it to fruition. Because our philosophies are the result of genetics, instruction, and other circumstances that have fused into cultural traditions, habits, and our setting, we might not question them. Significant segments of our generated or adopted philosophies might be dedicated to vindicating why they do not enable more happiness. Then again, as long as we perceive deficiencies, we may search for or be open to remedies.

In these permutations, our genetic, acquired, and other personal and environmental circumstances determine the extent of our individual forays compared to our acceptance of external influences in our considerations. Yet, even if we are independent-minded, we are prone to be overwhelmed by the difficulty of developing our own existential philosophy. In the absence of a philosophy that reveals and speaks to our wishes and needs and helps us respond to them with knowledge, we may try to fill our lack of confidence with external help. Even if we recognize the necessity of individual trials, we may see ourselves unable to go forward with them. The pervasive impact of our idiosyncratic needs on our happiness would require us to intensely and broadly engage in trials to find better let alone ideal ways of satisfying our needs. Further, we may not have sufficient clarity about our existential needs and their requirements, their interaction, or the relation between idiosyncratic and existential needs. Considering the scope of our insecurities, we may not consider personal trials a feasible option to improve our pursuits, except perhaps in some circumscribed areas that may be mostly of a technical nature. We may claim to possess neither the necessary resources nor a competent plan to undertake the extensive discovery that appears to be indicated. We may fear that our trials might overwhelm us, not appropriately reward us, or trigger adversities. We may presume that the adoption of external philosophies may give us reprieve from personal trials. We may prefer subscribing to an already

implemented philosophy in search for predictability. To gain a measure of happiness under the purportedly thought-out scheme of such a
philosophy, we may be willing to compromise some of our pursuits.

In our search for reliable guidance, we may disregard scientific
speculations by because they disclose their premises and the speculative character of their concepts. Their lacking assurance and our aver-
sion against experiments may inspire us toward nonscientific philosophies that seem certain in their claims. We may follow them provided
that they can deliver a trustworthy impression on us, manage contradictory evidence, and give us sufficient indications regarding the reliability of their advice. They might achieve this in part by surrounding
speculative claims with claimed corroboration and by making claims
of resolution that, while they cannot be proved, also cannot be readily
disproved. We may accept their unproven representations and speculations because we want to believe them. Our desire to find solutions
to our fear and pain focuses on them because we see no other or better way to improve or even maintain our happiness. This voluntary investment of belief may be complemented by assertions of such philosophies that their teachings must be unquestioningly accepted if we are
to benefit from them. These self-inflicted and external indoctrinations
may subdue our critical thinking. We may allow them to dispel doubt,
inconsistencies, and failures not only by externalizing blame but also
by creating imaginary present of future adjuncts to our world in which
they claim all problems are or will be resolved. That removal of issues
from reasonable consideration may afford them with a position of unassailability no matter how nonsensical their averments may be.

Notwithstanding, this strategy alone may not suffice to keep us
enthralled if our dissatisfaction is not resolved or increases under their
leadership. To entrench and preserve their position, nonscientific existential philosophies may resort to proven practical strategies that may
exist independently of them. They may take up popular objectives and
pursuits that are already successful and confer upon them philosophical legitimization. This may make them and their ideas seem to be the
source for the prosperity to which they attach a philosophical expression. They may also incorporate proven aspects of scientific existential
philosophies and claim such concepts to have been authored by them.
They may further set forth some valid practical advancements of their
own. The collection, reiteration, and possible advancement of insights
by such philosophies may appear unobjectionable past possible claims
of plagiarism. But such a practical philosophy might be illegitimate for
several other interrelated reasons. It may constrain its followers' considerations to a limited focus dedicated to the fulfillment of proximate

needs and wishes. This might forestall individuals from developing a more comprehensive philosophy. The extensive, familiar fulfillment of needs within the confines of the philosophy may make it seem largely unnecessary to develop additional insights. That lack of coverage may lead to manners of pursuit that benefit subjects in some respects but damage them in other respects and ultimately even the concerns that appear to be the focal points of such a philosophy. A limited practical philosophy may render subjects of that philosophy prone to manipulation because they may be merely aware of some needs and distracted from others. If concerns not addressed by such a practical philosophy break through in subjects' minds, they may needlessly suffer because of a systematic disregard for such concerns. Even if individuals realize that such a philosophy does not represent all of their aspirations, they may not want to jeopardize its successful representation in the areas it covers. Such an appreciation and reluctance may leave an incomplete practical philosophy intact and its supporters with dispersed and incomplete philosophical views on issues they deem or are made to believe to be collateral. They may accept that it is upon them to find answers in supplemental or individual philosophies in harmony with the principal practical philosophy that seems to secure their existence.

However, the limitation of its scope may also translate into unrest that may affect the stability of its established aspects. To keep the effects of needs they cannot or refuse to cover at bay, practical philosophies may propound reasons, possibly comprising otherworldly satisfaction, why such needs cannot or should not be pursued or met, even if such claims were not the origin of such a philosophy. But nonscientific philosophies that originated in notions of belief may use the convincing power of incomplete practical philosophies as well to instill or reinforce allegiance to their beliefs. The trust individuals extend to a philosophy that seems to reflect and resolve many or all of their basic existential concerns may motivate them to trust its speculative aspects that exceed these concerns. Its practical basis may constitute a lure to make them accept speculation. Such mechanisms, whether intentionally or coincidentally installed, may use both belief and proven aspects to gloss over doubt, inconsistencies, or failures. More than that, they may detract us from exploring and proving aspects that do not agree with their dogma. They might even have us renounce insights we have already confirmed. They may remove aspects of our life from our consideration. Nonscientific speculative philosophies may therefore arrest and reverse our progress as individuals and as a species. Their combination with scientific speculative and practical philosophies may render such detrimental philosophies difficult to discern or fight.

The delinquencies that allow belief-based and incomplete existential philosophies to gain influence and persist appear to be caused and advanced by our lack of determination to fully develop our philosophy. Our absence of insight that such a development is possible or even missing may prompt us to approach philosophical matters largely as a task of interpretation under guiding philosophies or of topical treatment that is overshadowed by the organized import of the philosophies we adopt. Their domination may contain our dissatisfaction for some time, and we may find adequate outlets for our frustrations. Yet, as we stall, the pain of unfulfilled or underfulfilled needs advances. Our lack of relief may eventually sway us to engage in experiments that the speculative nature of belief-based philosophies and the open issues of incomplete existential philosophies suggest. Our unresolved pain may reach states where we fail to limit efforts to carefully paced and limited experimentation. It may force us to engage in increasingly tenuous and hazardous speculations and enactment adventures. This willingness may be used and channeled by the claimed coverage of belief-based philosophies that might even have caused our desolation. It may also have us fall prey to other nonscientific philosophies.

In deciding whether and to which extent we should follow external philosophies, we weigh our pain and fear about current nonfulfillment and our apprehension regarding our engagement in our own trials against concerns about following a philosophy. Misinformation or lacking information about philosophies as well as misconceptions about personal trials we would face and the intensity and scope of our future deprivations may sway us. We may further evaluate our capacity to improve our happiness independently as inferior because of our apparent disability to remedy undesirable conditions and because we discount our ability to formulate alternative strategies. Our purported knowledge of our dissatisfactory capacity and prospects may seduce us into adventures to rise above our deprivation by investing in the relative unknown of an external philosophy. The inducement to follow a philosophy grows with rising pain or fear in unfavorable circumstances. Yet, even if we merely believe that our experiences do not present the most happiness that we can achieve regarding a need or a range of needs, we may give a philosophy that promises to improve our happiness a try, provided we do not believe there is a prohibitive downside. Our search for ways to increase our happiness may render us open to existential philosophies that we presume to hold sufficient promise in providing them. If they contain no features that clearly signal incompatibility or other trouble, we may be willing to invest some trust and effort even if the indication that they might assist us is slight.

We may be susceptible to impressions that others have brought or can bring talents, insights, and implements to bear that exceed our reach, that they can observe the world in more detail and with a wider scope, better acuity, or superior rational or emotional wisdom. We also may be prepared to believe that recipes for happiness were given to others by mysterious or mythical forces or other authorities that are beyond questioning and cannot be explained or confirmed. These impressions may be supported by tolerating a philosophy to be encoded in language and practices that make it unapproachable to nonexperts or by shrouding it into concepts that leave nonexperts confused. Our inability to access, trace, and understand methods, justifications, and sources of an external philosophy we regard as superior may represent additional causes for us to resign to its leadership. These factors may greatly reduce our incentives to scrutinize the merit of a philosophy.

In our search for indications that warrant trust, we may not only look for signs of superiority. We may also require indications that the objectives and methods of an external philosophy are aligned with ours. Such an assessment must stay necessarily incomplete if we have not yet identified many of our objectives and methods. We may be attracted to philosophies that appeal to fundamental laws because these are universal. We may take these indications of congruence as causes to trust remaining aspects of existential philosophies that they represent to constitute fundamental laws or logical deductions as well. We may moreover be tempted to identify with a philosophy by indications that idiosyncrasies appear to be shared or accommodated. We may be attracted by features of a philosophy, its creators, proponents, or surrounding circumstances that comport with our internal and external conditions, experiences, or objectives. An impression of similarity or identity of interests that is attributable to such indications may motivate us to let trust overcome reservation and critical thinking. We may believe that the philosophy, its creators, or its proponents have our interests in mind or have the same or parallel interests. This motivates us to cooperate with them or to emulate them. They may move us to abandon previously held different opinions and to share the conclusions and instructions of a philosophy or of authorities that purport to represent it. Even if aspects that induce such effects might be intentionally or unintentionally attractive attachments to a philosophy that are not integrated into its substance, we may not notice that shallowness if we base our trust on poorly explored semblances. An apparent logical process and systematic nature of a philosophy may additionally increase our confidence that we have found an applicable approach to happiness. Moreover, the fact that others have already subscribed to such philosophies may sway us to assume that they have familiarized themselves with its objectives and techniques and have found them beneficial. Critical reviews may also be moderated by examples that a philosophy has proved its capacity to deliver happiness to us or other individuals we regard as similar. In that respect, we may not demand broad practical proof. The fulfillment of one or a few needs may lure us into the belief or hope that other as of yet unproven parts of a philosophy are accurate as well and will benefit us. Further, we may not parse whether benefits are attributable to the merits of a philosophy, an ancillary ploy, or unconnected and merely coinciding with activities of a philosophy. We might even deem a cessation of deterioration that may be ascribed to a philosophy as sufficient indication for its reliability. Although we might have the opportunity to critically assess a philosophy, indicators of reliability may weaken or eliminate our resolve to ascertain or investigate into its premises, argument, or consequences or to scrutinize the intent of its originators or supporters.

The perceived level of resonance may cause us to ignore or discount incongruities. Even if we discover potential or actual incompatibilities, we may have confidence that the benefits in some areas warrant the risk or actuality of incompatibility in other areas. We may be willing to entertain a philosophy if the unsatisfied needs it promises to address are critical enough and we are at a loss for practicable alternatives. A crisis in our ability to fulfill our needs may render it obvious that our principles of how happiness can be achieved have failed. The resulting vacancy and our particularly low self-confidence constitute a unique opportunity to be filled with a theory that promises a cure for that deprivation. Our desperation to soothe our pain in that condition may prompt us to accept the risk or reality of extensive incongruities and contradictions, and we may be prepared to suffer some damage. A lack of alternatives may even cause us to accept a mere promise with no or only little proof that a philosophy can help us. We may commit to settings that superimpose foreign thoughts, emotions, and behavior on us even if these call for extensive sacrifices or confront us with uncertainty. While such an attitude may damage large segments or even the entirety of our existence, we may prefer the pretense of guidance to the reality of a painful conclusion that such guidance does not exist. We may prefer hope of salvation to the harsh reality of failure, confusion, and struggle. We may willingly subject ourselves to the governance and manipulation by others if we believe that, by participating in their schemes, we can build overall profitable structures and processes for us that would otherwise not be possible. As our state of deprivation grows more desperate, we may be willing to sacrifice our search

for ideal happiness and safety for the sake of survival and merely getting by. Particularly if our basic survival needs are threatened, we may
place trust in philosophies that promise to protect and support these
needs and we may tolerate requirements such a philosophy poses that
might be at odds with or outside our objectives. Feared and actual deficiencies may be powerful motivations to devise or accept ideas that
diverge from or surpass our personality and experiences. We may in-
tend to limit such nonconformities to exigent circumstances and may
hope to transition to more congruent aspects of a philosophy or even
to move on to more congruent types of philosophy once our exigency
ends. But we may also conceive or concede that we and possibly other
aspects of our environment have to go through extensive adjustments
according to a philosophy to reach higher levels of happiness.

Our delusional approaches may have us follow nonscientific existential philosophies even if they are demonstrably inapplicable to us.
Nonscientific existential philosophies might be applicable as a matter
of intuition or coincidence. Yet the complexity of human needs and
particularly the variety of idiosyncratic human needs make it extremely unlikely that such a philosophy would constitute a properly developed instrument of guidance for us in more than rather rudimentary,
commonsensical aspects. It is equally unlikely that such a philosophy
would limit itself to rudimentary insights. We may therefore be well-
served by shunning nonscientific existential philosophies at least until
they transition to a scientific form that reveals all their relevant premises, arguments, and conclusions. There is also a danger that we may
uncritically accept even a scientifically derived existential philosophy
that discloses its speculative nature in all respects. Its disclosures cannot guaranty that we would peruse these and base our determination
whether to follow the philosophy on adequate consideration. Our inability or unwillingness to obtain clarity about our needs and their pursuit through our independent reflection may render us prone to adopt
such a philosophy with insufficient comprehension and thus a partial
distortion. Even if we understand its treatments, we may fail to grasp
its speculative nature and its function as a foray of consideration that
still awaits confirmation. In our zeal to find practicable recipes for our
pursuits, we may exhibit an excessive conviction in its implementation
and may lack tolerance toward other speculative constructs. Scientific
speculative philosophies may hence be commandeered by individuals
who abuse and pervert them. This may bring speculative philosophies
on which they draw into disrepute and disqualify them from further
consideration. A mistaken insistence concerning scientific speculative
philosophies can easily develop from experimental settings that probe

their validity. It may be difficult to sustain an appropriate reserve because individuals considering and applying speculative principles may become invested in the capacity of these to serve their interests.

Our propensity to seize on ideas that might improve our happiness without much prior consideration makes it easy for nonscientific existential philosophies. As long as they can influence us without disclosure, they are disinclined to undertake it. They might also refuse to rationalize themselves because that would mean to lay open their inapplicabilities, at least if we would gain clarity about our views on their stated positions. Stating their premises, arguments, and conclusions may set such consideration in motion. Philosophies that try to influence us underhandedly may therefore retain the lack of clarity in their derivation. By subscribing to and proceeding under a philosophy that does not meet our needs, we become willing, although potentially unwitting tools in providing benefits to those whose needs it is able to meet. We place other forces in charge that might use us for their purposes with our protection and support. We may be to blame for much of the undue influence of external philosophies over us and their deleterious consequences. We may follow others even if they undertake no actions to impress us or even if they try to keep us at a distance. However, they may also fabricate an existential philosophy that is acceptable to us to take advantage of our susceptibility to surrender to such a philosophy, or our submission may instigate them to engage in abuse. They may undertake to instrumentalize us for their benefit, realizing that the philosophy they promote is not or not primarily geared to our interests. They may investigate the tipping point in our considerations that causes us to trust their philosophy and try to steer us toward that point. They may emphasize concordances over dissonances and try to gain our trust through assistance. They may purposely confuse us and weaken our resolve and ability to develop autonomous philosophies of happiness. They may place us in positions of deprivation and dependence to increase our willingness to submit to external leadership.

Not all endeavors to extend an existential philosophy to others may be driven by nefarious objectives. Promoters might be genuinely under the impression that the philosophy they advocate is applicable and beneficial to subjects of their efforts. They may seek to derive satisfaction from benefiting other individuals by disseminating the philosophy they have devised. That may be a laudable objective with regard to philosophical principles that have been proved to be generally applicable or specifically applicable to others. It may also be acceptable for speculative insights whose relevant premises, arguments, and conclusions are disclosed if the recipients are able to reflect on such presentations without being improperly influenced by them. But individuals may exceed such boundaries in the spreading of their philosophy because they are immersed in their needs, wishes, and knowledge or imagination of means and strategies and tend to register phenomena exclusively through the prism of their viewpoint. They have a propensity to interpret, produce, and use objects and events in ways that confirm their position. Caught in such references, existential philosophies become closed systems whose concepts may not escape the perceptions, rational interpretations, and emotional mechanisms of their proponents. Because philosophies appear to match their outlook, they may be unaware of the subjectivity of their viewpoint. This impression of objectivity may grow by a lack of experiential awareness that other individuals generate happiness in different ways. Proponents of a philosophy may not be acquainted with the multiplicity of contours and pursuits that happiness takes and may therefore not have correct, let alone profound knowledge about what makes other individuals happy. They may have typically experienced homogeneous environments and may be rooted in their influences. These experiential limitations may strengthen them in assuming that other persons' mechanisms of happiness are identical with or similar to theirs. Even if they are aware of variations in individual needs and preferences, they may be convinced of the superiority of their philosophy over all other ways of achieving individual and collective happiness. Their dispositions and experiences may induce them to consider other concepts of happiness as pathological, disingenuous, erroneous, frivolous, ineffective, or inefficient.

Arguably, nonscientific existential philosophies that individuals develop based on their impressions might not even apply to their proponents because they may not give them reflective clarity about their relevant premises, arguments, and conclusions. Their lack of transparency may also embolden them to assume that their philosophy applies to others. That may infuse an additional degree of error into such philosophies. However, even if initiators and proponents of a philosophy would be completely clear about their philosophy and thus elevate it to the status of a scientific existential philosophy, they might not wish to share that clarity with others whose compliance can serve their objectives. They may not consider their philosophy to be speculative and therefore have no hesitation to impose it despite its unproven nature. They may even be accurate in their conviction of its applicability concerning their person. But they may not be aware of or respect the possibility that their philosophy might not be applicable to others. They may believe that other individuals who do not share their views would illegitimately reject their viewpoints against the interest of these individuals. Even if promoters of an existential philosophy originated it as speculative and gave complete disclosure of its premises, arguments, and conclusions, they might still be tempted to induce others to invest themselves in their philosophy. They may want other individuals to take note of what they set forth, discuss it, take it seriously as a possibility, and engage in trials to test its practical merit. They may want the philosophy they endorse to prove correct and find acceptance. The competition by speculative philosophies that vie for the same position and the resistance by entrenched attitudes and philosophies may intensify their resolve to influence possible subjects. Hence, there may be a considerable risk that objectively formulated philosophies might be promoted with subjective bias. The advocacy by their promoters may negligently, recklessly, or willfully influence proposed subjects to take considerative shortcuts. Many promoters of philosophies may be unimpaired by the threat of such transgressions. They might not even hide behind the notion that their philosophy is superior to the philosophies held by others. They may impose their instructions of pursuit in excess of their appropriate boundaries to benefit their goals regardless of whether they lose their integrity and damage others.

Regardless of the reasons proponents of a subjective philosophy advocate its applicability beyond its boundaries, their excessive claim causes them to favor the conversion or at least neutralization of dissenting individuals. The recognition of nonconformities within its asserted scope of applicability as legitimate would reveal a philosophy to be at least partly duplicitous or erroneous. As a consequence, an overreaching approach to happiness is likely to reject differentiating ideas as subversive and hostile. To achieve and maintain an unnatural position of domination, it has to induce a sufficient number of dissenting or uncommitted individuals to adjust their pursuits and to replace or modify their concepts or lack of concept with a promoted philosophy, and if it is only for considerative and trial purposes. To secure that objective, an overreaching philosophy has to preclude subjects from following competing viewpoints and deny competing viewpoints the capacity to exist or at least to compete. It may therefore try to restrain or eliminate different ways of reaching happiness and seek to align individuals holding such ideas within its asserted scope. If it cannot win over all individuals to whom it declares to apply, it will want to influence hesitating individuals sufficiently to not interfere with its establishment. It will also want to restrain individuals it does not assert to cover from interfering. Even if a philosophy does not apply to them directly, they have to be convinced that its establishment will not unduly interfere with their affairs. Such strategies may not distinguish over-

reaching philosophies. All existential philosophies that require or can
benefit from cooperation or noninterference may create strategies for
individuals to think, feel, or act in accordance with their demands. All
existential philosophies that attempt to convince others may publicize
their advantages. But promoters of overreaching philosophies may also resort to manipulation and coercion to fulfill their objectives where
the content of their philosophy fails. Such strategies may be most ar-
dently pursued by an ideology. To attain the quality of an ideology, an
existential philosophy would not have to claim to have found universally applicable, objective truth about human happiness and hence be
nonspeculative. It may limit its scope to a certain group of individuals
and shared aspects of their needs. Its distinguishing characteristic is
its claim of objective truth and exclusivity in the creation of happiness
for the individuals and areas it claims to cover. That exclusivity may
extend to an acknowledgment that other manners of generating happiness exist that is eclipsed by a claim of superiority. The claim of representing the sole or the best manner of organizing happiness for certain types of individuals radicalizes ideologies. Due to their unquestioning conviction, they tend to be particularly ruthless in the original
application and escalation of means. Because of the insistence by ideologies on objective truth and exclusivity within their claimed scope of
applicability, the execution of their course appears uniquely legitimate
to them. The resistance or nonparticipation of claimed subjects might
appear illegitimate. They would stand in the way of their own happiness and forestall the happiness of others if their contribution to the
ideological plan is helpful or required. Ideologies infer from this position of righteousness an unquestionable license to align deviating intended subjects by any means required to accomplish their objective.

    Nonideological existential philosophies may have more scruples
because they do not declare objective applicability. Their acknowledgment that individuals within their purview may have different ideas of
happiness and that such ideas may be valid for those individuals may
render them tolerant. It may stimulate considerations that respecting
one another's particularities might be beneficial and that applicability
assertions might have to be adjusted. Then again, a finding of different
usable manners of pursuit by other individuals does not automatically
cause an existential philosophy to abstain from interfering with the interests of these individuals. It may resort to similarly harsh strategies
as an ideology if it deems the subject matters it represents sufficiently
significant relative to the virtue of respecting the objectives and pursuits of individuals with other needs. To implement its concepts as designed, a nonideological existential philosophy might foist itself on in-

dividuals even if it realizes that they embrace different objectives and modes of pursuing happiness. It might patently subject them and take advantage of them. To inspire its intended beneficiaries for that challenge, it may organize them in an ideology. However, its requirements may go further. To build the structures and processes that such a philosophy claims can convey happiness for its intended beneficiaries, it may benefit from or require the assistance in significant breadth and depth by individuals on whose benefit it does not focus. For this reason, it may overrepresent its claim of coverage and the substances and processes of its benefits to make all designated participants in its establishment believe that it can make them happy. To undertake such a scheme, its true overreaching nature might not even be shared with intended beneficiaries. Knowledge may be reserved to a small group of functionaries or its intended results may be embedded in its instructions to come to automatic fruition as it progresses. The nonapplicability of such an overreaching philosophy results in unwarranted calls for individual adjustments and organizational changes. It may require significant alterations in our nonhuman environment as well. The restructurings and advancements it demands may entail lengthy and involved development processes before they can prove the claimed benefits of their purported function. The requirement to comprehensively invest time, effort, and other resources into a system that has not yet proved its functionality creates a massive opportunity for deceit.

Even if a philosophy has not been conceptualized for such abusive purposes, convincing subjects of the feasibility and utility of its concept so they will stand by the philosophy until its purported fruition forms an essential condition. An existential philosophy that pronounces far removed achievements may not be able to give us much present assurance of its usefulness. It may prevent us from confirming its applicability until its processes and structures become reality. We may have to decide the merit of a philosophy by preliminary and collateral aspects. We may be asked to commit before we possess clarity whether our commitment is warranted. We may not obtain such clarity until we are far invested into implementing a philosophy. This may cause substantial and even existential problems if we should find ourselves mistaken or misled. In consideration of the uncertain and possibly deferred effects and momentous changes a philosophy requires, many individuals may hesitate or not fully commit to the implementation of a philosophy or even to meaningful experimental forays on its behalf, thus decreasing its support level below its requirements to become a working reality or prove its applicability. Overcoming these attitudes of resistance is often the reason for ideological radicalization.

Arguably, such ideological radicalization is justifiable if an applicable or promising speculative philosophy encounters unreasonable resistance that cannot be overcome by attempts to convince intended beneficiaries. But this presumes that a philosophy can be sufficiently qualified before its application or trial to warrant ideological imposition. It also assumes that such imposition can replace voluntary cooperation and that it will eventually result in voluntary cooperation once its benefits emerge. However, unless an ideological imposition focuses on standards that can be scientifically proved to correctly correspond to and ameliorate the circumstances of all subjected individuals, such assumptions are wide open to error and speculative insecurity.

In cases in which an existential philosophy proceeds with ideological impositions without sufficient assurances of its applicability, its proponents are implementing its requirements with the understanding that they are or might be suppressing the happiness of others and take advantage of them. This inherently weakens their conviction of authority and subjects them to concerns. These include that their regime is illegitimate and under risk of being overturned if this becomes apparent to their victims, and that they might be punished for their overreaching in ways that might reach or exceed the severity of their usurpation. This fear may spur them on to become even more fanatical in their impositions, but it may also have them consider means of imposition that do not use coercion. While proponents of an ideology are not subjected to this self-consciousness, even they may fear repercussions of harsh imposition methods. The aggressive assertiveness of ideologies seems to create resistance and strife that might be circumvented with less confrontational but still effective forms of promotion. Promoters of a philosophy who wish to accomplish dominating results have a variety of manipulatory schemes available that can overcome or moderate such disadvantages. To subject individuals unconditionally, they may apply mechanisms of allegiance, commitment, membership, and similar constructs that create a strong emotional bond. They may further try to systematically direct and streamline subjects' thinking in accordance with their requirements with the assistance of indoctrination. Beyond that, they may achieve conformance by making the pursuits and the fulfillment of subjects' needs dependent on compliance with the system. If such mechanisms of dependence can be successfully created and maintained, subjects may not be able to escape an ideology because large parts of their existence would be tied to its existence. They may not know how to cope without its implements. Only where these are insufficient to inspire allegiance may coercion be applied to keep intended subjects committed or at least from objecting.

Such a moderation of ideological strategies renders them more interesting and more manageable to overreaching existential philosophies whose proponents do not have ideological conviction. Such proponents may also be drawn to such approaches because an ideological claim of applicability may render the system they venture to establish more successful in orienting the blame for subjects' unhappiness away from the system. It may be more effective in deflecting questions why circumstances have not progressed or why reaching certain stages has not resulted in the promised improvements of happiness. Rather than seeking or allowing the answers to be located within itself, the radical self-confidence of an ideology is more likely to blame external interference or claim a lack of commitment by its followers. Its conviction and influence may turn the threat of negative results in its implementation into a strengthening factor. It may be able to convince supporters that they need to subscribe more comprehensively to its principles or work harder. It may impress them to increase their efforts, to fight circumstances that allegedly keep it from coming to fruition, and to extend their patience because they believe that there is no viable alternative. Such techniques may succeed temporarily in adjusting reality or impressions of reality to match the claim of an ideology. It may be able shape its environment to a degree where some of its principles are or appear to be successfully implemented. This may produce a certain degree of happiness or at least expectations of happiness because subjects may gain confidence that happiness can be reached in its application. Such a restructuring of reality or of its perception may reach far. Still, unless an ideology can permanently assimilate and transform the reality of existence as well as the needs of its subjects, its superimposed constructs and modifications remain ultimately incompatible. If its doctrine does not arrange itself with how its subjects generate happiness, contradictions between its assertion to improve happiness and the deficiencies it leaves in the emotions of subjects' lives are destined to become conspicuous in time. When expectations are eventually disappointed without credible excuses and incompatibilities become undeniable, disillusionment sets in. Individuals who for all such time intensified their efforts and bore other hardships because they were successfully misled may turn against their manipulators and avenge their betrayal. As a result, manipulatory ideological strategies may ultimately generate significant repercussions for those who apply them.

The fundamental problem of incompatibility may be shared by philosophies that desist from availing themselves of ideological impositions. The revelation of incompatibilities may hinder the implementation or maintenance of their scheme. But they have the advantage of not needing to insist on infallibility to survive. They may adjust to the requirements of their subjects, including demands for a pluralistic society and governance. They may acknowledge their station as one philosophy among others or retreat to a common philosophy that can be shared by all or the vast majority of philosophies in a society. Ideologically phrased philosophies cannot resort to such an adjustment without endangering or abandoning their tenet of objective truth and exclusivity. An ideology is characterized by its unwillingness to compromise or to otherwise accommodate opposing positions among its purported subjects and by its determination to abolish these positions. It might adjust if opposition is so formidable that it cannot be overcome or if the related struggle might jeopardize its benefits or existence. It might strategically and temporarily provide semblances of coexistence and compromise and hide its nature until it can resume its course.

Then again, an ideology might not be able to commit to truces without endangering its existence because plurality constitutes a contradiction to its totalitarian claim. A change of strategy might be misinterpreted as the abandonment of its claim by its supporters and critics and it might not be taken seriously by other interests. As a consequence of these factors, an ideology might not only be unwilling but also unable to retreat. It may be unable to continue to exist as a pluralistic philosophy because much of its strength is built on unquestioning obedience by its subjects. The destruction of its claim of absolute truth leaves its aggressive assertion devoid of justification. This may prompt an ideology to become particularly defensive. That defensiveness may be shared by a nonideological philosophy that takes cover in ideological manipulation and enforcement mechanisms. By casting itself as an ideology, it restricts its options to respond to threats. It might compel itself to take a stand and risk falling as an ideology rather than being able to transmute into forms that allow it to compromise with other philosophies and might enable it to survive at least to some extent. A revelation of ideological pretense may even subject its proponents to additional adversities because of their intentional misrepresentation. The existential danger that actual and simulated ideologies bring upon themselves may oblige them to continue their ways as the only feasible choice to survive as long as possible even after it has become clear that they cannot ultimately succeed. With the effectiveness of manipulation waning, they may increasingly resort to coercion. This insistence may greatly increase the damage they create and accelerate and increase the intensity of their destruction directly or by response. Hence, neither ideologies nor their emulations appear to be effective manners of imposing existential philosophies over others.

The falseness of ideologies and their emulations is regularly revealed in the contradiction between their totalitarian claim and their radical efforts to suppress or eliminate other existential philosophies or less organized dissent. If there were no reasonable alternative to the path they describe, there would be no reason to be so insistent because their philosophy would necessarily prevail. Arguably, this might require efforts to popularize its ideas. Still, it could generally trust that intended subjects would unavoidably discover the advantages it offers and eventually subscribe to its principles. Even if that might not initially occur by experiencing its benefits, subjects would be eventually led to try this philosophy after all others have failed. That a philosophy would not rely on this mechanism and instead engage in manipulation or in coercion seems to demonstrate the untruthful character of its claim. It appears to show that such a philosophy does not possess sufficient self-confidence that it is superior or the only way to happiness. The aggressive nature of ideologies and their emulations seem to uncover that they do not trust the legitimacy and effectiveness of their ideas. Yet there are exceptions to such a rule. We may not possess the luxury of trying other philosophies or slowly warming to a philosophy. Adopting a philosophy might be so critically important for individual or collective survival and thriving that we could not afford the delay connected with its natural absorption. We might impose fundamental rights on others in an ideological manner under the justification that these spring from shared requirements and because we might be unwilling or unable to wait until abusers come to their senses.

However, ideological pursuits or defenses of fundamental rights must be practiced with utmost restraint. Great care must be exercised to block the influence of idiosyncratic positions on the interpretation of fundamental rights. The assertion and defense of pure fundamental rights may be burdened by error and by attempts of subjective interests to adopt their position of objective unassailability to afford objective status to their views. The ability of fundamental rights to assume absolute authority as an ideology destines them to be particularly attractive to idiosyncratic subversion. It provides idiosyncrasies with a full arsenal of enforcement tools and a mantle of legitimacy. The danger of error and subjective usurpation continues as long as the definitions and the boundaries of fundamental rights have not been settled. Containing this risk may require an ongoing assertion, discussion, and agreement of all competent individuals. Such an agreement might be difficult because of idiosyncrasies and because individuals or their divisions may assert interpretations against one another with ideological resolve. This jeopardizes human coexistence with continuing, uncompromising overreaching and strife. Thus, it may be necessary that we reserve ideological treatment and enforcement of fundamental rights to features beyond reproach. Such features might be established as a matter of science that validates the existential importance of a fundamental right and the scope necessary to safeguard its fulfillment. They might also be recognized by overwhelming acclaim and a lack of justifiable dissent under acknowledged fundamental rights. Regions where views of existential needs are individualized without distinct evidence that they violate core tenets may invalidate claims for universal application as a basis for intervention. Such evidence seems easier to establish for basic survival needs than for collateral needs because of differences in traceability. Ambiguities might have to be addressed in the manner in which other idiosyncratic differences are treated under the guidance of fundamental laws. Different viewpoints may compromise to continue a common society or give rise to separate organizations.

The task of conducting compromises and distinctions of non-fundamental philosophies may be complex because it may involve the reconciliation or disjointing of a multitude of incongruent idiosyncratic positions. It implies an inquiry into and statement of multiple viewpoints and underlying needs and the arrangement of our pursuits with other individuals in a manner that minimizes mutual interference and maximizes constructive cooperation. An approach of our happiness in this manner may require that we individually state and argue our positions. That may appear to us as a dubious and bewildering challenge. The statement and negotiation of positions and the potential of conflict that are involved in finding compromised solutions with a variety of individuals may appear to us as sources for danger and insecurity. We may fear the potential of uncontrollable consequences if negotiations or arrangements fail. Moreover, this practice appears to remove us from finding solutions that resemble our ideals. We may therefore consider entering into a variety of alliances and subscribing to multiple limited philosophies that better support and protect our positions. Even then, maneuvering with and among a plurality of limited existential philosophies lacks the plain clarity and direction of a streamlined, comprehensive arrangement under a single philosophy or a few compatible philosophies. We may deem ourselves unable or unwilling to arrange our pursuits for ourselves, let alone with those of others, even as indirect participants in organizations. We may seek the order of one existential philosophy or of a compatible set and may be willing to make concessions to find backing in it or them. We may rather subject ourselves to the compromises in such an arrangement than suffer the unpredictable complications of arranging ourselves with others.

But our propensity to attach ourselves to the idiosyncratic phi-losophies of others may come at a high price. The history of upheaval and pain that has been brought on by the adoption of such philoso-phies demonstrates that they are unlikely to improve the fate of those subscribing to them, much less of those further affected by them. It is almost inconceivable that the anguish they cause began with the de-sire to be happy. It seems equally inconceivable that the negative rec-ord of adopted idiosyncratic philosophies would not decisively dis-suade us from following them. Their continued popularity evidences our lack of understanding or desperation. Even if we subscribe to phi-losophies that are willing to compromise, we risk pouring efforts and hopes into pursuits that do not represent our needs because they are likely to only represent parts of our interests and not to be reconciled with our other needs. Our continuing susceptibility is a testament to the power of individuals and groups to wield undue influence over us. But it also proves that we have not properly developed our ideas about our happiness and how to shape our existence according to them.

While it may be true that we are actively looking to attach our-selves, we may live in an environment rife with ideological predations and more moderate endeavors by other existential philosophies to in-fluence and govern us. Social, economic, and religious movements are likely to compete for our allegiance and try to hoist their ideas of hap-piness upon us. They may seek to incorporate us into their structures and processes to render them more viable in competition with other philosophies and to install and maintain the requisites of their plans. We might be aware of their overreaching nature and may avoid their approaches at least in certain areas where we dissent. Even if we can-not withstand their meddling entirely, we may be able to get by with a minimum of responsiveness and reserve a large section of our pursuits for our contemplation and determination. Nevertheless, overreaching philosophies and their mechanisms might continue to disturb our cir-cumstances. Even if we can resist being converted and can avoid their direct pressures, we may be indirectly affected by others who abide by them. Operating outside their system may be unfavorable. That is not only because philosophies may try to compel us directly or indirectly into compliance or because our pursuits may conflict with their struc-tures and processes. If we persist beyond their reach and they perceive that enforcing compliance does not yield a sufficient benefit for their system, they might try to exclude, abuse, or eliminate us. Even if com-plying with such a philosophy would be detrimental, a position sepa-rate from its system may further deprive us of protections and means and lead to more deleterious consequences for us than membership.

Although the attitudes of overreaching philosophies toward individuals within their claimed scope who distance themselves may be dominated by punitive motives, such philosophies may not necessarily be hostile toward individuals beyond their claimed purview. Admitted limited applicability might imply insight regarding the legitimacy of a plurality of needs among humans, even by limited ideologies, and a willingness to come to arrangements of peaceful coexistence and even constructive cooperation. Any limited philosophy should be interested not to be disturbed by humans outside its purview, and it may rightly guard and defend itself against such interferences. But the impression that certain individuals or groups are functionally irrelevant for a philosophy might also prompt a philosophy to operate without regard for their survival or wellbeing. This may be particularly so because the exclusion of individuals from its scope is likely to be based on disqualifying criteria. That disqualification may cause it to make their exclusion or annihilation as competitors for resources or as potential sources of interference permissible or even mandatory or may permit or endorse their exploitation. A philosophy may target and depend on predatory behavior toward others without including them into its system. It may rely on their availability without a requirement of managing them. Its overreaching may occur without any pretense of conferring benefits.

We may expect that foundational insights of existential philosophies into the universality of fundamental rights guard against such infringements. But idiosyncrasies and parochial attitudes engendered by these may rule within such philosophies over fundamental rights. Philosophies that engage in the support or protection of fundamental rights beyond their intended beneficiaries to others affected by their demeanor may be scarce or incomplete. The at times extensive claims and consequences of overreaching philosophies may make it hard to evade their infringements. Considering their ubiquitous presence, our best hope might be that a sufficient number of them keep competing and that inconclusive attributions of allegiance might prevent any of them from gaining overbearing status or sole power and from fully installing their direction. Yet, even if they contain one another in competition, they may encumber or thwart effective and efficient interaction and burden those directly or indirectly exposed to their claims. A standoff between philosophies may not or not profoundly improve the fate of their claimed subjects or others. It may have a settling and radicalizing effect. The pervasive conflict and the impasses resulting from competition among overreaching existential philosophies may further counsel them to understand that it is in their interest to establish lasting arrangements of compromise or even collaboration among them.

Arguably, a view that existential philosophies tend to expand to other individuals through a relationship of leaders and followers may not represent the entirety of how existential philosophies can grow. As an alternative, individuals with similar interests may pool their resources and strategies to pursue their shared objectives together. That seems plausible in the area of fundamental rights because their basis is equally shared. But the joining of individuals for more idiosyncratic purposes and even in areas of fundamental law that are susceptible to idiosyncratic interpretations seems to be subject to different dynamics. The fact that idiosyncratic predilections can differ widely is likely to reduce the number of possible candidates for joint undertakings in these areas. Even if individuals share an idiosyncrasy, that commonality is likely to be surrounded by different idiosyncrasies that provide a different setting for a shared idiosyncrasy in each member's context of wishes. This would appear to severely restrain the scope of a common undertaking in idiosyncratic affairs. Individuals may find it relatively easy to join in the production of certain means that they subsequently use in their individual pursuits as they deem fit. However, such levels of cooperation only represent a very narrow and generic philosophy. More extensive particularized cooperation seems only possible in very rare circumstances where idiosyncrasies and their positioning among other needs coincide. Finding such harmony merely between two individuals seems to be already a challenge. It becomes increasingly difficult as more individuals gather. Idiosyncratic existential philosophies would therefore necessarily be restrained to few members if individuals joined under full awareness and reservation of their remaining idiosyncrasies. That would be so even if the philosophy would exclusively represent a specialized objective because the priority of that objective and its coordination with the other objectives of individuals is likely to differ. Individuals may establish enterprises that pursue such purposes within the confines of compromised common denominators. But this might reflect on the effectiveness and hence the attractiveness of such organizations. That idiosyncratic philosophies with substantial membership and range of topical coverage exist may show that their members find value in a corrupted cooperative agenda. It may also demonstrate that they are not aware of or were compelled to hand control to a rule that is unlikely to represent their objectives in many respects.

Beyond oppression by larger-scale idiosyncratic existential philosophies, we are being exposed to a multitude of attempts by personal philosophies or small associations thereof to subject us to these philosophies. Such efforts to influence, replace, or counteract our ideas of happiness are pervasive in most aspects of our life. As pursuits become increasingly interdependent, individual endeavors to influence others increase as well. Such influences may not rise to what we might consider philosophical heights. They might focus on mundane topics and be limited to one idea for one incident. They might pertain to a small area of concerns and few participants. However, their prolific presence may render them cumulatively as important as comprehensive philosophies. They might be even more difficult to counter or avoid because of the variety and dispersion of their sources. In pursuit of their primary agenda of making themselves happier, individuals try to sell one another on ideas that serve that agenda under the claim that following these ideas will render the other person happier. Their attempts may not rise above the equivalent of a suggestion. If they have difficulties to succeed on open terms, individuals may be willing to enhance their influence by manipulation. If that fails as well, or even without such prior escalation, they may be willing to force others to their purported happiness or they may give up all pretenses and blatantly sacrifice the happiness of others for their own happiness. In either case, they may try to punish, marginalize, or eliminate those who resist their efforts. Even without such an opposition, they may objectify other individuals and seek to exclude, exploit, or eliminate them to serve their own purposes. Such impositions are particularly probable if individuals believe that their ideas represent the best or the sole possible manner of pursuit for them. If they see no valid or sufficiently satisfying alternatives, they may consider themselves entitled to interfere in the existence of others to realize their own wishes without scruples. They may resort to strategies that are similar to those taken by organized aggressive idiosyncratic philosophies and may differ from these only by scale.

We may have different thresholds before we impose on others. Yet, like all other humans, we possess core tenets that we deem essential to fulfill our needs and whose pursuit we are prepared to impose and to defend at considerable risk and cost. We include the benefit of others only in our wishes to the extent it satisfies our needs. Our exclusive motivation to prosecute the satisfaction of our needs seems to necessarily cause us to view others as sources of interference, neutral, or resources. This may prompt us to preclude or prey upon others, to ignore them, or to seek out their cooperation. Our fervor to align others with our wishes may contain features aimed at assisting them. To secure the successful pursuit of our needs, we may seem to espouse a philosophy that endeavors to advance our happiness less or at least no more than the happiness of others. Nevertheless, the only reason we would be interested in the happiness of others is that their happiness, its pursuit, or its results matter for our happiness. Our efforts to help others draw their motivation exclusively from needs that produce fulfillment from such activities. That we are governed by considerations of utility in our relations and that our behavior is selfish may strike us as the opposite of our ideals. However, if claimed ideals demand behavior that is not rooted in our needs, if they impose a duty on us that is not reflected in our desires, they do not constitute our ideals. Moreover, we might unfairly prejudge what our needs, if fully revealed and considered, would command. Even initial impressions of our ideals reflect a material emphasis on the happiness of others as an important means for the fulfillment of our needs. This should render us optimistic that our happiness and the happiness of others can, and probably must, exist in constructive harmony. These impressions, together with indications that we might be able to construe and correlate our needs as ideals, might inspire us to explore the establishment of a comprehensive set of ideals and to thus bring forth a philosophy of our own.

Short of that or to enhance our own process, we may find external philosophies helpful and even essential in areas where concepts apply regardless of idiosyncrasies. Such objective applicability exists in the area of existential needs, fundamental rights, and their derivatives. It also applies in areas of technical concern. In that respect, we might think primarily of technological, economic, and social structures and procedures that might be verified to be objectively capable of achieving certain objectives. But there also might be techniques that we can apply to identify our idiosyncratic needs regardless of what these idiosyncrasies are. These techniques would result, together with substantive insights, from the scientific exploration of needs, our human and nonhuman environment, and their correlation. We may call methods that instruct us how we can derive insights about happiness procedural existential philosophies. We may distinguish such procedural philosophies from substantive philosophies that try to instruct us directly in what will satisfy us. Considering other individuals' substantive and procedural philosophies may assist us in developing or obtaining access to generally shared and contrasting concepts of our own. Still, we must distrust external philosophies to produce correct answers to our questions about happiness. We have to scrutinize their methods and substance before we adopt any part of them. Even if a philosophy has shown that it can bring happiness to some, we must assess its applicability to us. Even if it benefits us in some aspects, we cannot be certain that it will do so in other aspects. If we want to find competent guidance in existential philosophies, we must become adept in discerning parts that comport with our happiness from aspects that do not. The next chapter reviews strategies to establish such an understanding.

CHAPTER 13
CRITICAL EXAMINATION

There appear to be two complementary ways by which we can determine the applicability of an existential philosophy or of any part of it.
We can investigate its components and mechanisms. We can explore
its premises, its arguments, and conclusions and determine whether
we agree with them. Notwithstanding, we may distrust such a theoretical and apparently rational treatment because happiness is an emotional experience. We may presume that we do not possess sufficient
references in our experiences to determine whether a philosophy can
make us happy. We may therefore prefer to determine its applicability
depending on its results. Proof by implementation represents a clear
method for finding out whether an existential philosophy can provide
us with competent guidance regarding our happiness. Existential philosophies that claim applicability to our person would have to allow us
to verify them by putting the claim of their applicability to the test. To
be legitimate, an existential philosophy must be able to withstand our
empiric scrutiny. Otherwise, it cannot validly claim to pertain to us.

    Such a verification method for a philosophy may appear to be
unscientific and primitive. However, it is the embodiment of fundamental scientific confirmation to insist that the instruction provided
by an existential philosophy leads to the predicted result. If it does not
lead to the predicted result and such failure is not due to extraneous
circumstances, it is incorrect and we may decide to abstain from further application. If following the instructions of an existential philosophy in assembling certain components produces its promised results,
we may regard the explanation of that philosophy as proven. We may
assume until we find otherwise that its hypothesis poses a complete
explanation for all circumstances of an experience within the claimed
range of the hypothesis. These categorizations may become refined by
the evaluation of similar incidents. If instructions always fail to confer
the promised happiness, they fail to account for a necessary ingredient
and are therefore false. If the allocation of the described components
produces the predicted result part of the time, the hypothesis can only
account for some circumstances that are pertinent to its claim. It may
miss some ingredients or not account for interferences. It is a working
theory that, although it grants some guidance, does not represent the
last word. It is only partly true because it does not account for all aspects to generate the result it claims to describe. It constitutes a preliminary explanation for a phenomenon that might be superseded by
another explanation that can account for all observable incidents.

If we consider external existential philosophies to be provisional models and apply empiric exploration modes, we should be able to keep sufficient distance from them so we do not succumb to aspects of them that are not in our interest. However, an approach of empiric verification may not be efficient and may cause problems in our pursuit of happiness. We may not be able to obtain or assemble the circumstances that the philosophy requires to create happiness. Hence, we may not have an opportunity to determine whether it has the potential of making us happy. Yet, even if we could obtain and assemble the required means for an empiric verification, we may incur similar problems we encounter in trying to derive an existential philosophy of our own from trials. Empiric verification carries the systemic disadvantage of potentially high risk and cost. A philosophy's claim that it is applicable to us may focus that risk and cost to particular trials. But it may also intensify risk and cost because it may prompt us to comprehensively invest trust, other mental efforts, tangible resources, and patience. Its incompatibility with other manners of pursuit and the resources it demands may prohibit us to try other philosophies contemporaneously. By the time we find out that a philosophy does not serve our happiness, we may have lost important, most, or even all alternative opportunities or the will or resources to actualize them. Applying a philosophy to find out whether it can bring us happiness may then expose us to unconscionable risks. These risks appear particularly high where a philosophy cannot point to a record of prior implementation.

We might fare better if we could determine the compatibility of an existential philosophy in a theoretical state without implementing its instructions. Instead of trying to build the structure suggested by a philosophy, we would examine its building plans to determine whether we approve its principles of construction. Even if we can sufficiently judge whether the result would be to our liking, we have to investigate whether it can be soundly constructed under the given scheme. To determine in advance whether a philosophy is compatible or more compatible than other philosophies with our needs, we have to investigate its constituents and its processes. If there are no technical flaws in the argument, the cause for disagreements among philosophies must be a difference in the ingredients of their argument. It must lie in different premises that stem from a discrepancy in what they assume to be true or false. Such a difference may be attributable to aberrations in purportedly empiric data, their perception, or their other processing that form the premises on which their theory is built. To establish whether an existential philosophy is compatible with our dispositions for happiness, we must find out whether we can agree with its premises.

In reviewing an existential philosophy, we may have to review several layers of premises. We would regard the ultimate conclusions of an existential philosophy as hypotheses that must be substantiated. Each hypothesis would have to be shown to follow from the correlation of its premises. That correlation would consist in the interaction of premises according to properties and interactive laws by which they have to or tend to abide. These properties and interactive laws would constitute premises as well. The interrelation of true premises is presumed to produce true results. The conditions needed to prove a main hypothesis are divided into two categories. The first category is represented by premises that can be relied upon without additional proof because they are accepted as true by those examining the truth of a hypothesis. The second category contains subhypotheses whose presence still has to be proved. The proofs of these subhypotheses constitute subroutines of the main proof. These subroutines would follow the same formal principles as the proof of a main hypothesis. Each of these subhypotheses would have to be traced to premises that can be relied upon without additional proof because we accept them as true. Once a subhypothesis is confirmed, it can be categorized as a premise that now can be relied upon as true in a higher level of argument.

Because a hypothesis rests on its necessary premises, we cannot agree with its truth unless we can agree with all of these premises. To identify the ultimate premises, we have to follow the deductions of its arguments from the ultimate proof in the reverse direction upstream. We have to investigate the arguments until we arrive at a class of assertions that are not questioned or deduced any further. By reversing the synthesis of an argument, we may be able to trace back to ultimate premises that we can accept as true, dismiss as false, or classify as indeterminate. Our acceptance of a premise as true, our dismissal of it as false, and our final determination of it as uncertain are founded on whether it matches our direct or indirect impression of how the world works. Both types of experiences have sources at different processing levels. In its most basic form, what we regard as true will be based on experiences that result from our direct sensory exposure. These acquisitions lead to concepts in our mind from our impressions and interpretations of what we sense. We attribute properties to objects and to events and their components. We infer causalities and principles from their interaction. We may also obtain such concepts with the help of other sources. Such indirectly obtained concepts are divided into sensory information and interpretations of sensory information as well. A segment of this purported external sensory and interpretive information will be verifiable by our experiences. However, we might not have any previous experience of a premise and may not be able to institute an adequate experience by direct experimentation or observation. The source of external information or its interpretation may be so removed that, in spite of the investment of all our efforts and the assistance of external sources, we may be unable to determine its truth or falsity by direct indication. Where external premises do not lend themselves to a direct witnessing or substantiation, we eliminate these sources from our consideration or concede such information in consideration of its circumstantial credibility. Depending on our reliance on secondary information, what we regard as true or false may then largely be a matter of trust. That trust may be manipulated by external sources or by us without influences. But trust is not limited to external sources.

We also apply trust to our mental facilities in the processing of information. We use our judgment depending on how far we trust our own sensory perception, our interpretation, and the absence of manipulation. We are likely to form a repository of topics whose truth or falsity we cannot determine and with regard to which we must withhold judgment. Because the determination of what we regard as true, false, or inconclusive is a matter of our judgment, our ability to render such judgment properly is critical. Our judgment is largely formed by our preceding determinations because we ponder newly emerging information on their basis. New experiences are subject to our perceptive, rational, and emotional processing capability as well as our personality traits and previous experiences that might have been involved in forming and might more immediately influence how we apply that capacity. Our mental capacities may limit our absorption and consideration of available information. Even if we possess sufficient perceptive capacity, our rational or emotional convictions may limit, falsify, or block the registration or the subsequent processing of information. Further, our emotional traits may sway or prevent us from accessing or fully using our rational capacity. They may interject wishes as perceptions or facts into rational or emotional consideration. Moreover, our personal and our environmental circumstances may lead us to different exposure to information and a divergent desire for it. They may focus our perceptions, inquiries, and consideration on the experience of certain events and objects rather than others. The resulting state of mind may provide individuals with dissimilar understandings of how the world works or should work. This divergence of views on what is settled or unsettled, what requires inquiry and what does not, on what is true or incorrect, poses a problem for philosophies. It affects whether and to what extent they appear agreeable to us. If we do not share their premises, we will not likely be able to share their conclusions.

Identifying the premises of a philosophy can be a difficult task. A philosophy tends to focus and explain its own gains in knowledge more than it would dwell on something it considers as already established. In laying out its argument, a philosophy cannot well develop and prove all underlying relevant facts from the beginning of time. It may be counterproductive to describe all necessary premises, including those that its originator regards as obvious and unquestioned, and even more to prove their truth. Most of the originator's efforts would be spent on such traces instead of laying out the purported philosophical development that builds on them. Certain circumstances have to be assumed as an established basis. Beyond the removal of premises from proof requirements, many premises may be considered to be so unassailable and universally understood that they do not even have to be stated. Out of a greater number of purportedly undisputed premises, the originator of a philosophy will then pick a limited number that are regarded as required to create proof for a hypothesis. An additional determination will be made whether to merely state these premises or whether demonstrating their truth is necessary. It is often unclear how this decision whether to state or prove a premise is rendered. The purpose of proposing a philosophy is to convince others of its applicability. For that reason, its originator will likely make that determination according to the supposed level of acceptance of certain premises in the targeted audience. As a consequence of this assessment, the architect of an existential philosophy might stop short of developing an argument sufficiently far into its premises to obtain our acceptance. If we consider such a philosophy worthy of continued consideration, we have to engage in the dissection of premises ourselves or call upon external assistance to arrive at premises whose veracity we can judge.

Even if we should be able to locate and agree with all relevant premises of a philosophy, we may not possess a guaranty that following it will improve or maximize our happiness. The reason is that happiness cannot be purely based on rational derivation. The structure a philosophy proposes to shape has to resonate with us emotionally as well. We do not think happy; we feel happy. Besides tracing the premises of a philosophy, we also must establish that its deductions are in conformance with our emotional preferences. If we lack the ability to identify emotionally with the derivative settings of happiness of a philosophy, it may not be able to bring us the happiness it promises. An existential philosophy may postulate an arrangement of circumstances and behavior that surpass the conditions we have experienced so far. We may have difficulties imagining the composite and specific experiences of happiness in its described ideal world. When we produce an ideal system of happiness in our mind, our perceptive vocabulary and our capabilities of rational development and structuring may precede our ability to emotionally evaluate the effects of these imaginary concepts. But even our perceptive and rational capacity to imagine the totality of what is proposed might be overburdened. Beyond the logical comprehension of premises and deductions, we might have difficulties following described concepts with our imagination of a practical environment. To discern whether the ideal world of a philosophy is feasible and represents our ideal, we might imagine such a world and place ourselves into its environment in our mind's eye. We might be able to envision some of that setting and its emotional effects by populating it with similar experiences we have already had. In areas without parallels or sufficient references, we might supplement these features with more imprecise desires of departure generated by the pain of our deprivations. Such a manner of forecasting the feasibility of a philosophy and our emotional reactions to it might not be reliable because of the topical and incomplete nature of our vision. A philosophy might pose perceptive, rational, or emotional circumstances that are so removed from our experiences that we cannot anticipate them and their consequences. Because their ideals have not been verified in our experiences, we are asked to take a leap of faith concerning their feasibility and capacity of granting us the desired type and intensity of happiness.

To develop this trust, we may be relegated to collateral indicia. It may be established in similar ways as our trust regarding indirect information. Still, in this case, a greater investment of trust might be required because of the possibly more comprehensive effects that following a philosophy might have for our fate. Our investment in trust rises as philosophies present us with aspects of their imagined system that are fundamentally new. Such trust might even have to be invested by the originator of an existential philosophy. Although a philosophy will be in large part based on experiences, it may not represent a mere account of these. It may correlate and extrapolate experiences in ways that exceed anybody's experience. An existential philosophy may begin as an expression of a desire, of hope to locate a system of order and guidance. It may spring from the imagination of an ideal setting where the originator's wishes are resolved. As a result, the hypotheses of such a philosophy may exist initially in the originator's mind without a conscious deduction from premises. Proving the applicability of that ideal may be an afterthought to achieve and prove the grounding of a dream. The purportedly deductive development of an existential philosophy may succumb to wishful thinking. Even if a logical deduction can be construed, it may not convincingly carry the deduction.

Because of this wishful origin, an existential philosophy may be disposed toward displaying only corroborating possibilities. Even if we agree with its premises, processes, and deductions, there might be factors or interferences that the philosophy does not adequately consider and accommodate. Its implementation is not only a matter of logical deduction from premises. It is further a function of the environmental setting in which the designated sequence of events is to occur and the motivation of its proponents. The mere theoretical possibility of connecting steps to build to a result does not necessarily inform us about the strength of such an approach, about its likelihood of success, or its costs. This is particularly so when we try to gauge complex systems of happiness that depend on multiple sequences by multiple actors. We might not be able to predict whether a particular philosophy can succeed in establishing or maintaining the conditions to make its promised benefits available. Nor might we know whether its successful realization would improve or maximize our happiness or the happiness of anyone else. To find a dependable resolution to these issues, it seems inevitable that we implement a philosophy. Without our commitment and the appropriate participation of other individuals, we may not be able to achieve sufficient knowledge about the feasibility and applicability of an existential philosophy. Even partial participation may not be sufficient to give a fair assessment of its potential. This places us in the difficult situation where we must weigh the positive and negative implications of following a philosophy against the implications of not following it because of incomplete information. In addition, we might have to weigh multiple philosophies against one another. The number and indeterminacy of avenues and choices may confound us.

Yet, before we even arrive at these potential problems of selection, we would have to overcome internalized obstacles that do not allow us to fully examine the potential of a philosophy. We do not usually find ourselves in a situation where we live free of existential philosophies and are approached by them with a fair chance to evaluate their applicability. Most of us live within a framework of one or more existential philosophies that have already gained a following, obtained common accord, or reached institutionalized status. We may find our world saturated by religious, social, economic, and cultural viewpoints and traditions. Their impositions may override and preempt our free consideration of them or of other philosophies, or the development of our own existential philosophy. Their instructions on how we should think, feel, and conduct ourselves may have established themselves as an integrated, structural part of our mind, our society, and our tangible conditions. Their pervasiveness may largely determine the dispositions and circumstances that guide our choices. They may have permeated us and our surroundings to such a degree that we are incapable of separating us from them. They may be so settled that we regard them as reflections of objective facts rather than subjective theories.

This conclusion may not only be the consequence of direct indoctrination in which philosophies claim applicability of their theory. It may also be the result of indirect absorption from our environment. When we learn about our world, we may become exposed to philosophies through the surroundings they have shaped. The facts they have created may cause us to adapt to them to meet our needs. Implemented philosophies might enter our mind through their results even if we would not know of them directly. By their implementation in our surroundings, their subjective claim of how happiness is to be obtained attains a semblance of objectivity. They shape our reality in conformance with their claim and constrain us to pursue our happiness within their parameters. These parameters may prevent awareness of or sufficient familiarity with alternatives. If they offer some way to pursue our needs, we may believe that we have all possible means available to obtain and maintain our happiness. Our missing knowledge of other objectives or manners of pursuits may cause us to regard sanctioned objectives or ways as exclusive or superior. Our direct and indirect permeation by existential philosophies may foreclose us from questioning them or their installations. This renders ingrained existential philosophies sources of prejudgments. They may compel us to view ourselves and our world through the prism of their explanation and direction.

Emancipating ourselves from existential philosophies that surround us and have permeated us often requires great effort. To decide competently whether we wish to embrace them partly or entirely, we first have to be free from them. We must gain detachment from views we have come to accept as an ingrown and natural part of our reality. To begin that process, we have to realize that their content might not be genuinely ours and that they might not represent the ideals of our happiness. Gaining such an initial insight might already prove to be a challenge. The burial and suppression of our own ideas of happiness and the formation of our ideas by external philosophies may leave us with little awareness. We may not possess a manifest record of the replacement of our autonomous ideas with foreign influences. We may believe that we are independent thinkers and do not abide by any philosophy obliviously. Even if we are aware of the influence a philosophy exerts on us, we may be of the opinion that we freely chose to follow it. This may lead us to protect the disingenuous, external state of our ideas about happiness as our own against any criticism and doubt, including our own. Because ambient philosophies are regularly absorbed under the bypass of our critical abilities, we might not be able to apply finely tuned critical mechanisms to them later. Once a philosophy has become uncritically absorbed, it may cause us to act and react according to or similar to instinctive conditioning. Its motivations may not be conscious to us, and we might react with predictable responses to certain stimuli. This relegates us largely to the function of a relay device for those directing a philosophy. Once we are taken in by an existential philosophy, overwhelming contrary evidence may be necessary to disabuse us of the notion that it represents applicable ideas of happiness. We tend to hold on to such a philosophy stubbornly in spite of painful results. Rather than holding a philosophy responsible or even questioning it, we may try to blame its erroneous or insufficient application and other factors that interfere with its application. Our adherence is regularly assisted by a reduction of philosophies to conclusory principles or their symbolic representations in persons, places, or objects. These simplifications may not be a mere result of traditions and of the correlated institutionalization of structures and practices. They may be intentionally conceived to preempt our independent consideration. Our individual and institutionalized societal internalization of them and our instinctive obedience when they are cited as legitimization for activities to support or protect them may be powerful instruments to keep us compliant and acting against our interests.

Even where philosophies have not progressed to shape our personality, we remain capable of gathering some reflective distance, and know of or suspect deficiencies in them, we may continue to hold on to them. We may find it hard to distance ourselves from them because we remain surrounded and held captive by the environmental reality they have produced or they dominate. That domination may cause us to conclude that we have to put up with a philosophy that is to some degree incompatible with our happiness to enjoy the remaining benefits. We may not even distinguish whether a philosophy has created or usurped environmental conditions. We may consider our interests too connected to a philosophy or to the system it governs to explore or to act upon our secretly held opinions or doubts. We may fear losing the advantages we derive under the existing regime. We may believe that we have already too much time and effort invested in what we might have to discard. Changing our position may require the admission that we were mistaken or ineffective and wasted a piece of our existence. We may be concerned that a modification will not permit us to maintain relationships that we believe impossible or difficult to substitute. We may fear the impairment or loss of our authority, influence, status, capacity, or support structure if we deviate from familiar circumstances. We may also hold back because we lack confidence that we possess sufficient capacity or preparation to assess for capable approval or disapproval the philosophies that surround us, judge matters of our happiness independently, or cultivate our personal existential philosophy. We may not know with sufficient security how to obtain distance and assessment powers or how to act effectively upon receiving the resulting insights. We may not possess access to critical information or to alternative philosophies. We may be uncertain whether another value system can successfully replace a philosophy to which we are currently subjected. We may be afraid that if we do not hold on to our current direction, we stand to lose our value system and become directionless. These factors may form a prohibitive disincentive to our development of a separate concept of what we want. They may dissuade us from undertaking critical assessments or dramatic changes. We may rather attempt to find happiness under current principles than look for better guidance in the unknown. We may try to adjust principles or their applications to serve us better. But as long as circumstances reasonably meet our needs and we do not possess a firm knowledge of conditions that could dramatically improve our fate, we may give in. We may preserve or at least suffer a habitual system and, by implication, its ruling philosophy even if we deem it useless, deficient, or detrimental.

Our subservience to philosophies in our environment is prominently demonstrated by our extraordinary reluctance to consider other philosophies, let alone to contemplate adopting any of them. If humans were successful in obtaining an independent view, there should be much more, and more intense, consideration of established philosophies and development of autonomous philosophies. The prevailing scarcity of diversification cannot be explained by the customization of resident philosophies. Most do not represent specific reactions to conditions that are only present in their area of prevalent entrenchment. Even if they represent particularities, the distribution of such particularities among humans should make such particularized philosophies more widely distributed. If they are general, the similarity of humans beyond their differences should enable their spread as well. Nevertheless, the coverage by philosophies seems to be largely a matter of geographic, ethnic, or cultural context, or of political and military power. The absence of critical activity may lead us to conclude that individuals subjected to resident philosophies are satisfied with the guidance these philosophies provide and that the lack of application elsewhere is merely a function of insufficient publicity. Conversely, it may be argued that an incompatible philosophy survives because of a lack of information about more applicable philosophies. However, these arguments regarding publicity lose power as access to information grows. Even if sufficient information is available, external and internal mechanisms and pressures of adherence continue. Populations' persistence in a prevailing philosophy may be due to indoctrination, compulsion, fear, lethargy, error, or to combinations of these causes. It may also be attributable to their inexperience how much more happiness could be gained through other philosophies. To compare philosophies, individuals would have to immerse themselves to these and render informed selections among them free from internal and external influences and pressures. External difficulties and their own resistance to avail themselves of such options may arrest individuals even if they feel discontented and information about alternatives is available. This makes inquiries about how happy individuals are with a philosophy unreliable. But even if they could freely sample other philosophies, they might be insufficiently impressed by these to leave or change their familiar environment because these might not offer sufficiently better prospects.

Beyond influences from external principled campaigns or presences, principles we create ourselves may hamper our consideration of happiness. Our internalization of experiences may independently give rise to intransigence. We may fashion principles based on a single experience, but their recurring application and utility infuse them with added authority. After we generate a principle or find it confirmed, we are not likely to recollect the particular circumstances of each incident that contributed to the adoption or maintenance of that principle. We tend to remember less than all of the relevant constituent objects and events, and we may not clearly recall the objects and events we do remember. When we encounter circumstances that appear to be similar to objects or events we remember to have given rise to a principle, we are drawn to apply the related principle as an automatic response. The partial disconnection from sources and mental processes that made us form and affirm a principle may position us to misapply that principle. Our failure to accurately recall the underlying circumstances makes it difficult if not impossible to distinguish and possibly adjust the application of a principle to dissimilar circumstances. Without the context of its origin and rationale, the principle becomes a rigid and imprecise directive. This disconnection of principles may have physiological reasons. As our memory of constituent objects and events fades, the derived principles may grow gradually disconnected from their sources. We may also bar our mind from questioning and correcting our principles and their application for reasons that may closely resemble the grounds that keep us committed to an external existential philosophy.

Not all reasons for our adherence to such principles are negative. They can be important for acting effectively and efficiently in our
environment. Our ability to abstract our experiences into generalized
principles permits us to categorize similar events by their essence. We
can then apply that essence in the assessment or construction of other
circumstances. This rationalizes our decision-making practice. When
we face a task of assessing or developing circumstances, we can take
guidance from our principles by comparing these circumstances with
those that gave rise to our principles. Principles permit us to shorten
considerations when we find sufficient congruence between the facts
that caused them to be formed and facts we newly encounter. But we
lose their benefits if we let them prevent us from considering disparate circumstances in addition to similarities. By holding on to principles without questioning them every time we apply them, we incur a
risk of error. We become oblivious, automated executors of a program
that may not apply. When we enter a decision-making process with a
preconceived notion and we are set to sustain that notion, we reverse
functions. Instead of having our categorizations serve us, we end up
serving them. To optimize our response to a new situation, we cannot
forget about the circumstances that formed a principle and blindly repeat only the result we derived based on some similarities. We cannot
impose conclusions without scrutiny of the present facts and comparing them with facts that gave rise to our principles. We must consider
situational information before we act or react. We have to inquire how
the present circumstances differ from previously encountered circumstances and whether they might warrant a different response. We further have to ask whether they warrant a new principle, an exception to
an existing principle, its modification, or its abandonment. Because
such considerations yield superior responses, we must not permit our
experiences to program us so thoroughly that our responses are automatic. We have to continue to learn and adapt. Our libraries of principles can rationalize considerations by presenting possible patterns of
causalities that may amount to explanations as well as recommendations for our reactions. But they cannot supplant our considerations.
Principles remain defined by the facts from which they were obtained
until we ascertain that new facts follow the same principles.

The continued questioning of a principle may be relaxed if we
have populated its pertinent range of applicability with sufficient examples to be confident that phenomena within that range will behave
consistent with the principle. That is particularly so in the application
of laws of nature. Yet, in many of our pursuits, we do not investigate
our activities under these laws. The principles by which we act are fre-

quently of a purported higher, human-made nature aimed to help us cope with complex amalgamated functions of nature or of human design. We search for principles that help us act and react in our natural and created environment without having to investigate each situation presented anew. We are trying to reduce a multiplicity of substances and laws of nature that are at work in us, other humans, or other objects or events to manageable, combined essences and rules. Even if everything we and other individuals experience, are, and do can be investigated into its components, their properties, and their interaction, our mind does not regularly function on that level. For the largest expanse of our development, we did not have access to a full technical investigation. Many of the technical details relevant for our decision making remain beyond our grasp even as such investigations become increasingly possible and available. Further, the great number and interaction of details make us search for higher-level objects and events and for principles by which they act, including principles by which humans act to simplify our life. Our ability to effectively and efficiently pursue our needs necessitates that we build generalized schemes of recognition, action, and reaction at higher levels. On the other hand, the complexity and variety of objects and events and their interaction make a situational review before we can apply such higher-level laws particularly important. We still must understand the relevant underlying facts or types of facts that led to the laws we connect to them. We must inquire whether newly experienced circumstances are sufficiently similar to the originating facts to sanction the application of the law or whether they warrant a different reaction. This deliberation threatens to derail our application of higher-level laws and the benefits we hope to derive from them. Our potential lack of knowledge about participating factors, as well as difficulties in sorting out immaterial factors, in correlating remaining factors, and judging the results, threaten to overwhelm us. They burden our existence with insecurity. We may strive to decrease that insecurity by adhering to principles even at the risk of misjudging some circumstances. We may take refuge and satisfaction in the notion that the application of principles we have adopted yields overall acceptable results even if it fails us sometimes.

Because principles are often necessary or helpful for us to function in our world, it is to be expected that we would maintain a bias in favor of them. We are tempted to treat a new constellation of familiar components or a constellation in which we recognize familiar components according to established principles. Even if we understand that it is important to explore the congruity of circumstances we encounter with the circumstances that gave rise to a principle, our awareness of a principle that is recalled by certain aspects precedes our exploration of relevant circumstances. The existence of a principle thus carries a procedural presumption of validity. It serves as a working model, a start of our consideration. Yet, more than that, our tendency to hold on to principles seems to be based on our experiences that have found them to be adequately applicable. If we have already committed substantial attention to forming and confirming a principle, it appears reasonable to give diminished continued consideration to whether our position is correct. Even if we are not closed to the eventuality of deviations, we are protective of the utility of such models until we become convinced differently. Unnecessary confusion of established principles might imperil our ability to act and react effectively and efficiently. A defensive bias in favor of our principles filters out facts that are irrelevant to a particular pursuit. It would be unreasonable to question what we have repeatedly determined to be true unless there is a compelling reason. Moreover, it often takes principled and steadfast approaches to pursue an objective successfully and to bring it to the desired conclusion. To persevere in our pursuits, we may have to have an attitude that is not easily dissuaded or discouraged. We cannot preoccupy ourselves with investigating whether a fact should alter our understanding unless its relevance has been demonstrated or we have reason to believe that it has potential relevance. Until we are convinced on the basis of our experiences that circumstances are material enough to warrant a review of our position, it seems prudent to follow proven notions.

To overcome an established principle, a potentially amending, modifying, or superseding experience may therefore have to pass a rational defense mechanism. This mechanism requires positive proof or initially at least a reasonable indication that an apparently appropriate established principle is in fact inapplicable. This defense mechanism tests whether an experience is sufficiently relevant to modify or to discard a previously derived principle or to establish a new principle that deserves exception status or a different categorization. It may require a significantly higher burden of proof for deviating occurrences than for those that are in conformance with established principles. In the extreme, we may refuse to grant credence to nonconforming evidence until it irrefutably confronts us. Such a defensive stance may prevent us from considering and responding to changed circumstances, or it may cause us to react insufficiently or with delay. We may then conclude that the same mechanisms of building and adhering to principles that might serve us well in some respects may also be hindrances for the fulfillment of our needs in other respects, particularly as we or our circumstances develop in more complex and accelerated ways.

The difficult task we face is to distinguish and weed out irrelevant circumstances so we can consider those that may warrant the revision of our views. Arguably, we have to review every new aspect because we do not know whether it might change our mind. However, we might be able to speed up our review. During times when we are less experienced, we may lack sufficient references to draw competent distinctions between relevant and irrelevant changes. Every object and every occurrence has the potential to form, change, or destroy a rule. In such periods, it is vital for us to consider each circumstance and to learn how it fits into the concerns of our happiness. Even principles established by others have not yet gained sufficient depth of repeated personal experience to be wholly corroborated. While instructions, incentives, and repercussions might at least initially keep us in compliance with such principles, we might be willing to explore a variety of experiences that test their foundations and their confines. Such tests could result in our abandonment or modification of these traditional principles and the construction of our own, deviating principles. We may further encounter spaces where we can or have to experiment to establish autonomous principles without previous prescriptions.

Still, as we become more experienced, we may settle down and cast our thoughts, emotions, and demeanor increasingly into a system guided by principles. Parallel with that hardening, and possibly due to our behavior as its consequence of it, unprecedented occurrences that could challenge our principles become less frequent. Even if constellations might change, they are increasingly composed of familiar constituents and patterns. Our rising knowledge of circumstances that relate to our principles may permit us to distinguish extraordinary circumstances. Then again, observing our principles repeatedly and even regularly confirmed may create a contravening potential of inflexibility. Although our evolution of principles may render us more adept in predicting the effect of situations, the resulting assuredness may cause complacency. As we increasingly encounter situations that are essentially familiar to us and we observe no material deviations, we will also increasingly form an opinion about the likelihood that material deviations will occur that would cause our principles to change. We will be progressively disposed to estimate the likelihood of change to be low or nonexistent. Even if we observe partial deviations, previously undisturbed experiences of conformance may impress us toward the belief that these are inconsequential. With this assumption, we may become less inclined to investigate circumstances and question our principles. We may ignore or discredit circumstances that should cause our views to change and instead act or react in keeping with our principles.

The risk that our decision-making process should grow inflexible seems to become even more pronounced as we connect our principles to form a systematic existential philosophy. In building this philosophy, we may strive to harmonize and complete our principles so that all our experiences fit into the resulting scheme. Rather than giving attention to unruly circumstances that our philosophy does not seem to cover competently, we may try to ignore or explain away such circumstances. We may defend parts of our philosophy that should be adjusted because we fear that its overarching configuration might be affected by concessions. If we subscribe to existential philosophies established by others, we would be even more exposed to the dangers of inflexibility because the origins of their principles are further removed from our insight. Moreover, the dependence of a multitude of individuals on philosophies to guide them, and that other individuals will act pursuant to them as well, renders modifying the doctrine of a philosophy a potentially momentous undertaking. Those who rely on a philosophy to give them guidance might weaken in their reliance if they witness its adjustment. They might wonder whether other aspects will be or need to be revised or retracted. Such questioning and independent thinking may create an environment where individuals are not unreservedly following a philosophy anymore. This affects the security of those who rely for the fulfillment of their needs on others to follow a certain philosophy. As a consequence, the modification of established philosophies to better reflect circumstances might be avoided in an effort to prevent the destabilization of entrenched reliance.

However, the modification of a philosophy might be necessary because it might not provide competent principles to deal with occurrences it purports to address. It might not have captured all relevant circumstances or formulated the best possible principles in response. Even if a philosophy would offer complete and correct interpretations up to its establishment, these may not apply to changed circumstances that had not occurred at the time of its establishment and were not foreseen. All existential philosophies are necessarily constructed from and based only on experiences and derived principles up to the time of their creation and take a point of view based on such experiences. Unless existential philosophies are successively adjusted to correct deficiencies or include changed circumstances, they are bound to remain or become misleading. The intransigence of a philosophy against better insight weakens it because it does not permit itself to intensify or maintain its competence. Even if it may temporarily succeed in defending and stabilizing its position, the failure to adjust may create an even bigger problem by fostering dissent and withdrawal of support.

Rigidly subscribing to a philosophy does not necessarily mean that we would not involve our mind in the endeavor to find our happiness. Still, even if we try to apply rational investigation to our issues, our doctrine institutes anchor points and barriers for our perceptions, thoughts, emotions, and behavior. These form strictures and impediments to finding and implementing what makes us happy. It is easier to detect such a state of captivity in others than in ourselves. Our distance in a different point of view empowers us to identify with relative ease how others are being influenced, dominated, and commanded by rigid guidelines that seem to impede their happiness. We can observe how they seem to be impaired, appear to be controlled, and seem to have lost their independence. We can examine expressions that reflect their skewed perceptions and interpretations. We can bear witness to their compulsions to adjust their circumstances to their fixed ideas of how the world is and how it should be according to their existential philosophy. Discussions with such individuals often take the form of mere declarations of position and rhetorical maneuvers. Their rigidity may cause them to reject a serious consideration of any other position or of the possibility that present circumstances might require the reconsideration of their principles. While we may criticize such obvious extremes, we may exhibit a similar rigidity and antagonism to growth beyond what we have come to accept as truthful under an existential philosophy. Some of these positions may exist because following them has proved to be necessary or useful for our happiness. But we may also discover that we take positions without exactly understanding why we take them or why they should rule superior to others. We often do not recall and do not critically investigate how our views came about. Even if we may be able to think of a rationale, that process may constitute an attempted justification after the fact of acceptance.

Piercing such a state of complacency and defensive inertia may be difficult enough with respect to philosophies we developed on our own. Yet our ability to accurately scrutinize principles theoretically or practically may be further impaired if we follow external philosophies. Our intensified adherence to them may build on deficits in our capacity, skill, or willingness to determine their truth or falsity. We may not conduct a theoretical verification. We may not follow arguments up to their premises to detect errors or deficiencies in those premises or arguments. Our failure to do this may be created or supported by a philosophy that wishes to gain our support. A philosophy may obstruct the tracing of its theoretical soundness by failing to lay open how it arrived at its conclusions. Its proponents may be motivated to manipulate or omit premises and arguments that they deem might not meet with the approval of intended subjects. That might damage its influence on those who insist on tracing its premises and deductions. On the other hand, it may gain support overall by aligning those who are disposed or manipulated to not examine it sufficiently to comprehend its flaws. To compensate for and distract from deficiencies in its proof, a philosophy may emphasize premises, arguments, or conclusions that find broad acceptance. It may use popular views as premises, hypotheses, or to short-circuit or conceal an argument regardless of whether such views are structurally necessary for their philosophy. By championing agreeable positions, a philosophy may make its claims appear as a representation or logical inference of what intended subjects already assume to be correct. Our practical inability to determine the truth of a philosophy may largely flow from the esoteric and unrealized nature of that philosophy. To the extent its suggested structures and processes are matters that await future implementation, we may have difficulties to currently test its deductions and even some of its assumptions. Even where present empiric verification of aspects would be possible, a philosophy may encumber our practical verification by failing to set forth clear instructions. If a philosophy cannot assist us in certain areas, it may patently exclude them. However, such limitations may subject a philosophy to competition by philosophies that assert coverage of such extraneous areas and whose claim overlaps with areas claimed by the incomplete philosophy. This gives philosophies an incentive to pronounce a wider competence than they possess. To prevent us from recognizing that they cannot provide guidance in certain regions, they may leave their instructions in problematic areas general and open to interpretation. This renders them less effective in these areas but also less prone to opposition. Moreover, they may succeed in detracting us from their weaknesses by concentrating our attention on subject matters where they can demonstrate utility that serves our happiness.

Even where empiric and theoretical investigation would be possible for us, and even if a philosophy would not seek to manipulate us, we may rest on only partial verification and shy away from a closer examination. The comprehensive and often complex nature of a philosophy and requirements to invest substantial resources may be reasons enough for us not to take philosophies to task in an exhaustive manner. We may be willing to determine our allegiance to a philosophy on account of an abbreviated review. We may investigate some parts of it regarding their rational premises, arguments, and conclusions, and we may put some of its aspects to the test of whether they bring us happiness. We may take resulting evidence of compatibility as a reason to curb exploration instead of letting it encourage us to undertake a full investigation. Particularly if we find a sufficient extent of agreeability regarding immediate concerns, we may be swayed to subscribe to its other parts without further reflection and verification and even without much care whether we agree otherwise. Regardless of whether we make the selection of the aspects we review or they are suggested, allowing circumstances or influences to outmaneuver our theoretical or practical verification renders us vulnerable to influences that counteract our happiness. Following unconfirmed philosophies exposes us to a risk that they or their promoters will place us in their service instead of serving our interests. Even if such abusive motives are absent, unconfirmed philosophies may lead us astray and impair or block our ascent to happiness or its preservation. Our failure to examine an existential philosophy for incompatibilities or our readiness to suffer them on account of its actual or its purported strengths may ensconce us in a system in which a significant part of our compliant activities is disconnected from our needs. It may also install in us a high threshold for reconsideration and reorientation. We might not revoke our allegiance until failure affects the topics that caused or supported our allegiance. However, at that time, the trust, protection, and support by us and others like us may have created facts that we cannot overcome. A system built in relation with a philosophy may be so firmly installed that we might not be able to change it or even escape it anymore.

Our ability to resist undue influences and to avoid corruptions of our needs necessitates that we understand critical methods and are able to bring these methods to bear and that we can exercise our independent judgment regarding the truth of premises. But we can only securely disabuse ourselves from misinvesting our confidence or from having our confidence misguided if we know what we want. We are then returned to the notion that the utility of existential philosophies in assisting us is contingent upon our independent awareness of what will serve our happiness. Without such an independent compass, their assistance cannot be effective or efficient and may be dangerous. Critical review methods provide significant instruments to disqualify disingenuous and obviously incompatible approaches and to prepare the field of possibilities for our selection. They might indicate areas where we have to gain additional experiences to make an informed judgment whether to adopt a suggested manner of pursuit. Yet, ultimately, we are reverted to our perceptive, rational, and emotional experiences for confirmation. Our ability to raise our happiness depends on our ability to evaluate experiences correctly and to competently conduct explorations in areas where we are lacking experience. The next chapter addresses difficulties we face in these independent undertakings.

CHAPTER 14
IDEALISTIC SCIENCE

Before we adopt an existential philosophy or any portion of it, we may want to ascertain that it is technically feasible and that it can yield the happiness it promises. Even if we limit an existential philosophy to us individually, we may engage in a process of verifying it for our own account. If we assert a broader application to other individuals, we may have to demonstrate its feasibility and effectiveness to them. To serve that purpose, philosophies may assert that their principles have scientific quality. They may openly claim that they were derived from empiric studies. In that instance, they will concede that their foundation is based on experiences from which their principles were derived. Alternatively, philosophies may shroud the empiric genesis of their principles and claim ideal inspiration without empiric construction. However, even then, they regularly contend that their principles can withstand scientific scrutiny to demonstrate their practical applicability.

In as far as our needs are based on existential requirements for individual or collective survival and thriving, scientific proof should be possible. We should be able to establish fundamental rights as a matter of science. That should be most readily achievable regarding basic survival needs. Even the existential nature of collateral needs might be established by following the processes that depend on them and their importance for human survival and thriving. To the extent these processes can be isolated and reduced to physiological reactions, convincing scientific proof seems achievable. Yet, beyond basic survival needs, the task of scientific tracing and confirmation of our needs becomes exponentially more difficult. The often indirect and mentally involved ways in the pursuit of collateral needs, the complexity of interaction among perceptive, rational, emotional, and tangible factors and individuals in their pursuit, as well as the regular combination of collateral pursuits can render scientific proof arduous. Scientific tracing seems even more difficult regarding idiosyncratic aspects of any needs. The individualized qualities of happiness cast substantial additional doubt on whether scientific proof can be carried through because the sourcing of such needs seems to be concealed in our mind. At low levels of scientific development, problems in tracing needs threaten to impede even rudimentary existential philosophies if we insisted on scientific proof. We might therefore replace such proof for the time being with indications of trustworthiness and belief. Still, because this exposes us to error and manipulation, we may favor the development and application of scientific insights in all areas of existential philosophy.

As we apply scientific methods to needs, we must be aware that such methods generally, and their application to our needs particularly, are fraught with hazards that threaten the purity of the process and its results. These hazards arise from the fact that the mechanisms of our needs innately overlay with the mechanisms of scientific research. Our needs present the principal premises from which our motivations and activities for their fulfillment emerge. Beyond that, they form the objectives of all our activities, the conclusions we try to meet by our pursuits. Each need encompasses both a state of deficiency as its beginning and a claim that fulfillment can be had. It poses a hypothesis. Defined by the span between pain and satisfaction and by its instinctive and related experiential content, each need also contains the organizing principle and some information how we can move from deprivation to fulfillment. It provides criteria and direction for the identification and qualification of practical ingredients. These are measured according to whether and how well they serve the satisfaction of our needs. Interspaced between the definitional span of pain and pleasure, the function of means is to eliminate that differential. Our needs thus form or inform the hypothesis, premises, argument, and conclusion of our pursuits. In matters of happiness, the process leading to its occurrence cannot be constructed without the wish that spans between its beginning and end. Because all our activities, all our rational thoughts and our emotions focus on satisfying our needs, it is hard to preclude this same permeating focus from infecting scientific processes.

In a scientific process, every hypothesis is already a conclusion. We or someone else has already derived a generalization, a principle, or at least a supposition regarding the workings of an observed object or event. A hypothesis usually has a record of constituents that trigger it, impressions that shape an idea. Even if an idea is new, there has to be some conceptual basis for it to arise that is sourced in experiences. Our incomplete knowledge causes us to speculate about what we may find. We form an opinion of what we will find before we have the results of a related scientific process. This is the hypothesis that guides our exploration process. In this process, we ask what conditions would have to prevail to generate our experience and how these conditions would have to contribute. We form a hypothesis because our lack of knowledge deprives us of a potential means for our pursuit of happiness. Immediately, we are deprived of knowing the workings of an observed object or event. In a greater context, we may desire to establish knowledge generally that will permit us to use what we have observed consistent with a utility that we may imagine based on our experiences. In either event, we have a wish to confirm a hypothesis of utility.

Consequently, a scientific process can resemble the pursuit of a need. We begin with the desired result contrasted by a status of deprivation. We subsequently select or form the remainder of the process, the means of proof, to bridge our deficiency and meet the desired result. We work backward from what we are trying to achieve to securing the necessary premises. If science is an instrument we develop and use to implement and satisfy our needs, this type of approach would seem appropriate. Our purpose would be to make circumstances work for us or at least prevent them from working against us. Science fulfills that purpose if it can help us to find and arrange objects or events to deliver results we desire. This function of locating ways to satisfy our needs appears to be the reason we began to engage in scientific exploration and categorization. Much of our scientific research seems to be motivated by that interest. Our approaches toward finding happiness and toward science may therefore be largely indistinguishable because they represent essentially the same undertaking. Science seems to be a more focused manner of trying to develop an existential philosophy. It serves our wish to be happy in all our needs. It is then not surprising that we would undertake to prove a scientific hypothesis in the same manner we try to plan for the fulfillment of a wish. Since we begin and pursue our efforts with an ideal result we desire to reach, we may call the scientific methods that serve such a pursuit idealistic science. Because idealistic science is driven by fulfilling an objective of which we are currently deprived, it is not satisfied with what exists and can be shown to exist. Rather, it leaps ahead of what can be shown to a result it wishes could be proved. It tries to fill the discrepancy between what is and what we wish matters to be. This makes it the scientific embodiment of a wish issued by our needs. If we introduce a scientific process that includes such wish patterns to matters of building an ideal of happiness, we increase the likelihood that such a scientific process can serve our needs. We focus it on creating means that help us reach and maintain fulfillment of our needs. To the extent science is motivated by the wish to address concerns of our needs, we unavoidably infuse our needs into the scientific process. As useful as this infusion might seem to focus and motivate our research, it may also render the scientific technique less effective. The interest by our needs in its outcome may not stop at determining the subject matters of our inquiries. Defining its objectives may inexorably affect how we try to reach them.

There appears to be an integral risk that a scientific progression might be influenced by the wishes of the scientists who are engaged in the goal-driven nature of scientific development. By using science in the pursuit of needs, the scientific process may be more influenced by what we hope to find than research that does not have such a practical purview. To develop our practical scientific insights and technological capabilities efficiently, we may depend on a scientific process that infuses the desired outcome and concentrates on ways to accomplish it. Yet such a restricted focus threatens to prevent us from detecting, understanding, or properly assessing circumstances in their entirety. We may lose sight of or discount the importance of relevant aspects that detract from desired insights. If science is not open to detect circumstances as they are and rather concentrates on aspects that are conducive to the objectives it wishes to accomplish, it may be an incomplete or faulty, and thus less effective tool in understanding and using our environment to our benefit. A bias in favor of our hypothesis of utility could have the opposite effect of what we are trying to accomplish. To improve and maximize our happiness, we have to deliberate potential interferences and weigh the advantages and disadvantages of different pursuits impartially. On the other hand, broad, aimless investigations expose us to the risks of increased expenditures, unproductive inquiries, delay, and potentially damaging encounters. To resolve this dilemma in scientific methods, we must take a closer look at them.

We may inquire whether the bias of idealistic science can be reformed in an effort to foreclose negative consequences. Idealistic science is prone to bias because it is based on prejudgment. Arguably, we could eliminate its bias if we could manage to disconnect science from the pursuit of needs. However, that may be incorrect. A prejudgment may not only be due to influences from particular needs or the general compulsion to find means that assist our needs. It also seems to necessarily exist in any technique of scientific exploration as a function of our rational processes. When we observe a phenomenon, our rational mind attempts to make sense of it in the context of our experiences. It attempts to detect similarities to known objects and events. It tries to supplement incomplete information about the new phenomenon with associated information from our memory. It takes reference to experiences in which the same or similar components participated. We tend to categorize new observations according to our knowledge base. Even if we cannot find exact matches, we can home in on similarities and dissimilarities that might allow us to understand new observations.

The formation of this rational process may often be motivated and supported by our needs. But it also appears to have the nature of an automatic mechanism in our rational mind that we cannot seem to escape. The sorting procedures for new information inevitably touch upon related impressions. We are compelled to compare newly made observations to our fund of existing experiences. This unavoidably results in a determination of similarity or difference. We form a rational opinion, a hypothesis, about a phenomenon. We prejudge an associated result based on what we perceive to be correct before we know it to be correct. Our judgment endows us with an interest in confirming its truth. We become invested in proving our hypothesis. A bias is established by the mere formulation of a hypothesis because it is a statement that is believed to be true. Even if we cannot pass firm judgment on an observation by a comparison with our knowledge base, we form a similar bias if our comparison has returned a potential explanation. We tend to form an opinion about the probabilities of alternative explanations and to subscribe to an explanation that we consider to be the most probable, that we deem to have the most potential for truth. We then champion that explanation at least until circumstances dissuade us. Such a bias appears to be constructive in several respects. Its categorization of new events according to similarities helps us to construct our understanding of a new phenomenon. It gives us a starting point for research and experimentation. It may further provide essential guidance in situations in which we must react quickly. However, there are several disadvantages connected to such guidance.

One potential problem arises because of the close correlation of our rational processes with our needs. Rational considerations seem to be inevitably recruited and drawn into the service of our needs. That can cloud our focus and our judgment. Our needs may introduce additional bias that may interfere with the assessment of empiric knowledge and logical deductions, or they may reinforce rational bias. They may also fill the void of missing information regarding a phenomenon with information that is derived from our imagination of ideal circumstances. But even if we can avoid such influences by desires of utility, our rational bias seems to be subjected to emotional aspects that can be problematic. When we formulate a hypothesis, we inexorably wish it to be accurate and that we could prove its truth. The hypothesis becomes our wish. Even if that hypothesis is not biased by utility, our needs still appear to influence our rational exploration processes. They seem to unite in their wish to confirm the competence of our rational mind. In the pursuit of all our needs, we want to be secure in our reliance on our rational mind to explain the world. Our resulting wish to prove a hypothesis represents the differential between a current pain of not being able to prove the hypothesis and the imagined satisfaction of proving it. The same can be said if we try to disprove a hypothesis. The mere fact that we are trying to disprove a hypothesis means that we are partial to disproving it. We wish the hypothesis to be false and that we could prove its falsity. The destruction of the hypothesis becomes our wish. That wish represents the differential between the current pain of not being able to prove the falsity of a hypothesis and the satisfaction of disproving it. Although it is possible that a hypothesis would be propounded under the inclination that it is wrong, such a stance is unusual. We carry no natural inclination to posit hypotheses about factual assertions that we perceive to be wrong or to prove our own hypotheses wrong. We tend to want to be right in our hypotheses because it signals that we understand a part of our world and can use that understanding to find or build means for our pursuits. Hypotheses that prove assertions wrong do not usually serve that purpose as well as those that can be positively confirmed. The relative worth of proving the factual assertions of a hypothesis as correct is higher than proving them wrong. There are regularly many more facts and combinations of facts that do not serve the fulfillment of a need than there are facts or combinations of facts that advance that fulfillment. Therefore, proving the falsity of an assertion is often less helpful in pointing us into the correct direction than proving its correctness. Proving hypotheses wrong is commonly reserved to others who disagree with our ulterior wishes or do not share our perceptions and conclusions.

A general bias in favor of affirmation, at least regarding a scientist's own hypotheses, is then understandable. Nevertheless, such a bias is dangerous because it may be continued in the factual focus taken to prove a hypothesis. Our bias in favor of a hypothesis may make us partial to establishing the presence of required premises to prove the veracity of our hypothesis. If we have a wish to prove a hypothesis, we will attempt to locate and select facts that support our hypothesis rather than facts that detract. Our bias may continue even if we try to be mindful of circumstances that could disprove our hypothesis. We may be so focused on finding premises that help us establish the truth of a hypothesis that we may commit mistakes. We may convince ourselves that required premises are present when they are not. We may further mislead ourselves and others in presuming causal connections among components and claiming sequences that live up to a hypothesis when such connections have not been proved. Arguably, this bias is not of much import because there are merely two possible results. We either succeed in establishing all necessary premises and steps to prove a hypothesis or do not succeed. There should be no problem in ascertaining and distinguishing these two possibilities. Yet, besides appearing in obvious missteps, bias may also reveal itself in not immediately detectable ways. We may be able to construct a path of scientific deduction from ascertainable premises to the proof of a hypothesis. Still, the exclusion of contradictory evidence would render that deduction tenuous. We may underestimate, fail to explore or detect, disregard, marginalize, or dismiss circumstances that undermine our hypothesis. Instead, we may build a sequence leading up to our hypothesis that only contains favorable circumstances. We may find legitimate conditions of proof under the use of these circumstances. Only, our narrow focus may cause various deficiencies in our method that can render its results unreliable and the exclusivity of their avowal erroneous because we concentrate on the best circumstances for deduction. We may establish hypotheses, premises, and deductions that may be so rare or so prone to problems that they cannot serve us well. If we do not or do not adequately consider possible detractants of a deductive sequence, we cannot ascertain how effective or efficient it is on its own account. Nor can we determine whether it is inferior or superior to other possible sequences. Yet, even if we contemplate other avenues, we may let our zeal for reaching fulfillment of our preferred hypothesis cloud our judgment in assessing the relative feasibility of possible approaches.

The narrowing of our focus on features that agree with our hypotheses threatens to leave our scientific endeavors incomplete, shortsighted, and invalid. To pursue our wishes effectively, we cannot allow our judgment of reality to be dictated by our wishes. We cannot let our wishes of how the world should work determine our understanding of how the world does work. We must secure and maintain rational independence for our methods and reserve judgment until after we have derived objective results. It would appear that we could foreclose bias and ascertain objectivity in our scientific research by taking our preferences, our wishes, and needs out of our investigations. Such purity might be achieved if we confine ourselves to the abstraction of the substances of our world and the principles by which it functions without any ulterior purpose. Such an empiric research that is undertaken without any objective or hypothesis in mind constitutes an inquisitive form of accounting. It scrutinizes and registers what exists, how it behaves, how it works, what its components are, and how combinations of particular objects, events, or components behave. It classifies these phenomena together or in contrast with one another. Such a manner of research has a better likelihood of yielding objective results because it takes utilitarian motivations of researchers out of their process. Only after substances and principles are found would we deliberate their use. This concept of science that is not carried out in the service of our wishes may sound appealing. We may idealize such a mode of exploration. We may view it as the only manner of scientific research free of undue influences by concerns of utility and desires of being right. We may regard it as the sole pure manner of scientific exploration.

However, it is questionable how successful such a general scientific process could be. We may possess little incentive to investigate unless we have an idea that we might be able to use our findings directly or indirectly for the satisfaction of our needs. Arguably, most scientific exploration results might become useful at some point, and we should eventually venture across knowledge that is useful at our stage of development. On the other hand, we might waste efforts in gaining knowledge that is of no consequence to our advancement at this or even any future point. Further, playing through all possibilities without any ambitions regarding the result presents us with a workload that stands to delay the derivation of useful results. Nontargeted research may slow our ability to improve our conditions. It may leave the fulfillment of needs that could be provided languishing, exposing us to pain and possibly existential danger. But even if we had the luxury of engaging in unbridled research without practical considerations and without following indications, we might encounter problems of bias. To keep pure, our only motivation during research would have to be to gain knowledge for its own sake, without an expectation that we could use the results in any way. This may be difficult to accomplish. Even if the process is begun without a specific motivation, the considerations of our needs may inevitably arise as we derive knowledge. It may cause us to make choices in research that we believe more likely to yield functional results. This effect could only be avoided if all our needs were fulfilled and we were assured that they would remain fulfilled. It is also difficult to imagine how aimless research would escape the tendency of our mind to speculate based on preceding experiences about circumstances before we encounter them. We might not be able to avoid forming hypotheses and taking an interest in proving these in spite of the generality of our research. Even to generically expand our knowledge, we have to form a wish to apprehend concepts that we do not know. That wish alone may fill us with anticipations that may introduce bias. More particularly, achieving scientific order implies the ambition of transcending an initial stage of having to observe or experiment in a nondiscriminatory manner without any concept and to arrive at substances and principles that make further observation and experimentation unnecessary. That objective is an anticipatory ideal.

A forward-looking approach is essential to maximize the use of our potential. We must expand our grasp beyond the circumstances in which we are passive, coincidental recipients of information. While a passive mode may work well initially, new knowledge does not lie anymore on the surface as our insights progress. The chances that scientific insights would be accomplished by random combinations of what we can immediately find or that we could immediately engage in such combinations become increasingly unlikely. We have to capture them by ever more elaborate machineries and by interventions that are only feasible through targeted research and production techniques. Even if it is not possible to imagine what we might find or we can resist theoretical speculation, we will have to develop means for the extraction of that knowledge through observation and experiment. If we refused to give any consideration to what we might find, we could not very well put the requirements for our observation or experimentation in place. We must have at least a general idea of the knowledge we might gain to competently detect its representations. The formation of an ideal of what we hope to find is therefore a requisite of scientific exploration. Thus, keeping a purely objective stance of research may not only come at an unacceptable cost. It may also be fundamentally impossible.

Arguably, many difficulties of bias for or against a particular result could be avoided if a researcher would not have formed an opinion on the subject being observed or tested, possible results, or the desirability of results. Although such a starting position seems preferable in the neutrality of its intent, it is unrealistic. It is unlikely that someone without a previous connection to a science and without any ambition would develop an interest to research an advanced topic or area in it. Nor is a novice likely to have the necessary knowledge to form a meaningful idea of research, the skill to undertake the necessary empiric studies, or the ability to interpret and to understand the resulting data. We may be substituting the risk of bias with a lack of drive and incompetence. Finding scientists who have not formed an opinion before engaging in or reviewing a study may be achievable in new fields of science that address new substances and principles with little or no connection to previous insights. Yet, because scientific progress is typically incremental, it seems unavoidable that a scientist preconceives a possible next step before being able to produce proof of it. The more we know about a subject matter, the more we are able and probable to form an opinion regarding its development. Even if a science is new, it may initially be perceived on the basis of existing notions. Our ability to avoid bias is impeded by the limitation of our research and speculation to concepts already familiar to us. The means to extract additional knowledge are founded on what we already know. Moreover, we are bound to base our anticipation of what we might find on substances and behavior we already know. All we can imagine is their modulation in ways we can already perceive. Discoveries beyond such extrapolations might not only encounter our bias but also our inability to understand them at least initially due to a possible lack of references.

To the extent our capacities or capacities of machines we devise cannot engender new reflections, our discoveries may be limited. We may meet boundaries of general impossibility. But our bias threatens to curtail and block scientific development long before we encounter such boundaries. In matters of science, what is considered as known is expressed as a doctrine by arrangement of accepted authorities on the matter. Those who originated or support a doctrine frequently have a personal stake in maintaining it because their status or other benefits may depend on its continued acceptance. If they cannot benefit more from a scientific development than the current state of knowledge or capability, they will be worried about the effects of new insights. This engenders bias against developments that question or disprove established science. Even if scientists and their beneficiaries should be open to progress, they might wish to conduct or allow changes only in ways that do not negatively affect their interests. Restrictions on the development of science may be particularly possible if exploration is controlled by individuals or groups vested in the current state of science. The institutionalization of science provides proficient instruments for such a control. This might impose a momentous obstacle on scientific progress. Nevertheless, even the shrewdest influences and restrictions may not be able to forestall it. Established interests may be unable to refute the objective proof of scientific insights. Nor may they be able to suppress their application, particularly if developments significantly advance the fulfillment of needs. They may only be able to defer or to guide it. Such powers may be crucial if they are undertaken for legitimate reasons. Making utility the focal point of research might prompt bias in favor of scientific proceedings that indicate utility and against indications to the contrary. It seems vital to provide incentives for scientists to create better insights by rewarding them. But it also appears prudent to have their predisposed focus supplemented by skeptical review of their results by scientists who would profit from disproof. This might assist in determining the correctness of a scientific result and in weighing its application ramifications. Both advancing and restraining interests fill necessary functions in achieving deliberate progress. Our best hope to avoid scientific bias may be the free communication and consideration of insights and arguments to reveal and address bias.

It would then appear that prejudgment and the resulting risk of skewed objectivity afflict all of science to some degree. The purposeful manner of empiric science turns it inescapably into idealistic science. In addition, in the pursuit of our needs, idealistic motivation for scientific advancement may not only be unavoidable. An ideal seems necessary to make empiric science relevant to our existence, to give us sufficient motivation to engage in empiric exploration. Without an ideal, we would stagnate. Without the direction of our wishes, we could not concentrate our scientific research on what we need. The solution for the problem of potential bias of such orientations lies in the fact that idealistic science is in its core empiric. Its ideas, as fantastical and unrealistic as they may be, are formed from combinations of experienced aspects and have to prove themselves in empiric application. Idealistic bias may not necessarily overwhelm the empiric aspects of science if a biased attitude is confronted with an opposing stance that reveals the weaknesses in its claims. Our self-interest in succeeding motivates us to seek empiric testing and confirmation of our ideas before we apply them in our pursuits. Falsifying distortions can be identified and corrected through techniques of critical review that emerge from the nature of empiric science. The techniques and results of empiric inquiry are disposed to examination because they consist of factual phenomena that can be measured, recorded, and rationally traced. That potential for transparency of an empiric process can serve to establish the reliability of observations through data derived in the process.

If objects and events, components, methods, participating constants and variables, as well as the resulting functionalities are all recorded, scientific claims can be examined. Where scientific experimentation, observation, or deduction is performed in ways that favor conclusions or premises over others, such bias will find expression. It will be reflected in the selection of test or observation subjects, settings, and processes, in the data collection or its assembly, or the interpretations and conclusions drawn from the resulting data. Adherence to an empiric approach in the confirmation of a scientific idea can uncover subjective influences. The timing, detail, and formalities of the record accompanying the work are thus vital for giving research credibility. If there exist deficiencies in the record, the process itself is deficient because it did not establish itself as derived from observed circumstances. Its empiric basis and its conclusions may therefore be deemed unreliable. Once research data is recorded, it is difficult to create interpretations that contradict or skew the content or its meaning without such deviations being detectable. The recorded facts form the premises for any interpretive argument. If these premises are disclosed, subjective interpretation is restricted by them. Subjective influence is further constrained if we lay open the logical steps of our interpretation. Although it is possible to falsify data, verification processes can reveal its truthfulness. A record that complies with accepted standards of obtaining, measuring, and describing observations and that discloses the devices and conditions of research exposes the perceived occurrences

and their characterizations to causal investigation. It enables an independent establishment of the accuracy of observations through a re-
observation of the underlying occurrences or a study of similar occurrences. Even if practical confirmation is not possible, a detailed record
of observations, the conditions of their collection, and the processes of
their interpretation can make a partial showing whether proper methods were employed that should have yielded objective results.

We can prove the correctness or falsity of a claimed sequence of
causality by following the claimed steps in reverse. We may take the
description of asserted factors and functionalities as a formula for re-
constituting the declared starting position. If we review a process of
synthesis, we should be able to trace the process back to its ingredients. We should be able to dismember the result or a similar result into its claimed constituents. If we review an analytical process, the reversal should enable us to synthesize the observed composite object or
event. We should be able to reconstruct the investigated or a similar
object, event, or array of components from the provided descriptions.
If we can reconstitute the premises of a deductive process through its
reversal, its descriptions are correct and complete. If we fail, the record does not describe all parameters and steps required for tracing it
back to its beginning or it is otherwise erroneous. This indicates that
the analyzed object or event or synthesized components are not completely understood because they are not fully governable. Underdeveloped insight, technology, or availability of means may not allow proof
by reversal. If empiric processes are only provable by one-directional
repetition rather than a reversal, we may settle for such an incomplete
proof as satisfactory to establish the correctness of a scientific deduction. However, only if both directions of proof succeed can a scientific
deduction be deemed established beyond any doubt of completeness.
Complete proof requires a complete cycle of analysis and synthesis or
its reverse. Controlled settings reduce the risk that unobserved causes
participate in engendering the described results, but they cannot exclude such causes unless we are aware of the existence of such causes.
As long as we cannot be certain that we are aware of all circumstances
that might influence the outcome of an analytical or a synthetical sequence we are trying to prove, we cannot be certain that our deductions are correct. Unidirectional proof carries a higher possibility that
such undetected grounds could be existent. A repetition of sequences
does not remove that risk because they might be subject to the same
unobserved causes as the original. That risk is also present in a proof
by reversal. But the reconstruction of the beginning from a result reduces the possibility that unknown circumstances might participate.

Assuming that we can become comfortable with the accuracy of scientific results, we still have to confront the question what we will do with this knowledge. We have to determine what part of it and resulting capabilities serve our purposes best. We have to justify why we select certain aspects of what we know and are able to implement over other aspects. After all questions of what is true, what our possibilities are, and what we can do have been resolved, after we have found out how everything in us and in our surroundings works and what can be undertaken with it, the question remains which of all these means will make us happy. As long as science cannot fully trace the production processes of our needs and measure whether they are satisfied, there is substantial risk of error. Our investigation of our needs and wishes may be particularly impaired because our mind is at once the examiner and the subject of our examination. Our dual involvement may subject our endeavors to empirically explore and develop matters of our happiness to our bias. This bias might not necessarily induce our philosophy to remain within our experiences. Our ideas about happiness may also develop in nonconformity with our familiar notions because of our frustration with them. They might feature conditions or experiences that we do not possess but deem to be superior. What our needs and wishes are and what we would like them to be might therefore not correspond. Still, even such speculative concepts would arise from our reactions to our impressions of our current happiness and unhappiness. As in all science, our empiric exploration may be conditioned by our wishes. Yet, in this case, these wishes also constitute the subjects we hope to uncover by our research. Since our wishes guide their own revelation, we might only confirm what we already believe to be our wishes. The circularity of our research may not allow us to find mistakes or shortcomings in our wishes and underlying needs.

The negative consequences of this circularity might be confined if we examine our own happiness. However, the particularities of our needs and our experiences in trying to meet their demands are bound to inform our views on happiness generally and the happiness of others. Our scientific claim becomes problematic if we attempt to devise an existential philosophy for other individuals from more than human commonalities. But even if we try to avoid idiosyncrasies, our particular genetic and environmental traits and experiences in pursuing happiness with these settings form inescapable references. They influence our determination which concepts of happiness we view to be worthwhile possibilities or certainties and which concepts we doubt or reject. In examining happiness in general or the happiness of others, we may never be able to separate ourselves entirely from our preexisting notions. Although we might try to apply an objective process of fact-finding and deduction, it may be difficult to accept forms of happiness that we cannot experience as genuine or valid. We may be arrested to interpret what individuals wish and should wish to be happy from the viewpoint of what we know or wish regarding our happiness. Even if we purport to engage in reasoned procedures, we may judge circumstances as right or wrong, worse or better, efficient or inefficient based on our own notions of happiness. As a consequence, our premises, hypotheses, and arguments may be biased even if we could discover our own principles of happiness. This is likely to lead to repercussions for others who seek guidance in our explorations. As humans studying an aspect of human nature, we have difficulties excluding ourselves from our observations even if we include other individuals or entirely dedicate our efforts to them. We may also look for confirmation and a development of our own idea of happiness in a scientific process because we remain personally interested in the results. We may even seek to influence scientific exploration of happiness to serve our ideas of happiness. Our intentional and inadvertent bias and its concealment tend to be supported by a widespread lack of scientific proof in the research of happiness. Hence, scientific research into matters of happiness remains subject to a significant risk of error and manipulation.

However, bias in scientific procedures may not be our principal problem at this juncture of our research. We face an additional type of bias that reigns because we have not sufficiently advanced to a scientific treatment of happiness. To the extent there are no scientific procedures regarding matters of happiness, we may be wholly exposed to the unbridled bias engendered by our needs. Because we lack a scientific concept of our needs, we lack a counterforce to that bias. This insight compels us to a sobering conclusion concerning our quest to improve our happiness. Future generations might manage to escape the circularity of their needs or intentional falsification of research. Even if their needs might not incentivize such an undertaking to overcome their own bias, someone might explore and apply scientific means to countermand oppressive philosophies imposed by others. Further, the course of independent technological advancement may disclose scientific tools that enable independent scientific insight. But we may still find ourselves considerably removed from exact scientific knowledge of our needs, particularly our idiosyncratic needs. We therefore face a situation where we must either abandon our undertaking to improve our happiness in a systematic fashion or find an alternative method to overcome the deficiency in our scientific capabilities. The next chapter probes how we might find the inspiration to devise such a method.

CHAPTER 15
IDEALISTIC DISSATISFACTION

That we have not discovered sufficient guidance on what will make us happy by empiric or idealistic methods does not necessarily mean that our life has to be a disaster. These methods may provide us with some basic guidance, with general parameters within which we can subsist. Our embeddedness in our environment may present us with additional acceptable modes and choices that allow us to survive and thrive in some respects. Asking for more may seem to be unrealistic and overwrought. We are taught and we tell ourselves that we have to fit into what is available, into what is possible. Our experience assures us that the world is filled with adversities. To the extent we cannot overcome them, we have to cope with them. But we also know that we may never get what we want if we do not know what that is and if we do not pursue it. If we want to maximize our happiness within what is or can be made available, we have to follow our dreams. This is an intuition that we all appear to have. The problem seems to be that we might not know very well what to do with that insight. What we want and how to best pursue what we want may not be developed very well in our mind. While our needs and our experiences are likely to give us some ideas, their vagueness may remind us of the notion we retain from a dream. This may be the reason we identify our ideals as dreams.

Identifying our dreams of happiness and making sense of them appears to be difficult. We may not have certainty how many of our objectives are genuine. Needs mandate that we act in certain ways or ranges of ways to satisfy them. Yet our other needs and our environment provide further parameters for our activity. Our pursuits are entangled with one another and the behavior of other humans and other independent forces. This interchange may form and influence our perception, rational thoughts, emotions, and behavior. In the correlation of our needs with one another and with our environment, distinguishing the sources that shape our circumstances is often hard. Our needs shape one another. Also, we shape our environment according to our needs, and our needs and their expressions have been and continue to be shaped by our environment. What we genuinely want might easily be barred from developing or become overcast, convoluted, varied, directed, or lost in these complexities that dictate our existence. Not being familiar with what will make us happy may make us travel down a pathway that does not satisfy our needs. It is likely to prevent us from living true to ourselves. We, other persons, and circumstances may set us on a track to think and feel in ways, to conduct ourselves in manners, to internalize and represent principles that are disingenuous. We take a profession, select relationships, choose surroundings, and pursue a lifestyle within the possibilities of our circumstances. Before we realize it, our life is set onto a course over which we only seem to have limited control. Once we have embarked on our path, the momentum of our trajectory does not seem to favor significant deviations even as new influences appear. Our mind seems to be set on continuing that trajectory with no or few enduring deflections. As we become familiar with the conditions that keep us on our pathway, we may become increasingly adept in complying with the demands of that trajectory. Although we might be nominally successful, we may not be able to find sufficient satisfaction. This may prompt us to conclude that we need to increase or intensify our pursuits rather than consider whether we might be going down the wrong avenue. An additional blindness may befall us if or as long as we do not technically succeed in our pursuits or only succeed after incurring significant risk or cost. The complexities of our relation with our environment and our lack of understanding ourselves may prevent us from knowing whether our unhappiness stems from the frustration of capable pursuits or whether our pursuits are inherently incapable of securing the satisfaction we seek. We may continue to struggle for purported feats of happiness without knowing whether our pursuits can bring us the happiness we desire.

The occurrences of unquestionable success that present us with inexplicable desolation may be rare because our pursuits regularly remain imperfect and offer us remaining reasons to worry. Yet we may sense that our behavior and circumstances are not in all respects what we desire, that aspects of our needs are being shortchanged, underdeveloped, forgotten, or suppressed. We may detect in a variety of ways unrealized wishes that are going unlived. Our body may send us signals of upheaval and strain. We may feel that we are wasting our time, that our existence is without purpose. We may lack interest in matters that should be exciting and rewarding. We may feel empty, have problems concentrating, or wish time to pass. We may sense that our heart is not invested, that we are being held back. We may feel uncomfortable, alienated, subdued, or trapped. We may rather do something else, be somewhere or with someone else, or turn into someone else. What we have experienced and stand to experience may not appear enough. We may sense that there is, or wish for, something more. We may fear we might die without having found fulfillment. Our struggle with such or similar symptoms demonstrates that something in us compares our state of happiness with an ideal. However obscured, we all possess an impression of happiness in us that may contrast with our state of affairs. We all carry an inherent but undefined knowledge of happiness, and we possess a dream of an existence in harmony with who we are. Even if the specifics may be elusive, we can recognize if our experiences are removed from our ideal of happiness. That ideal may be negatively defined. As long as we feel pain, we have not reached it. But we may also have strong positive indications. We may know that a higher state of happiness exists and can be achieved because we are likely to have experienced it in our childhood when our needs might have been reliably satisfied. The love of caretakers, the security of being attended, the warm feeling of effortless satisfaction let us experience happiness as a seemingly endless present without worries. These experiences joined a broader basic predisposition toward happiness. It extended to the awareness of our tangible and mental faculties. It included our senses, the gifts and possibilities of the world around us to sample and use, and an apparently unrestrained potential to experience and enjoy them. These conditions did not only convey contemporary happiness. The ease with which we experienced happiness created an innocence that imparted us with confidence that the future would be as happy or even happier because we would grow and learn. In the absence of contrary experiences, we trusted that the world was friendly and that we could create happiness for ever more with the help of our faculties and our environment. We believed that pain and its causes would not last, and we had no awareness of the limitation of our life by death or that our experiences would haunt us. Anything we imagined seemed possible. That feeling itself formed a great source of happiness for us.

Arguably, such idyllic circumstances might have been reserved only to some and maybe none of us. Our existence may have involved hardships and denial from the earliest time of sensation or soon after our arrival. We may have suffered traumatic neglect or abuse. Much of the pain and fear we may feel may have arisen from the denial of our needs and resulting poor conditions for happiness in our childhood. But we are bound to have experienced at least some incidents of satisfaction with regard to some of our needs. These occasions continue to serve us as general paradigms for what it means to be satisfied. Even if we were happy only for moments and these experiences were far from ideal, there appears to have been a time when we could be happy as a state of concentrated consciousness that filled us completely and permitted us to forget at that moment everything bad. We had this open mindset in spite of experiencing pain or understanding that it would catch up with us again. While we may look to regain particularities of happiness we felt as a child, we may also yearn for the purity of happiness we could experience then even if its occurrences were rare.

This original happiness was subsequently flawed by our discovery that circumstances differed or changed from what had formed the basis of our consciousness of happiness. Our existence was soon encumbered by experiences of repeated and lasting limitations, of struggle against deprivation as our habitual state of our being, and of difficulties to recover from frustrations. These adversities, our exertions to learn how we might surmount them, our fight against them, and the experience of not being able to overcome them subsequently came to preoccupy a large portion of our existence. Worries and fears crept into our mind that ever since seem to loom over us and overshadow and weaken every accomplishment. At times, we are reminded of our early impressions of pure happiness. We may even have occasions in which we approach our childlike enjoyment. For a moment we appear to be able to forget our struggle, its costs, and our despair of not being able to reach the happiness we seek. Yet, in the end, our grasp for unconditional bliss is immediately surrounded and subdued by memories, impressions, or anticipations of pain. We seem to have lost our ability of experiencing pure joy. We also appear to have lost our resilience, our expectation, possibly even our hope that our future will be happy. We may have rational explanations of why the purity and optimism of our original happiness could not continue. We may dismiss it as a childish illusion. We know more about the imperfections in us and the world around us. We have grown up and are hence charged to watch out for ourselves instead of being pampered. We have more complex wishes and needs. Then again, regardless of such insights, we mourn the loss of the unconditional, unbridled, simple happiness we once knew when something good happened. We grieve over our loss of confidence that whatever bad may happen can and will be overcome. We may be certain that these states will be unattainable, but we cannot help yearning for them. This may form our greatest challenge as adults.

Our childhood impressions of happiness give us powerful ideas of what happiness is. They create memories and expectations of wellbeing that are hard to erase from our mind. Although we may forget the specific incidents of this happiness, vestiges stay with us for our entire existence and define our ideal of happiness. What makes these fundamental experiences of happiness so particularly powerful is that they transpired for the most part without our effort, planning, or implementation. They were free of risk and cost concerns. They resulted from the caring by others, our attitude, and circumstances. They were often caused by small and inconsequential delights. We were unconditional recipients of this happiness as a gift. We did not have to earn it in a pursuit. Because the circumstances of that happiness are remote from our contemporary and recent circumstances, they may assume a dreamlike and mythical quality and may be enhanced by our embellishment. The same circumstances that made us happy then might not keep their former joyous import if we experienced them now because we are different. Nevertheless, our recall of this original happiness sets the benchmark for what we consider as happy. It constitutes our ideal, and we cannot help striving to experience it again. The contrast with persistent difficulties in the satisfaction of our needs fills us with dissatisfaction. We might sense frustration, sadness, or anger about this unrewarded desire, that we fall short of constructing the happiness we once had or deemed possible, that we cannot live up to our memories and ambitions of happiness. Our failure to attain our ideal in spite of a commitment of all our capacities, all our studying, planning, and implementation efforts inflicts lasting pain on us. The specific causes as well as their presence and strength may be different in each of us. Impressions of this pain may occasionally strike our mind or may form a general undercurrent. Our lingering inability to soothe that pain unavoidably increases its intensity. Eventually, these signals may become too strong for us to ignore and urge us to address their causes.

If we are not sufficiently knowledgeable or equipped to remove the causes for that pain, we have impulses to find releases or absorption for it. We may focus on pursuits of needs in which we can reach satisfaction. But as these become exhausted, we understand that their fulfillment cannot effectively surmount our remaining pain, or if such deemed replacements are unavailable, we may turn our focus to manners of pursuit that can offer a respite from our pain by diverting our mind. To serve that objective, a diversion must produce its own tasks. By solving diversionary tasks, we may be able to decrease our frustrations that we projected into these diversions. Yet a resolution of a task would terminate its function. We may therefore also seek diversion in new, reiterative, or continuing challenges. Although this might add a second layer of problems and of coping requirements if we cannot resolve these tasks, that pain may be easier for us to carry. We may even welcome it to distract us from the original pain. Notwithstanding the temporary effectiveness of such distractive mechanisms, the original pain may remain unaddressed and unresolved and may keep festering. It may require increasingly strong coping mechanisms and an increasing share of our resources to hold it at bay. Both aspects may combine to render a strategy that was intended to help us cope with our pain to instead increase our pain. In some of us, the failure to resolve the underlying pain and the dissatisfaction with diversions may develop to a point at which we cannot cope any longer. We may find the discrepancies between the reality we experience and our ideal of happiness unbearable. The contradictions may be so severe that we cannot continue in this mode. Our unresolved and growing pain may drive us to reorient our efforts from its suppression through diversion and to take fundamental action to change our state of affairs. Reaching such a situation might be dangerous if we cannot instantly ascertain or develop a competent strategy to improve our happiness. If we dismiss our distractions but cannot find a way to remediate our inability to find happiness effectively, we face our pain without a buffer. This immediacy and apparent inescapability may overwhelm us. It may cause us to resort to desperate self-destructive or externally destructive actions. Not knowing how we can escape our pain, we may attempt to end it without addressing its sources. Instead, we may attack our sensory and our other mental equipment, the physiological structures that allow us to register and suffer the pain. We may turn against ourselves, or we may lash out against persons and other aspects of our environment that we may falsely or overproportionally hold responsible for our pain. Even if we legitimately fight external causes, this can only cure a part of our deprivations. Many of them may only come to bear because we do not understand our needs and do not competently pursue them.

Our fear of being unable to cope with our pain in the absence of distractions may prompt us to continue distractions while we try to mend the deficiencies they cover. We may be able to establish parallel mechanisms by which we can address part of our frustration with distractions and another part through countermeasures. We may find a middle ground that permits us to live with our pain. With such an approach, fewer of us may be driven to extremes of desperation. Yet, by offering relief, such a pattern may prevent us from building our motivation and skills to comprehensively remove the causes of our unhappiness. We may be prepared to settle into such a mediocrity. If we can find or fashion pursuits that fulfill the principal functionalities of our needs, remaining discrepancies between our ideal and our reality may be manageable by distractions without further addressing their causes. We may continue to suffer and become skilled at managing moderate forms of pain while keeping our existence on a stable and familiar track. We may successfully avoid examining our lack of happiness and its causes more closely. We may regard this compromised but relatively stable existence as an accomplishment that takes us as far as our circumstances allow. Although we might be open to and hope for improvements, we may keep our lingering disappointments subdued. But we might also reject any idea of betterment to avoid having to acknowledge a seemingly unfulfillable desire that causes us pain.

The reluctance we sense in dealing with the source of our pain more fundamentally is only superficially attributable to our fear of the technical burdens of trials or the availability of competent diversions. The pain inflicted by technical burdens may soon be matched and exceeded by the pain of failing to solve the dissatisfaction of our needs. Further, diversions cannot offer a permanent solution. Their very purpose is to accommodate the source of our pain, to make it more bearable. At best, they can merely subdue or modulate our dissatisfaction. Our willingness to suffer that pain instead of resolving the underlying pain has deeper roots. It is based on our ignorance of what our needs are or what will satisfy them and our resistance and deemed inability to find out. We may also doubt whether we can obtain and successfully apply the means required to make us happy. We may resent being drawn into trials and uncertain pursuits, particularly if they constitute a radical departure from our familiar ways. We may be exhausted from trying or afraid to be hurt by false hope. As long as our circumstances are bearable, we may try to hold on to them. We may be accustomed to them and reluctant to jeopardize their relative benefits and security. We may feel uneasy about replacing our faulty but familiar situation with a promise of more happiness. We may fear that we have followed our path too far to be able to change or that we might fail in our departure and incur more pain. We may be concerned that we will unearth deportment that makes us ashamed, disappointed, or angry with ourselves or that may cause such reactions toward others or toward us in others. We may refuse to admit that a portion of our chances to experience happiness has irreversibly been lost. We may dread the judgment by others and possible recriminations connected to change. We may want to forget the pain of the experiences that shaped our limitations. We may be afraid of failing again, of reencountering helplessness, embarrassment, and frustration. We may suffer from the apprehension that the pain we may incur in attempting to address our pain may be worse than the pain we would feel from not addressing it.

As a result of these fears, we may seek safety and stop short of covering the complete distance of our desire. The threat of additional pain if we should try to address the pain of certain unfulfilled wishes creates a counterbalance that can motivate us to turn away from the fulfillment of our needs. As a result, we may try to settle into a condition where our fear of examining our needs and following our wishes more intensely keeps our pain of disconnection from our ideal of happiness at bay. Depending on the intensity of desire and fear with regard to each of our needs, a point may be reached for each need where our desires and fears hold each other in a stalemate. These stalemates may be embattled in the beginning. Still, in time, we may not struggle much with our positions anymore and learn to live with them. Much of our behavior induced by these standoffs may become habitual and automatic. Habitual impasses may be adjusted and boundaries may be occasionally moved by incidents that increase or decrease our desires or the fears that are holding us back. Yet, to protect us from the pain of ongoing struggles, we may be able to create a state that causes the disengagement of our desires and fears and provides us with stability most of the time. The boundaries between our fears and desires may therefore not be delineated too well. Rather than constituting distinct lines, they may resemble danger zones into which we dare not venture or dare not venture too far. As long as we do not push the fulfillment of our needs past the neutral zone and invade the area of our fears, we may perceive that there are no internal boundaries for the pursuit of our needs. We may be able to conceal our fears because our activities may remain within an area where they are not being activated. But the unrelenting force of our needs is bound to push against these boundaries and protections. If we experience dissatisfaction in excess of what can be diverted, our needs will eventually encounter our fears.

Where our fears are confronted by our needs, they may disguise their resentments by references to purportedly rational reasons. They may suggest that our wishes are not in our interest, that they damage our chances for happiness. Moreover, we may pretend to find advantages in what we do not dare to change. We might tell ourselves that our situation is sufficient, that we can be satisfied with where we are. We might induce the belief in us that we are doing exactly what we want to do, that we are exactly where we want to be. Even if we do not pretend to like our circumstances, we may talk ourselves into sticking with the choices we made. We may try to make reticence and intransigence our virtue. We may persuade ourselves that our circumstances are unchangeable. We may resign to the idea that we will have to cope with them to get by, that they are part of how the world works, that we need to adjust to reality. We may tell ourselves that we are not going to run from the responsibilities we have incurred, that we remain true to our principles or our obligations. We may try to find solace in the notion that we are sacrificing our happiness for a greater cause, for somebody else's happiness, and that this compensates for our loss. We may talk ourselves into the notion that we did make the right decision and that any doubts must be invalid, must be signs of temptation or temporary weakness. We may determine that our doubts are not real, that we experience lapses in judgment or bouts of temporary depression, or that our unease is caused by superficial disturbances.

Many of the pretenses fueled by our fear and lack of knowledge are linked to diversion strategies. This combination may result in an underdeveloped will to succeed. It may prevent us from acting upon the pain of unfulfilled or underfulfilled needs. We may resign to an existence permeated by an undercurrent of unease, an often nameless sense of loss, pain, and frustration. We may hope that happiness will find us someday. We may soldier on and try to keep our deeper-seated misgivings to ourselves. We may try to console ourselves by thinking that it could be worse. We may be glad to escape the deeper questions we cannot seem to answer and the deeper challenges of our needs we cannot seem to overcome. Still, in spite of all our attempts to convince and soothe ourselves, continuing the impasse between our fears and the pain of dissatisfaction about unrewarded desires necessarily translates into less than blissful conditions. It renders us prone to manipulation by those who can profit from our lack of confidence, fear, and weakness for subterfuges and diversions. At best, it produces an existence of quiet and uneventful denial and suffering. The parameters we set for ourselves or permit others to set for us combine and interweave with the factual circumstances of our existence that place restraints on how much happiness we can achieve. We may accept external limits for similar reasons and under similar subterfuges as those we apply to our internal boundaries. We may fear the pain and upheaval that revealing and attacking these external boundaries might bring.

The subjective and objective parameters in which we operate to fulfill our needs may leave us in a situation that is neither greatly happy nor greatly unhappy. Much of our existence may take its position in a purgatory of getting by. In this state, we may even build resolve, investigate, plan, and prepare to take charge, yet merely to hesitate and stall. We may expend vastly more time in this purgatory of happiness than in the pursuit of our dreams. Our experiences of happiness may appear like islands of brightness that are endangered to be swallowed by a sea of darkness. These impressions may incentivize us to adhere to these islands and to avoid venturing too far from them. Some of us manage to live in this condition without ever addressing the causes of our dissatisfaction. But such an existence where we keep the signals of our dissatisfied wishes under control comes at a price. We face a lifetime of investing resources to keep our dissatisfaction limited and to control the fallout of our coping efforts. There is no victory in enduring such containment efforts. However small the discrepancy between our reality and our unanswered needs might be, maintaining it results in a steady drain on our strength and in dissatisfaction. Because our wishes will not subside, we have to dedicate a portion of our efforts to keeping us from trying to reach them and addressing our pain over that fact. These efforts are wasted. They are missing in endeavors that could bring us happiness. Beyond that, they create an existence that is tarnished by fear and haunted by unfulfilled wishes, regret for lost opportunities, and wondering what could have been. We cannot escape bitterness over times spent in suspension of our wishes and under the influence of our fears. We cannot avoid the impression that we have not been living up to our potential. The continuing standoff between our desires and fears causes unrequited desires to transform into pain. Although that pain is canceled by our fears in terms of motivation, it combines with our fears to form an encumbrance on our happiness.

If we are to overcome the established stalemates in which our defense mechanisms stand pitted against improvements of our happiness, we must take countermeasures. It would appear that if we could reconnect with sensations of our original happiness and contrast these feelings with the present condition of our happiness, we might derive sufficient motivation to regain what we have lost. Recalling the tenets of our original happiness might permit us to recapture a basic orientation of what matters to us and might assist us in building clear objectives for our wishes. Yet, even if this approach can develop our readiness to improve our happiness and deliver some insights regarding the roots of our needs, it may be inadequate to develop a full insight into what will make us happy. The unencumbered happiness we felt then appears impossible now. The naive impressions of potential, of boundless opportunity and resources, of an everlasting present, and of a benevolent world have been replaced by mounting contrary experiences. We are now on our own. What once came about without our effort or only with little prompting now appears impossible or to generally require our assiduous planning, engagement, and the marshaling of resources that are relatively difficult to obtain. With these challenges, an improved ability to understand our limitations and our chances to fulfill our needs has set in. Our personal capacities have dramatically improved. That should help us substantially in devising strategies to obtain happiness. However, we and our ambitions have changed not only in terms of awareness and technical responsiveness. In the course of our development, our needs have become more complicated. We did not understand the full scope of our needs then. They have expanded and transformed in many respects. Some were only present as beginnings or potentials, and all have become more articulated. These complications indicate that identifying what will render us happy is not a matter of focusing back but that we have to find our current ideas of happiness. The next section investigates such a new approach.

SECTION FOUR
EXISTENTIAL APPROACH

CHAPTER 16
SEARCHING FOR A BETTER WAY

Our review of empiric and idealistic approaches gives us indications of utility. Either method may render fundamental objectives available to us based on the commonalities among humans. Both offer techniques by which we can investigate our concerns of happiness and pursue our goals more effectively or efficiently. An examination of both fortifies us with warnings regarding corrupting or misleading influences. Still, these methods leave us in grave doubt whether they can provide sufficient instruction on what will make us happy as particularized individuals. Individual empiric approaches may deliver some insights, but developing these insights may expose us to high cost, delay, and error. Individual idealistic approaches are hampered as well. Our view seems to be obscured and restricted by our emotional inhibitions. Even if we gain a sense of our ideals by the way we feel about the satisfaction of our needs, our imagination of ideal circumstances is often undefined and insecure. Accordingly, both individual empiric and idealistic approaches leave us wanting for guidance on what will make us happy.

Considering the systemic inadequacy of these methods to improve idiosyncratic aspects of our happiness, we may wonder what alternatives we have left. Since both empiric studies and idealistic constructs seem to fail in designating what will make us happy, we may conclude that it is impossible to derive a coherent existential philosophy from them how to achieve individual happiness. For certainty, we appear to be reduced to pursuing our needs in a generic mode that is based on our commonalities. For individual guidance, we seem to be limited to trials in our pursuits led by often unclear notions of ideals. We can detect whether pursuits meet our ideals of happiness, but may not be able to define these ideals very well. Even if trials succeed, we might be missing a systematic, comprehensive approach that can optimize the fulfillment of all our needs. By building experiences based on where our trials guide us, we may in time develop worthwhile and relatively stable manners of pursuits. Much of that may be due to our increasing technical proficiency once we have identified needs. Only, that identification may come at a price of painful errors along the way, may never come, or arrive too late to relieve much pain. Moreover, the utility of principles we construct from our experiences may be limited because changes in our needs or in other circumstances in which we must or choose to pursue our needs may impose new challenges. The improvising, fragmented nature of our pursuits may limit us in acquiring timely and complete knowledge of what will make us happy.

Awareness of this situation may engender despair and resentment toward ourselves. We may blame ourselves for not being wiser, for not anticipating outcomes. In addition or instead, we may hold our environment responsible. We may ascribe fault to its creators or governors, other groups, individuals, and even objects and events for our inability to generate and maintain the level of happiness we crave. We might oppose a variety of purported adversaries and obstacles. Some of them may indeed limit or work against our happiness, and our interests may require that we stand our ground against such forces. But we may also battle restrictions or infringements on our activities that assist our happiness. We may not be able to grasp the difference if we do not possess a comprehensive understanding of our happiness. Even where we correctly identify limitations and infringements on our activities, we may not be able to counteract them effectively or efficiently. We may act mistakenly when we identify causes, attempt to defend against them, or try to overcome the opposition of our environment in providing means. These errors may waste resources as well as unnecessarily damage our relationship with our environment and make cooperation problematic or impossible. We may further focus on obtaining means without a genuine requirement for them or specific understanding of their utility. We may regard the pursuit and high esteem of certain means or types of means by others as indications for the potential of these in our pursuits. Not possessing or having difficulties in accessing them may move us to deem them even more desirable. Our needs might contain general notions of means. Yet these notions may be too undifferentiated to assure or enhance positive results. Without knowledge which means are better or best adapted to our needs, and which might cause us trouble or the extent of that trouble, or whether and how they might have positive and negative aspects, we may erroneously fight for or against a variety of means. Even if we could designate suitable means, our unconsidered manner of their pursuit might cause us to engage in activities that are not in our best interest.

In our awareness of the relative futility of our efforts, we may become wary, lethargic, and disappointed in an existence that fails to meet our desires in spite of our apparently best efforts. We may try to cope with our despair and resentment toward ourselves and our surroundings. Our helplessness is often such that we feel compelled to contort ourselves and our circumstances to forestall the pain of needs and pursuits we cannot sufficiently define. With such resigning strategies, we tend to solidify the deficiencies in our knowledge and other resources and our lack of motivation to overcome them. We may thus make no or only few meaningful strides to improve our happiness.

If we refuse to give up, we may keep struggling under the odds we are handed and develop coping mechanisms and diversionary abilities for the pain that we unavoidably incur. Still, despite that accommodation, we may wonder whether this is the best we can do. We may examine empiric and idealistic approaches we have identified for signs that we might be able to rise from the disappointing state of our happiness. We may review these approaches more intensely because, notwithstanding their shortcomings, they are the only available methods for understanding and interacting with the world, for the formulation and the pursuit of our wishes, for the fulfillment of our needs. Both result from, fortify, and represent the pain-pleasure mechanism that lies at the heart of our pursuits. Both the empiric and idealistic aspects of our pursuits are born from our experience of needs, pain and pleasure, the more comprehensive factual correlations of these experiences, and our mental capacity to process these factors. Both aspects are essential conditions for the successful pursuit of happiness. Without taking account and looking forward, we could not create happiness. What will make us happy is a combined subject of empiric and idealistic aspects. We ask what our circumstances are and, if they are painful or give rise to fear, we ask what we would like them to be. This intimate correlation makes it confounding that empiric and idealistic methods should not be able to collaborate to give us satisfactory answers to our question of what we want and that they seem to have only limited utility.

Not being able to imagine any methods beyond them, we may consider the possibility that we might not be using these methods in a manner that is appropriately considerate of their functionalities, that we might misapply their capabilities. Their utility lies in offering us an arsenal of techniques. It is up to us to identify, select, and relate these to find answers to the question what makes us happy, and to use them in implementing the answers. This function of empiric and idealistic techniques appears to be similar to many methods that allow us to explore and produce an array of substances for a variety of uses, that allow us to find and implement content. These techniques do not tell us for what to search, what product to create, or what process to operate. The derivation of a particular product is built into a technique as part of its possibilities. However, it may constitute only one of many products that can be generated through or with the support of a technique. This tends to turn techniques into general methods that can be adapted to various objectives. Because they are separated from the specifics of our motivations, they do not contain the answer to the question of our choices, of the purposes for which we might use them. The direction to seize upon possibilities they offer and the subjects of their en-

gagement must come from different sources and have to be developed
under different standards. They spring from emotional impulses that
our needs issue, and, because our happiness is a function of our needs,
our needs govern what will satisfy them. Empiric and idealistic methods cannot pose or deduce motivations independently. Nevertheless,
we may be able to apply them to coax our motivations out of us and to
bring their intent into reality. They may enable us to render our desires conscious and to build a concept of our happiness from these desires. This has already become apparent with regard to commonalities
of needs. Empiric and idealistic techniques can assist us in delineating
shared principles of happiness, building them to their closest approximation to shared ideals, and in deriving a philosophy that comprises
general insights about the nature and the workings of happiness and
its fundamental requirements. The task now is to build on these general aspects to include our idiosyncratic aspects. Such an expansion is
necessary because subjective aspects are of an essential importance for
our happiness. They carry importance not only as surplus installments
to be considered in addition to the general aspects of our happiness.
Our idiosyncrasies are often inseparable from the common aspects of
a need. Without their accommodation, we might not fulfill underlying
existential needs, let alone derive sufficient happiness. They modulate
the basic ingredients of a need to form a particularized, consolidated
entirety. Although we may be able to derive universal basic truths and
basic fulfillment from commonalities, our idiosyncrasies insist that we
advance beyond these. The individuality of our needs requires that we
employ empiric and idealistic techniques in particularized ways. If we
do not comprise our idiosyncrasies in defining and building happiness
and our philosophy of it, we create incomplete and thus substantially
ineffective guidance. We have to narrow the potential of general needs
to our individual requirements if we want to advance our happiness.

    We must scrutinize why empiric and idealistic techniques have
been instrumental in affording us general insights but have failed us
in more particular inquiries. There appears to be an obvious reason for
this failure. The commonalities of our needs and the nature of happiness are highly accessible to reason because they reflect objective requirements for individual and collective survival and thriving. In contrast, our idiosyncratic modulations appear to be a profoundly subjective aspects of our personality. Individualized needs may appear to be
only partly traceable by reason. They consist mostly of emotions that
do not seem to be a cogent or even a useful reflection of objective circumstances. Rather, many of them seem to constitute irrational deviations from sensible pursuits. That may make it appear as if individual-

izations of existential needs were of a different quality and may foster doubt whether the exploration of idiosyncratic needs can make much use of our general insights. Beyond a lack of objective association, difficulties in accessing, measuring, and communicating emotions seem to leave it to us individually to ascertain our idiosyncratic traits.

We may interpret our unique potential of insight as isolation. We may believe that we are left to our own devices to find who we are. But that is not entirely so. The prevailing subjectivity of what we attempt to find does not require the method for finding it to be subjective as well. The advantage of an objective method to elicit subjective content would be that, although we might have to undertake most or all of the work in revealing it individually, our exploration could rely on preexisting procedural knowledge and guidance. Such a technique could reduce error and enhance our odds of finding our happiness. It might save us considerable individual effort, leaving us free to concentrate on deriving the essence of what makes us individually happy and on moving forward with the implementation of our insights. The requirements of such a methodology for finding and pursuing individual happiness are demanding. It would have to be able to help us establish what makes each of us individually happy and how that happiness can be accomplished, maintained, augmented, and maximized. Its procedures would have to be applicable regardless of who we are. It would have to be neutral with regard to our personality, experiences, culture, beliefs, education, geography, technology, or economy. That presents a challenge. To keep the undertaking pure, one would have to look for universal procedural principles by which individual happiness can be determined yet abstain from suggesting what to think, feel, or implement substantively. As difficult as this task may seem, we have reason to conclude that it can be accomplished. The details of what we want may be highly subjective and may critically depend on our individual circumstances. Nevertheless, we possess indications that we may find a technique of revealing what we want that is common to all humans. The basic commonalities among humans in the fundamental character of their needs and their shared physiology, as well as the shared characteristic that they customize shared needs by idiosyncrasies provide the foundation for such a technique. They suggest that a general procedure might be devised that all humans would find helpful in extracting the particularities of their nature. We have previously tried to derive valid principles of happiness from commonalities and, because of particularities, have only succeeded in part. But our focus was then on finding substantive guidance. We now are using insights from that search into the nature of happiness to build a general methodology.

Initially, the claim that a general methodology of revealing happiness might exist is only a preconceived notion. It is an unsubstantiated claim that is derived from direct and indirect experiences and interpretations by its originator. Hence, there is a risk that the premises and arguments proving such methodology as well as the details of its method might be influenced by the originator's subjective viewpoint. Like any other theory, the claim of its existence begins with a hypothesis, an idea that is bundled with a wish for its affirmation. The claim that a general methodology of happiness exists is a proposition that its proponent wishes to be true. Thus, there is a potential that the premises and argument may be slanted in favor of proving such a claim. All precautions against the danger that we might be misled should therefore prevail until we become convinced of the methodology's objectivity. Then again, the claim that a general methodology exists by which we can find our individual happiness should not be greatly susceptible to substantive bias by its originator. After all, it proposes a technique by which we each are supposed to be able to identify, collect, comprehend, organize, and implement our own substantive tenets regarding happiness. Its immediate focus is the empowerment of individuals to discover and to examine their idiosyncratic substance by following the general method. Its goal is to assist individuals in the formulation of their own substantive existential philosophy. If the development of a general method could be kept free of substantive premises, assertions, or conclusions about happiness, substantive bias could be avoided.

But it is neither possible nor helpful to limit the development of a general method regarding happiness to procedural aspects. The form of establishing a personal philosophy of happiness cannot be entirely separated from its substance. The substance of our needs and our experiences according to their commands inform our development of a methodology for identifying our needs. This methodology takes on a substantive quality because it leads and connects to substance, however broadly defined or varied that substance might be. Without our notion of our needs, we would not be able to devise any useful procedural strategy for illuminating them. We would have no subject matter toward which we could orient our procedures. We would be aimless because we would not know what we are trying to find. Therefore, a procedure for the revelation of our needs cannot be created without a general concept of the substance of our needs. To the extent our research deals with substances and laws of nature, bias should be relatively easily excluded. These empiric aspects of our experiences naturally lend themselves to scientific review. Yet, because we explore our needs and what will fulfill them, we have inextricably chosen our ideals as the subject matter of our research even if we are looking for a technique to identify them. Due to their involvement, the empiric derivation of a procedural theory about finding the content of our needs, as well as its application, is in continuous danger of being taken over by conclusory shortcuts to what we presume to be our ideals. What we find is in unavoidable danger of being influenced by what we hope to find. Nevertheless, we must not ignore our wishes because they are the subject of our research. Rather than excluding them, we must register and learn to understand the dangers of circularity that emanate from our needs for the derivation of a method regarding their discovery. The circularity of common existential needs may already create a challenge for efforts to identify such needs. But their rational foundation in human survival and thriving makes this challenge manageable. The subjective influences of idiosyncratic needs appear to be distinctly more problematic. They may infect attempts to find a general method similarly to how they might taint the derivation of a more substantive general existential philosophy. Even if our logic seems sound to us, we may pursue strategies that obtain results ordained by our idiosyncratic mental traits. In our inquiries, idiosyncrasies might be difficult to separate from their existential underpinnings because it is in their nature to govern these for their benefit. We are necessarily hampered in our undertaking because we have not used the technique yet. The method we are trying to identify must take the possibility of such circularities into account and disable them. It must reveal our needs without giving them a chance of influencing the revelation process. We may be able to thwart such undue influence in the conceptualization phase of our method with relative ease because we are not approaching particular needs yet. We may obtain a general notion of our common needs and that idiosyncratic needs might interfere with common needs and attempts to identify these. We may also grasp that idiosyncratic needs might strive even more to interfere with revelation efforts that focus on their nature and activities. Still, to devise capable countermeasures against such influences that might hamper the development of a general method and a concept of our happiness, we must comprehend the substantive positioning of existential and specific needs better.

Understanding our needs fundamentally requires the reconciliation of their idealistic ambitions to their empiric roots. This is necessary to create clarity because an idealistic approach constitutes an outgrowth of the empiric method. The reconciliation of idealistic aspects with their empiric sources is based on an acknowledgment that ideals, needs, and wishes spring from physical phenomena, from the interaction of substances and laws of nature. This forces the conclusion that they must be decipherable in an empiric, scientific, objective fashion. The empiric method finds fertile ground in the research of human affairs because of the great commonalities in the physiological setup of humans that can lead to the establishment of some general substantive rules about the nature of happiness. Such general rules are extensions of the principles at work in creating and maintaining our shared physiology. They refer to natural substances and principles in their application. This framework affords us empiric access to our existential needs. But it also assists us in ascertaining and judging our particularities. The particularities of our traits are grafts onto our shared physiological substance. They must correlate with and therefore conform to a certain extent to the framework of our common needs. That framework lays a universal basis for idiosyncratic needs and the parameters within which they can range. This appears to create an empiric foundation, a common denominator that helps us to formulate a scientific method for defining idiosyncrasies by their deviations within its parameters of existential functionality and beyond. It also provides a scientific basis for the possible modification, suppression, elimination, or even the creation of idiosyncrasies. The shared substance of our needs further supplies a basis for the development of derivative laws. These give direction regarding the practical applicability of that substance in the relationship of needs in us, among humans, and with our nonhuman environment. Because these laws spring from our common basis, their more detailed categorizations constitute commonly shared principles as well. Their more immediate practical relation with substances and principles from which our world is organized imposes these in additional detail as common foundations on our endeavors. Together, these human and natural laws posit the parameters by which we can identify idiosyncratic nonconformities and by which idiosyncratic pursuits must be judged because they must abide by them to succeed.

These general requirements may narrow a pursuit of happiness to one feasible choice regardless of our personal idiosyncrasies or specific circumstances. We may encounter general principles that require close or precise adherence to a particular manner of pursuit. But that does not seem to be the case in many instances. Most of our common needs appear to permit a considerable variety of possibilities to satisfy their substance. The general requirements of our needs may be sufficiently expansive to allow flexibility in their definition and fulfillment. That is demonstrated by the range of idiosyncrasies among individuals we detect in the successful individual satisfaction of a common need. The requirements for the fulfillment of most existential needs occur in the form of parameters within which we may operate and still secure their fulfillment. Within these parameters, we may distinguish conditions that are better or best suited to bring forth success. Thus, our insight into general conditions causes us not only to determine that certain substantive concepts are viable or not viable to meet the generalized purpose of an existential need. It may also permit us to differentiate a gradation among viable concepts in relation to their advantages and disadvantages in meeting that need. The idiosyncratic aspects of our needs superimpose onto this background. Still, the principal categorizations pursuant to general criteria of our existential needs tend to persist. A pursuit that is not viable to support a common need cannot become viable because of the particularization of such a need. If it cannot satisfy our underlying need, it will not be able to satisfy the composite of general and idiosyncratic features because idiosyncratic modulations cannot occur independently. However, the narrowing of existential needs by our idiosyncrasies appears to make it possible that conditions that fulfill the underlying need fail to fulfill the composite need because they fail to satisfy its idiosyncratic aspects. Further, idiosyncrasies may impose divergent gradations among the remaining solutions. Idiosyncratic particularizations may also disagree with derivative regulations and the definitions of their foundations in fundamental law. Their individual contraction of the range of capable pursuits and their variations in the ranking of pursuits may not leave a general substantive existential philosophy with much practical relevance.

Missing correspondence between general utility and individual preferences may lead to difficulties and possibly tragic results for the fulfillment of our needs. Our particularizations of common needs consistent with our individual personality traits may create demands that situate us beyond a sufficient approach to satisfy underlying needs by principle or available means. They may also exclude better or the best solutions within a general parameter. These problems might be aggravated by incongruences among idiosyncratic needs. Meeting requirements set by common needs comprehensively may already challenge us and call for compromises that restrict our ability to pursue each existential need according to its own criteria of success. But our internal particularities are bound to introduce requirements among our needs that additionally narrow our options. This would only be useful where strict guidance is necessary or helpful for the overall beneficial fulfillment of our existential needs. In all other incidents, it deprives us of opportunities to succeed or to excel in our individual or collective survival and thriving. In addition, idiosyncratic needs may considerably augment the incongruities that might already exist among individuals on account of their separately centered common needs. Competition

among individuals based on common needs might also be overcome
by the application of common needs. But idiosyncratic needs seem to
lack this capacity to harmonize. This may render them impediments
to the fulfillment of common and idiosyncratic needs among individuals that may be difficult to resolve. These causes may weaken our position and enable other adversities to have more severe consequences.
Our idiosyncrasies may position us to where we can meet our existential needs less well or where meeting them becomes less likely or impossible. Their demands may also impede their own fulfillment or the
implementation of other idiosyncratic needs. As a consequence, they
may depress or eliminate our chances of individual and collective survival and thriving or at least curb our chances of reaching happiness.

Hence, we may regard idiosyncrasies in our needs as potential
threats to our happiness. This may appear absurd because they define
in part what makes us happy. Still, the happiness they might produce
might not be worth incurring the pain or the risk of pain they might
cause. Any attempt to advance our happiness would have to take this
consideration into account. It would have to support the adjustment
of idiosyncrasies to approach and meet optimal settings for satisfying
their fundamental common needs. Arguably, differentiations in objectives, abilities, and pursuits may be important for reaching, improving,
and maximizing the fulfillment of our common needs in a cooperative
manner and for the development of humanity. Yet specialization may
not have to be a function in accord with idiosyncratic preferences. At
times, it may flow from particular talents that we may possess regardless of our preferences. Conversely, it may result from shortcomings in
our ability to fulfill our needs at the levels they demand. If we had all
the capacities of other humans, the only required or useful differentiations among humans would be situational. We might fulfill a variety
of functions individually or assume a variety of positions in a cooperative undertaking. But these differentiations would not rise to the level
of entrenched particularities. We might vary our pursuits as required,
to broaden our experiences, and to disrupt the monotony and lack of
freedom of specialization. As our mental and tangible abilities develop, we should be able to meet our common needs better through versatility. This should particularly cause a significant leap in the satisfaction of needs that rely on our individual application or personal aptitude because it would alleviate our suffering from individual and personal impossibilities. Any advantages from a development of humanity through alterations that are initially idiosyncratic could be assumed
and increased by planned, tuned modifications on a broad scale after
restricted testing. Arguably, even if we possess versatility, idiosyncrat-

ic personality traits may continue to optimize pursuits by motivating particular efforts. That we can undertake a variety of occupations does not mean that we find any, let alone optimal, fulfillment in them and pursue them energetically. However, we might not require idiosyncrasies for such motivational purposes. We could think of a best reconciliation mode under an assessment of our common needs alone. To the extent our mental powers have not yet arrived at a level at which they can supplant idiosyncratic preferences in the facilitation of specialized utility, these may perform constructive functions. But our preferences may not correspond to our requirements for specialization. They may be founded on genetic or acquired modulations that are not responding to challenges we face, are ill-conceived or ill-constructed, or are in response to challenges that subsequently transform or subside. To the extent that is the case, we must obtain the capacity to modify, subdue, or eliminate such traits if we wish to improve our happiness.

Still, we may hesitate regarding the adjustment of our personality because we consider it as the essence of who we are from which we have difficulties separating. In addition, we may remain apprehensive concerning external engineering of our personality. Much of it already appears to be formed by external influences without our participation or over our objection. We may therefore be reluctant to allow external influences even more power over us. Although we might acknowledge that external influence might be used to our benefit, we might fear its erroneous application and abuse. At most, we might agree to give individuals whose needs strongly include the promotion of our wellbeing some forming authority. Yet, even there, we may frequently have grounds to suspect that their formation of our personality serves their needs more than ours and afflicts us with transferred or otherwise instilled idiosyncrasies that pose additional obstacles to our happiness. We may not trust anybody with the reformation of our personality except ourselves. Even if it is inevitable that we obtain formational influences from external sources during phases when we are immature and impressionable, we would likely want to be in charge of later adjustments and judge whether an alteration is to our advantage. The problem with such an undertaking is that our personality may already be shaped to a point where it becomes difficult for us to identify or implement beneficial changes to our personality. In particular, our motivation to increase our happiness may be hampered by motivations of detrimental idiosyncrasies to remain. Their motivations may be pitted against motivations by impaired needs to liberate themselves. In this confrontation, our desire to overcome unfavorable self-restraint fortifies our desire to gain a better understanding of our idiosyncrasies.

We may define emotional idiosyncrasies fundamentally by distinguishing them from common aspects of our needs. Such a distinction also gains in importance because we may not accord to them the protection and support of common needs and because we use common needs as standards to judge the utility of idiosyncratic deviations. All this makes it necessary that we construct a complete general substantive existential philosophy. Scientific research might help us to reveal underlying existential dimensions of our needs. Yet, even if we discover a competent physiological method for measuring happiness, we might not be able to distinguish general from idiosyncratic aspects in the reactions of individuals. To the extent physiological indications are not available or sufficient, the distinction might be left to the registration and communication by individuals in whom these phenomena occur. However, because of the consolidated character of common and idiosyncratic aspects of a need, individuals who feel happiness as well as others who evaluate their expressions might not be able to distinguish them. This would reduce our exploration to identifying common denominators through uncontroverted affirmation from individuals that a certain cause makes them sense a certain type of happiness or unhappiness. This low standard might be necessary to obtain agreement on very basic definitions of fundamental rights. But it might not be sufficient for defining the full extent of common needs and rights.

That the scope of applicability of a general substantive philosophy should be described by the scope of its acceptance appears to be a fair requirement. No theory about human happiness that proclaims its applicability to other humans can deny the legitimacy of personal verification. It must be able to withstand the critical theoretical investigation and empiric verification by those to whom it claims to apply. For a theory that asserts general applicability, requiring general approbation is merely a matter of matching this assertion with its reality. If its principles are to be generally applicable, its underlying characteristics would have to be present or elicitable in each of us. Our critical theoretical investigation and its empiric verification should naturally meet with the concordance of underlying causes in us. We have a threefold safety mechanism at our disposal that allows us to evaluate the veracity of such a theory. First, we should be able to confirm its premises by comparing them with our perceptions of reality. Second, its argumentative steps and conclusions would have to comport with logic. Third, to prove that its general principles can offer guidance, we should be able to implement them successfully. By these measures, we each can individually and directly judge the soundness of a substantive existential philosophy through our own critical exploration and application.

Nevertheless, even if a common factor exists, its general approbation may not happen. This may not only be attributable to the foreclosure of our awareness, approval, or willingness to conduct verification by our idiosyncratic mental traits. Other genetic or acquired dispositions, experiences that do not give rise to traits, a lack of instruction, or the unavailability of resources may negatively affect our verification capacity. We may not have had occasion or the need to confirm or disprove the existence of a purported general rule. External circumstances may restrain our activities by prohibition or by manipulation. These factors may hamper practical verification even if the underlying commonality is provided. Such adversities may foreclose our ability or willingness to confirm general substantive principles as well as a procedural general existential philosophy. The grounds that keep us from recognizing general principles of happiness and other factors that fill the void may be unorganized. They may be the result of circumstances that are not aimed at setting parameters or giving instructions for our mind and activities. But some reorientations and impositions that undermine or block our recognition of the essence of our happiness may be more systematic. The entrenched quality of our idiosyncratic mental traits and other conditions may be considered as systematic even if their causes were not systematic. In addition, we may be subjected to systematic efforts by other individuals to impose a philosophy on us.

The offer of theoretical and practical verification by an existential philosophy may place such a philosophy in contention with other philosophies or with their constituent ideas because these might have to match that openness to persist. This contest may occur in individuals' minds as well as in a societal context. It intensifies with the extent of overlap in asserted coverage. Particularly a philosophy that declares general applicability is likely to be placed into an adversarial position with other philosophies or rudimentary philosophical concepts. Established concepts may try to preclude a new general existential philosophy to plead and prove its case. They may try to hinder its verification process. Resident personal or more widely held attitudes may attempt to influence our ability or our willingness to explore and reshape our notions of substantive happiness or of how happiness can be revealed because their existence might be at stake. They may engender adverse bias and fear that militate not only against change but even the consideration of change. They may make it hard for us to free our mind or our external physical circumstances to engage in dispassionate reflection and meaningful verification. They may induce us to forgo or may preclude us from considering, testing, recognizing, or acting upon the recognition of benefits even if they present themselves to our grasp.

In these strategies, established points of view may relate to an innate apprehension regarding change. Implications of change by new philosophies may create fear of the unknown, of upheaval, and deprivation of presently secure benefits. We may therefore already autonomously develop sufficient apprehension to make us turn away from concepts that might benefit us. But established external philosophies may effectively use and cultivate such a fear against insurgent philosophies. These impediments might make it difficult or impossible for a valid existential philosophy to convince us of its applicability. Even if we are exposed to its teachings, we may hold on to confusion, inabilities, or erroneous pursuits. We may also follow those who purport to clarify our confusion and try to explain our failures with familiar references. We may favor established philosophies for the relative security they offer. Their ingrained mechanisms, societal sanction, and approval by persons we respect suggest that they offer valid manners of pursuit. We may cling to this notion against contradictory evidence.

The collective resistance by internal and external obstacles may render the derivation of common aspects of our needs difficult. It may also hinder the adoption of a common procedure that might assist us to derive more individualized substantive insights. Even if individuals could settle on general principles or at least common foundations for them, differences are likely to emerge when these fundamental principles or foundations are applied and to be given definition, thus resulting in disagreement. We may therefore have to settle on less than unanimous approbation results. The best preliminary indication of a common principle or a common foundation of a principle we may be able to obtain is majority consent. Yet the presence of competing existential philosophies and personal dispositions and circumstances may render even such a manner of consent difficult. Although we may find confirmation that certain foundations, principles, and assortments of such principles in a philosophy apply to most humans, their rejection by some individuals gives rise to the possibility that we might not be dealing with universal essences. We may try to save the concept of a general theory by claiming that it typically applies to all humans, except for aberrations. However, casting dispersions on those who disagree and their opinions and designating them as erroneous could not forestall the fact that our theory misses its proof by general applicability. We may not be able to show the difference between a general and a limited theory, between principles that are founded the commonalities among humans and subjective particularities. The margins of consent regarding general principles may overlap with margins of widely proliferated idiosyncrasies or unrelated erroneously held principles.

If a philosophy should not achieve universal corroboration, it must submit to such insecurity even if that is deemed undeserved by its proponents. Asserting the applicability of a philosophy over the objection of purported subjects would render such a philosophy into an oppressive ideology. In avoidance of assuming such characteristics, a philosophy that fails universal acclaim must console itself with the notion that it may at least provide guidance for some or perhaps many. But it would have to abandon its assertion of general applicability and could not be trusted as a universal guide in the pursuit of happiness. Arguably, the difference between general and more limited applicability of principles regarding happiness should matter little because all theories must prove themselves in our review before we accept their applicability to us. Still, we may be more motivated to test an alleged principle if we perceive that it might be generally applicable because this represents an increased likelihood that it can help us. A recipe with a smaller circle of approval bears less likelihood of compatibility with our needs and situation. We should be less inclined to try such principles unless there are other strong indications of their applicability. Hence, the appearance of general tenets of happiness is important for our individual orientation in how we might find happiness. Then again, widely cast principles may be slated toward the benefit of certain parties at the cost of others. The broad acceptance of a principle does not allow us the conclusion that it should be beneficial to us.

Even if we must maintain a critical stance on the proliferation of philosophies, the ascertainment of general tenets of happiness is also important for pursuits in social settings. If we can refer to common values and principles of pursuit, we can more easily fashion modes of cooperation and peaceful coexistence. Basic commonalities allow us to support and protect at least the core of our interests because these interests and the need for their advancement are shared. We may regard our commonalities of pursuit and the general principles that can be derived from them as the basis of a fair social order, as the foundation of just laws. The establishment of general principles of pursuit hence becomes critical for building and preserving our happiness in a world where we must, or have the opportunity to, correlate with other individuals. The inability to gain universal approval for a general philosophy might then constitute a significant obstacle to the establishment and advancement of our happiness in a social context. As we express idiosyncrasies in the pursuit of our common needs, our cooperation and our coexistence are burdened by individual differences. We might console ourselves with the idea that we might limit the establishment of a social context to individuals who are agreeable on most facets of happiness that are affected by their contact and who are able and willing to manage their differences. Yet such a group of similarly minded individuals may not be sufficiently numerous or coherent to provide the functionality and harmony we desire. Further, contacts with disagreeing individuals and groups might be inescapable and induce discord. Thus, the inability of humans to reach agreement on guidelines for happiness forms a significant impediment for their happiness.

We might conclude that a systematic comprehensive improvement of our condition according to general substantive principles of happiness is largely illusory past a very basic level. We do not appear capable of categorically separating common from idiosyncratic needs beyond that level. We might only establish approximations of pure existential needs. Because our idiosyncratic needs combine with our existential needs to form a composite need, we might uncover existential needs to some extent by peeling away aspects we can recognize as idiosyncrasies. We might achieve additional progress in ascertaining common principles and bringing them to free expression by increased levels of scientific consideration and confirming agreement. Arguably, the genetic and possibly a generally conditioned acquired sourcing of our existential needs makes them persist even if they are covered by idiosyncrasies. They might be merely concealed, dormant, scattered, neglected, unreflected, or suppressed. But this common underpinning might also be reduced and contorted to where it becomes idiosyncratic. Even if we could find common substance, its oppression by our idiosyncrasies and our preference of them might depress its relevance.

To the extent idiosyncrasies obstruct our achievement of maximum fulfillment for their underlying existential needs without compensatory advantages, they would have to be neutralized. Moreover, if we could direct idiosyncrasies, they would work best for us if we could train them to help us select and achieve the best manner of pursuit for the underlying needs. Arguably, this is or it should be the focus of upbringing and education. Additionally, the superior performance by individuals whose genetic disposition stimulates them to engage in appropriate demeanor for individual and collective survival and thriving should favor the strengthening of such genetic idiosyncrasies. Both influences would contribute to establish positive idiosyncrasies that are most advantageous for the satisfaction of common needs. But the extent as well as the utility of such positive idiosyncrasies seems debatable. Our common traits already seem to contain ample motivations for their optimization and may already be the result of many idiosyncratic optimizations that have attained commonality. Further, optimization often requires more flexibility than idiosyncratic traits can tolerate.

Beneficial idiosyncratic motivations seem to compete with genetic and environmental causes that result in malformations and the proliferation of idiosyncrasies that damage the fulfillment of existential needs for those afflicted by them and others. It appears difficult to gauge which types of idiosyncrasies are more prevalent, which will finally succeed, or whether their competition will continue. Over time, this contest, its modalities, and its outcome may resolve whether humanity can survive or at least how successful and happy it can be. Yet how much idiosyncratic aspects of our needs interfere with our individual and collective survival and thriving is also essential for our current affairs and deserves to be more immediately addressed.

Current shortcomings of idiosyncrasies necessitate that we adjust their negative features and not merely depend on generational adjustments. If we do not let other individuals adjust our personality, we each have to address our own idiosyncrasies. We might try to regulate them if they produce more impairment than benefit or, if they already produce more happiness than pain, to make them more effective or efficient. If we decide that the benefit they generate is not worth the risk or cost they engender, we might try to modify, eliminate, or suppress them. If we determine that the happiness we receive from idiosyncrasies could be ameliorated, we may change them as well. But any such engineering may prove to be a daunting challenge. Features of needs that damage our happiness or fail to optimize it still contribute to our happiness during their pursuit and upon their fulfillment and detract from our happiness upon their nonfulfillment. The immediate damage to our happiness when we affect such aspects of needs may prevent us from taking action even if that would benefit our happiness. We may fear the elimination, restructuring, or inhibition of needs because we equate it with a partial death similar to our death as an entirety. If we are successful in eliminating or recasting them, a part of our personality will come to an end. We may associate painful consequences with such a purported partial death that we imagine to be similar to those we fear to loom upon our ultimate demise. Only, such consequences may seem more likely during our lifetime because we are certain to be aware of our deprivation. Even ideas of suppression may arouse claustrophobic reactions similar to our fear of death. We may build an apprehension against the elimination, revision, and suppression of idiosyncratic needs that may already arise during our assessment of negative idiosyncrasies. This may transform our concept of happiness to an ambiguous stance without reconciliation. The influence of idiosyncrasies we might have to adjust to improve our happiness may grow particularly strong if we are more successful in their pursuit than in the pursuit of objectives that reflect more positively on our overall happiness. Our frustration about the state of our happiness may cause us to place additional emphasis on pursuits that reward us more readily.

Even if we recognize the damaging or the less than optimized effects of an idiosyncrasy, we may not be technically capable to affect it fundamentally. To the extent we cannot permanently transform or eliminate a damaging aspect, we are relegated to suppressing it. But this may only be a constructive choice where we receive more damage than benefit from it. Further, the continuous efforts required for suppression expose us to a mounting accumulation of pain and loss of resources. That detriment may prompt us to accommodate detrimental idiosyncrasies. We may find the pain resulting from the pursuit of a damaging need more bearable than the pain resulting from its continued denial. We may also find that a compromise between these states suits us best. However, regardless of whether we can eliminate or permanently revise a damaging need or we are reduced to suppressing it, confronting detrimental emotional traits and possibly other types of mental traits that contribute may be difficult. Idiosyncratic traits may customarily fail to appear to us as distinctive from their underlying existential needs. Even if we can identify damaging or nonoptimized aspects, we might not succeed isolating these traits. The attachment by idiosyncratic needs to underlying existential needs may enable them to control and call on defense mechanisms of these to enter the fight on their behalf. This may make them formidable contenders.

To identify the grounds for idiosyncratic resistance and address damaging or nonoptimized idiosyncrasies, we must have clarity about their sourcing. We must separate genetic and acquired mental dispositions from particularities that are more superficially imposed on us. Our pursuits are also determined by impediments originating outside our mind, as well as by the quality and quantity of obviously physical means in us and means generally in our surroundings. These conditions might dictate to us that we pursue our needs in manners that are damaging for our happiness or fall short of our ideals. Some of them might be improved. Others may present insurmountable individual or general impossibilities. These conditions form the setting in which we must try to find our happiness. By describing what is or may be possible, the objective facts defining our body and our environment leave an area of available possibilities among which we may choose means and strategies for the fulfillment of our existential needs. This area often only partly overlaps with the area of what will satisfy these needs. Not everything that is possible will be desirable. Nor will everything that we want on behalf of our needs be possible. We may have some flexibility to adjust our possibilities to our wishes unless impossibilities are absolute. We may attempt to expand our maneuvering space into areas of current individual or general impossibility. To the extent our idiosyncrasies foreclose or hinder the selection of choices, we may venture to enlarge them by their revision, elimination, or suppression. But the competent management of our idiosyncratic needs may place a significant burden on us. Neither what we want according to our existential needs or according to idiosyncratic modulations nor what is possible may have crystallized sufficiently in our mind for us to render a determination concerning our most appropriate course of action. If the partial congruence of what we might want and what might be possible presents us with sufficient space to provide alternatives in one, the other, or both categories, we have to select. We have to determine which desirable or feasible solutions are acceptable, more acceptable than others, or most acceptable for a particular need. We further have to place what is possible and what might satisfy us into the context of our entirety of needs and the future fulfillment of the same need. We must systematically weigh the advantages and disadvantages of each available course of action to select the most suitable course in view of the entirety of our happiness. We have to govern our purview.

Still, if we worry about the technicalities of means and strategies while we try to understand our needs, we may introduce practical prospects into the definition of our needs that may confuse what we want with what is feasible, effective, or efficient. We may misidentify practical aspects that we consider to be potential means, obstacles, or boundaries with our wishes and needs. Such a commingling of principles can short-circuit our determination process to where we cut the extent of our needs to what is feasible. As a consequence, we may not know our needs and may not improve our practical abilities to match our needs. We may stunt the growth of our happiness. We may place our resources into technicalities that fail to match the demands of our needs or do not correspond with their ideals. To avoid these mistakes, we must gather awareness of our needs first before we look for practical means for their fulfillment. We must also refrain from prematurely judging our idiosyncrasies during their discovery because that might prevent us from fully developing our insights of their features. To adequately estimate the utility or damaging character of our idiosyncrasies and to address them competently, we must obtain a true impression of them. We must begin our undertaking to improve our happiness by allowing our needs to come forth and express themselves unfettered by concerns for requirements or consequences. We must find the pure substance of our needs whatever that substance might be.

To do that competently, a method that claims to help us derive such substance must itself be neutral regarding substance. If we cannot conceive of a method to reveal our needs ourselves, we may turn to external guidance. Invoking such assistance would seem to give rise to the same potential problems of possible undue influence as in the area of substantive philosophies. It seems that there is no way to exclude this risk entirely. Nevertheless, we can minimize undue influence in the assistance we use if we limit external advice to the investigational method and undertake the observations and interpretations ourselves. This might still expose us to some undue influence through the choice of suggested methods. But if a method that claimed substantive neutrality excluded certain substantive insights or guided us toward certain substantive insights over others, those allusions should become obvious because of their content. To forestall such an eventual bias, we must review the submitted methods concerning their neutrality. Moreover, we will have to be mindful not to introduce substantive bias of our own construction. Substantive neutrality is not only important to ensure the applicability of the method to anybody and to prevent external influence. It is also critical for our individual application of the method to yield an unbiased statement of our needs. Only if we obtain such an account can we engage in a fully competent substantive appraisal and treatment of our needs by comprehensively exploring their properties and interrelations. Maintaining such a critical position of neutrality appears difficult because our prejudgments may influence our application of methods. External and self-generated distortions of our needs may extend their damaging influences over our mental processes to this investigative phase. To minimize such influences, we must initially keep ourselves from placing our insights into a context of what we presently consider as proper, useful, frivolous, embarrassing, or dangerous. We must hand the idealistic sections of our mind over to our empiric facilities for a mere accounting. Our assessments must be reserved until later when we are sufficiently informed to make a judgment about what we discover. At that time, we will decide which features of our personality we want to keep, change, shed, or subdue, and which features should have priority over others.

Before we engage in self-discovery in application of external advice, we must verify our agreement with its premises and the correctness of its logic. In addition, verification that we have applied a proper procedure would ultimately be provided if it reveals our needs and enables us to implement those needs better. We will discern whether a suggested method works by whether it can assist us in improving our happiness. This constitutes a built-in device for uncovering the shortcomings of the method. If we do not succeed, we may be able to trace our difficulties to the method. Then again, failure may also show that we have not applied the method to its greatest potential. We may not have followed the method accurately or our defense mechanisms may not have permitted us a good, comprehensive look at who we are. We might have to repeat and possibly improve the processes that give us insight into our needs. Our application of that method might be examined and critiqued by other individuals. Such an undertaking might be helpful, but it may also present the same problems that we already encountered with regard to finding substantive guidance for our pursuits. It might be difficult if not impossible to give competent advice on procedural issues without considering the results of methods. Even if procedural advice can be kept pure, it might easily constitute or be construed as a substantive intervention because it leads us to substantive conclusions. Therefore, we might exercise caution in engaging external procedural assistance in our self-exploration. We might only involve such assistance if we cannot proceed adequately on our own. Such a point may be reached if we cannot identify or, in a subsequent stage, reconcile our needs or pursuits in spite of our best attempts. We might further enlist assistance to eliminate, modify, or suppress idiosyncrasies that unduly disturb the pursuit of other needs if we cannot adequately address these problems ourselves. Depending on our situation, such services might be essential for our success. Still, even with assistance, we may have much to explore, learn, determine, and possibly to correct that could not be undertaken by assistance for us.

Those who are looking for ready-made, easy methods to mend their issues with happiness might be disappointed that the development of our happiness requires methodical, careful involvement. They might be perturbed that there is no quick fix to their ailments, that they cannot simply engage someone or something to find and create happiness for them. However, we should be used to the idea that happiness is not easily understood or accomplished. Based on our experiences, it should come as no surprise that any approach that might improve our happiness would involve our commitment and effort. Expectations of shortcuts or that we could be delivered from the burdens of our pursuits without the related labors might likely be causes for much unhappiness because we would place our hopes and resources into strategies that are likely to fail. If we turn away from such pretenses and explore a procedural method to reveal the entirety of our needs, we enter new terrain. We leave preconceived notions of our needs and how we should pursue them behind and concentrate exclusively on what we find in us. The next chapter begins that discovery.

CHAPTER 17
OUR INNER ESSENCE

When we explore our needs, we may categorize them as mental constructs because they involve perceptive, rational, and emotional characteristics. We are inclined to define our mind as the repository of our awareness composed by these characteristics. That awareness provides us with a sense of self. Although we identify with our obviously physical aspects to some extent, we reserve a more intimate concept of self to our mental aspects, our inner self. We perceive our mind to be of a nonphysical, higher nature. This distinction is based on the pairing of a momentous deficiency of our mind with a remarkable aptitude. The deficient aspect is our lack of awareness of our mental structures and processes as physiological phenomena. The remarkable aptitude is our mind's ability to manufacture mental representations of our world and to develop these representations in its service into further representations that it can again process. It can thus build and rule an abstracted world. We tend to separate that inner reality and the mystery of its generating mechanisms from outward aspects that may find reflection in our mind. We designate our inner world and its generating mechanisms as our essence, and everything else as exterior matters.

These impressions give rise to the tendency of attributing our body to the outside world. We may recognize our body as a necessary host for our mind and that we must assist it to sustain its host functions. We may view it as a possession to which we may attribute various value. We may regard it as a separate adjunct with its own, automatic functions. We may seek to control our body to implement resolutions of our mind that transcend the body's support functions. Such a viewpoint leads us to distinguish our needs into those that serve our physical requirements and those that attend the purportedly more exalted functions of our mind. Maintaining this differentiation implies a split personality. It prompts us to view part of our personality as being composed of primitive, animal needs that are forced upon us by our support system but are not part of our inner self. It causes us to focus on more advanced, purportedly nonphysical needs that we regard as our true nature. Maintaining this artificial distinction may prompt us to degrade needs at the center of our individual and collective survival and thriving. If we are to be happy, we have to supersede our intuitive but untenable discrimination toward our body. While we can and, for an understanding of our self, must acknowledge and explore our mental functions, we must recognize them as integrated parts of our body. We must extend our emotional mind to encompass all our needs.

Cognizance of our inner self may be obtained by observing and measuring the structures and processes of our personality. To achieve these insights, we have to focus on our personality as an object of exploration. However, in this undertaking, we encounter a problem of circularity. To obtain observations and measurements, we have to be able to observe and to measure aspects that can be distinguished from the mechanism that observes and measures. If there is not such a distinction, if the facility engaged in observation and measurement is to observe and measure itself, the observation and measuring might fail. The facility might not be equipped to turn on itself as an object. That problem seems to apply to our mind. We have very little direct knowledge about the generation of our mental phenomena. We can identify our sensory exposure and the mental results it produces. But we cannot very well turn our senses inward and trace the physiological structures and processes that produce these results. Our mind presents us with results, and we are often left to speculate how it produced them. This may be regarded as an issue of missing sensory facilities. Arguably, that problem could be solved if we find technological assistance. With sufficient sensory impressions about its structures and resulting processes, an information processing device like our mind should be able to process information about itself. Yet our issues go deeper.

A problem of circularity also arises if an information processing device is employed to produce information about how it processes information. Because the investigation about the way we process information is processed by the mechanism that is the subject of our inquiry, the investigation could not follow other processing possibilities than the process we are trying to investigate. If the device and its exploration process are flawed or limited, its self-investigation is subject to the same inadequacies. Therefore, we might be unable to detect our mental flaws and limitations. Here again, we might employ technological assistance. That seems to be a promising prospect, except that engaging machines might not advance us if we or others pass the same mental inadequacies that disqualify us on to them. We might derive use from the processing by other individuals and their technological devices if they do not share the same deficiencies. Such assistance may be impaired by other deficiencies. But these would be easier to determine if we or other sources of assistance would not suffer these deficiencies. Ultimately, we may only be able to trust the adequacy of our or external processing if it stands up to the rigors of scientific proof. While we may refer to such a clarification generally, it may not be sufficiently available for many of our specific endeavors. Further, we may not engage them because we fear interference with our decision making or reputation, or unauthorized use of information by others. As a result, we may be detained in our mental processing disabilities. This may render us incapable of investigating or evaluating our mind. Our lack of self-awareness may translate into a lack of self-determination.

But the sweeping scope of such a conclusion does not comport with the way we experience ourselves. We do observe that we possess self-awareness, that we can reflect on our traits, our needs, and their consequences. We detect the ability to distance ourselves sufficiently from aspects of our self to determine their nature and validity in our pursuits. We notice that we can determine what makes us happy and that we can change our mind and ways to comport with these determinations. We sense that we possess some awareness regarding what goes on within our mind. We appear to be able to gain sufficient distance for at least some self-reflection. Still, these instances seem to be imprecise and transitory. The act of capturing, understanding, and describing our personality seems to be surprisingly difficult. Who we are inside mostly appears to us as an intuitive, nebulous notion. It is neither perceptible by us as a detailed image nor as a totality. Our direct exposure to our self does not equal comprehension. Beyond suffering from possible circularity of processing facilities, we seem to lack focus and resolve to know ourselves. These combined deficiencies of self-observation cause us to be largely unconscious of our self. This unconsciousness may prevent a closer understanding of what will make us happy. To gain insight, we have to overcome these obstructions. We might achieve that by applying an indirect empiric method to our personality. While we may not be able to directly sense our mental processes, we can perceive their results. These provide us with evidence that our processing of information might be accurate or deficient because our needs are being fulfilled or fail. We may use these insights to explore the structures and processes that produce these results.

Although we may refer to us as an undifferentiated singularity, a review of our needs makes us recognize that our personality is not a homogeneous unit. It is a conglomerate of separately conceived mental traits whose correlation produces who we are. That our personality may be constituted of distinct components does not seem to make our task of defining our personality easier. Another part of the difficulty in developing an understanding of ourselves is that so many of the ingredients and the mechanisms in us have come about without our involvement and outside our control. Some of our mental traits appear to be preordained by our nature as humans. They appear to be hardwired into our physiology by common genetic tradition. They may also be due to ubiquitous external physiological influences that bear on all humans manifestly or by perception. We may refer to these mental traits as common mental traits or common traits. They represent the basic mental dispositions in all humans in pursuit of shared existential needs. They are part of a broader commonality of dispositions that includes other, more tangible shared physiological dispositions. Another part of us may be determined by intangible and tangible dispositions that are not common to all humans. These encompass conditions that are caused by genetic mutation in fewer than all of us as well as dispositions that are produced by nongenetic physical influences that affect less than all humans. Such nongenetic causes include particular nutrition, biological, chemical, radiological, traumatic, and other physical exposure or sensory impressions during and subsequent to our development. These nongenetic causes may hamper our development pursuant to original genetic code or with the functioning of the resulting physiology upon its establishment. We may designate any genetic and nongenetic dispositions that affect less than all humans specific dispositions. Specific dispositions of mental traits may be designated specific mental traits or specific traits. While it might be possible that specific dispositions could be formed as separate phenomena, they regularly appear to occur as variations of common dispositions that render aspects of them specific. Understanding common and specific dispositions necessitates awareness that our environment defines part of our physiological essence more directly than through reactive genetic programming. Nongenetic physical influences may directly affect genetic physiological structures and processes. They may further influence the potential that genetic dispositions provide and thus create nongenetic physiological dispositions. In a departure from the relative predictability of genetic conditions and of general environmental conditions that directly and indirectly affect our body, our existential functions seem to be heavily exposed to specific direct environmental influences. But such an exposure appears to be eclipsed by indirect specific environmental influences that filter through our perceptions and impact our rational and emotional processing. Our immersion in sensory signals as well as our capacity and necessity to acquire, store, interrelate, and react to information create a potential of impressionability that offers countless opportunities for our environment to influence us.

All environmental effects on us, regardless of whether they consist of direct interferences or indirect, sensory influences share the attribute of not being genetically preordained in us unless they occur in execution of our genetic instructions. To the extent such effects constitute lasting phenomena, we may call them acquired dispositions in distinction from genetic dispositions. Our genetic and acquired dispositions form all aspects, all particularities of our body. Describing all of these dispositions would mean to pronounce the entirety of our substance and of our functions. We may discern genetic dispositions that form our mind as genetic mental traits or genetic traits and acquired dispositions that form our mind as acquired mental traits or acquired traits. The relative permanence of our mental traits makes it plausible that they relate to somewhat stable physiological structures. Regarding genetic mental traits, that is also indicated by their close connection to physiological functions and the regularity of their occurrence. A physical representation of environmentally influenced constituents of our mental traits is indicated by the physical nature of sensory impressions of objects and events and their representational processing by our mind. Yet, for much of humanity's history, the confirmation of mental processes as physiological phenomena was impossible because it involves identification and tracking of complex causal connections by technological means. Only as science reveals the physical functions of our mind can we overcome the intuitive assumption cast upon us by the secretive character of our mind that it is nonphysical. Someday we may succeed in completely tracing and revealing mental functions. To comprehend them fully, we have to ascertain physiological mechanisms as their foundations. We are becoming acquainted that a genetically initiated and administered infrastructure makes perceptions, rational thoughts, and emotional responses possible. We also know that direct physical influences can damage or support our mind's potential. It further seems that sensory impressions and the work undertaken by our mind on them contribute to the construction and alteration of our mental physiology. But to understand our mind more fully, we have to comprehend the functions of the physiological language or languages constituting perceptions, rational thoughts, and emotions in its structures and processes. All our mind perceives, considers, recalls, knows, feels, or derives appears to be symbolized by code. Through it, mental structures seem to be formed, function, and communicate.

Although we do not have immediate access to the physiological processes and formations that our perceptions, rational thoughts, and emotions create in our mind, we register them by our resulting mental capacity. There appear to exist physical structures and mechanisms in our mind that have the ability to register, store, and process our perceptions, rational thoughts, and emotions. In addition, such structures and mechanisms carry the capability to communicate perceptions, rational thoughts, and emotions without being expended in such a process. They appear to have the capacity to generate code that travels in our body with their messages. Some of these messages may be directions targeted at nonmental parts of our body that translate the code into physiological reactions, including the positioning of aspects with sensory facilities to obtain perceptive signals. Other messages are focused on facilities of our mind that register, store, and process them further. The content of this code originates from physical objects and events outside or within our body that impress upon receptors of our senses. When we initially perceive an object or event, the code generated by that perception consists of that object or event itself or physical emissions or refractions from it that are detected and processed by our nervous system. That system seems to contain mechanisms that may translate our initial impressions into traveling code. This code is relayed to rational and emotional facilities that enable our mind to process the initial sensory and possibly transformed messages. These facilities may keep the code in the received format or translate it. They may by themselves or in correlation with one another analyze information into its components and properties, and compare, categorize, store, or recall it. They may correlate and rearrange information and its components into new composites. There seem to be communications within rational facilities and within emotional facilities that enable such functions. All of these communications may be regarded as the sending and perception of participating facilities of the same general type. Moreover, rationally processed information may be sent by rational facilities and perceived by emotional facilities and emotionally processed information may be sent by emotional facilities and perceived by rational facilities. The complexity and variety of communication streams indicate the close coordination among our rational and emotional facilities. Such a coordination only appears to be possible if they share a common code or have the ability to translate one another's code and a similar ability to register originally processed perceptive information. Understanding our mind may only be fundamentally possible if we understand its parts by the code they send and receive, the content of that code, and the factors affecting that code.

The code by which our mind functions, the physiological structures built or influenced by this code, and the processes in which such structures engage are physical objects or events of a distinct character. Their presence and interaction do no longer rely on the original triggering objects or events. Original impressions from objects and events have become translated and incorporated into separate physiological structures in our body. These constitute or comprise abstractions that may have been derived from the physical sources of an original sensory impression. But they now appear to have obtained a different, separate existence. The mechanisms of our mind that work with this code may communicate with other mechanisms of our mind independently from the initial causes and from their immediate physical impact. The translated, analyzed, or synthesized nature of this code is a representation of original causes. Our mind generates symbols of them, their components, their properties, the properties of their components, and the correlations of these factors. These symbols form building blocks of, as well as instructions for the actions and interactions of, our mental traits. Our mind uses the symbols of abstracted code and their correlations to build an inner world that appears to have the capacity of functioning separately from the outside world. Upon their establishment, abstracted mechanisms of our mind and their interactions may constitute originating sources or triggers for further rational and emotional emissions, refractions, and combinations that may be reflected in perceptive impressions. They can cause or participate in the creation of mental derivatives that have their own physiological presence. These derivatives may be the basis for further derivatives. By the processing of representations in our mind, we may arrive at concepts that we can carry into the world by physical implementation through our body and technical assistance. As external physical objects and events receive reflection in the internal physical structures and processes of our mind, internal physical objects and events also find reflection in external structures and processes. Apparently, two physical worlds internal and external to our mind exist parallel to each other but find reflection in each other. This reveals their qualities that we initially perceive as real and representational as aspects of one physical world.

Arguably, the mutuality between the inner and outer provinces should lead to a unification of these spheres through human activity and development. Yet it may produce idiosyncrasies and differences in the ways we react to and we shape our environment. As particular environmental influences create or shape physiological structures in our mind, the facilities of our mind may grow to be sufficiently dissimilar from those of other individuals to give rise to noticeable differences in perceptive, rational, and emotional processing. We may develop a disparate sensitivity to information, different ways of thinking and feeling, specific acquired traits that distinguish our personality from other individuals' personalities. The development of acquired traits may interact or exist parallel with variances in genetic dispositions that may also significantly individualize our mind. Specific acquired and specific genetic traits may interrelate differently with one another and with common environmental and genetic conditions. Both types of differences may direct us toward particularized experiences. However, the development of acquired idiosyncrasies appears to distinguish itself in that it may be assisted by a particularly intense self-reinforcing mechanism. In as far as experiences shape the structures of our mind, these structures are likely to process our environment consistent with these experiences. Our mind becomes particularly receptive to experiences in conformance with these structures. Moreover, it will act and react in our environment according to the impressions that our experiences engender. We may try to convert our environment in reflection of our experiences regardless of whether these form traits. If we succeed with that undertaking, the particularized structures of our mind will gain support by the circumstances we create. We may construe similar self-reinforcing phenomena for specific genetic aspects of our mind. Particularized genetic traits may shape our acquisition of information and our shaping of our environment and thus provide a mechanism for a circular reinforcing pattern for the original specific genetic traits. But these effects are generational and are therefore much more attenuated compared to acquired circular reinforcement. Self-reinforcement may also occur regarding common genetic and environmental traits. Only, this might be less noticeable because of their constancy and ubiquitous nature. Beyond self-reinforcement, we may discover that all four types of acquired and genetic traits can influence one another.

All these varieties of possible interaction make it hard to trace traits to their origins. In the case of common traits, their refined and harmonious nature might render such a tracing largely irrelevant. We have more interest in specific traits because these form our idiosyncrasies. Here, we may be successful distinguishing overt physiological particularities that were caused by manifest physical influences or that can be traced to particular genetic instructions. Finding clarity about the establishment of specific personality traits may pose a substantially greater problem. Even where self-reinforcing or crossover mechanisms are not the primary driving source for the establishment of such a trait, we have often trouble tracing it to its origins. Both specific genetic and acquired traits often give our perceptive, rational, and emotional attributes a largely unconscious imprint. It is not difficult to understand the reasons genetic mental traits are enigmatic. They became part of us without participation by our mind. We found them preexisting as an unreflected, natural part of us. Acquired mental dispositions differ because we acquired them during our existence. Some of them may stand out because they were incurred willfully, imposed against our will, or were acquired under particularly perceptible or traumatic momentous circumstances. Yet many, if not most of them, were acquired without our awareness in small increments over time. This may give them a subliminal, unreflected, and even unconscious quality.

Many of our experiences may leave structures in our mind that can be reversed or adjusted by additional experiences with a range of efforts. We may even be able to overcome some genetic structures this way. However, if fledgling structures are reinforced by additional experiences, self-reinforcement, and crossover backing, they can become acquired traits that approximate genetic traits in durability. Some acquired traits pertain to perceptive or rational attitudes. Others pertain to the emotional sourcing of our needs. Although acquired emotional traits are originated differently, they appear to follow the same pain-pleasure mechanism as genetic traits to motivate us. Mechanisms that were acquired rather than built by our genes might differ in the depth of their entrenchment. Nevertheless, motivational forces they generate can be similar to those inherent in genetically sourced needs. The similarity of their motivational mechanisms empowers them to attach themselves effortlessly to our genetic traits and other acquired traits. Acquired needs assume a co-defining function in what we want, and our idea of happiness shifts to include them. We are not happy unless these nonoriginal needs are contented as well. Our ideal of happiness includes the fulfillment of all our needs regardless of whether they are genetic or acquired, and we usually do not distinguish accordingly.

It seems that becoming aware of our mental traits requires us to emerge from an attitude of passivity. We did not choose our perceptive, rational, or emotional substances or processes. We did not select our personality to produce a maximum of happiness and did not work backward from that ambition to assemble the necessary mental traits. What happened was quite the reverse. We were given mental traits or components of such traits by inheritance and developed other aspects by exposure to our environment. Our person, our physiological identity, including its mental aspects, was formed by genetic and environmental circumstances, not by us. As science advances, perceptive mechanisms seem most easily explained as physical phenomena. Further, we may find relatively direct access to rational structures and processes. This may appear hardly surprising considering that our rational mental constructs are specific or general reflections of obviously physical objects and events in the physiological devices of our mind. The emotional expanses of our mind appear to be considerably more mysterious and challenging to reveal. Their irrational nature removes them from an understanding of them as direct symbolic representations of the outside world. Their apparent failure to follow logic complicates the identification of their physiological foundations and a rational explanation of their sources and functions. We should be confident that such encumbrances will be lifted as we scientifically dissect our emotional structures and processes into their physiological components because these have to follow the same underlying substances and principles as any other matters we explore. But even if we could explain our mental phenomena in rational terms as representations of physiological phenomena, that understanding may not give us insight into how the acquired portions of mental traits came about.

Short of a full exploration of the genetic sources of our mind, part of the difficulty in deciphering the sources of our mind lies in the absence of a clear differentiation between acquired and genetic traits. Our mental traits have generally grown organically with and into one another during our development. Acquired mental traits may have become so integrated into our mind that they may be indistinguishable from our genetic mental traits. The differences in the accrual and underlying physiology between genetic and acquired mental traits make a distinction between them important to find suitable tools for their suppression, advancement, modeling, or removal. Another reason we might want to identify the genetic and acquired aspects of our mind is that they carry a difference of presumption regarding their legitimacy.

Our common genetic dispositions likely were delivered to us in a selection process favoring attributes that advance or are necessary for our individual or collective survival and thriving. Then again, it is possible that we all might be carrying some common dispositions that historically have been, have become, or are becoming liabilities. They might be misdevelopments or remnants of past requirements, of precursor stages that have lost their utility and might even have become damaging. That may seem particularly possible considering the apparently recent development of our mind. That development and its implications for the development of genetic traits and even more for the development of human technology and living conditions may engender dissonances with more fundamental genetic instincts. Still, an assertion that common genetic mental traits are damaging requires positive proof against an overwhelming presumption of utility. We might carry a similar assumption regarding common acquired mental traits. If all humans are impressed in the same way by a ubiquitous environmental factor, its forming influence may reflect a necessary or helpful constituent for human survival and thriving. Our common reaction to our environment might constitute an important supplement that can contain, channel, support, or improve our genetic traits. But it is also conceivable that all humans would succumb to the same deleterious general acquired trait. Our favorable presumption might be disproved again. That we are uniformly subjected to a genetic or acquired disposition does not routinely make a disposition helpful or necessary.

Our presumptions may be different in dealing with specific genetic and acquired dispositions. Here, the presumption appears to be warranted that such dispositions are not required for our survival or wellbeing, at least if other humans can survive and thrive in their absence. However, they may correspond to special or new general environmental challenges, or constitute an enhancement for our capacity to survive and thrive by modulating common dispositions even if circumstances remain the same. The challenges a genetic mutation can address might not be immediately recognizable. They might only become clear after extended periods. Past beneficial mutations are likely to have been first confined to one or few individuals and to then have proliferated through the favored propagation of individuals with superior properties. Such mutations may initially appear incomplete or inapplicable in addressing present or potential future conditions. Hence, we cannot validly presume that specific genetic dispositions, including specific mental traits, are useless for human survival or wellbeing.

It may appear that we can make a better case for a negative presumption when it comes to specific acquired dispositions. Their introduced sourcing and unique character create an intrinsic risk that they would interfere negatively with the program of our genetic and common acquired dispositions. Specific acquired dispositions may be the haphazard result of activities and of circumstances that were not particularly focused on us. In that case, it would be coincidental if they happened to benefit us. An even clearer negative presumption can be made when specific acquired dispositions are installed in us with the intended function of manipulating us to serve someone else. Their installation may not be primarily concerned with our happiness, not be concerned with our happiness, or may even require that our happiness be damaged. Even if external influences are exerted in an effort to advance our needs, they continue to carry the possibility that they might not serve our happiness. But these factors do not categorically override the possible benefits of specific acquired dispositions. Specific environmental challenges may occur faster than specific genetic dispositions can adjust to them. Even if a challenge is common for humanity and calls for a response in the form of a general acquired disposition, that challenge may originate with a limited range and a response may begin with a specific acquired disposition before it expands and eventually grows to be common. Apart from that, specific acquired dispositions might act parallel to general acquired dispositions and contain, channel, support, or improve instructions provided by specific genetic dispositions. For these reasons, we cannot well presume that specific acquired dispositions are useless for human survival or wellbeing.

We may determine that, although we can establish some valid presumptions in favor of general dispositions, the character of our dispositions, including of our mental traits, as genetic, acquired, specific, or common does not clearly resolve whether they constitute constructive factors in our quest for happiness. Nor does it seem right to categorically contend that acquired dispositions are superior or inferior to genetic conditioning. We will have to consider every disposition on its own merits to determine whether it promotes our happiness, whether we would prefer to keep it untouched, modify it, or transcend it. This determination requires the review of each disposition on its merit and its systematic investigation in correlation with all other dispositions. To make a competent decision, we must identify our dispositions and must comprehend their composition, their reasons for existence, their functions, and their consequences. That might be relatively uncomplicated when we consider more obvious physical dispositions. Our mental traits promise to be more of a challenge because we cannot as easily grasp and separate their nature and functions. We may compare our mind to a manufacturing facility for highly processed products. These products give us only limited information about their ingredients and the stations of their manufacturing process. Examining a product may permit us to identify some ingredients and processes that were used and to refer to its manufacturing in general terms. Yet the more complex a product is the more we have to observe how every manufacturing stage contributes to the product or its components to comprehend how the result comes about. That understanding is also essential if we want to modify the product or improve the production process.

Our investigation concerning the utility of mental traits is additionally challenged because we have to account for perceptive, rational, and emotional traits although they act as integrated aspects of our mind. Distinguishing perceptive traits seems to be relatively straightforward. The processes of reception of objects or events or their emissions or of refractions from other objects and events, their translation, and the transport of impressions by our nervous system appear to be distinct from other mental traits. This phenomenon is clearly based in physiology and therefore physical. However, the distinction of perceptive traits blurs when we connect them with the rational or emotional aspects of our mind. We may consider the interaction among rational aspects of our mind as separate. Still, at least in part, it consists of the emission or refraction of rational concepts that are subsequently perceived by other rational facilities. The sole difference seems to be that these concepts may not require translation and may involve different code than the reception, transport, and registration of exterior signals.

A similar claim can be made concerning the interaction among emotional aspects. Further, perceptive functions appear to connect the rational and emotional sections of our mind. The emotions we rationally register as well as the constructs and processes we rationally build to which emotional traits react all seem to have perceptive involvement. The initial transmission by perceptive processes and their involvement in the interaction among rational and emotional aspects make it possible that perceptive traits would influence these aspects. Because all our mental processes can be defined in terms of communication, perceptive mechanisms are aspects of rational and emotional traits without which these cannot be conceptualized. Such traits are extensively formed and influenced by perceptive facilities because they must rely on these in their internal and correlative functions that entail the receipt of code. Conversely, perceptive facilities stand to be influenced by rational and emotional aspects because these give rise to perceptive impressions. Hence, perceptive traits may be difficult to separate from rational and emotional traits in wholly internal mental processes.

The problems regarding the distinction of our perceptive facilities do not abate with the involvement of perceptions from the world beyond our mind. Here, the physical features of perception appear to govern. Our perceptive facilities receive whatever falls within their detection range, translate this information into transportable code, and forward that code to other parts of our mind through the nervous system. These signals appear to be responsible for building large parts of our rational and emotional mind. We are not solely influenced by external influences that are transmitted. Perceptive traits may influence our rational and emotional traits as well since they are the messengers through which our outside influences must pass. They constitute a filter, conversion, and relay system that transforms received information even at its best. However, we can also distinguish a reverse influence. The processing by rational and emotional aspects of our mind may alter the information received through perceptive facilities. This change may be automatic by a translation into code that these traits can process. But it may be more targeted in many of their functions. Rational and emotional traits evaluate everything we perceive according to how it might correlate with already established notions. They judge how it fits into our pursuits or what adversities it might present. Rational or emotional traits may interpret what they receive from the viewpoint of their already established structures. Depending on the capacity or motivation connected to such structures, they may filter, alter, suppress, or block information. While these processes may succeed a transmission of external information, rational or emotional mechanisms might

be able to interfere in perceptive processes. They might instruct perceptive facilities about modes or details of registration, translation, or
transportation of information. Further, our rational or our emotional
mind might direct our body to prevent our sensory facilities from receiving information that contradicts our rational or emotional settings
even if perceptive facilities remain unbiased and properly functioning
within their capacities. Consequently, mutual influences between our
perceptive and other mental facilities seem to be conceivable throughout the range of internal and external perceptive functions.

The mutual influences also seem to exist between our rational and
emotional traits. Although we appear to be able to distinguish rational
and emotional traits as concepts, they do not arise separately. We cannot undertake thoughts without feeling about them in a certain way.
Nor can we preclude rational consideration of emotional phenomena
as factual events. That may be partly based on similarities in their processing when they relate, categorize, store, and retrieve perceived representations of objects and events. Further, emotional functions overlap with rational functions because emotional traits use rational traits
to solve emotional tasks. Close collaboration by rational traits appears
to be essential to afford our emotional traits capabilities of pursuit in
excess of those ordained by their instinctive programming. While our
rational traits then present themselves as adjuncts, as instruments of
our emotional traits, we can also observe that rational phenomena deliver much of the interpretive information from which emotions arise
or by which they are shaped. Consequently, distinguishing emotional
traits from rational traits seems to be difficult in some respects.

The division of our mental functions into the activities of perceptive, rational, and emotional traits appears to be an oversimplification. Although such a model serves to typify the prominent character
of mental phenomena, its categorizations cannot be regarded as categorical separations between perceptive, rational, and emotional functions. The reciprocal dependences and influences among mental traits
suggest that we must explore all of these aspects together if we want
to understand our mind. Still, we will not fully comprehend its functions without taking note of the hierarchy among perceptive, rational,
and emotional aspects of our mind that places emotional traits on top,
followed by rational traits, and finally perceptive traits as instruments
that serve both of the higher categories. Nor will we be able to change
our mind without developing strategies that take this hierarchy into
consideration. All our wishes and all our efforts to improve our happiness as a practical matter will have to contend with the governance of
our mind by needs. They will encounter needs as motivators, adminis-

trators, and judges of our conduct and as gatekeepers to the functions of our perceptive and rational facilities. Moreover, all our activities in exploring and changing our mental traits would be governed by our needs and the mandates they impose on us. Our needs arrange for the incentives, objectives, and decision-making for all our activities. If we want to improve our happiness, we must find the key to unlock them. Against this task, improving our practical powers through perceptive and rational traits seems eminently solvable and almost mundane.

When we approach our emotional traits as a subject of inquiry, we observe that they communicate through impulses. Our emotional mind registers these, together with the preceding awareness of deficiencies, as needs and to which the rest of our body reacts with action. To comprehend our emotional traits and their functions, we must explore these impulses. To the extent emotional impulses originate from common emotional traits, they inform us, together with a sense of deficiency, whether we meet our existential needs and they motivate us to satisfy these needs. We should discover what makes us happy if we surrender to our impulses. This conclusion would be justified if all our impulses were constructive for our happiness. Then again, chances are that we possess impulses that are not aligned with our overall happiness. Such impulses may represent what we want at a certain point in time. They do represent needs. Yet, even if following such an impulse may give us immediate satisfaction, our pursuit may cause damage in the fulfillment of other legitimate needs that exceeds its benefits. We may acknowledge that such a risk might be created by incompatible idiosyncratic needs. However, existential needs may give rise to detrimental impulses as well. They may harm us because they are preprogrammed responses with the mission to commandeer our mind in the interest of their issuing traits. Because impulses only address the concerns of needs that issue them, they might produce unbalanced results with regard to our other needs. Accordingly, following all our impulses, and even the impulses of needs we have found to be constructive, indiscriminately may lead to unintended unhappy consequences. We cannot trust our impulses. Following them would render us liable to skip from one command to another and would disable our pursuit of an overall reconciled strategy of happiness. While they might use our critical thinking to execute their commands, their motivations threaten to bypass reflective services. Left unchecked, impulses function like short circuits that preoccupy and determine our judgment led by their spontaneous concerns. If we abide by them without considering their merit, we desert control over our circumstances. We suspend the possibility of a considered judgment about what will make us happy.

Apparently then, we cannot rely on our emotional mind and its impulses if we desire to develop a plan to maintain and improve our happiness. Our considerations may lead us to the conclusion that we need a comprehensive system in which all our mental traits, but particularly our emotional impulses are being considered and are being given their most appropriate function in the advancement of our happiness. In that system, our impulses can only be first indicators in the formulation of wishes in promotion of our happiness. By generating the insight that following an impulse would be detrimental, we should be able to formulate a countervailing wish that neutralizes, adjusts, or at least weakens such an impulse. Our considerations may be complex because we have to determine how a particular impulse and its consequences comport with an overall regime for our happiness. To undertake the necessary consideration, we must prepare. It would place us at a severe disadvantage if we had to delay our reflection until an emotional trait presented us with an impulse. Usually, an impulse is sent when we are in present apprehension of a deficiency. At that point, we may not have the luxury of considering the qualities of impulses. We may be under pressure to enter a momentary resolution according to their demands and, because of our anxiety, may be in danger of making a wrong or less than optimized decision. It would create a stressful existence if we were blindsided by our impulses until they confronted us and compelled us to decide. Reviewing preceding similar impulses, our reactions to them, and their consequences allows us to generally predetermine how we want to deal with a particular type of impulse.

A supervisory capacity over our impulses is not a novel position for us to take. We are already exercising this capacity to some extent. We have the distinct impression that we are more than the sum of our traits. We possess strong indications that our mind contains a switchboard-like mechanism where we attempt to exercise discretion among our emotional traits, where we reflect whether and how we bring an impulse to bear and where we determine our behavior as one to optimize our overall happiness. This authority may be poorly developed. It may be fraught with errors and shortcomings. Still, it appears to constitute a capability that might enable us to maximize our happiness if it is sufficiently developed. That we can take the position of our overall happiness and not allow ourselves to be driven by individual emotional traits suggests that our decisional core structure is independent from any one individual emotional trait. An obvious candidate for this leadership position would appear to be our rational mind. Our rational mind seems to be the only aspect of our mind that is capable of reflecting on and therefore distancing itself from our mind. Our power to reason and explore facts appears to be able to relatively easily over-come factual assertions or rational thought sequences or patterns that have hardened into rational traits. All that would seem to be required is proving them to be incorrect. We may regard the apparent reticence of rational traits against such enlightenment to be sponsored in large part by emotional traits that have an interest in maintaining conform-ing rational structures or processes. A similar argument can be made regarding perceptive traits. Rational reflection should be able to lead us to optimized perception practices if it were not for the reticence of emotional traits. We may think that we can overcome this opposition and that we can maximize our happiness if we follow reason, and the factual proof to which it attaches, as the supreme organizational prin-ciple over our emotional traits. Our rational mind seems to be unique-ly equipped to investigate, assess, coordinate, and if needed, find ways to restrict, modify, and possibly eliminate traits in favor of a solution that maximizes the overall fulfillment of our constructive needs. Our service to this purpose would have us account for and determine the objectives, requirements, and urgencies of our needs and all available resources for their pursuit. We would also determine the consequenc-es of their pursuit for one another's fulfillment. We would develop and adjust means and strategies in line with principles of efficiency and ef-fectiveness in the service of maximizing our individual and collective survival and thriving. These directorial functions of our rational mind would have to be permanent to be effective because emotional traits display ceaseless determination to make us follow their demands and display considerable resourcefulness to sway us in their favor.

The overall optimization of our happiness through the consid-eration of all our traits might then appear to be a consummately ra-tional function. But closer examination establishes that the leadership of these functions is reserved to our emotional mind because our ra-tional mind is fundamentally unable of generating any type of motiva-tion to engage it in optimizing our conditions. Our principal needs to secure our individual and collective survival and thriving appear to in-struct and back the arbitration function of our rational mind. We be-come emotionally attached to the effectiveness and efficiency gains of rational methods in the arrangement of our needs and develop corre-sponding wishes. The comprehensive direction by our principal needs seems to be in charge of liberating us from following the programs of subordinated needs when they do not attend to these principal needs. Still, a presumption that principal needs exist and that they constitute separately organized, controlling phenomena appears to derive from a functional oversimplification that does not accurately reflect reality.

Rather, it seems that our principal needs represent composites of all needs that appear to serve them. The regularly interwoven character of multiple needs in our pursuits gives us an indication for this proposition. We rarely find traits operating distinctly in the planning and execution of strategies. To survive and thrive, we may not possess the luxury of pursuing each single need separately. We may regularly have to combine the pursuit of several needs. Even if we could afford to dedicate our efforts fully to one pursuit at a time without existential danger, other needs may demand that we pursue our tasks without violating or disadvantaging their objectives or that we advance their objectives contemporaneously. This places us under a requirement to select compromised courses of action that support multiple needs or are at least mindful of them. It would appear then that many of our pursuits are directed by a committee of emotional traits. We cannot presume that all participating emotional traits would necessarily cooperate for the joint purpose of producing a product with a particular intermediate or ultimate quality. Rather, each emotional trait appears to be only interested in a product to the extent it serves that trait's satisfaction. Our emotional traits may cooperate to the extent their interests are aligned, or they may agitate against one another where this is not the case. The push and pull between positions of pain and pleasure for every need propel and draw our planning and implementation into different directions with possibly dissimilar intensities. This may regularly shape our wishes and activities into composite strategies.

Multilateral interests and participations by emotional traits in our pursuits threaten to render an arrangement among our emotional traits a complicated undertaking. Guidance by multiple needs can materially restrict the maneuvering space for our pursuits. That maneuvering space may already be scarce or nonexistent because of several types of internal limitations that may be inherent or attach to a need. Emotional traits might not only issue impulses for ultimate objectives but also regarding our choices of means for the pursuit of such ultimate objectives. We appear to be emotionally invested not only to fill the differential between pain and pleasure of a need but also to fill it in a particular manner. Such requirements may be rooted in common existential needs and in idiosyncratic particularizations. Idiosyncrasies may additionally narrow our ultimate objectives for a need. These restrictions are exposed to further limitations of external circumstances in which our needs must find fulfillment. The resulting requirements may not leave much flexibility for an optimized or even adequate pursuit. Each need may therefore assert itself and fight for the accommodation of its requirements at every juncture. The urging of a variety of needs and the pain we would suffer if we ignored that urging require us to compromise and sacrifice efficiency and effectiveness in the pursuit of needs for the sake of gaining efficiency and effectiveness in the pursuit of other needs. We may curtail our pursuit of one objective so that we can better achieve another objective. Conducted sensibly, this coordination among interested needs can minimize our overall exposure to pain and maximize our overall yield of pleasure. But succeeding in this enterprise appears to remain difficult. It is characteristically likely in a compromise that needs will not be able to insist on manners of pursuit that fully satisfy their requirements. However, the arrangements strategies we can make available may not even fall within a range of lesser, still functional strategies for some interested needs or they may only be fulfillable at a relative overall disadvantage. Moreover, the reconciliation of a multitude of needs that vie for satisfaction is not limited to an abstract and static plan. It must relate and adjust to the specific internal and practical circumstances of our pursuits as they vary. These practical concerns add to the complexity of our considerations during a plan's conception, and might also encumber us at any step of its implementation if there are deviations from the plan.

Depending on the subject matter we pursue and our fulfillment status, participation in this guidance system might be limited to less than all of our emotional traits. Still, the diversity of needs participating in a decisional process and pursuit may exceed the array of needs that may be directly affected by a decision. Even if a suggested pursuit does not touch upon the direct interests of an emotional trait, a proposed pursuit might involve resources or the pursuit of another need may have attenuated consequences in which it is interested. Thus, although an emotional trait might not actively participate in a pursuit with the objective of its contemporary fulfillment, it may weigh in to preserve or advance its present or future status. We may call the overarching mechanism by which our emotional traits interact with one another our council of traits or our conscience. It is the administrative mechanism of our mental traits that organizes our personality as more than the sum of its traits. The activity of our council of traits suggests that its independent authority is not formed by our rational capacity but that it arises from the correlation of our emotional traits and their impulses. Hence, it seems to confirm our impression that we are being governed by our emotional traits. Yet, in spite of being guided by the motivations of our emotional traits, the council is a forum in which all our mental traits can obtain representation. A council of traits might function solely based on the interaction of perceptive and emotional traits if the reconciliation of emotional traits is settled or automated by instinct. But rational information may allow us to further customize and improve our responses to challenges and opportunities. Many of our rational traits are indispensable for rendering our mental traits conscious by investigating, determining, categorizing, recording, and tracking them and their consequences. They can derive insights that provide factual orientation. They can provide rational considerations of relevant circumstances to prepare considerations by our emotional traits. They may even provide the factual recognitions and deductions that lead us to cast our reactions into an acquired emotional trait or influence the formation or the adjustment of such a trait. Our rational traits might then have great power in our council of traits. They may assist its functions with correct reflections and correlations or damage it by infusing our decisions with erroneous or incomplete notions. Regardless of whether they are engaged by our emotional mind or spontaneously process based on sensory impressions, they may present an independent result. Nevertheless, because our rational mind does not have its own motivations and is incapable of forming its own impulses, it does not have a stake in the contest among our needs. Therefore, our rational mind is not a supreme authority that rules and judges our traits, impulses, and personality. Rather, it constitutes a mere utility. Our perceptive traits take a similar posture. They are vitally important for enabling factually accurate judgments, and they carry a significant informational function with regard to acquired emotional traits. However, they have no motivation of their own and do not try to convince us. That motivation is uniquely reserved to our emotional traits.

Through its impulses, every emotional trait causes our mind to take its viewpoint temporarily. Assuming the positions of all our emotional traits in relation to the demands and implications of a particular emotional trait permits us to engage in a well-rounded review, argument, and possibly negotiation among our emotional traits. Reflective awareness of our emotional traits requires their distinction from us as the observing entity. Our rational mind naturally possesses that quality because it is limited to rational interpretations. This makes our rational mind an effective factual counselor. But the necessary motivation for that advice to be prepared and argued arises from the differing viewpoints of emotional traits. We can step outside our emotional traits, albeit only at the price of identifying with and being biased by other emotional traits. Yet the distance that is generated by the combined viewpoints of every emotional trait with respect to every other emotional trait gives us the ability to comprehend our needs and settle their pursuit in correlation with one another. The comparative review by our emotional traits is more than a mere jostling of impulses.

It can inform us of our perceptions and our rational insights regarding participating circumstances, risks, requirements, possible alternatives, effectiveness, efficiency, and the ramifications of pursuits for involved and further needs. The composite of these informed emotional viewpoints can present us with a comprehensive picture of the interests of our emotional traits. The sum of their positions produces an approximation of objectivity because it positions perceptions, rational arguments, and emotional reactions in context with one another. This interchange of vantage points also seems to create the best opportunity to minimize any blind spots in our self-investigation. By stating their position relative to one another and negotiating or refusing to negotiate with other emotional traits, our emotional traits make us aware of the facets of our self. To the extent there are differences, they might not only expose one another in this process. Their biased engagement of rational arguments and procedures of proof might be able to question and engender consideration of rational and perceptive traits and views as well. Such critical treatment seems often necessary because emotional traits tend to sway perceptive and rational traits to provide factual justification for their stance. They may use that justification to defend their position relative to other emotional traits or to motivate them to cooperate. Even without such intent, perceptive and rational traits regularly form settled adjuncts to emotional traits because of the interest by needs in securing their fulfillment. Our mental traits may then be regarded as integrated spheres of influence under the control of emotional traits. This integration may prevent or impede the consideration of perceptive evidence or of rational arguments that are incompatible with an emotional stance. Emotional traits might unwisely promote such strategies even if it damages our overall happiness or their own objectives. Rational and perceptive traits that have become attached to emotional traits may only be changed upon permission by such emotional traits or upon compulsion by other emotional traits.

The process engaged by our council of traits may lead our emotional traits to arrive at the same result as rational arrangements if we gave them the directive of maximizing our individual and collective survival and thriving. Superficially, that may be the impression we derive from the workings of our council of traits as an entirety. However, the imposition of that purpose and any deviation from it seem to be the prerogative of our emotional traits and to result from their reflection and relation of one another's objectives to their own objective. If we wish to secure our happiness, we must find a resolution among our emotional traits. Provided that we can get all our needs to participate, our council of traits can help us in that resolution. It allows us to determine whether we want to follow an emotional, rational, or perceptive trait based on the council's consideration whether such an act increases or decreases our overall happiness. Accordingly, we may view our council of traits not only as a mechanism by which we can reach full self-awareness but also fulfill our need for self-determination.

Some of our existential needs or some aspects of them might be products of common acquired traits. Yet the apparent presence of existential needs in the past of human development when the minds of our ancestors were not able to acquire traits would indicate that they are genetically based. Even if we cannot find direct evidence for such a presence, we might support such a conclusion by finding similar existential needs in species that are not able to develop common acquired emotional traits. Some existential needs may also be due to the higher genetic development of humans. Until we identify the genetic basis of existential needs, we might not know this for certain. Either way, our common emotional traits seem to have found a relatively stable mode of coexistence to the extent they are part of an established, integrated system of relationships that has been refined through eons of development. That process has not demarcated our general emotional traits in absolute harmony. Even common needs may engage in competition with one another. Depending on their satisfaction status, our common needs may clamor for our attention to motivate us to give them preference in fulfillment over other needs. Arguably, competition among traditional common needs remains necessary because it informs us of the relative urgency of deficiencies and permits us to focus our efforts where they are most needed. The relationship of our general emotional traits may benefit from optimization efforts that organize our pursuits beyond topical preferences they indicate. Reconciling the competition of existential claims may place fairly complex coordination demands on us because all participating needs are relevant to our individual or collective survival and thriving. But the beneficial character of traditionally participating needs, or at least of the resulting system in which they balance one another, carries a presumption of benefit.

This presumption does not exist with regard to specific genetic and specific acquired traits. The particularized sourcing of these idiosyncratic needs and the varying objectives of such needs make conflict among them and with existential needs likely. Their introduction into a system of general instructions heightens the risk of a conflicted personality without a consistent concept of happiness. The persistence of such nonharmonized needs and the impulses they issue makes it likely that we will continually suffer conflict. Specific emotional traits may be necessary or helpful to provide fulfillment for our existential needs.

To the extent their accommodation can create a higher overall level of happiness, including them into reconciliation might be a sensible undertaking even if they are difficult to accommodate. But the potentially uncoordinated character of specific emotional traits and the resulting conflict they cause threaten to negatively affect our overall happiness. Instead of the dynamics of our traditional existential needs that attend a constructive purpose, the participation of specific emotional traits may be convoluted, contradictory, and ineffective. It may be incompetent of producing coherent, optimized, or even adequate results for securing our individual and collective survival and thriving. Growing specific genetic and specific acquired needs threaten to overstrain the traditional reconciliation mechanism among common needs. The diversity and details of their extraneous demands may hinder its functioning. Curtailing frivolous and damaging specific needs requires that we expand our consideration and our management of these needs and their adjuncts in perceptive and rational traits. We may augment our happiness significantly by gaining the ability to curb, modify, or eliminate specific mental traits that hamper our happiness or do not adequately advance it, or to create beneficial specific mental traits.

This prospect of having to take active control of our happiness places us in a situation where we have to understand, define, and possibly redefine the details of our happiness. We cannot reach happiness simply by promoting indiscriminate fulfillment for all our needs. Not all our needs can be trusted to assist our existential objectives and to contribute to a harmonious entirety. Rather, we must cultivate the aptitude to comprehend the correlations among our needs so we can determine how we can achieve the most happiness for ourselves. The arguments among our emotional traits within our council of traits may assist us in determining which correlations among them and their adjuncts constitute the best advancement of our happiness overall. The dynamics of this determination are likely to be fluid in many respects. Depending on the fulfillment status of needs and their environmental conditions, they may try to urge us into obedient conduct with different resolve and backing. Yet, beyond gauging the relevance of immediate impulses and considerations, we have to consider what will serve our long-term individual and collective objectives. To produce such a reconciliation, our emotional traits have to find expression without restraints and comprehensively debate and persuade, compromise with, or possibly compel one another. To accomplish this, we must develop a thorough understanding of our emotional traits, their requirements, consequences, and backing by perceptive and rational traits. The next chapter addresses the foundations for such an understanding.

CHAPTER 18
PERSONALITY FORMATION

To identify our mental traits, it appears useful that we continue to investigate the differences between genetic and acquired traits. Genetic traits constitute the foundation for our existence. They are established before any acquired traits can affect us. A particular interest in genetic traits appears to be warranted because they represent our original essence. Even if acquired traits should prove to be advantageous for our overall happiness, they represent foreign modulations of that essence. They present attachments that could not exist by themselves. Beyond that, we attribute particular constructive import to our genetic traits. This quality might be drawn into doubt when we consider that human history appears to have innately been marked by destructive impulses. Still, notwithstanding that history, the underlying grounds for human survival and thriving can be found in genetic common traits. Common acquired traits may have had and may continue to have helpful or essential functions. Yet they constitute later accruals to our original genetic traits. Before we were sufficiently cognizant to react to our environment and develop acquired traits, genetic common traits had to be sufficient to empower human existence. Moreover, these common genetic traits represent the receptive basis into which all acquired traits have to be integrated to exist. Our common genetic traits most genuinely define us as human. We may have additional interest in specific genetic traits because they might show to us new horizons for human evolution. But even if their developmental potential should be inconclusive, our specific genetic traits seem to most genuinely define us as individuals. Genetic traits constitute the most tenacious and indelible of our characteristics because they are imprinted in and represented by every cell in our body. Although acquired traits achieve physiological representation as well, it is relatively superficial. Unless they modify genetic code, their adjustments to genetically based traits consist of superstructures that affect the expression of our genetic traits without changing their essence. Particularly if acquired traits arise from sensory experiences, but also if they arise from direct physical impact, they may be susceptible to alteration by simpler, nongenetic influences.

If we could segregate the superstructures of our acquired traits, we should be able to uncover our genetic traits. We should be able to lay bare a pure expression of our genetic traits by identifying and subtracting our acquired traits. By further subtraction of specific genetic traits, we should be able to arrive at our common genetic traits. Upon a cursory review, the attribution of traits among genetic and acquired sources would appear to be largely uncomplicated. Humans universally share common genetic traits. These should therefore display themselves in commonalities among humans irrespective of their environment. They should entirely or largely constitute our existential needs. If a trait is acquired from external circumstances, we will likely detect variety depending on these circumstances. Still, there is considerable room for error in this simple investigation. There may be uniform environmental circumstances that exert matching forming consequences for the traits of all humans regardless of other variations in our environment. Particularly, basic conditions that humans require to survive may place them into similar or identical environmental circumstances. Besides that, coincidental circumstances might be similar or identical for all humans. Humans may acquire common traits from these common conditions. It may be difficult to keep causations by general conditions separate from common genetic traits, and these may be set to interact with such general conditions. We might therefore have to distinguish common genetic and acquired traits by their coding alone. A similar complication in distinguishing the sourcing of traits may exist between specific genetic traits and specific acquired traits. Unusual traits may make it seem as if certain humans or groups are genetically predisposed. But they may also suggest that these traits are caused by environmental circumstances that are particular to or shared by certain individuals. For these reasons, we cannot render attributions between environmental and genetic causes without deeper exploration.

Such an attribution is difficult because the interaction of genetic and environmental aspects tends to meld them into one experiential phenomenon. Genetic conditions may enter a reaction with environmental influences into an amalgamated trait without clear separation. While the informational basis for genetic traits is present from the beginning of our existence, the expression of this information develops in our environment and may be subject to acquired influences. Conversely, an acquisition of environmental influences must connect and therefore conform in part to our genetic basis. The supplementary character of acquired traits makes their interaction with genetic traits inescapable. Genetic traits may hence significantly participate in the formation of acquired traits. They may originate the formation of acquired traits as adjuncts to their purposes or may at least influence the shape of acquired traits targeted at them. Even if genetic and acquired traits were to develop separately, they would not exist in pure form if they focused on the same concern. They would inevitably evoke, enhance, supplement, detract from, or subdue one another. Genetic and environmental particularities individualize these interactions.

Beyond this stage of coalescence, there is another degree of a more intimate relationship between environmental and genetic phenomena. Environmental conditions may change genetic code. This effect may be caused by direct external intervention in genetic code or through mechanisms by which our body translates environmental influences into genetic adjustments. But environmental changes to genetic code may also occur without such interventions. Genetic alterations may happen autonomously within an organism. Yet, by favoring genetic alterations that adjust a species to function better in its environment, environmental circumstances may validate genetic dispositions and influence their direction. The resulting development may be regarded as a response, an adaption to environmental influences. As a consequence, environmental conditions significantly influence human genetic development. On the other hand, this influence is increasingly accompanied by a reciprocal movement. As humans progress, they organize their environment in conformity with their genetic conditions. The effects of how humans treat their environment may generate environmental conditions that influence human genetic adaption, which may create environmental effects, repeating in cycles. Moreover, environmental conditions affect human behavior through acquired traits and more superficial, often topical considerations that form our environment in turn, giving rise to parallel cycles that connect by their environmental representation. This makes it difficult to keep genetic and nongenetic causes separate over longer periods because they become inherently linked. The basis of our difficulties is that genetic and acquired traits share the same type of sourcing in our environment. Although they are differentiated by time and mechanics in their facilitation and enforcement, their formational subjection and effect may be similar. Acquired traits may be regarded as temporary precursors of genetic adaptions. The more lasting genetic reflection of environmental circumstances may only form when particular environmental conditions continue and meet with genetic capacity to adjust to them.

Our exposure to the ensuing mixture of mutual influences may cause the distinction between genetic and acquired traits to be far less clear than we might presume. However, even if we should succeed in distinguishing genetic and acquired aspects of our traits, we are likely to find that they are inseparable in their existence. Our genetic dispositions are genuinely a seed. They represent a program that requires the presence of particular environmental factors to develop. This gives the characteristics of the organism that develops from the seed a predisposed genetic as well as an acquired quality. The seed is set to use certain environmental factors. It relies on the acquisition of comple-

mentary environmental influences because its genetic code arose from
an adjustment to prior occurrences of such environmental factors and,
originally, is indistinguishable from such factors. In its beginnings, the
combination of genetic code may have been a matter of connecting by
elemental substances according to their properties and the resulting
interactive laws with only basic environmental influences. The aspect
of elemental reactivity has remained applicable in the development of
genetic code. Nevertheless, with increasing development and resulting
complexity of biological interrelations, environmental conditions have
had increasingly detailing influence on the progression of genetic programming. The characteristics of organisms that develop from genetic
code then appear to be as much a result of genetic programming as
they are the result of environmental conditions. We may view genetic
traits as acquired traits that are reflected and passed on in our genetic
substance. To express themselves, they necessitate the reacquisition of
similar environmental aspects that led to their creation. Environmental correspondence is also vital if a change of genetic code arises independently of environmental influences. Because environmental factors
select which variations are viable and are passed on, genetic traits require the harmonizing presence of these factors to be effective.

All these interrelations between genetic and environmental influences may make their distinction meaningless in the long-term development of humankind. Their differences only seem relevant for the
consideration of shorter timespans such as a human lifespan, a limited
succession of generations, the continuance of a civilization, or historical memory. Relatively immediate genetic adaptions may be possible.
Yet a capable adjustment of genetic code to new environmental influences during the span of one or several generations is unlikely. Even if
environmental influences have a lasting effect, it is initially more likely
to take the form of an acquired trait than genetic customization. Particularly our mental acuity and flexibility and our ability to shape our
environment may accelerate the interchange between us and our environmental conditions to develop too quickly and significantly to allow
timely genetic reaction, at least until we can securely manipulate our
genetic traits. Thus, we may largely presume that alterations in human
conduct during historical times have been due to newly developed acquired traits or the reaction of already resident traits to new circumstances. The speed of adjustment that acquired traits offer compared
to genetic traits seems to be a great advantage. Still, fundamental difficulties of distinction remain. Distinguishing acquired traits may even
gain difficulty because environmental influences may produce new acquired supplements that reflect genetic attributes differently.

In an effort to gain clarity, we might turn to a scientific manner of exploration for assistance. We might attempt to distinguish genetic from acquired traits by exposing genetically identical persons to specific differences in their environments while keeping the remainder of their environments identical and subsequently comparing their traits. If they exhibit distinctions in their traits, we might conclude that environmental differences initiated these and that they are acquired traits. This conclusion seems legitimate. One might also try to conclude that a trait is genetic if identical individuals exhibit the same trait in spite of different developmental environments. But that might not be a valid conclusion. Identical traits might be acquired traits that were fashioned by shared environmental factors and not influenced by the environmental differences. Consistent general features of the environment might find reflection in acquired traits or otherwise set conditions for behavior that might be difficult to distinguish from a genetic basis.

Even to the extent we could succeed identifying environmental conditions as causes of acquired traits based on behavioral differences by genetically identical persons, the theoretical prospect of testing for causalities and clearly identifying causes is very difficult to implement. The extensive number of environmental influences that would have to be kept controlled and identical until the formation of acquired traits would pose colossal management challenges for such an experimental setting. Determining unambiguous causal connections would necessitate a finely tuned, elaborate, and long-term planning that would have to tightly administrate the environment for observation subjects from the inception of their existence. Studies would remain limited not only due to such issues but also because they could only be undertaken with genetically identical persons. If we were limited to naturally produced identical persons, we would have to draw our knowledge mostly from identical twins. Further, we might not be able to test multiple specific environmental variances because these may combine with one another or react with genetic traits in ways that might complicate the attribution of acquired traits to particular environmental aspects.

To create a robust field of observation, we would need multiple replicas of genetically identical persons positioned in controlled environments with controlled differentiations. Yet, as complex as such an arrangement may seem, it would not disclose much. It might allow us to understand the development of certain acquired traits by a certain type of genetically identical individuals. But we might have difficulties distinguishing traits from the repeated reactions that a person keeps choosing because of being confronted with the same challenges. We may not be able to distinguish practices that have been internalized as a need from consistent practical considerations. Moreover, we would have to subject individuals to manipulation and to control that would severely violate fundamental rights and might engender extraordinary acquired traits and behavior patterns. Even apart from such complications, the requirement for particularization to generate relatively clear results severely limits the applicability of insights. Understanding the formational results of a variety of single environmental factors and of their combinations would require an exorbitant multiplication of experimental settings. Finally, we might at best derive some understanding regarding possibilities of acquired traits with regard to individuals whose genetic setup is identical to that of the test subjects. However, such an experimental setting could not tell us which genetic aspects are responsible. Testing individuals with fractional identities to isolate these aspects would exponentially complicate the scope of experimentation and might introduce too many disturbances by different genetic dispositions to derive insights, requiring us to control these variables as well. Nor would a testing of identical genetic dispositions inform us how the same environmental factors would interact with different genetic compositions. To explore these questions, we would have to reverse the observation setting and instead introduce into identical environments individuals whose genetic code differs in certain features. To achieve that, we would have to select or produce individuals with particular genetic variations. In addition, we would have to create and maintain identical circumstances for all of them from the beginning of their existence through the relevant test period. The obstacles against achieving this are as formidable as the control of environmental circumstances for identical individuals. We would face many of the same or similar issues because we would have to comprehensively control genetic and environmental settings and the results under this research would be similarly limited as those of the reverse arrangement.

Short of extremely difficult to arrange and nightmarish experimentation, we can only observe compromised settings. We may only draw very rough and unreliable conclusions from these. Where we detect differences or congruences in personality, we might try to explore, but in the end might not have much certainty about participating factors and processes. The number and nuances of forming influences as well as among the possible characteristics of genetic and environmental traits, the complexity of possible interaction among forming influences, among traits, as well as between forming influences and traits, and the variety of circumstances in which traits find expression might not allow clear conclusions regarding causal connections. To isolate a genetic source of a trait, we would have to show that all humans who share a trait also share a portion of genetic code that is not shared by persons who do not display that trait. This identification requirement prevents proof of common genetic traits. To isolate environmental aspects as the cause for a trait, we would have to show that all humans who share a trait also share external circumstances not shared by persons who do not display that trait. This requirement prevents proof of common acquired traits. The described manners of distinction may be competent to identify specific traits as acquired or genetic. Nevertheless, because of the interference of other traits and circumstantial particularities, large expanses of our personality may not allow an exclusive attribution of a trait in this manner. We may improve our chances of being able to attribute traits to genetic or environmental sources by constructing a database of individuals that encompasses their genetic code, their behavior, and their environmental conditions. Given a sufficiently massive database and specificity of information, we might determine at least some causal relationships between genetic sequences and environmental settings and traits. However, considering the great effort and personal intrusion this undertaking would require, it is unlikely to occur. Even if it could be instituted, the complexity of a multiplicity of possible connections may not allow us to draw many conclusive results. To achieve reasonable certainty regarding the sourcing and nature of our traits, we might have to lay open the internal causes and processes by which traits develop generally and in particular. Unless we can accomplish this feat, our exploration will have to remain largely inconclusive. This is a result of which we were already aware to some extent from the failure of previous empiric and idealistic explorations to define our happiness. But now we have a better insight into the reasons. This may allow us to find a way to overcome this failure.

The mixture of genetic and environmental aspects in our traits that precludes clarity may be a representation of important beneficial mechanisms. Genetic traits may be in large parts built to allow or require environmental participation in their functions. This is a natural consequence of the formation of our genetic traits by our environment and their function to use our environment. Yet, in addition, our genetic programming may permit or call for the mechanisms it provides to be adapted to a certain extent by sources in our environment. This enables us to be more effective in relatively quickly varying circumstances. Accordingly, our genetic dispositions do not solely enable us to acquire contributions from external sources in a tightly controlled manner. Many of them also leave us room to acquire programming from our environment and to be thus intensely formed by our external settings during our life. Our mind is the facilitator of that influence.

Because our genetic dispositions are then positioned to react to and function in correspondence with environmental influences, both sources seem to be integral parts of our mental mechanisms. The contributions of environmental sources may contain necessary or useful direction that complements genetic instructions. Not all environmental influences have solidified into traits. But our genetic code may by itself not contain all the information that we seek to define personality traits, including those defining our existential needs. As we investigate the interchange between genetic and environmental aspects, we gain awareness that our mental traits are regularly not formed exclusively by one or the other source. Rather, we find that they are ingredients in merged structures. Acquired and genetic features comprise a miniature council of traits for each trait that is characterized by two fused aspects. This tandem of features determines the issuance and direction of our impulses for each of our needs. Genetic and environmental variations among individuals may complicate the derivation of general insights regarding the functioning of these tandems. Even for aspects of our genetic traits that are identical, the variability in the substance and intensity of acquired traits that are paired up with genetic traits is likely to lead to a wide variety of composite mental traits and resulting personalities. We may one day become able to trace and understand acquired and genetic traits by their physiological underpinnings. Until then, larger-scale scientific undertakings appear to be stalled.

We are thus essentially relegated to investigating and assessing ourselves. We may doubt that we should succeed where more general explorations seem to fail. However, there appear to be distinctions between genetic and acquired mental traits that are uniquely accessible to us as the carriers of these traits and that we can use to illuminate them. Our genetic traits appear to us as more concealed because their configurations were built as a matter of events that preceded us. Our mind does not possess a record of our genetic traits or how they were built. This would appear to preclude us from taking immediate cognizance of our genetic traits until we reach scientific insights into their physiological details. Although we might possess some of this insight regarding common genetic traits, our comprehension of most specific aspects will have to await additional scientific progress. Our acquired traits seem to be significantly more accessible to us. They entered our mind through our perceptions. We may therefore be able to retrieve memories surrounding their acquisition and other processing. While acquired aspects of traits are often involuntarily suffered, the physical manner of their acquisition is bound to leave a record in our mind. Methods that probe our recollection may lead us to the mental record left by the formation of acquired personality aspects. That record may enable us to trace these effects to their source. By recalling the origin and acquisition of acquired personality facets, we can develop a better understanding of their nature and how they contribute to or detract from our happiness. Illuminating acquired features of our composite traits also helps us to identify the remainder of our traits as genetically sourced. For that to happen with a reasonable certainty of distinction, however, we must investigate the entirety of environmental influences on our traits. The exhaustive identification of our acquired personality aspects may allow us to identify our genetic traits by subtraction. This can increase our understanding of the interaction among environmental and genetic factors in the formation of our traits as well.

An additional discrepancy between genetic and acquired traits consists in how we might affect them. Even if we could recognize our genetic traits, we might not possess much ability to change them. The genetic influences on our traits appear to be fixed until we obtain the technology to change our genetic code, the mechanisms of its application, or the physical facilities that are built according to that code. The technological demands seem to be highest in changing genetic aspects of traits imminently by accessing code sequences. We might more easily succeed in generational selection and deselection of genetic traits, although this promises to be a much less refined instrument. To affect genetic traits without such genetic technologies, we might be limited to suppressing or channeling them in their application or preempting or altering their physical results. The results of such interventions may be categorized as acquired traits. Their direct physicality joins acquired traits that are created or revised by direct physical processes without an intent to affect genetic structures or results. Yet acquired traits are currently typically acquired by sensory impressions in coincidental or intentional exposure. This may endure even as direct interventions become attainable. In our consideration, we will use the term acquired traits to denote sensory acquisition unless we indicate traits as directly acquired. The amendment of acquired traits by acquired traits appears to hold the most promise. We may further use impressions to customize genetically initiated and directly acquired traits. Acquired features may become seemingly inseparably fused with the trait they join. Still, their experiential sourcing makes them accessible to exploration and modification. In as far as acquired traits are already extant, we may alter, suppress, or remove them by supplementing or counteracting responsible impressions. Learning how acquired personality features develop and work may also lead us to a concept how to purposely construct acquired traits, possibly helping us to master our personality.

In our attempts to change acquired aspects of mental traits, we might not be able to roll back the acquisition process that has already occurred. But it may be possible to introduce experiences that interact with already established experiences to create a modified and possibly compensated entirety for each trait. It may be sufficient to bring past experiences back into our current, different awareness, placing them into context, and considering them under the judgment of our council of traits. We may not need newly sourced experiences to change our mind. The renewed experience of past influences alone may enable us to shape our traits to where they yield improved results of satisfaction. We may be able to resolve that what we came to be through environmental influences is not who we want to be, and we may be able to act effectively upon that resolution. We may be able to unlearn what we learned and diminish or abrogate the influences of selected forces. In addition, we may be able to design and construct acquired traits that we deem missing. To the extent we do not possess sufficient experiences or considerative ability to change our mind to our desired state by reconsideration, we may produce or find new impressions. By modifying or neutralizing acquired adjuncts to genetic traits or by building new adjuncts, we may modify the expression of our genetic traits. We can change our personality according to our ideals to the extent it can be affected by the presence or absence of acquired traits. This ability could provide us with freedom to shape the pursuit of our happiness in line with our ideals. In spite of their partial definition by acquired or by specific genetic traits, our ideals appear to be fundamentally defined by common genetic traits. Specific traits may accord uncommon importance to their particularities. However, our council of traits will recognize the importance of their foundations. In its context, specific traits are looking, apart from special favors by other traits, for a functioning organism that advances their existence and success. They are disinclined to support one another's idiosyncrasies at the cost of such a foundation. Their mutually critical attitudes tend to favor existential traits as dominant forces if our council's mechanisms are fully developed. To the extent specific traits advance common traits in an overall constructive manner, our council is likely to tolerate their pursuit. To the extent it considers them to be harmful, it is likely to oppose these traits and militate for their deselection, suppression, or change.

The deselection, suppression, and change of our acquired mental traits may appear to us somewhat like a second chance. Arguably, we would already have had a choice at the occasion of acquiring these traits. Because we seem to be forming our mental traits or allow their institution by admitting influences from our environment, we might conclude that we are responsible for traits acquired through our mind. But that conclusion would not be entirely justified because our acquisitions are being determined by outside sources and our predispositions. The traits we acquire through our mind result from the correlation of two components: information and its processing by our mind. Our genetic setup creates an infrastructure of mental capacity that has yet to be shaped and organized by substance. Still, that capacity may be particularized by genetic programming and direct physiological influences. In addition, our genetic setup also gives us initial processing instructions through the instinctive mental conditioning provided by our common and specific genetic traits. Here again, the development of the genetically programmed basis may be affected by direct physiological influences. The resulting mental capacity and focus constitute the ground structures and processes of our mental activity. Not all of these facilities and not the entirety of their scope may be formed during the early phases of our existence. Nevertheless, they install initial programming by which information is processed. Information, including information that might establish acquired mental traits, must pass through these initial mechanisms. Moreover, to be effective in merging with a genetic trait, acquired mental traits must adjust themselves. Although acquired traits may supplement or change our mind, this arrangement may partly reinforce genetic traits. As a result, our mental activities, including the development of our acquired traits, are significantly predisposed by our genetic instructions. Our mind's development remains significantly determined and limited by its initial structures and processes and by acquisitions that are formed by them.

Within the parameters permitted by our genetic and our physiological conditioning, the information we receive through our senses appears to have a significant forming effect as well. Our mental capacity provides the opportunity to supplement the instructions of our genetic traits with information and programming that might ameliorate our ability to satisfy our needs. Our genetic traits inspire us to make use of our mental capacity. But even without such encouragement, we might absorb environmental information as a matter of exposed capacity. As we accumulate impressions and as they are processed, they contribute to the development of our mental structures and processes that perceive, memorize, categorize, and further process impressions. They become part of a mechanism that manages impressions based on the facilities originally built by genetic traits and amended by impressions. At the outset of our existence, when our impressions are beginning to exert their formative influences, they may be at their most effective. They are less likely to encounter entirely formed and fortified mental configurations. Our lack of experiences renders our mind most open to formative environmental influences. Early life experiences can therefore have a decisive beneficial or detrimental function in forming our mind. They may condition us to readily incorporate new experiences and to adjust our mind to them. But they may also build conditions that integrate subsequent impressions only selectively in accordance with the mental structures and processes built by previous impressions and to reject change. The self-reinforcing mechanisms in the construction of traits are the same that cause our general propensity toward categorizing our world according to principles and of perceiving, thinking, or feeling about the world according to such principles. The hardening of our attitudes into traits constitutes an extreme result of automation that threatens to remove our response to circumstances from our control. To be effective, acquired standards by which we operate have to be policed by reflective and by corrective processes that tell us whether they are or continue to be warranted. This is necessary to keep experiences from building self-reinforcing mechanisms that fail to reflect reality. Yet, at the beginning of our existence, when such mechanisms are most rapidly built, a relative lack of experiences causes our reflective and corrective abilities to be feeble. Our capacity to learn outpaces our capacity to reflect on and correct what we learn. This weakness may not only be due to the state of our rational development. It may also be attributable to a relative underdevelopment in the definition of our needs and accordingly their functionalities in our council of traits. Together, these conditions favor the formation of acquired traits or entrenched principles that stop short of traits. The extended self-reinforcement processes of such principles and traits may make surmounting them difficult even if we are later exposed to countervailing information. Further, the proximity of our early conditioning may make it hard to connect to the original shape of our traits.

Our mind sets out to acquire environmental influences as soon as we can process sensory information, possibly before our birth. We acquire important aspects of our traits as the result of targeted influences that attempt to shape our personality. Some of that training is administered by our parents and other persons in charge of raising us. Ideally, the formative objectives and efforts of such persons would be congruent with a child's natural potential of development. They would assist a child in comprehending its existential needs and in acquiring the knowledge, skills, and possibly traits to satisfy these needs in an optimized and harmonized manner. They might impart instructions they consider to be objectively applicable to any human. To the extent general principles of happiness exist, teaching these does not constitute an undue imposition on a child's personality. It merely accelerates learning, and it preempts experiences that could be unnecessarily painful for the child and its surroundings. Beyond such general principles, particularized instruction may be required to enable a competent pursuit of fulfillment. That may entail consideration for the particularized needs and capacities of a child as well as for the individual conditions of the child's environment. The formation of particularized traits may be pursued to adjust genetic idiosyncrasies or adapt a child to a particular environment. However, such influences may not be in the child's interest. Persons responsible for its upbringing would only focus on its happiness because that usually serves their happiness. Yet the pursuit of caretakers' happiness might infuse motivations that do not serve their charge's happiness. Even if they focus on the welfare of the child, the peculiarities of their mental traits may not allow instruction free of limiting or damaging influences characteristic to them.

The preemptions of a child's choices by others are fraught with risks of bias, error, and abuse. Persons in charge of a child's upbringing may have to override a child's choices during phases when its capacity to make considered and informed selections is underdeveloped or compromised, at least if the instructional worth of such choices is exceeded by damage. If possible, a selection in such cases would have to be deferred to a later time when the child is competent. Some decisions that narrow the options of pursuit may have to be made before that time according to the best available indications. But persons raising a child may be tempted to venture beyond. They might instruct the child on behalf of other interests that pursue their own objectives. More likely, they might teach a child in line with their individual perceptions, thoughts, preferences, aversions, aspirations, and fears. They might attempt to live vicariously through a child to repeat or exceed their successes or to avoid their mistakes. They may encourage or venture to create traits they approve or desire. They may further attempt to suppress, channel, or remove traits or their development if they regard them as incompatible with their own. They may intentionally or unwittingly form the personality of a child consistent with their personalities, to compensate for perceived deficiencies in their personalities, or to pursue their desires. Such narrowing of a child's focus might be undertaken with good intentions to lessen a child's pain from trial and error, from unfulfilled searching for happiness. But it might have the opposite effect because it interferes with a child's development of independent decisional mechanisms. Frequently, preemptive instruction may be undertaken under the presumption that a child shares all or most genetic traits and environmental circumstances with its caretakers. Thus, the conveyance of information and experiences and the formation of acquired traits to assist a child in properly acting and reacting may seem helpful. However, a child's genetic traits may deviate sufficiently to make instructions not or less applicable. Even if the genetic traits are congruent, instructions may represent unhelpful or less than optimized responses. They might already have been inapplicable to the original conditions under which they were formed or environmental conditions might have changed or may change in a child's life. While formative efforts are primarily undertaken by biological parents and substitute caretakers, other family members and persons attached to families may reinforce or weaken such efforts. They may add deliberate or coincidental conditioning according to their own traits. Their influence raises the risk that a child might be preempted and used.

Besides our home, our school environments can have one of the most purposeful impacts on us during our formative years. The educational objective of most schools is oriented toward shaping the technical abilities and thus utility of students and making them compliant with governing philosophies. To the extent issues of happiness are addressed, subjects may be taught from cultural, religious, economic, or political positions held by the authorities that maintain schools. They may try to inculcate concepts that conform students to their goals rather than critical thinking or the development of an independent personality. Schools may place emphasis on compliance as an ulterior objective and a state of mind that facilitates educational objectives. They may undertake their educational objectives by imparting standardized information and aptitudes so that students can be subjected to standardized grading. They may use grading and the threat of demotion or expulsion as an instrument of compliance with their procedural and substantive demands. Hence, the formalities and substance of schooling often result in a curriculum that is not open to reflections, discussions, viewpoints, or variances and that is instead directed toward the suppression of self-determination in favor of submission to authority.

In addition to secular education, we may receive instruction in purported matters of our spirit or soul from religions. Most of that instruction is not aimed at encouraging or instilling the development of autonomous or critical personalities. Usually, religious instruction endeavors to inculcate standardized precepts of belief and conformance with substantive and procedural requirements said to secure our survival after death. Most religions institute an existential philosophy and dwell on customs and prescribed demeanor. Their authorities monitor and control our compliance with their dictates or may indoctrinate us with mental devices that cause us to control our compliance. They require by threatening us with repercussions that their postulates be accepted and their impositions followed without question. Investigatory skills and differing views may be tightly controlled and only permitted within unquestioned premises. Organizational, existential, and competitive requirements of religions may induce them to comprehensively control and direct our rational thoughts, emotions, and behavior.

Instruction and reinforcing threats may be essential or helpful to control deleterious impulses and give guidance, particularly as long as our mind has not fully developed. But if such controls do not comport with internal controls, they are a shell that may be broken or discarded. Not trusting the efficacy of inherent internal controls even after we mature, instruction may try to adjust our personality. Such approaches and even the override of our internal controls or their development may also be pursued for nefarious purposes. Either way, informal and formal instruction may be sought by forces that wish to govern us, our associations, or societies to have us serve their traits.

If government were constructed in the interest of the governed, its function would be to assist individuals in the pursuits of their happiness. That pursuit would only be limited by the equal right of other individuals to pursue their happiness. Government would be tasked to state and enforce such limits. It may also be assigned additional functions to improve overall happiness in a society. Opinions may vary on the best ways of increasing overall happiness in a society. There might be diverse views on whether or how much government should restrict and actively assist or shape individual pursuits. A society may sanction such opinions to arise and organize and to determine the functions of government consistent with such opinions. Moreover, it may incorporate mechanisms by which the rights of individuals who do not win in the contest of opinions are protected. In any event, government would be barred from interfering in excess of what is deemed to be required to maximize overall happiness. Then again, powers that direct a society may also try to create or preserve an advantage of certain individuals or groups over others. They may obstruct diverging opinions or activities to form, organize, or compete. Still, even governments that follow an ideal of constructive equality may try to manage the mind and conduct of subjects to some extent to fulfill their mission. Their function is facilitated if the governed naturally agree. But most systems of government have core tenets on which their promoters insist. To forestall their violation, they may not only install external coercive structures and procedures. They may also apply instruction as an essential instrument to maintain stability and may not shy away from trying to form mental traits compliant with what they believe to be right.

The principles that support the existence and functioning of a particular government might be originally shared or subsequently internalized by its subjects. In that case, control mechanisms can mostly restrict themselves to occasional reinforcement and instructing future generations in matters of compliance. There may also be societies in which governmental control is less extensively established or may be threatened or negatively affected by noncompliance or active dissent. In these contexts, governmental authorities and related interests may enforce an alignment with and prevent deviation from organizational structures and principles more intensely. Control instruments may be outright and obvious in restrictive rules, mandates, oversight, prosecution and enforcement against violators, suppression, discrimination, intimidation, and possibly requirements that subjects display their allegiance and backing. But such courses of action may induce dissent, unrest, and active resistance that might be dangerous or at least disturbing for the prevailing order and that might be costly to overcome. Governing authorities may prefer the subtler approach of forming and manipulating their subjects' perceptions, rational thoughts, and emotions to minimize disruption while maximizing compliance. In addition to formal instructional institutions, governing interests may utilize other settings of communication to form subjects' minds and their view of reality. Methods include the withholding, fabrication, or falsification of information as well as committing or provoking acts that stimulate conducive impulses and allow the short-circuiting of critical facilities. Governmental interests may take advantage of subjects' fears and desires. They may sustain, intensify, and direct emotions to serve their purposes. Their manipulation may cause subjects to accept false representations as true, conform, become indifferent, and act in blind allegiance against their interests. Forces that strive to assume governing power may employ similar schemes to have subjects question government actions, resist, or revolt. However, once such interests are in power, their promotion of destabilizing attitudes is typically replaced by the encouragement of alignment with governmental interests.

Accordingly, a number of formative forces may take advantage of our relative infirmity. They may generate, preserve, or amplify emotional, cognitive, and informational weaknesses that affect our capacity to judge what our happiness requires. They may utilize our underdeveloped knowledge of our happiness to implant perceptions, rational thoughts, and emotional responses. They may persuade us to take actions that are reflective of their mental traits, fulfillment status, and circumstances and that are of service to them. Although such influences might be most effective if they are introduced to us during the formative period of our youth, they might also wield significant power over us later if we fail in deriving an applicable concept of happiness. The formation of mental traits may not appear as the result of obvious indoctrination. Environmental shaping alone may translate into the formation of traits because subjects may adjust to their setting. Even if influences do not establish firmly entrenched traits in one generation, they may create gradual generational mindsets that steer subsequent generations into ever growing alignment. Further, the distribution of parallel formative influences through several purportedly independent sources of instruction and influence may allow manipulatory interests to develop momentous influence by subtle means. It may allow them to wield widespread dominance over the mindsets of subjects.

Traditional manners of mental domination seem to increasingly compete with a wider scope of other sources whose availability is enabled by technology. Yet many of these sources may be controlled by the same interests that are continuing to manipulate us through more traditional channels. Some alternative sources might be able to stop or roll back traditional or new manipulatory influences. But they may also be controlled by forces that seek to influence us to serve their objectives. Even if such sources seem to be opposed to interests that are currently in power, it might be similarly difficult for us to determine whether we share their objectives and whether their information is reliable. If information sources are independent, have no particular offensive or defensive agenda, and have therefore no interest to manipulate information to serve their goals, they are often underfinanced and thus less effective. Even if such sources persist, we may not select or support them. They may not succeed gaining our attention or esteem among a profusion of information sources that serve manipulatory interests, particularly because these lure us into favoring them. In such a setting, relevant information can be subject to widespread confusion and dissipation. Increased availability of technology to create and distribute information may add to this problem. In such an atmosphere, professionally produced, packaged, and marketed sources of information are still more likely to grasp and hold our attention. That conditioning may hide behind the free availability of multiple sources that leaves it to us to choose among information sources. Only, what may appear as a selection of our own volition may be directed by previous media exposure or other influences from more traditional sources.

Our environment and selections subject us to powerful messages about the world around us and us. Media messages purport to instruct us how to feel good, how to become wealthy, how to be desirable, loved, successful, and surrounded by family and friends, how to

gain life after our death, how to be happy. The opportunity to influence our mind through media has long been recognized by commercial interests that make sales the principal motivation for communications. But this power has not escaped religious, cultural, and political
interests. They engage in media efforts that rival, and at times exceed,
commercial influences to establish, shape, reinforce, weaken, or eliminate unfavorable philosophies, modes of behavior, or states of mind.
It might seem that the rivalry of causes that try to influence us should
contrast them sufficiently to raise concern and doubt and to incentivize deeper investigation. However, once we are taken in by a view, it is
unlikely that we will expose ourselves to sources that disagree with
the positions we have accepted. Our own tendencies as well as external influences may keep us from seeking, exploring, or acknowledging
contrary information. Interests that attempt to influence us may emo-
tionalize their messages to attract and to keep our attention and allegiance and to indoctrinate us surreptitiously. They may also use more
superficially emotional conditioning to distract us from inconvenient
circumstances. Such forces may not expect to indoctrinate everybody.
Rather, they may use rivaling positions to create much of the desired
emotionalization. Opposing forces may settle to play off one another
as adversaries to divide and attract a populace among them. They may
find that competing for allegiances through misinformation and emotional polarization affords them acceptable control and power. The resulting conflict may benefit all such forces because it permits them to
draw uncommitted individuals into their influence and to strengthen
the adherence and support by their constituents. Their formal or informal coordination of opposing information and activity offerings restricts subjects' selections and moves them to instinctively take sides.
This consolidates the governance of interests that steer these efforts.

     The vast combined onslaught of information and even our par-
tial exposure to it portrays a reality to us that is superimposed on ours.
What we experience through media may influence us as much as our
own experiences, or we may accept their content as our own experiences. We may incorporate what someone else intends to be our experiences, wants us to think, feel, or do. The placing of content into the
form of a shared medium necessarily implies an intent by its author
and publisher to affect the mind and behavior of the communication
recipient. As communications convince us of their messages, we are
being subjected to control. This risk increases with the arrival of technology that makes it possible to target media offerings specifically to
certain types of individuals or to specific persons. It further intensifies
as media experiences become more similar to real world experiences.

Together, the influences of powerful sources on our mind during our formative and later years place us at grave risk of being controlled by intentional programming and indoctrination. Some of these influences may be motivated by the idea that conformance with their instructions will advance our happiness. Notwithstanding, the motivation to benefit us itself stems from one or multiple needs of those who wish to benefit us. Even this motivation is therefore in danger of being biased by the needs of such individuals. Beyond that, a great number of influences are exerted to obtain a more direct subjection of others to the interests of those exerting the influence. In addition, intentional measures to influence might create unintended byproducts in their intended or unintended subjects through their messages alone, in correlation with other messages, or in correlation with preexisting traits.

Besides our exposure to intended and unintended influences by families, schools, religions, commercial interests, political movements, and governments, we are subject to less systematic influences. Growing up, we receive influences from peers, acquaintances, and friends. The frequency and range of encounters past these types of individuals usually increase as we mature. We become part of a professional and wider social environment. We connect with strangers that take on various functions in our existence. All individuals we encounter have an agenda and strive to use and adjust their environment to their needs. They might try to influence us or might affect us collaterally. The profusion of sources of influence appears to attenuate and distract from more systematic influences. However, if the same, similar, or complementary influences are widely originated or gain a widely distributed presence, their effects may compound, resonate in, and be reinforced by one another. The coincidental confluence of multiple sources of influence that might by themselves appear innocuous and separate may combine to have a decisive impact on us because they portray a consistent reality. Moreover, determined interests may generate a significant impact by influencing those who seek to influence or who influence without intent. They may attach themselves to popular sources of influence and succeed in spite of the diffusion and commingling of their impositions. Engineered and coincidental influences may reflect on acquired traits or lesser attitudes to where their content becomes the intent of influenced individuals and these are unaware that they serve others. Further, the concealing of the originators of influence by relays may preclude subjects from recognizing whom they serve. Influences that might gain momentum through distribution may therewith fashion our economic, social, cultural, and security environment and set the general parameters in which we must advance our needs.

All our direct and indirect influences form an amalgamation of acquired aspects in our traits and of more superficial impressions that may be difficult to differentiate. We may be able to identify many, in some cases maybe even all sources that have formed or influenced our personality or attitudes. But it is typically much more difficult to determine which particular feature of our mind was initiated or influenced by which particular source and how and to what effect it was formed or influenced. The cause for this disconnection seems to lie in the way most influences that we acquire through our senses form our mind. Only few experiences originate from key events that suddenly transform our mind. Most acquired influences establish themselves in small doses that are not memorable by themselves. The messages they carry become part of our inner self similar to how food becomes part of our body. We cannot keep track of the effect of each piece we consume and might not know its true composition. Our mind processes pieces of information and incorporates them into larger mental constructs. The building blocks of our mind may enter our awareness at the time they are assimilated. Nevertheless, the often incremental and concealed structures and processes to which they contribute may render it difficult to recognize them as parts of the assembled result. This can make it hard to discern not only whether an attitude or a mental trait is genetic or acquired but also what sources are responsible for it. More complications are contributed by the interaction of several factors. Messages that impress us may be compounds of influences from a number of sources that overlap. Each source of influence over our mind is likely to send out a variety of messages that contribute to multiple impressions. Influences may reinforce or they may interfere with one another or the mindsets they encounter. Mindsets and messages may change. Messages may have different strengths at different times and our mind may be dissimilarly receptive to them at different times. These effects may amalgamate in ways that are difficult to trace.

In consequence of the profusion and intensity of influences that surround us and others, individual agendas could be considerably affected and perhaps dominated by foreign influences. We and other individuals appear to largely share a fate of lacking self-determination. We all may have adopted and may execute and infuse into others foreign sources of programming. We may at least in parts be unwitting agents for the pursuit of other individuals' objectives. It is not surprising then that we might have difficulties finding satisfaction or realizing what our needs are. Our sense and pursuit of happiness may have been buried in layers of instructions, impressions, ideas, and accordingly shaped mental structures and processes that are not ours.

Our programming by external sources is so powerful because it seems to coincide with our fundamental willingness to engage in conforming perceptions, rational thoughts, emotions, and behavior. Our deficiencies in understanding us and the world and our incapacity to sustain ourselves at the beginning of our existence cause us to emulate others with little or no reflection. That drive appears to be genetically inculcated in us. We are also disposed to accept our environment as a standard of normality and tend to seek happiness within its confines. This regularly continues into adulthood. We are prone to accept general conditions and behavior around us and to fit ourselves into that reality without greatly questioning its legitimacy. We not merely gravitate toward imitating and following others if we have concrete indications that they are more competent in pursuing their happiness. There appears to be a herd instinct in us that makes us follow the example or influences of others if we do not consider ourselves able to determine clear directions for our pursuits. Although environmental sources may try to program us to conform to their wishes, we appear to have a predisposition that renders us receptive to environmental programming. Eventually, we may become aware that following others and adjusting ourselves to our environment are not necessarily in our interest. We may find out that permitting external influences to shape our circumstances, needs, and other aspects of our mind can decrease our happiness. If we let this motivate us to ascertain whether and to what extent acquired traits are in our interest, we may be able to correct them.

The abilities to reflect on and to regulate acquired dispositions of our personality may depend on how widely and how deeply our experiences have configured our mind. Arguably, perceptive and rational structures and processes by themselves should be easily changed with a proper showing that prior perceptions and thoughts are incorrect or unwarranted. Unless we have an emotionally motivated objection, we should welcome well-founded expansions or corrections to our knowledge or perceptive or rational capacity because they help our pursuits. It is more difficult to adjust the structures and processes of our emotional mind and of their reliance on perceptive and rational underpinnings. They may display a stubborn determination to persist. Our impulses may insist that we follow their directives against perceptive and rational evidence. We may not succeed in addressing these commands until our council of traits finds them to be contrary to our interests. Even then, incompatible emotional traits may resist as if they had an independent existence and an autonomous interest to carry on. Overcoming their opposition may require considerable capacity, skill, and energy and may create sustained conflict and pain within ourselves.

Our experience does not uniformly reflect that a development toward the maximization of happiness by the collective wisdom of our mental traits is inescapable or even probable. Some of our emotional traits may resist adjustment and removal successfully even if we recognize that they and other mental traits committed to them distract from our overall happiness. Some emotional traits may command our mind relative to other traits to such a degree that they exert domination or at least a veto power. They might not permit other emotional traits to assert themselves sufficiently in the collective of our traits to undertake necessary adjustments in the interest of our overall happiness. This control may not only weaken the implementation of a resolution of our council. It may already suppress the investigatory or argumentative contributions of other emotional traits and their support sphere and thus the decisional facilities of the council. The resulting weakened capacity of our council of traits may leave us with only little and undefined awareness of our mental traits. We may have an insufficient understanding of controlling traits and may sense the dissatisfaction of suppressed needs without identifying the damaging sources and causalities. Eventually, our continuing or recurring pain may provide sufficient motivation for us to investigate and address its causes.

To advance the regulatory mechanism of our council of traits, we have to become aware of our traits. To exert control and to regain control we have already lost, we must rally these traits to examine the influences that have formed us and the influences that continue a tendency or intent to shape us. We must determine which influences we allow over us and have to develop strategies for deflecting, curbing, or eliminating influences that we reject. We may undertake a similar inquiry with regard to our genetic traits although we might attribute to them a higher presumption of validity compared to acquired traits. In fact, as long as we have not identified and subtracted acquired traits from our composite traits, we can only judge our genetic and acquired traits together. We will only be able to identify our genetic traits after we have traced the acquisition of our acquired traits and understand how they contribute. But all of these activities are contingent on thorough preparatory work. Before we can pass judgment on our composite traits, refine that judgment between genetic and acquired components, and before we can engage in a judgment of remedial action, we must identify our traits. We must ensure that each trait is present in our awareness and expresses itself without restraint. Only then can we properly evaluate the function of traits or aspects of traits in relation to our happiness. The next chapter deliberates the fundamental issues we may encounter in trying to achieve the necessary knowledge.

CHAPTER 19
THE STRUGGLE FOR OBJECTIVITY

To many of us, an exploration of our personality might seem intuitively redundant because we are what we are trying to explore. We may not acknowledge the possibility of being uninformed. We may believe that we should be well aware of and familiar with our self because our mind has been witnessing all along everything we perceive, think, feel, and do and is exposed to all that we are at present. We should be able to recognize our traits by focusing on our exposure to them without much additional inquiry. Notwithstanding, many of us seem to possess only a superficial knowledge of our personality. This becomes apparent if we pose to us the question of who we are. The answers may not come easily. It is unlikely that we can readily marshal a sufficient detail to cover all or at least the principal facets of our personality.

On occasions when we want or are prompted to communicate who we are, we might appear to have a sovereign grip on such a representation. Most of us have learned to render short presentations about us. We may state our name and our occupation. We might explain in more detail what we do and have done, our professional experiences, and our opinions. We might describe our family, where we live, where we grew up, and how we arrived at our current station. We might talk about our leisure endeavors, possessions, nonprofessional experiences, social affiliations and activities, and possibly our religious and political attitudes. Different occasions may require or allow selection or preferences among these descriptions. We may further portray information about us by our accomplishments, status symbols, and demeanor. All such communications might be important in our cultural, social, economic, religious, and political interchanges. Still, they are expressions of our outward existence. They give only indirect clues about the person within. We shy away from revealing too much of our personality. On occasion, the provision of deeper insight into our personality to others or ourselves may be unavoidable or appear useful or necessary to pursue our needs. But such events seem to be extraordinary. Most of them are marked by exigencies that lay our emotions bare or designate them as a means of pursuit. We might strive to limit these occasions. We may shy away from revealing our personality to others for fear that they might discover an insight that disadvantages us. Yet we also appear inclined to avert our mind from who we are. We seem to resist acquiring insights about our personality or keeping them in our awareness or considering them after they become apparent. This may prevent us from taking full or even partial account of our self.

Many of us may not see any obvious reasons for delving deeper into who we are. Our perceptions, thoughts, emotions, and demeanor regularly go unnoticed by us as indications of traits. The preset, automatic, amalgamated nature of our mental traits may not let them rise to prominence in our conscious mind. Rather, they impress us as undifferentiated, natural expressions of our person. As much as our traits may engage in competition with one another, their automatic interaction may prevent or materially restrict this competition from entering our awareness. Even the activities of our council of traits appear to us as intuitive and subliminal. We might assert that this largely unconscious mechanism has worked reasonably well, that our existence has been satisfactory without knowing ourselves in detail. Where we cannot convincingly maintain that, we might refer to our demanding and eventful circumstances as preventing us from pausing and reflecting more deeply about our character. Our mind may be preoccupied with countless tasks. We may be struggling to keep up with immediate and ever-changing challenges, to get by from one day to the next. We may not have the time or the energy for fundamental contemplation. Then again, we appear to reserve time and energy for diversions, entertainment, and pastimes. This might cause us to ask whether our claim of being too busy for self-exploration is not a pretext or an indication of a shield we built. We may wonder whether we are merely unskilled at introspection or avoid facing ourselves. Do we fear insights or that we might have none? Are we apprehensive that we would not know what to do with what we expose? Whatever the claimed reasons might be, we may not have investigated our self exhaustively. Yet, without self-awareness, our genetic and acquired programming works largely in an automated fashion. We find ourselves at the mercy of what unregulated mental traits or extraneous occasions might trigger. We may have immediate awareness of our impulses, thoughts, and perceptions. We may try to engage them at that immediate level. However, we may not be aware of their causes, how they came to be, and whether they serve our happiness, serve it better than alternatives, or serve it in the best possible manner. We cannot be certain that our emotional traits engage in competent determinations or that they prompt the rest of our mind to obtain, investigate, review, and correlate information in adequate ways. We may at any given time follow the needs that issue the strongest impulses with little or no contest or deliberation.

Because we may not have dedicated much effort to the exploration of our inner dimension, our aptitude for self-investigation may be underdeveloped. If we do not know very well who we are inside, it is not surprising that we have trouble understanding what we want from our existence, what makes us happy. Given our lack of access and skill in investigating ourselves, it is not probable that we can suddenly gain this access and skill simply as a matter of determination. Finding admittance to our inner world may be more of a challenge than we first realize. Our mental traits are programs, routines that cause us to deal with issues in particular, set ways. Once these programs have been installed, they tend to defend themselves against attempts to destabilize them. This is a necessary function if they are to succeed and survive in competition with other traits and with functional obstacles. But it also poses a barrier in the investigation of our mental traits. Because that investigation is motivated by the ultimate intent of obtaining power over them and possibly interfering with them, our mental traits may raise their defenses. Such defenses may be inculcated not only in the natural persistence of established mental structures and processes as traits. Our perceptive and rational traits may be additionally protected by the leadership of emotional traits that depend on them for support and protection. As a consequence, we may be contending with sophisticated mechanisms that include all three types of our mental abilities and may include coalitions of emotional traits. The integration of such mechanisms into the communications of our mind allows them to notice our intent or its potential and to evade detection and scrutiny of their nature. They may have access to many of the awareness and assistance functions in their efforts of evasion that we attempt to rally in their capture. The focusing of our mind on itself thus seems to create obstacles that exceed inherent circularity with attempts of evasion.

Defense mechanisms appear to be particularly vigorous in traits that already maintain disagreements with other traits or our council of traits or that are struggling with themselves. If they cannot deflect attention, they might instill defensive concerns or combine with favorable concerns set forth by other traits. We might resist exploring them for fear that we might weaken needs whose pursuit is already under pressure. We might fear that we would reveal and inflame aspects that cause us pain without an effective ability to heal them. We might recall failed remediation attempts whose recurrence we might attempt to prevent. We might have become despondent about our inability to address demands successfully or to establish balance among them. We might lack confidence that we can harmonize our traits. The resigning obstruction resulting from these concerns is unproductive. If there is unresolved conflict or dissatisfaction in our personality, if we continue to accept and reinforce internal barriers in the pursuit and fulfillment of our needs, we sentence ourselves to carry their burdens. By registering and reviewing these issues, we gain a chance of resolving them.

Arguably, it should be easiest to review our perceptive and rational traits because these can be measured by how well they reflect reality that we can describe through scientific insights. To the extent there are discrepancies, we should be able to find functional deficiencies in the mechanisms these traits represent and use. But there may be problems in drawing insights from scientific attention to our mind even if we should make impressive advancements in science and technology. We might have general blind spots in our comprehension of human perceptive and rational traits. Humans might be incapable of detecting incongruities of our perceptive or rational facilities with the substances and principles of nature because we apply these facilities to detect incongruities. The impressions of substances and principles of nature we derive might be shaped to comply with these blind spots. We might find some indications that our perceptive and rational traits are inadequate when we observe aspects of nature that seem to breach logic or specific principles of nature. Rather than considering that we might lack capacities to perceive or understand, we may claim that nature acts in ways that allow us to deny our shortcomings. As long as we can create purported scientific explanations and apply them in the pursuit of needs, we may deem our views sufficiently confirmed, even if we leave inconsistencies unresolved. Machines we devise may confront us with our blind spots and help us overcome them only if we do not pass our disabilities on to them. That might happen if we understand our limitations and construe machines to step into such areas. We might also construe machines that coincidentally alert us to blind spots or contribute to their remediation. Even if we fail to detect blind spots, machines we produce might become able to develop themselves to independently increase their perceptive and rational capacities beyond ours. Defining the general human perceptive and rational blind spots then appears to be an undertaking that we must largely leave to scientific and technological progress. Besides some obvious extrapolations of our spectral ranges, it appears to require the surpassing of our mind by an exterior, nonhuman intelligence that can investigate our world, including our mind, without being caught in our restraints and avenues of perceptive and rational processing of information.

Machines might assist us in the expansion of perceptive and rational capacities. But they may also visit perceptive and rational horizons in excess of our capabilities that remain removed from our mental grasp. Even if we avoided implanting them with human perceptive and rational deficiencies and thus eluded reiterating our blind spots in them, we would filter their results through our perceptive and rational facilities, including the shortcomings of these facilities. Our acknowledgment that there are ranges of perception and rational thinking that exceed our capacity does not make these areas accessible to our senses and thinking. The construction of machines to appropriate an extended reality might suggest to us that we are capable of imagination beyond our perception and thinking. But such an imagination can only consist of rearrangements of the aspects we are already perceiving and thinking. We may possess much room for such rearrangements within our perceptive and rational capacities and may make much scientific progress under the use of our imagination. Still, our perceptive and rational capacities pose natural limits to our imagination. Machines we devise can only assist us to supersede these limitations to the extent they can translate matters outside our reach down to matters within our perception and thought. That we can conceptualize and construct such translation mechanisms is based on experiences that certain allocations allow us to measure effects emanating outside our range. We can only perceive an image and deductive concepts of what is being translated. We try to explain what is being translated in terms of the behavior of that image. While this may allow us some conclusions that we may deem scientific due to their stability, our indirect exposure to phenomena may leave us with substantial deficits in our understanding of the phenomena themselves. At some point, our inability to perceive or rationalize phenomena may leave us unable to interpret their effects in our perceptive and rational parameters with much success. Machines we can construct may meet limits of what they can detect because they are still bound to our capacities. If we created machines that could independently evolve and develop their perceptive and rational capacities, they might develop into such a distance that similes we could understand might not capture much or anything they could conceive or compute. We might only be apprised of it by vague metaphors or by products that we can perceive or consider in our range.

Our understanding of the limitations of our perceptive and rational capacities appears to be generally confined by these limitations. We only accept areas external to our capacities if we are confronted by their results within our sphere of perception and rationality. To go beyond the limitations of this mindset, we would have to change our capacities. We might undertake that through genetic manipulation or by integrating our mind with technological supplements that are capable of perception and rational operations in excess of our natural capacity.

Scientifically affirmed or developed perceptive and rational capacities typical to humans as well as general restrictions to them may be considered to be general perceptive and rational traits. There may be significant individual variances to these general standards. Similar to emotional traits, these other mental traits may be differently developed and distinguished in individuals due to genetic or environmental causes. Here again, science and technology should be able to assist us in ascertaining individual perceptive and rational traits. Even in an individual, not all perceptive or rational facilities might be developed or variegated equally. They can vary depending on different types of subject matters being processed. Hence, there may be differences in and among individuals that we may describe as specific perceptive or rational traits. But differences in perceptive or rational processing may not only happen as a matter of differently shaped capacities. They may further stem from variations of operational conditions individuals encounter due to exposures and influences that might assist or restrict the use of their capacities or preoccupy them. The external and often temporary nature of these conditions distinguishes them from traits.

We may measure perceptive acuity by how well we can acquire information from scientifically measurable phenomena. We may also measure rational acuity, our intelligence, by our ability to recall, understand, associate, and invent. Arguably, such tests should yield objective, scientific results that can inspire suggestions for improvement. While tests we undergo in education and licensing may provide some of such results, we may otherwise avoid subjecting ourselves to independent objective testing of our perceptive and rational traits for fear of repercussions on our internal and external standing. We may only accept such testing if it is required to obtain or maintain a position. We may still undertake informal inquiries to gauge whether and how well we can accomplish perceptive or rational goals. But determining our related traits on our own may be difficult. We may experience individual blind spots in our perceptive and rational faculties, and humanity may have similar difficulties to supersede them generally. We might be incapable of perceiving or imagining capacities that diverge from our current capacities. Further, we might not realize that, within our capacities, it is possible to perceive or think differently. We might not acknowledge limitations or errors that lead to an incorrect or an incomplete reflection or processing of circumstances unless we apply our insights, that application fails, and other causes for failure are excluded. Then again, many of us might not be compelled to such clarification because our pursuits may present us with bearable results in spite of perceptive or rational limitations or because we find plausible other attributions of responsibility. In addition, our pursuits may not have us apply perceptions or thoughts in ways that show their incorrect or incomplete nature. As a consequence, we may carry perceptive or rational blind spots without any or much awareness of them.

Arguably, there might be conditions where we might not profit from becoming aware of perceptive or rational blind spots. However, we might not know that until we explore what we have been missing and reach such awareness. Added perceptive or rational ability or capacity carries a strong presumption of a potential to improve our existence. This may incentivize us to try to transcend their limitations. Their scientific exploration might impress us as preferable because it may provide us with certainty. But the number and variety of issues with which we have to contend may not lend themselves to a scientific treatment. Further, we may not possess the necessary resources or be willing to invest them. Nor may adequate scientific resources be available for such specialized purposes, except in conditions in which our existential functioning is at risk. This may frequently leave large areas of our perceptive and rational idiosyncrasies unexplored by science.

In these areas, we may use our experiences to examine whether our perceptions and rational operations are correct or lack effectiveness and efficiency. We may engage in explorations through observations and experimentation of our own. Yet we may fall prey to the circularity of our perceptive and rational traits or less permanent settings investigating themselves. Moreover, it seems difficult to separate emotional impressions from our perceptive and rational assessments. We seem to have difficulties gathering impressions about perceptive or rational aspects without an emotional connotation that threatens to influence or take over our impression of what we perceive or think. Any perception or rational thought we have is immediately evaluated concerning its utility and its detriment for the contentment of our needs. This threatens to taint our assessments of factual reflection with emotional bias. To avert such problems of subjectivity, to evade the problems of circularity, and to gain a better understanding of our perceptive and rational mind, we might supplement our perceptive and rational experiences by comparing them with those of other individuals. We may establish our perceptive and rational capacity and operational peculiarities relative to other humans by differences and similarities in reaction or in communication regarding perceptive and rational phenomena. We may participate in explorations regarding possible causes of differences. Others may be amenable to granting information about their perceptions and thoughts to ascertain their perceptive or rational conditions. But the benefits of such comparisons seem insecure because each individual might employ different variations of subjectivity and circularity in the derivation and description of perceptive and rational phenomena. These effects are enhanced if we rely on others to assess our perceptive and rational mind. Each individual observes and evaluates others through the filter of that individual's perceptive, rational, and emotional facilities. In addition, numerous situational biases of observers may contribute to their assessments. The results may then be as much a reflection of the observing as of the observed individual. The threat of bias may increase if evaluations of other individuals are not confined to perceptive or rational features. This is understandable given the difficulty of deciphering other individuals' minds and because being aware of and understanding their motivations may be crucial or helpful in our pursuits. We will also want to compare our emotional bearings with those of others to know whether we are processing other mental aspects correctly. But we may miss opportunities for cooperation and peaceful coexistence if we do not distinguish perceptive and rational conditions in others from emotional motivations. We may impart additional bias if we do not keep our emotional positions separate from evaluations of other individuals' minds. We must make an effort even if excluding emotional aspects entirely appears to be impossible unless we proceed pursuant to scientific protocols.

There may further be a risk of bias if evaluations are not mutual because they may lack disclosure or understanding of evaluative foundations. Others may be able to better hide their propensity to judge or influence us according to the biases of their mental traits. They might mislabel their blind spots as ours, identify our disharmonies with their interests as blind spots, or render false evaluations to benefit their interests. They may abuse insights about us without reciprocal risk. But a mutuality of evaluation may also incentivize individuals to act disingenuously to attain favorable judgment in return. Effects similar to deception may occur if we fail to comprehend the mind of others. If we cannot find acceptable results in mutual disclosure, we may try to gain safeguards by involving individuals whose judgment we trust not to be tainted. We might ask them to register and evaluate our circumstances, our mental management of these circumstances, and possible reasons for variances and problems. Only, identifying such individuals already requires a level of capable judgment that we may not possess. In either case, we may be drawn to trust the judgment of individuals who display similar traits or situations without their or our grasp of the differences. Even if they are similar to us, their judgment may not be useful because they might have the same or similar blind spots. In addition, we may trust the judgment of individuals based on an impression that they care for us. Beyond an exposure to uncontrolled traits or situational conditioning and the risk that our presumption of their care is false, their care might bias them to evaluate us incorrectly. Any relationship from which trust emerges carries a risk of false positive evaluations if an individual we trust wishes to build or preserve the relationship. Combining the two criteria in our attempts to exclude exposure to undue influence, abuse of information, or error may foreclose corrective insights because of their compatibility with our mindset.

Considering such risks of bias, we may seek the evaluation by individuals who stand removed from direct relationships with us and thus have a diminished or no interest in how we affect their pursuits. We may regard this as a big enough advantage to accept an increased shallowness of evaluations because of lacking contact and diminished interest by such individuals. We may trust that they want to advance human affairs for their proximate sake or in the interest of their need for collective survival and thriving. We may trust they act in the hope that they could be beneficiaries of unbiased evaluation efforts by us or others. We may believe that these motivations can make them bridge their distance and can sufficiently engage them to provide meaningful evaluations. Such assistance may suffer if we do not sufficiently know about individual differences. Still, large numbers of assessments may balance individual particularities and may thus approximate an accurate assessment. We may therefore prefer to rely on the evaluation by a larger group of individuals to minimize effects of idiosyncratic bias. We may believe that we can gain useful direction if we draw a median of opinions or focus on a large enough preponderance of opinions.

But such a participation may be difficult to mobilize and its occurrence would not create certainty who is right or wrong. Incapacity, error, and treachery can afflict large numbers of individuals. Additionally, individual particularities may differ quantitatively or qualitatively so much that it may be impossible to establish useful accord or middle ground. An amalgamation of observations and of assessments that are tainted by skewed mental conditions might fail to approximate a true portrait of perceptive, rational, or emotional traits. This renders it indispensable that we undertake comprehensive inquiries regarding the traits and positioning of individuals before we consider their opinions in any circumstances where these might impact their evaluation. This requirement makes finding adequate evaluations of our mental traits by others a complex undertaking. Arriving at reliable and sufficiently thorough results appears to require a breadth and a depth of involvement with other individuals that we might not be able to achieve or willing to build. We would have to divert considerable resources and might create closeness that would counteract necessary detachment. We therefore appear to be reverted to trials in which we test the effectiveness and efficiencies of our pursuits to make adjustments within the flexibilities and capacities of our mental traits. Such a restriction may be unworkable because we may not muster necessary motivation or skills. That may direct us toward considering evaluations by others even if we have indication that such evaluations may be tainted.

As imperfect as the detection or confirmation of perceptive and rational standards with the assistance of individuals who have different bearings might be, it often seems to be the most convenient tool to give us a comparative sense of reality. It also may give us orientation regarding the eccentricity of our emotional positions. Even if the views of us issued by others are contaminated by differences in their mental traits and situations, we may take their statements as indicators for further investigations into their and our positions. Evaluations by other individuals of subjects other than us may assist us to recognize and understand their and our mental traits and more superficial positions. Engaging with different positions seems preferable to a dialogue with persons whose judgment is affected by similar blind spots.

Even if we found little use in the exchange of insights to illuminate our mental positions and even if the views of others about us are incorrect, we might not be able to ignore them. We might have to be aware of and address how other individuals evaluate us because these views influence the demeanor of others toward us and our interests. Beyond that, we may more generally explore the attitudes of other individuals whose behavior matters to us. In a social context, individuals commonly engage in the examination of mental traits and opinions of others and compare them to theirs to anticipate the behavior of such individuals and plan appropriately. That purpose may be assisted if we open ourselves to them in an exchange of expressions that opens their views to us. Individuals may then engage in a disclosure process not only to explore and improve their own shortcomings. They might also try to gain information about and possibly affect the traits and resulting behavior of others or to adjust their own positioning toward them. These processes may be embedded in a larger process of information sharing and more tangible cooperation by which individuals strive to improve the pursuit of particular needs or to generate a general socialization that can serve as the basis for the pursuit of various needs. Besides trying to discern our mental traits to possibly improve them, we may look for similarly minded or complementary-minded individuals with whom we can successfully interact in the pursuit of our needs or who will not or not unduly interfere. That objective may have negative consequences for our mental growth. The constructive and defensive mechanisms of our mental traits may join in arrangements with each other to surround us with an environment in which doubts about the applicability of our pursuits can be suppressed or postponed because their application is optimized with the assistance of other individuals. Defensive apprehensions that may motivate us to seek evaluations and affirmations from individuals whose mentalities resemble or complement ours may commingle with our legitimate tendencies to look for harmonious coexistence, guidance from individuals with similar experiences and dispositions, and compatible cooperation partners.

Even if we can attain objective assessments of our mental traits from others, such disclosures might be ineffective. We might not realize differences even if they are pointed out or upon receiving instructive experiences because we might be confined by the capacities of our traits or solidified patterns within our capacities. If we gather an impression that features are different in us than in others and some notion as to how these might be different, this may not induce us to address mental deficiencies. Rather, we may blame dissatisfactory experiences on deficiencies in other humans or other aspects of our environment. Multiple incidents of inadequacies and examination may be necessary to make us comprehend that our mental profile deviates injuriously from a general profile. This realization may never arrive because our condition may appear legitimate by its ostensible normality. Idiosyncrasies of others may further render it difficult to distinguish a contour of normality. Also, we may not strive to commonize our personality. Idiosyncrasies may insist on their characteristics as valuable defining elements of our personality. If we notice differences, we may consider them tolerable, helpful, or necessary. Even if we could come to realizations concerning our deficiencies alone or with the assistance of others, we and they might not know how to remediate these.

We may thus not succeed or our success may be lessened without professional assistance. Such assistance might be encumbered by limitations, contortions, and fears similar to those burdening nonprofessional assistance. Education, experience, accreditation, and the policing of standards may minimize or exclude such issues. Still, all outside assistance might be hampered by its separateness from our mind. While its distanced perspective may be beneficial because it provides an opportunity for an objective view, it might exacerbate the general problems in qualifying, quantifying, and affecting mental features and interactions. Professional assistance might overcome these issues. We might also weigh concerns of economy if we are to pay for assistance. Regardless of valid concerns, the very deficiencies that should make us pursue external assistance may try to deter us from seeking or heeding such assistance. Our dispositions and experiences may cause us to incorrectly evaluate benefits, risks, or costs in rejection of external assistance. We might not be able to overcome these obstacles on our own.

They may cause us to reject constructive assistance even if it is initiated by others. The more skewed or limited our mind is, the less we may
be amenable to the possibility of such a condition, that we should adjust, or that we might require or otherwise benefit from external help.

Mental blind spots might not be curable with the processing of
information by conventional conduits. More fundamental adjustments
might be necessary. Such adjustments might be undertaken through
genetic or other physiological interventions. While the targeted remediation of perceptive, rational, and emotional blind spots might be regarded to be a matter of technical acuity, the motivations to engage in
such interventions have to issue from emotional traits. Unless we become subjected to the will of others, we have to develop such motivations ourselves. Notions that there are perceptive, rational, and emotional aspects that are different or beyond the present scope or focus
of our traits might incentivize us to search for them and render them
accessible to improve our happiness. That motivation may arise from
our observation of others who have undergone similar adjustments or
from other impressions that prompt us to consider a different state as
superior. But we may also deem it in our interest to adjust the minds
of other individuals, as they may deem it in their interest to adjust our
mind. There appears to be a legitimate dimension to such an undertaking if it assists contorted, suppressed, or disjointed sections of individuals' minds or other mental growth. It is particularly unobjectionable if individuals request assistance and remain in decisional control.
That this might assist needs of other individuals who suggest modifications does not detract from the legitimacy. It seems equally justifiable to adjust the minds of others defensively if they cannot be otherwise dissuaded from illegitimate infringements. But the modification
of other individuals' minds by compulsory intervention carries a great
risk of abuse, if not error. It therefore has to be strictly evaluated and
controlled and might have to be reserved to egregious circumstances.

To the extent external sources eschew direct intervention, they
will have to work with the emotional mind of individuals as the central authority concerning all their current objectives and pursuits and
potential developments and alterations that might improve their happiness. Such interactions might be challenging because the identification of traits that require correction and the development of our motivation to change them may draw resistance from emotional traits that
consider themselves endangered by such actions. Such traits may also
object if we try to affect our traits without outside assistance. The processes by which traits are chosen and committed to change require an
investigation of our council of traits as the forum in which our traits

interact. Its proceedings appear to involve more than negotiations or a vote. It may involve investigations and a commitment by traits to restrain or shape their own character or pursuits or those of other traits. To fare well in council proceedings, emotional traits may brace themselves with diverse strategic options. These may encompass the use or threat of compulsion. More ordinarily, they may seek to convince other traits of the merits of leaving them intact or of protecting and supporting them. They may back their positions by perceptive and rational presentations. To succeed to the greatest possible extent in the satisfaction of our needs overall, an accurate representation of the world, including of us and our traits, is in our interest. A functioning council of traits should therefore be able to bring such positions in line under the combined pressure of our emotional traits. But such work may be complex and uncertain because perceptive and rational traits may not be entirely shared by our emotional traits. They may be at least partly subdivided into attachments to single or allied emotional traits.

The chances of this to occur may seem to be low. At the beginning of our existence, our perceptive and rational facilities should apply to all our emotional traits because these have not been able to take any influence yet. On the contrary, it appears that our perceptive and rational traits would have significant influence in the construction of emotional traits at that juncture. The development of emotional traits builds in part on our genetic basis and direct physiological influences. It additionally depends on our mental assimilation of external circumstances. That assimilation depends on the circumstances we encounter and the processing of information concerning them by our perceptive and rational mind. Hence, an important part of emotional traits may be formed by perceptive and rational traits. If these are uniform at the time, that should have a levelling effect on the operation of our emotional traits. Because our emotional traits would assume the same perceptive and rational blind spots, the resolution of each such blind spot should be a singular undertaking effective for our entire mind.

Yet complications may arise from the genetic and acquired differentiations among emotional traits. Each emotional trait establishes subroutines centered on its objectives. These are in their core defined by genetic or acquired instincts that interpret perceptive and rational information, derive decisions, and issue instructive impulses. The automatic nature of instincts may not only entail set manners of how information is processed by them. It may also shape perceptive and rational adjuncts they regularly use in their operations. Such instinctive mechanisms should be interested in applying perceptive and rational traits that reflect the environment in which they must operate and not falsifying these. However, instinctive programming of emotional traits may not follow such an imputed interest. It may not be shaped to logically accomplish its objectives. Our emotional traits may not be well-founded or generally applicable reflections of the world. They may not be well-adjusted to their particular purposes or to the overarching dedications of our individual and collective survival and thriving. Common features of emotional traits and their arrangements with one another may give rise to deviations. Emotional traits may further be contorted by idiosyncratic genetic mutations or manipulations and in reaction to the selective presentation of facts. That selective presentation may be externally intended or coincidental, or may be due to the genetic or acquired common or idiosyncratic receptivity of emotional traits. It may also stem from the fact that distorted common and idiosyncratic perceptive and rational traits may affect emotional traits. Finally, the underdevelopment of mental traits may distort their operations. As a result, emotional traits may be shaped in ways that compel perceptive and rational facilities to comply with ineffective or inefficient movements. That may be in addition to ineffectiveness and inefficiencies already afflicting such facilities on their own account. Each emotional trait may impose or trigger its particularized disfunctions in our perceptive and rational traits. Once these are installed, they tend to reinforce in a composite of emotional traits and perceptive and rational adjuncts with combined, mutually compounding blind spots.

The effects of this interaction may not only occur in our mind. Because our perceptive and rational facilities form instruments to reflect the outside world, they are purveyors of influence from our environment on the acquired portions of our mental traits. But our emotional traits project these influences back onto our environment. The reflection of mental traits in our activities creates aspects in our environment that can influence our mental traits. The shaping of our environment according to our mental traits provides a setting whereby our mental traits and our surroundings become aligned with each other. Yet, ultimately, our mental traits have to comply with the allocations, substances, and laws of nature presented in our environment and us. This should prompt our emotional and other mental traits to adjust to empiric circumstances. Our environment has also sourced our shared and our specific genetic and acquired traits or sanctioned and shaped them through their compulsion of having to exist in it. These formative impositions join more direct physical strictures and influences to form a rigid framework. Still, within the zone of activity that our environment tolerates and in accordance with the mental patterns shaped by it, emotional traits conduct our response to environmental circumstances. Their alterations to our environment may generate apparent confirmations that perceptive and rational positions they advocate are correct because these find some reflection in the outside world. Emotional traits may thus splinter our existence into partly different realities that appear to abide by their own perceptions and rationalities in some respects and leave our quest for happiness disjointed.

Emotional traits may be reflections of our world, and these reflections may be significantly influenced by our perceptive and rational traits. Nevertheless, emotional traits reign supreme among mental traits because they motivate all our undertakings, including their own, alone or through our council of traits. Our perceptive and our rational traits appear to be largely intermediaries in the forming mutuality between emotional traits and the world outside our mind. The overbearing nature of our emotional traits creates problems for the independence of our perceptive and rational traits. They may establish spheres of command and influence over perceptive and rational traits as they deem necessary to pursue their objectives and to preserve their integrity. Their influence may not necessarily install itself to a level of permanently shaping perceptive or rational traits. They may merely guide their application or suppress them. They may not only apply such tactics in their immediate domain but may endeavor to impose their perceptive and rational treatments on emotional traits whose deportment matters to them. They might even invent these for the particular purpose of misleading other traits. Emotional traits may interfere with already existing perceptive and rational capacities or their development. They may wield influence if such capacities are built or maintained by the acquisition and processing of information or by posing physiological conditions. They choose whether and to which effect we interfere with our perceptive and rational traits through direct genetic technology. They may regulate whether and which of our genetic perceptive and rational traits survive by directing our procreation, and they control whether and to what extent we impose acquired traits on others.

Our perceptive and rational traits might be dominated by emotional traits in ways that only allow glimpses of their deficiencies. We may become aware of undue influence exerted by our emotional traits if we catch ourselves resisting scientific or less formal empiric proof. But that resistance may be concealed and rationalized. We may escape acknowledging such resistance by calling indications or proof in question under purportedly valid reservations or interpretations. Our pursuits may habitually encounter sufficient interferences and imperfections to blame most of their deficiencies on extraneous factors and to spare ourselves internal examinations. Moreover, our emotional traits may produce interferences or give instructions to focus on them. They may also avoid the exploration, presentation, and correlation of facts. Many pursuits may grant us the opportunity of avoiding justification because they constitute relatively unordered amalgamations of objects and events that are not easily accessible to empiric insight. Even if we should have to justify perverted perceptive or rational processes, emotional traits may train perceptive and rational traits to act in conformance with their direction by limiting their purview or biasing their review proceedings. Where scientific proceedings would be possible, we may renounce them in favor of less accurate methods that grant room to empiric evasions or irregularities. Under the influence of emotional traits, we may further more openly abandon pretenses of empiric rationalization. We may posit emotional arguments to override the cogency of factual insights. We may assert that our needs or their reconciliations require manners of pursuit consistent with ideals or compromises in deviation from technical proficiency. While that might be a valid interjection, we might use it without full consideration whether a deviation is warranted. We may proclaim it and conduct ourselves according to it because our impulses are inadequately reconciled.

Notwithstanding the possibility that our emotional traits might use their power to impose on our perceptive or rational traits, they also contain the incentive to escape contortions and restrictions in such traits because these are likely to be reflected in painful experiences of failure. Such experiences may incentivize us to recognize and conquer or at least manage the existence of perceptive or rational inadequacies regardless of whether they originated in these traits or are imposed by emotional traits. Finding the necessary motivation appears to be relatively easy if we do not have the interests of particular emotional traits attached to the maintenance of these inadequacies. However, such attachments may be common because of emotional contortions and restrictions. In either case, an uncritical attitude may not only be a consequence of unawareness or misinformation due to emotional, perceptive, or rational inadequacies. We might be inclined to negate mental inadequacies of any kind because it may be painful for us to concede a permanent or even only a temporary personal impossibility or that we committed an avoidable failure of adequately processing information within our capacities. We may much rather seek fault in external circumstances or even accept shortcomings in our physical capacities or possessions. Moreover, if we require assistance to comprehend or address our limitations, needs that are attached to personal achievement might object. Other needs might fear undue influence or our subordination. Even if we would not rely on others, needs whose impressions of achievement would be weakened might object. On the other hand, our failure to acknowledge our mental disfunctions and shortfalls may result in additional, potentially repeated pain because we did not adjust our pursuits according to applicable insights. The incompatibility with reality of the results of our actions and the mental constructs on which our actions are based may be an effective corrective. Unsuccessful endeavors may have us question perceptive or rational traits even before we question emotional traits. Our fear of acknowledging inadequacies may be resolved if we recognize that we can overcome them or that addressing their unremitting presence can moderate their detrimental impact. The resolution of such functional deficiencies should be motivated by negatively affected needs. Needs that instill fear in us concerning the mode or consequences of gaining awareness and overcoming inadequacies might be addressed by providing sufficient participation and governance of the process by us. The resistance of traits might not be so firmly entrenched that it could not be overcome, even to the satisfaction of resisting traits, with the intervention of a considered argument. But we may harbor emotional traits whose interests in maintaining inadequacies might be more difficult to counter.

Such traits may engage in deceptive schemes that we may understand as a derivative of our wishes in whose nature it is to long for something that is not. To fulfill a wish, we normally operate based on facts upon having attained knowledge of them. The deception consists of contriving false impressions of facts or in providing incomplete impressions by withholding correct impressions of facts. It may be perpetrated by emotional traits in persuasion of themselves or other emotional traits of incorrect past, present, or future circumstances in a bid to manipulate reactions for a purportedly constructive purpose. It may also arise in protective mechanisms that are overwhelmed by practical demands of reality. To find some release from the pain of deprivation, emotional traits may pretend that they have already achieved their objectives, have the means, or are on their way to achieve them. If they cannot deny failure, they may pretend that, barring interference, they did have, could have had, or would now possess the means or success they desire. Arguably, emotional traits should never succeed in entirely deceiving themselves because they would have cognizance of their deceptive actions, particularly with the help of reflection through other mental traits. But their paths of processing may not allow such a reflection or may not allow it to be accurately considered by them. Even if they could reach some awareness of their deceptive practices, they might be able to override such an awareness at least to some extent by understanding their emotional reactions to certain factual stimuli and by generating such stimuli to outweigh contradictory concerns. Emotional traits may apply similar schemes to direct other emotional traits in support or protection of their interests or to foil their interference.

While self-deception can be a temporarily effective, superficial remedy, it keeps us from surmounting existent deficiencies and from avoiding possible deficiencies because it does not address actual causes and might issue motivations that lead us further astray. It may also motivate us to invest considerable resources into the evasion, suppression, or discreditation of awareness aspects that might correct our illusions. Our self-deception may extend to unwitting attempts to mislead others, and our conviction may add credibility to these. It may allow us to overcome scruples about overriding other individuals' needs and wishes by deception or other, more compelling methods. But we may also exert deception of others with clarity about the disingenuity of our positions. We may have traits that demand or permit deception of other individuals as means for our pursuits. These traits may dominate other traits that oppose such tactics. If we assume that the deception of other individuals is a sign of disfunction among our own emotional traits, we seem to employ a composite of self-deception and external deception. Our self-deception may be instigated, enhanced, and directed by external deception that ascends from the self-deception of others or their intentional deception of us. Interaction of internal and interactive deception may build among individuals in a linear or circular fashion to produce pervasive and profound illusions. If emotional traits predictably react to information, and such or other traits or other individuals benefit from that response, deceit might not be necessary. A manipulation to steer our emotions into certain directions may succeed by supplying accurate facts that trigger the desired reaction.

If our emotional traits are not entirely reconciled and have not explored our perceptive and rational traits to identify and to neutralize their bias and other defects, they may be prone to drive or permit the short-circuiting of our mental functions. This short-circuiting and its maintenance under the leadership of emotional traits may not only lead to far-reaching consequences for our ability to pursue our needs within ourselves but also in correlation with others. Due to the individualization of mental traits, each individual may entertain a particular perception and understanding of circumstances that is dominated by the individual's needs. Additional difficulties may be infused by differences in the fulfillment situations of needs among individuals. Reconciling differences among individuals is difficult under conditions of emotional involvement because objective, rational evidence must contend with subjective, irrational attitudes. These may prevent individu-

CHAPTER 19: THE STRUGGLE FOR OBJECTIVITY   353

als from coordinating their pursuits according to the same criteria unless their emotional traits happen to coincide. This may hamper constructive cooperation in pursuits and arrangements to lessen and minimize interferences. While similar challenges might exist based on different perceptive and rational traits and experiences alone, emotional
influences threaten to harden mindsets and to deprive humans of fundamental common references in the management of their relations.

    Although our perceptive and rational traits are tools in the ser-
vice of our emotional traits, they can fulfill their functions only if they
remain independent and grounded on reality. To pursue our needs effectively and efficiently, we must be able to connect to the factualities
of us and our environment so that we can unfold our capacities, maximize the utility of our and of our environment's resources, and prevent damage. Our perceptive and rational traits constitute the instruments by which we detect and process impressions about our world. If
we replace or taint their reflections of what is by what we would like it
to be, we preclude their proper functioning in assisting our emotional
traits. By changing perceptive or rational information or limiting what
we sense or think, we delude ourselves and we disable our mind from
competently organizing itself and interacting with our surroundings.
We disable a proper definition of our wishes and hence the fulfillment
of our needs. Further, our bias deprives our council of traits of a competent shared basis for reconciliation. It may foreclose our emotional
traits from evolving to solutions that maximize our overall happiness.
The utility of our perceptive and rational traits might already be challenged by genetic deficiencies, low states of development, and physiological damage. It may also be challenged by insufficient, false, or improperly correlated and thus misleading information in the building of
perceptive and rational traits and of less entrenched operational idiosyncrasies. Our emotional traits fulfill an important function in overcoming such challenges. They may be instrumental in protecting the
soundness of our perceptive and rational facilities and in supporting
them to apply their capacity to the highest degree and to extend their
reach so that our mind can match circumstances of our world. Hence,
our emotional mind may be a corruptor, beneficiary, and savior of our
perceptive and rational traits and through them of itself and of all the
objectives for whose pursuit it is responsible. Its connectedness with
perceptive and rational traits can make it difficult to clearly identify it.
Although we can recognize emotional traits by impulses, they necessarily take reference to our perceptions and thoughts in formulating
wishes and means. Moreover, we might not possess reflective or even
a direct awareness of our impulses, fully represented facts, or entirely

researched perceptive and rational traits. Absent detailed inquiries, we may be unable to decide whether, which, or to what degree emotional traits affect our treatment of facts. We can subject perceptive and rational assertions to empiric and logical proof. According to their functions, they must conform to observable conditions and an explanation in substances and principles of nature. Emotional traits may impede such proceedings or these may be unavailable. Still, our repeated failure in similar tasks without convincing other causes suggests that we suffer from inadequate mental traits and may cause us to inquire.

Only the testing of such problems under conditions that might attenuate or disconnect a possible influence by emotional traits might permit us to attribute our deficiencies among the three types of mental traits. Our detection of the involvement of emotional traits is predicated upon their autonomous acquiescence or the compulsion or revelation by other emotional traits. It also depends on our capabilities to establish constellations of circumstances in which perceptive and rational traits can be observed in manners that are unrestricted by emotional influences. If we could comprehend our perceptive and rational traits in this manner, we might identify and move to a remediation of their shortcomings. But the resolution to engage in scientific or in less formal empiric procedures to reveal our perceptive and rational traits free from emotional bias and to engage in remedial action has to arise from our emotional traits. Frequently, the only way we might proceed to such an unbiased resolution is through a mutual counterbalancing of bias by emotional traits in our council of traits. Pursuant to its mission to maximize the overall contentment of our needs, the assembly of our emotional traits may battle influences on perceptive or rational traits as well as more immediate impulses that detract from that mission. The proper functioning of our council of traits may not only rely on emotional cognition but also necessitate assistance from adequately advanced perceptive and rational faculties. Similar to how emotional traits might without council proceedings be inadequate in their definition and presence, perceptive and rational traits might be revealed, adjusted, or developed as our council of traits advances in its proceedings. Where emotional impositions on perceptive or rational traits exist, other emotional traits may requisition perceptive and rational facilities to build counterpositions. Disparate motivations and resulting positions among emotional traits have them engage in arguments that we notice as contests among different interpretations that assert factual and logical fidelity. Our council of traits may then be essential not only for the reconciliation of our emotional traits but also for reconciling perceptive and rational traits to reflect the factual circumstances of our pursuits. Its reconciliation of needs may collaterally neutralize holds by emotional traits on perceptive or rational functions. Through its comparison of factual assessments and investigation if they are incompatible, our council of traits may succeed in deriving one unified perceptive and rational stance. This may permit us to identify and to address remaining functional perceptive and rational shortcomings.

Objectivity then seems to be a condition for and result of emotional reconciliation. The superseding of distorting impositions from internal and external emotional traits appears to be a critical condition to unlock the potential of perceptive and rational traits in support of our emotional traits. It appears essential in achieving the potential of our emotional traits. We must ascertain the genuine character of information, consider its consequences, and uncover possible internal and external agendas to direct our perceptions, thoughts, or emotions. We must reserve emotional attachment until the completion of factual investigations. Even then, we must continue to reconsider our judgment when new facts rise to our attention or we become apprised that our previous considerations might have been incomplete or incorrect. Passively awaiting information may be insufficient. To reach an accurate and complete understanding of the world and of our activities in it, we must seek new perceptions and thoughts and expose our mind to the possibility that perceptions and thoughts, as well as resulting or independently arising emotions, might be invalidated in parts or their entirety. As a condition for accomplishing all this, and for the sake of the ulterior objective of advancing our happiness, we have to reconcile our emotional attitudes so that they apply our perceptive and rational traits in ways that maximize the overall fulfillment of our needs. The mutual appraisal and acknowledgment of integrated and ultimate purposes by constructive traits focuses us on a common interpretation of reality, if not within traits by their reconciled views. This joint reflection of facts in our mind may be as close to reality as we can come.

We may find it difficult to believe that we should be able to develop our council of traits to a level where it can arrange our traits in their relationship and if necessary in their character. This may indeed be impossible. Our mind may be underdeveloped or may be deformed in ways that foreclose its internal mechanisms from functioning with sufficient competence and flexibility to attain a reconciliation of our needs or an accurate reflection of reality. Such conditions may be partial but severe enough to forestall a well-rounded reconciliation of our mind. We all, most, or many of us might be suffering from such irreversible conditions. We might have to live with mental flaws that do not permit us to become whole. To the extent impediments to reconciliation might be resolvable, the comprehensive scope of review and possible intervention may exacerbate the problems that afflict topical endeavors to ascertain and correct mental inadequacies. The ambition of the undertaking may exceed our capabilities. Our mind may not be sufficiently skillful to comprehend, or resolute to acknowledge, its inadequacies or to achieve comprehensive remediation. Our efforts may compound inadequacies and unite traits that fear for their integrity in opposition. Our efforts may be successfully constrained by mental aspects we would have to mend to attain higher levels of happiness.

Individuals who do not suffer these limitations may assist us to ascertain obstacles to our reconciliation, address issues that can be resolved, or acknowledge and cope with problems that cannot be cured. Comparing our mindset, capabilities, pursuits, and results with theirs may provide us with helpful or required insights. They might also become more actively involved in ascertaining problems in our mind, assessing their consequences, adjusting or constraining damaging traits, promoting underdeveloped traits, and reconciling our traits. For best results, assistance in reconciliation of our mental traits might have to address them as an integrated mechanism. This implies a complexity and intensity of engagement that may exceed the willingness and capability of other individuals. It might also exceed our willingness to allow others insight to assess and to possibly reform any part of our personality. Even if others are trustworthy and willing to assist, they may lack skills or capacities of individuals with professional qualifications. The comprehensive ambition of reconciliation may make professional assistance even more necessary or helpful. Yet our opposition to this assistance may surge because the entirety of inadequate traits is challenged by the possibility of being suppressed, altered, or eradicated.

Such a determined resistance may necessitate the imposition of compulsory assistance. Warranted and unwarranted resistance at lower levels might be solved by the socialization of individuals in a manner that allows them to sample, understand, and trust others, encourages the exchange of mental reflections, and creates mental and practical ties that allow and motivate the detection and addressing of unreconciled mental states. Societal assistance for individual reconciliation is likely to interpose with reconciliation activities among individuals to advance their happiness through peaceful coexistence and constructive cooperation. If this becomes the primary objective, socialization increases the risk that individuals might be pressured into alignment against their advantage. Even if a society should not exert such a pressure willfully, personality traits that do not benefit the community might be adjusted or suppressed under the pressure of having to exist within the community. Arguably, such an alignment might be a desirable outcome and should independently be in the interest of individual members. Yet to be conducive to individual happiness and achieve sufficient stability, it would have to happen voluntarily unless procedures can be applied that supplant personality traits. A society seeking interpersonal reconciliation therefore must solve the potential contradiction of making room for individual reconciliation while also imposing constrictions that do not tolerate violations of principles indicated by such reconciliation. It has to decide how far it will go to align individuals for societal advantages, or even out of a sense of responsibility based on needs relating to others or mutuality. Alignment only seems legitimate to affirm or defend rights of individuals in question or others. If possible, alignment has to exceed coercion to promote reconciliatory capacity as a condition for functioning individuals and societies.

Beyond required or helpful assistance, and possibly in conjunction with it, there may be settings in which humans can sort and improve their own mind. Self-regulating mechanisms might succeed unless they are pathologically impaired. Emotional traits engage in council proceedings by their nature once we actuate them by making them conscious. Their drive to succeed impels traits to evaluate the relative merits and disadvantages of one another. They are prone to continually point out weaknesses and errors in one another's perceptive, rational, and emotional aspects and encourage aspects they deem constructive. The insight that we can improve our happiness if we permit our emotional traits to come forth and interact with one another in such a critical fashion focuses our efforts on identifying our emotional traits.

It may be possible to discover particularized or underdeveloped emotional traits if they noticeably distort the common acuity of other traits. But our emotional traits may not lie on the surface of our mind. Absent direct access to them as physiological phenomena, we can only detect them by their expressions. We must observe, if necessary draw out, their indications. Because they might defend against their discovery, we must limit our investigations initially to collecting mental impressions in an immediate and unconsidered state without attempting to categorize or otherwise evaluate. We must unqualifiedly gather and record perceptions, thoughts, and emotions without judging their relevance or authenticity and considering whether or to what extent they are expressions of emotional traits. We leave it to a second, diagnostic stage to organize, assemble, and interpret what we find to identify our emotional traits. A third phase is reserved for the examination of their interactions. The next chapter addresses how we can comprehensively collect information that may allow us to distill our emotional traits.

CHAPTER 20
GATHERING PERSONAL INFORMATION

To elicit expressions of our emotions, we might pose questions to ourselves that pertain quite openly to our needs and our happiness as our highest good. We might ask: How do I feel about my existence? Am I happy? Have I ever been happy and do I think I will be happy? What makes me happy? What makes me sad? What bores me, excites me, makes me angry or peaceful? What do I like or dislike? What matters to me and what does not? How beneficial or damaging to my happiness do I rate objects or events and how do I rate them relative to one another? We might focus these open-ended inquiries on past or present object and events, or on our imagined future. We might also ask more pointed questions about our conditions and how we feel about them. Why and how did I select my profession, friends, love interests, where I live, or any other aspects of my life? What are my fondest and least favorite memories? What do I perceive, think, and feel regarding persons I know, certain types or groups of people, or humans in general? What do I like best about myself? Is there anything I do not like about me? Do I have enough time for me? Am I alone? Is there something missing? Do I harbor regrets? Of what am I most proud? What would I like to change? Do I have any hopes and fears? What are my ambitions? Is there anything keeping me from pursuing them? What does my ideal existence look like? Where would I be? Who would be with me? How would I live? What would I be doing? What would I do or be if I could do or be anything? What new experiences, what additional abilities would I like to have? If I had to be an item of a certain kind, what would I be or want to be? What do I expect to happen after my death? What do I imagine heaven and hell to be like? If there is a heaven or a hell, where do I expect to be? These are some of the questions that might lead to indications about our essence. Although they are existential questions, we may not have a ready answer to many of them. We may have to search our mind and deliberate extensively before we can give an answer we deem accurate. Yet even with contemplation, we may have difficulties finding satisfying responses. That can lead to essential self-awareness as well. But the demands of such questions may exceed our investigative or evaluative capability at this time. In addition, questions of this type may trigger defensive mechanisms. Hence, they might not cause the enlightenment we might expect.

Eventually, we may have to ask these or similar questions to assume control of our existence and fulfill its potential. As we advance to cover the entire expanse of our personality, it may be unavoidable that we encounter the defensive barriers of traits, no matter how carefully we might pace and modulate our exploration. These may be positioned at different points and may be of various severity for each of us. But we must strive to defer encountering them until we have obtained better knowledge of our personality and are better equipped to overcome their defenses. We must have collected sufficient information at that point to prevent emotional traits from credibly denying their existence or from falsifying their nature. Once we understand the existence, constituents, and outline of emotional traits, it is harder to block or mislead our access. At that juncture, other emotional traits may be able to motivate us to deepen our knowledge so they can better deal with traits as actual or potential competitors. This motivation may be sufficient to defeat opposition by obstinate traits. Their resistance at that point may draw our interest and help to illuminate them.

To avoid provoking defensive action by our traits, we might try to avoid directly addressing objects and events that could have formed our traits or might pertain to them. We might inquire about our perceptions, rational thoughts, emotions, and behavior regarding matters that are unrelated to our life. We could ask what we would think, feel, or do if we were inserted into the plot of a movie, play, story, or book, the conditions of other individuals, or imagined situations. We might inquire about our views on purportedly superficial matters that do not seem to pertain directly to the essence of our traits. We could inquire about favorite and least favorable music, movies, shows, games, books, events, seasons, or characters in actual or imaginary contexts. The impressions garnered from such inquiries may give us important insights into aspects that occupy and define our emotional mind. The superficial information we receive may point us to common and idiosyncratic structures and processes and illuminate them. However, it might not clearly delineate underlying components to supply us an unobstructed picture of our emotional traits. Moreover, the amount and quality of information we can derive this way may remain limited. Based on our understanding that we undertake inquiries to discover our emotional traits, these are in danger of being channeled in ways that allow suspicious traits to conceal their nature. No artful indirect inquiry may be able to outwit them to an extent that allows the gathering of sufficient information without encountering their defenses. In an effort to outmaneuver these defenses, we may have to stray so far away from relevant inquiries that our answers become trite and do not lead to any revealing information. By contorting inquiries to avoid defense mechanisms, we may play into their hands and wind up with information that fails to reveal traits that opt to conceal themselves. The resistance by such traits to inquiries that we detect as unease and the unproblematic revelation of other areas may alert us to areas where additional scrutiny might be warranted. But defensive traits that hide in such areas are alerted as well. They may have such influence over our mind that they might succeed in averting our resolve to examine such areas more closely or to perceive correctly and process rationally what we find. They might even be able to curtail self-critical inquiries altogether to prevent us from isolating the problem areas governed by them.

Obtaining useful information may therefore at least initially require a different approach that avoids prompting our mind for reactions. Instead, we may begin by giving detailed attention to the natural occurrences in our mind. This strategy takes account of the components and processes that we have normally at our disposal, our remembered, current, and anticipated experiences and the thoughts and emotional responses we attach to them. We monitor and register our perceptions, contemplations, and impulses and possibly proceedings by our council of traits. Our mind may volunteer a significant amount of important information if we listen. Beyond background and collateral releases from traits, we may receive targeted offers of information because our stance signals preparedness of our council of traits to take account of and harmonize our traits. Traits that deem themselves disadvantaged may take this opportunity to plead their cause. They may call out other traits that rather would remain concealed and go about their pursuits undisturbed. Confronted by opposition, such traits and openly dominating traits may feel pressed to counter. They may assert their position to preclude the accommodation of claimant traits or to channel our treatment of such traits. The ensuing debate may lead to an unrestrained exchange of arguments among interested traits during which concealing maneuvers might be futile. We may thus be able to collect all necessary ingredients for a proper determination by our council of traits. Only, at this point, we allow our traits to come forth and to argue without making up our mind. We assume the position of observers, taking full account of all our traits and all their arguments.

Recording as much detail as we can is required at this juncture. The language or the presentation of our traits may not be succinct or coherent. We may not readily recognize what we detect or its source. We may have to capture features that are individually innocuous but may permit us a deeper understanding of our traits upon their subsequent assembly. We may be able to use these basic components to obtain a descriptive depiction of our emotional mind similar to how we would approach the assembly of a jigsaw puzzle. The only fundamental conceptual difference would be that we do not have the benefit of a

sample image beyond general notions of common traits to orient ourselves. As in a puzzle, it is essential that we collect all the pieces and
set them forth in front of us so we can assemble them. Single pieces
might portray traits in their entirety. Then again, pieces might describe traits together with others. Each sensory, rational, or emotional
experience is likely to be connected with other pieces. Together, these
pieces form clusters that, in turn, are connected to other clusters, and
so on until they give a picture of our emotional traits. We now have to
find and collect the pieces that represent them and place them into
view so we can determine how they compose our emotional mind.

We may be able to collect pieces and clusters of our mind simply by monitoring and capturing them as they traverse our mind. However, we may also prompt them by techniques that evoke impressions.
Under circumvention of pointed questions that might provoke our defense mechanisms, we may engage our memories. We may explore our
emotional traits by sampling the historical range of our experiences.
We might travel back through our memory and register perceptions,
thoughts, and emotions that come to mind. We might ask how we felt
about perceptive and rational information, how we perceived rational
and emotional information, and how we thought about perceptive and
emotional phenomena. Our answers to such inquiries come naturally
because perceptive, rational, and emotional events are closely linked.
An inquiry regarding one aspect unavoidably raises the other aspects.

Our recollection may be assisted by present impressions of objects and events that took part in forming our impressions in the past
or that are similar to those objects or events. By engendering a partial
similarity of our present impressions, we may be able to stimulate our
memory. Based on the recollection of some aspects, we may remember additional aspects. To facilitate this associative discovery, we may
revisit objects, events, and persons associated with our memories. We
may see persons who had a positive or negative influence on our life.
We may reencounter individuals who cared for, neglected, loved, hat-
ed, rejected, accepted, constrained, freed, hurt, or healed us. We may
visit persons whom we admired, from whom we learned, to whom we
felt a bond, to whom we felt enmity, ridicule, pity, envy, shame, un-
easiness, or fear, or even people whom we regarded as irrelevant. We
may also reconnect with people who were in the reverse positions of
such types of relationships with us. We may see people with whom we
shared good or bad times or who in other ways might have the same
or similar memories. We may return to where we made our memories,
the open areas, neighborhoods, houses, and rooms where we used to
live. We may go again to our schools and workplaces, the stores, and

leisure locations we frequented. We may re-experience or remember our toys, treasured possessions, clothes, foods, smells, music, habits, peculiarities, and events of the time. We may review documentary and emulated recordings of any kind that can bring us closer to objects or events of our past. We may recall and reconstruct objects or reenact events that impressed us or that coincided with experiences. We may let repeating events, seasons, and other similarities in auditory, visual, or other sensory experiences carry our mind back to us then.

Many facets of former stages in our existence may strike us as childish. We may have left many of the subjects we encounter behind for good reasons. We may wonder how some of them could have held so much power over us. Notwithstanding our changed attitudes, many of our former impressions remain alive and continue to influence us by their reflection in structures and processes of our mind they helped to form. We are likely to have developed since our youth or later periods. But the person who came into being during that time continues to be a large part of us. Some experiences of earlier periods may gain relevance in our awareness only now that we can look back with some distance and appreciate the consequences. The changed perspective may give us an opportunity to understand forming influences that had previously evaded us. Going back in our mind also gives us an opportunity to put our current condition in perspective and compare it. The more rudimentary and developing versions of us that we meet while we recall our past may appear more authentic than who we are now. They were closer to our genetic origins before they were modified and overlaid by acquired influences. Connecting back will evoke essential questions. How much have we remained the same? Why did or did we not change? Do we like who we were or have become? Are we glad or do we regret having or not having left certain aspects of us behind?

Such considerations and questions may help us to assemble the necessary background and the motivation to adjust our traits once we have connected the underlying information to comprehend them. By focusing on our past, we are likely to regain access to areas of our personality that have been overshadowed, marginalized, and covered by various causes over the years. Compared to our later existence, earlier stages appear full of possibilities. They represent a time before we and others made decisions that formed much of our present. They may have been less affected by pressure, commitment, or the consequences of our decisions. They represent a time in our life when we did not yet suffer from extended periods of frustrations by our inabilities, lack of assistance, interferences, or general events that pulled us along. Some of that potential may have been channeled, cut off, repressed, abraded, lost, or dissolved as an illusion since. Remembering our beginnings may give us a chance to reconnect to them and to decide whether we can or should continue something we left behind. We might wish to regain or advance on former circumstances, talents, ambitions, or passions, or we might determine that the curtailment of earlier traits or tendencies was warranted. Such insights make remembering the way we were potentially valuable for our self-realization and growth. That these traits, components of traits, or possibilities of traits lapsed our mind may mean that we purposely reoriented ourselves. It may also mean that alternative traits developed in us or were inflicted upon us without our control and have held these aspects in abeyance. Either way, the intent and processes by which stronger traits repressed these hidden traits, components, and potentials may continue. By reanimating hidden aspects through recollection, we may reactivate competitive mechanisms and dynamics that led to their suppression or abandonment. Searching in our past and remembering how we used to be may thus threaten to throw us into the midst of a struggle that we are striving to reserve to the interpretive phase of our exploration. Resisting such involvement now will be rewarded by a fuller panoply of information that will facilitate our interpretation. We may record the perceptive, rational, and emotional impact of our discoveries as part of the information we collect. Yet, in the interest of gaining a full array of information without the infringement of prejudgments, this is not the time to dwell on them or to scrutinize their causes and effects.

In addition to the impressions we can collect from our present and our past consciousness, we may extend our inquiry into the unconscious regions of our mind. We may believe that we can access this side by recording, collecting, and eventually interpreting our dreams. What occurs in our mind during our dreams has a markedly different quality compared to our mind's activity during our waking hours. Our consciousness takes on a different quality. Some of our dreams appear to be largely continuations or repetitions of situations and events we experienced when we were awake. Then again, our dreams frequently do not reflect that reality. Although much of what we dream draws on familiar places, persons, and events, all of our dreams confront us with various degrees of unfamiliarity, with divergences from waking reality in which apparently new content is intertwined with familiar aspects. That new content may be familiar by type, or it may constitute a fantastical concoction of familiar elements. The resulting story may present us with realities ranging from close similarities to what we have experienced or could experience in our waking reality to twisted and mysterious worlds that are incompatible with more of possibilities of a waking reality. Either way, these mental occurrences are enigmatic to us. We do not perceive ourselves as their author. When we dream, we seem to be immersed in a strange, fully appointed surrounding reality. Still, none of the elements we observe are so bizarre that we could not have imagined them. Our dreams appear to be a product of our mind. Except for sensory impressions we might obtain during our sleep, all constituents must have already existed in our mind before they were fabricated into a dream. Our dreams are apparently rearranging these constituents in stories to which we can relate. Nevertheless, we struggle determining their purpose in consideration of what they contain.

This mystery about the purpose of our dreams prompts us to speculate. Are they based on random nerve discharges that our mind perceives as sensory signals and of which it tries to make sense? Is our mind trying to fit experiences during our waking hours? Is it ordering, connecting, or building some of its structures and processes? Is it repairing damage? Is it preparing for future tasks that are indicated by experiences? Are dreams exercises to keep unused parts of our brain from deteriorating? Possible as any or all of this may be, it does not seem to explain fully what we experience. Our dreams appear too coherent to be accidents and too elaborate and odd to be utilities. They also appear too varied to be part of a continuing program. Our mind incurs the effort of positioning us into intricate, elaborate productions with lifelike detail. We can have happy and unhappy dreams ranging over the entire spectrum of our needs. Either way, what takes place in our dreams keeps our sleeping mind captivated and highly functioning. We are experiencing our dreams from our viewpoint and with a continued sense of our identity. We sense, think, and feel largely in familiar ways or within the range of our potential. Some of what we dream may be of a perceptive and rational nature. We may engage in complex external observations and contemplations. Yet many of our dreams feature prevalent emotional concerns and related perceptions. While external factual aspects might appear nonsensical in our waking appraisal of dreams, dreamed emotions and related perceptions appear to be authentic throughout at least in their potential. Any emotional traits and related perceptions that we experience in our waking mind may also be active in our dreams. The intense preoccupation of our self in the plot of our dreams with all our mental facilities gives us the notion that our mind is busily working on something important. The complex, inscrutable character of our dreams may prompt us to believe in the existence of a mostly hidden, powerful layer of our mind that we may designate our unconscious. It strikes us as absurd that we should have awareness of its existence and should be able to refer to sporadic recollected samples of its activities or at least their expressions but that we should be unable to understand the work to which this sphere of our own mind is committed. Our lack of comprehension leaves us with the impression that we are missing significant knowledge about us. We may regard the inaccessibility of an evidently highly functioning part of our mind as a challenge that we must resolve.

Our motivation to delve deeper into the unconscious regions of our mind further gains from the appearance that our unconscious is the repository for our mental traits. Many of the steering functions by our mind regarding our body entirely bypass our perceptive, rational, or emotional awareness. These vegetative functions constitute a type of mental trait on their own. But the other generation processes of our mind do not seem to be any less automatic. Our conscious mind appears to be a separate, exterior entity that takes notice of some production results without being involved in the production. It may have an impression of control because it has awareness of perceptive, rational, and emotional results. While some of these may arise obviously without our will, many occur because emotional traits act and direct our perceptive and rational facilities. Only, the motivations for these actions and directions are not directly accessible to our consciousness. Any process by which our emotional traits come into their own, contend, and reconcile through our council of traits is a function of these motivations. We witness aspects of these phenomena and take ownership of them because they occur in our mind. But our awareness as an entity in conscious command of itself seems to be an illusion. Eventually, we may comprehend the formation and functions of our mental traits through science. Yet, even then, our connection to them would remain immediately unconscious and only accessible to our awareness by measuring their structures and tracing their processes. Our awareness would remain indirect and our determinations to interfere with our unconscious settings would still be driven by our unconscious.

We may not object to such a detachment and illusion of command as we long as we can afford our traits with the necessary knowledge so they can control one another and the rest of our mental traits in a fully considered manner. In the absence of scientific insights concerning our unconscious, or as a way to guide a more detailed scientific inquiry, we may speculate that we can shed light on our mental traits by investigating into the mechanics and purposes of our dreams. Understanding the functions of our dreams may be essential for gaining full comprehension of our traits. Dreams may fulfill an important function in their construction, preservation, and activities. Hence, we may deem an inquiry into our dreams to be a worthwhile undertaking in our self-discovery. Yet, strangely, a short time after we awake, we forget most if not all of what just strenuously preoccupied us in our sleep. This may be easily and satisfactorily explained if we have no interest in our dreams because their twisted or alternate reality does not appear able to carry solutions for our problems. Further, their content may be disturbing. It may bring to light or renew fear and pain from which we may want to distance ourselves. We might therefore want to forget such dreams. But dreams in which we experience pleasure fade just as quickly as our unpleasant dreams. Our inability to keep dreams present does not appear to depend on motivations and efforts of our conscious mind. It seems to be a function inherent in their nature or the nature of our unconscious. Then again, our conscious mind has lingering awareness of our dreams immediately after we awake from a dream. We may speculate that its failure to keep that awareness of our dreams results from the failure of such awareness to hold value for our conscious mind. One might take the position that, if such value existed, our mind would be more interested and would have developed in ways that absorb dreams into our recollection. That our mind has not developed this way appears to support the notion that the function of our dreams is adequately or better satisfied without the participation of our conscious mind or that they have no function. Making dreams conscious without interpretive distance might produce adverse effects because we might not be able to distinguish their content from waking reality. These are not necessarily considerations in which we engage. We might take our fleeting awareness as a sign that humanity is at the edge of being able to make dreams conscious and expanding its awareness. Still, currently, the phenomenon seems to prove that high opinions about the capabilities of consciousness are unwarranted.

There seems to be reason to question the representation of our unconscious mind through dreams. After all, the structures and processes that result in our perceptive, rational, and emotional traits and their workings seem to be focused on securing our survival and thriving in the world we perceive as reality. But our dreams neither reliably reflect the circumstances of our existence nor do they reliably abide by precepts of logic, natural laws, or even human laws. They do not seem to contain much practical information that we could use in our waking existence. They do, however, effectively confront us with pain and pleasure. The intense emotional challenges in our dreams suggest that we might have to concentrate on their emotional involvement to explain their function or attributes. The placement of dreams in a self-contained emotional mechanism that works below our awareness poses an enigma we may have to solve to fully understand our traits.

In our dreams, instincts appear to respond to sensations of deprivation without a factual context that we recognize as real. As a consequence, they search our memory for facts that can be fitted to connect with their factual patterns. Dreamed needs may result from emotional traits that cannot motivate us appropriately when we are awake. The frequently primal types of needs and circumstances governing our dreams suggest that we experience needs in them with less inhibition than during waking hours because our conscious mind does not interfere. Maybe even acquired instincts that forestall their pursuit retreat. We may witness the relative state of our deprivation and procedures by our council of traits at basic levels. The emotions we dream may be expressions of formative events by which emotional traits develop and maintain themselves. Emotional traits may require different processes in these undertakings than perceptive and rational traits. Our perceptive traits are present and active in our dreams. But our dreams do not seem to labor with matters of external perception. In that regard, perceptive traits may be wholly developed as a genetic condition with acquired influences early in our life and may require no or only limited maintenance through our mind. To the extent such development and maintenance are necessary, our waking hours when we are exposed to external sensory impressions would seem most relevant. Similar observations can be made about rational aspects. Our rational mind may differ by being highly dependent in its development and maintenance on mental activity throughout our life. Yet, here again, we appear to obtain most benefit from processes during our waking hours because we are then preoccupied with rationalizing our impressions. Although integration, construction, or other functions pertaining to external aspects of perceptive and rational traits may occur during our sleep, our dreams do not seem to be connected to such functions. Possibly, they spellbind us to allow these functions to occur in the background.

More generally, the alternate reality of dreams may be necessary to preoccupy our impulses to prevent them from interrupting our sleep. Our emotional mind may also utilize dreams to undertake preparatory work. It may build emotional and related perceptive capacity that enables us to properly process experiences or to help us to withstand emotional trauma. Dreams of pain and pleasure may be a calibration mechanism for our compass of pain and pleasure, for our concept of good and bad. Feeling these emotions in our dreams may establish or reinforce the motivational range of an emotional trait, or it may be a precautionary and protective mechanism. It may be an exercise to keep us from incurring actual experiences of pain and to have us seek actual experiences of pleasure. Our mind may try to address needs we have not satisfied by reinforcing our sense of deprivation so we take action. To the extent we experience fulfillment of needs in our dreams, they might carry the function of impressing us with the desirability of their resolution. Our experiences in dreams could have any, any combination, all, none of these, or some other reasons.

As long as dreams present such fundamental questions that we appear unable to answer, they cannot help us garner a better understanding of our mental traits. For now, we might have to turn to other ways of investigating the unconscious aspects of our mental traits and making them conscious. The detection and reconstruction of unconscious sources by effects that reach our awareness may be inexact and insufficient. We may impose interpretations on such information according to terms and parameters that may have little or no relevance in the realm of our unconscious. To access our unconscious, we may have to find ways to leave our waking mind behind. Because the unconscious parts of our mind dwell beyond the confines of our awareness, we may gain the ability to detect them by altering our conscious mind. We may use chemicals or other stimuli for that purpose. While this may facilitate access to our unconscious, it may also distract. We may not possess certainty whether our perceptions with external assistance are completely or partly experiences caused by this assistance or whether they reflect a pure piece of our unconscious mind. Nor might the difference in states allow us to render our unconscious experiences conscious. We might merely fall into a dreamlike state. We might not be able to transport our conscious mind into that state. It may only appear this way, similar to how we seem to be conscious during our dreams. Nor might we advance in committing these experiences more to our conscious memory or understanding. Nothing might be won.

To explore unconscious reality without disabling our conscious mind, we may strive to gain access to our unconscious mind through meditation. We may regard techniques that are guided or enabled by other individuals helpful in this undertaking. However, to exclude the risk of external influence, we may prefer to achieve access to our inner self without external interference or with only a minimum of facilitation. We may gain insight simply by letting go of purposeful exploration, by being tranquil, empty-minded, and listening into us. Our unconscious mind may voluntarily impart impressions to our consciousness that might be usually overlaid by superficial preoccupation with stimuli that require attention. Thus, at this point of apparently highest extension in our exploration, we may come back to the starting point of our exploration where we listen to what our mind volunteers. Only, this time, we might be freer of restrictions and more sensitive.

If we intently look into ourselves and employ exploratory techniques, we can find a great range of information about ourselves. But finding that information does not mean that it is necessarily organized to where it is useful to us. We need to take account of the presence of all pieces of our mind we found and assemble them into a picture of our inner self. When we consider how we can derive a clear picture of our personality from all the impressions and insights we gather, the parallel to a jigsaw puzzle game continues to serve as a helpful illustration. To derive a picture of our inner self that makes sense, we have to allocate and assemble the pieces we have found. In a complicated puzzle game, we cannot commit the shape and content of each game piece to memory independently and merge the puzzle in our mind. A similar problem seems to exist regarding the assembly of a composite from impressions of our personality. We cannot well hold on to each impression in our mind while we look for other pieces or while we try to assemble the picture. As with puzzle pieces, we need a physical representation of the pieces of information about our personality to put them together. We need to see them in front of us to account for them and gain an understanding how they might fit with one another. We need to find a representation of our impressions outside our mind.

Initially, we might choose a variety of media to fulfill that function, including writing and vocal or visual recordings in a diversity of storage and retrieval technologies. One of the most effective and most familiar means for us to formulate and capture our impressions externally would seem to be through writing. There may also be occasions where, at least initially, voice recordings form a superior record of our impressions in the most immediate manner. It may be easier or faster for us to voice our impressions than to state them in writing. Voice recordings may carry additional information in their tone and mode of delivery. Visual recordings in which we verbalize our impressions may supplement that information because they also capture our nonverbal communications. Depending on the ease of recording or importance of visual communication, audio-visual recordings may take the place of voice recordings. Beyond preferences caused by the particularity of circumstances, some of us may feel more spontaneous and fluent if we can speak our mind. Expressing our impressions in writing increases the risk that we may become more careful. We may distrust and be reluctant to disclose our self in writing because writing is a manner of memorializing information that can be immediately acquired by others without any display device. As long as we carry the suspicion that others might read what we write, we may scrutinize and edit what we commit to writing before, while, and after we write based on that possibility. We may care about impressions we might cause in others. We may be influenced by what they might think and how they might react, and we may try to gain a favorable or lenient response. We may justify and explain, embellish, hold back, omit, or falsify. Then again, we may encounter a similar problem with voicing our impressions in aural or audio-visual recordings. The direct recording of our voice or our body and behavior may add an air of immediacy and undeniable authorship that may caution us. The removal from immediate recognition and the complication of having to find a playback device hardly seem to be distinguishing obstacles to their proliferation. Convenient distribution systems for such recordings and a lower threshold of effort to review them relative to writing may heighten our concern that others could access our recordings and that they might be publicized as items of voyeuristic curiosity. Even if we are not concerned about the secrecy of our recordings, we have to secure them from disclosure. The expectation or suspicion that they might be accessible by others may influence our expressions. It threatens to paralyze and falsify our recording of impressions. We might address this problem by selecting a repository for our impressions that is inaccessible to others.

However, in many cases, our problem with communicative aspects is more protracted. Even the assurance that others will not have access to our impressions might not avoid all hesitation or ensure our honesty. Because writing as well as our voice and our demeanor are generally means of communication to other individuals, we might automatically be guarded in what we write, say, or how we behave when we are being recorded, even if there is nobody to receive our communication. Although we would record ourselves exclusively for purposes of communication with ourselves, the externalization of our internal processes in an act of communication may trigger inhibitions to fully express ourselves. If we are not used to such practices, it may take effort and familiarization to overcome this inhibition. This may be particularly so when we hear our voice or know that our image is being recorded because vocal signaling and visual exposure are traditionally exclusively reserved for our communication with others. Writing may seem like a more familiar, a more intimate way of expressing ourselves to build and preserve a record of mental aspects. Yet even writing may appear uncomfortable and embarrassing because it continues to carry the connotation of a communicative objective. We may also feel awkward because most of us are not accustomed to exploring and expressing much of our inner domain or having that content represented externally. We may be unaccustomed to such an exposure of our self and sense awkwardness until we become familiar with our reflection.

If we detect stronger adverse reactions, these would have to be caused by an objection from one or more emotional traits. Defensive mechanisms might strain to prevent us from becoming aware of their presence, activities, or effects. Our apprehension that impressions will expose unwelcome information about our self might influence the expression of our impressions when we commit them to a medium. This apprehension might subdue the collection of potentially troublesome impressions regardless of the medium we might select for memorialization. We might already approach the induction of impressions with trepidation. At this preliminary stage, our defense mechanisms may be less concerned because they may still be confident in their reliance on familiar procedures to stifle painful impressions. But these mechanisms lose power after we commit an impression to a medium. Even if induction methods for generating impressions can circumvent our defense mechanisms, these mechanisms may be particularly alert at the moment when we try to memorialize impressions because this represents an important line of defense. We may sense a repulsion to express our impressions in any medium because it forces us to part with an impression and commit to it by instilling it with an exterior existence we cannot deny anymore. Our fear that we will summon painful occasions by recalling impressions may increase when we grant them exterior existence. The memorialization of our impressions might be a point where our desire to improve our happiness has to contend most intensely with our fear of encountering painful events in connection with our improvement efforts. If we allow our defense mechanisms to consider our impressions before we commit them to a medium, these mechanisms may interfere and we may not be able to safely transport our impressions to the next stage in our self-realization endeavor. Our mindfulness of perceptions, thoughts, and emotions without immediately recording them may grant mental traits an opportunity to reflect on them, to detect incompatible elements, and to raise objections. To minimize the risk of such interference, it is important that we record our impressions immediately as they cross our mind without further consideration or evaluation. We cannot allow ourselves to ponder our impressions before we commit to them as correct or as ours. We must not even worry about placing them into coherent descriptions.

We may be apprehensive that writing, aural, or audio-visual recordings might not preserve the meaning we attach to it. We may not be cued into reading our nonverbal expressions. Moreover, verbalizing places our ideas outside our immediate mental processes. We may be concerned that words have difficulties inducing the characteristics of our mind that we try to memorialize in them, even if they should be

accompanied by vocal or visual exposure of our person. We may suspect that a part of the content will not be reconstituted in our mind
because the medium of words intersperses an abstract and generalized
distance. Such concerns may be diminished because we communicate
with ourselves. As long as our mental concepts remain within the purview of our mind, words may serve as effective placeholders for them.
It is therefore likely that we will be able to reconstitute perceptive, rational, and emotional concepts we memorialize by verbal representations or references in excess or modification of their plain meaning.

Even if we represent our words in writing, their reconstitution
seems to be facilitated by the fact that the acquisition of information
from written concepts appears to travel along traditional channels for
auditory and visual acquisition of information that humans developed
long before the invention of writing. Employing auditory and visual
processing may remain important to make the best use of our mental
facilities regarding writing. As written representations, words are visual symbols for voice signals. Upon reading them, our mind seems to
initially reconstitute them into the types of internal signals caused by
aural impressions. We can detect this connection in our natural inclination to mouth words if we have difficulties determining their pro-
nunciation in a written medium or to read text aloud if we have difficulties understanding it. Even under normal circumstances, we seem
to form vocalizations from written words in our mind. Upon such vocalization, our mind can process these signals under the use of its traditional facilities for language. Beyond the vocalization of words, their
visual representation in writing alone may constitute a symbol for circumstances we would acquire through all our senses. They evoke described objects and events in our imagination. Our mind can thereafter process these memorized signals under the use of its traditional facilities for sensory processing. Because written words combine aural
and visual representation, they may be particularly effective and efficient in memorializing and reproducing impressions. While more direct representations of objects or events may have a more precise and
succinct impact, the use of words for creating impressions seems frequently superior because they can specifically name aspects. The representative quality of words we apply is further improved in our mind
because we connect with each word concepts of our experience or imagination that are associated with other experiences. Our association
of words additionally enriches their meaning. While verbal communication of our impressions and their associations might seem ambiguous to others, they may form effective and efficient representations for
us, even if our collection of impressions consists of cryptic references.

A recording of perceptive, rational, and emotional impressions in form of descriptions inexorably entails an interpretation and fails to preserve the immediacy of what comes to our mind. We must strive to minimize this effect by using descriptions that serve to retain in us a memory of the impressions that gave rise to them. Such a representative recording of our impressions may be encumbered because we may not be able to find an exact description for our impressions in words. Impressions may strike us in ways that do not lend themselves to succinct expression, or they may impact us in an indirect manner short of their underlying essence. We may have to engage metaphors, descriptions that, although they are not accurate in terms of the plain meaning of their expression, approximate the substance of our impressions. Metaphors may assume various, including nonverbal, forms. The metaphors in which our impressions find expression do not have to be our own. We already describe impressions in form of established symbols, illustrations, figures of speech, scenarios, and archetypes with a generally accepted meaning. In a way, all words constitute metaphors because they communicate a concept by a medium that represents but is different from the concept. Emotional impressions might particularly benefit from metaphoric representations. But they may also suffer the most because of the limited capacity of words to represent emotional content. This may prompt us to construct more elaborate descriptions of circumstances to describe an emotional state than would be necessary regarding perceptive or rational concepts. The difficulty of translating emotional content into words and to decipher it from them may further motivate us to attempt communicating it by its representation in visual, aural, or other sensory media alone or in supplementation of one another or words. Only, many of us may deem themselves unable to provide sufficiently clear and strong expressions in such media.

When we choose words, a short situational expression may suffice or we may require a more elaborating explanation to reinvoke an emotion. However, because our impressions may often be mere glances, extended story lines may not appositely describe them. This is particularly so if we use imported references. The additional components contained in such representations may confuse more than the congruences might assist, and they may dissipate or modify what we attempt to express. But we must stay clear of taking refuge in clichés that may overwhelm a nuanced represented meaning and preclude deeper personalized insights. Unless externally supplied metaphors that come to mind happen to irreplaceably fit our impressions, we may be better off creating our own. We might be able to rely on well-chosen metaphors without a substantial loss or distortion because we communicate with ourselves and can therefore link our recollection to them. Then again, their vagueness may render even our own metaphors prone to confusion. The inherent imprecision of metaphors places us at risk of attenuating the meaning of an impression and changing its essence in their interpretation. They may leave openings for defensive mechanisms to affect the memorialization of our impressions. To avert such a usurpation, we have to try to name circumstances as they appear in our mind whenever we can. Attempts to find a metaphor may cause more damage to the memorialization of impressions than an incomplete or even imprecise initial recording. We may have to use metaphors as initial tools during collection for lack of better descriptions. We may have to resort to them as markers to save impressions from being forgotten, suppressed, or falsified. However, where we cannot escape metaphors, we will have to penetrate them as soon as possible thereafter to make certain we recall the original mental processes that led to them.

Many perceptions, thoughts, and emotions we accumulate may be represented by aspects, fragments, and partial insights. We should not expect that we can put them in context right away and make sense of them. This piecemeal quality of self-discovery is not a disadvantage. It renders the daunting task of self-identification manageable. It increases the chances that our impressions will be in synchronicity with the length of time we can dedicate to recording them. Most of all, registering the raw impressions that strike our mind helps us to circumvent or defer the defense mechanisms of our mental traits. It keeps us honest in our effort to find our personality because we may not know their meaning and consequences. If we find and record the pieces of our mind without or with only partial context, without evaluating and correlating them, we lower the risk that we adjust these pieces to render them compliant with a predetermined notion we may have of our inner self. That notion may be directed and biased by certain mental traits. But even without their interferences, we may try to make sense of what we find. We are tempted to round off perceived rough edges, to fill voids in an incomplete picture, and to make pieces fit. We might even conceive puzzle pieces that do not exist. This disingenuity might lead our effort to recognize our mental traits astray. Beyond recording our impressions immediately in the condition in which they cross our mind, we must resist connecting our impressions to one another before we have accounted for them as completely as possible. Trying to put the puzzle together before we possess all or most relevant pieces would unnecessarily frustrate us. It would sabotage the natural flow of our realization process and impede or prevent us from connecting the pieces with the relative ease that the possession of all or most relevant pieces provides. These troubles might reinforce our apprehension that we might not succeed with our ambition to gain clarity about our personality and allow our defensive mechanisms to claim an easy victory.

Preserving the immediacy of our impressions is problematic because our mind is disposed to place all our impressions into context as they are being recalled and to retrieve together with them associated memories. This natural drive to associate impressions cannot be effectively suspended. It seems unavoidable that our impressions trigger an exploration of other pieces, particularly if our first impressions are not complete. They may stimulate our memory to produce additional important impressions. We may welcome and try to foster such associations. But we may not be able to forestall impressions by association that are manufactured by pressures of conformance with previous impressions. Nor may we be able to stem the influx of other manipulatory elements. The control by defensive traits may be so strong that capturing controversial genuine elements might be difficult. They might be buried in disingenuous impressions. To capture as many relevant impressions as possible, we may have to be amenable to induced impressions at the risk of subjecting inquiries to manipulation. Still, we must try to delay a contextual expansion of impressions and reserve it to a separate, second round of inquiry at which time we may have collected enough genuine elements to question disingenuous aspects.

We may try to forestall the interference of defense mechanisms by monitoring our expressions regarding their authenticity. However, that monitoring and our determination whether an expression is authentic may play into the hands of defense mechanisms. If we tried to disqualify disingenuous elements at the collection phase, we might allow entrenched defense mechanisms to subject genuine aspects of our personality to their disqualification efforts. In addition, we would exclude from our consideration the very features of our personality that might stand in the way of its harmonization. We would disregard the subjects of their manipulation efforts together with them. A record of unencumbered impressions can greatly assist us in evoking, exposing, and ultimately defeating defensive mechanisms. Their threat can only be contained if we bring their objections to our awareness and record them as well. We must take account of them not only because they interfere with finding our personality but also because they constitute expressions of traits that define or attempt to define our personality. We have to record the impositions they generate, the triggers of these impositions, our preventive or remedial reaction to these impositions or our lack thereof, and the consequences. We must gather the courage to look in the mirror and not avert our eyes from disagreeable features, disfigurements, wounds, or scars that nature or others have inflicted on us or that we have brought upon our self. We must further gather the courage to identify and to describe the mechanisms we and others have created to prevent us from seeing our self as we are. Registering information regarding these mechanisms is a necessary step to becoming self-aware and self-determined. We will want to elicit them because they reveal important insights without which an assessment of our mental traits would be deficient. However, to make our inquiries as effective as possible, we will have to avoid pushing them to take preemptive action until we have elicited as much as possible about the subjects of their preemption. The best way to undertake that seems to be not to qualify our impressions during their collection phase.

Our efforts may reveal elements that recognizably describe our personality as well as information that does not appear to immediately pertain or does not seem to pertain at all to our exploration. Much of the information we have gathered in our observational collection may not pertain to our mental traits in a definitional sense, but it may be more superficial. Much of what crosses our mind may seem irrelevant or distracting. Some of it might be coincidental clutter. Nevertheless, the fact that information occupies our mind may indicate that there is an ulterior reason for its presence. Although such information might not directly describe the essence of our traits, it may represent a general or a particularized expression of our traits that allows us to draw conclusions on the essence of our traits. It may also represent aspects that are on their way to establish or to shape traits. We must therefore do our best to ascertain as many pieces of our mind as we can regardless of what kind they are before we focus on what they mean and before we start putting them together and decide about their legitimacy or importance. We will know when our search has been exhausted because our discovery will increasingly yield repetitive impressions and will eventually cease to produce new insights. After we have completed the derivation of impressions through general collection methods, we may apply more pointed lines of inquiry that we previously avoided for fear that they would raise defensive maneuvers by our traits.

Up to this point, we have developed our general understanding of wishes and needs and of mental traits, discussed methods for exploration and registration of information about them, and collected and recorded information about our emotional traits. We now have to assemble and assess that information with the support of our general insights to reveal and reconcile our emotional traits so we can optimize them and the circumstances they conduct and influence in the interest of our happiness. The second part is devoted to these matters.

www.ingramcontent.com/pod-product-compliance
Lightning Source LLC
Chambersburg PA
CBHW022112080426
42734CB00006B/102